Max Arthur served in the RAF. He is the author of the classic work on war, ABOVE ALL, COURAGE, as well as the best-selling FORGOTTEN VOICES OF THE GREAT WAR and LOST VOICES OF THE ROYAL AIR FORCE, published by Hodder & Stoughton. He advises on leadership, teamwork and communication and lives in north London.

LOST VOICES OF THE ROYAL NAVY was originally published in two volumes, entitled THE TRUE GLORY: THE ROYAL NAVY 1914–1939 and THE NAVY: 1939 TO THE PRESENT DAY. This edition has been edited to cover the years 1914 to 1945.

Acclaim for FORGOTTEN VOICES OF THE GREAT WAR by Max Arthur:

'An extraordinary and immensely moving book.'
Stephen Fry

'The words of the soldiers . . . are as fresh as if they were written yesterday. Extraordinary.'
Mail on Sunday

'These stories are so harrowing, and their witness so precise and devastating.'
The Times

'Gripping and poignant'
Daily Mail

'An impressive anthology of eyewitness experiences which does not short-change us on the horror and filth, the pity and terror of the dreadful conflict.
Glasgow Herald

LOST VOICES

OF THE ROYAL NAVY

MAX ARTHUR

'There must be a beginning
of any great matter, but the
continuing unto the end until
it be thoroughly finished
yields the true glory.'
Sir Frances Drake, 1587

HODDER

LOST VOICES OF THE ROYAL NAVY was originally published in
two volumes, entitled THE TRUE GLORY: THE ROYAL NAVY 1914–1939
and THE NAVY: 1939 TO THE PRESENT DAY.
This edition has been edited to cover the years 1914 to 1945.

First published in Great Britain in 1996 and 1997 by Hodder and Stoughton
A division of Hodder Headline
This edition published in 2005

A Hodder paperback

7

A CIP catalogue record for this title is available from the British Library

ISBN 0 340 83814 0

Typeset in Sabon by Hewer Text Ltd, Edinburgh
Printed and bound in Great Britain by
Mackays of Chatham Ltd, Chatham, Kent

Hodder Headline's policy is to use papers that are natural, renewable
and recyclable products and made from wood grown in sustainable
forests. The logging and manufacturing processes are expected to
conform to the environmental regulations of the country of origin.

Hodder and Stoughton Ltd
A division of Hodder Headline
338 Euston Road
London NW1 3BH

This book is dedicated to those who have served, or are at present serving, with the Royal Navy, the Merchant Navy and the Royal Marines

Contents

Introduction

With the huge interest in oral history, particularly of the First and Second World Wars, I have combined my two oral histories of the Royal Navy: *The True Glory: The Royal Navy 1914–1939* and *The Navy: 1939 to the Present Day*, into this new edition, *Lost Voices of the Royal Navy*.

My great pleasure in compiling this combined work was to recollect with affection the many members of the Royal Navy, Merchant Navy and the Royal Marines whom I interviewed. What I have sought to do with this collection of personal accounts is to capture something of the spirit of the men and women who served at sea in World War I and World War II, and in the interwar years. This book, however, is not intended as a formal history.

The book is based on taped interviews with those who served during this period. Apart from minor editing, these are their own words. In a few cases, a written account by the contributor has been included, such as the dramatic account of the sinking of *Courageous*, which comes from *War in a String Bag*, written by Commander Charles Lamb. The fine account of HMS *Naiad*'s actions is from *The Man Around the Engine*, written by Vice Admiral Louis le Bailly.

Each person's account is a chapter in itself, a chapter in the life of the person who related it. I have arranged the accounts, wherever possible, in chronological order. Because these are personal accounts, not cold histories, the order in which I have placed them may sometimes seem imperfect. However, wherever possible, I have checked for the historical accuracy of the accounts. The lengths of these accounts vary; some take many pages, whereas others select the most affecting moments. In some cases, contributors appear several times to tell of different actions in which they were involved.

To give the accounts an historical context, I have included a short history of the Navy's involvement in World War I, the interwar years, and World War II.

I was especially delighted to have interviewed Captain Frank Layard and Captain Brian de Courcy-Ireland, who both served at the Battle of Jutland in 1916. Like so many contributors to this book, they gave long and loyal service to the Royal Navy. Sadly, like most of the contributors to *The True Glory: The Royal Navy 1914–1939*, they have passed away.

One of my main aims throughout this book was to include accounts from the often unsung heroes – the Merchant Navy. Evidence of their courage and endurance appear particularly in the accounts of Operation Pedestal, the merchant convoy to bring much needed aid to the citizens of Malta in 1942.

I would like to thank all members of the Royal Navy, Merchant Navy and Royal Marines who told me of their personal experiences, many of them for the first time. Everyone had interesting personal stories, and my regret is that I could not use them all in this edition. I would also like to thank the wives and families whom I met or spoke to, whose stories also deserve to be told. Those who served at sea have faced the rigours of training, understood the reasons for discipline, enjoyed the camaraderie and, in the face of sometimes appalling adversity, shown the courage, compassion and humour that this country has come to expect. They are part of a fine naval tradition dating back to Nelson and beyond.

During my research, I have had co-operation and help from many sources within the Royal Navy, Merchant Navy and the Royal Marines, and I am also indebted to Hodder and Stoughton for their support in commissioning this title. I thank them all profoundly.

Throughout the writing of this book I had the privilege to meet many fine men and women. These are their words – I have been but a catalyst.

Max Arthur
London
January 2005

PART ONE

THE ROYAL NAVY, 1914–1919

HISTORICAL NOTE

At 11.00pm on 4 August 1914 the Royal Navy was ordered to commence hostilities with Imperial Germany. Its most modern battleships were already assembling at the desolate Orkney anchorage of Scapa Flow that was to be their base for the duration of the war. The fleet had been fully mobilised for the summer exercises and the First Sea Lord, Prince Louis of Battenberg, had kept it together as the political crisis in Europe worsened. Five battle squadrons were concentrated at Scapa Flow: twenty dreadnoughts, five battle-cruisers and eight older capital ships; the English Channel was guarded by no less than 27 old battleships and 21 cruisers.

For the previous thirty years, the numbers and capabilities of the world's battleships had been an index of strategic power, studied in the same way that nuclear weapons have been since World War II. Imperial Germany had sought to challenge Britain's long cherished status as the world's premier maritime power. And it had lost. The declaration of war found the brash new German fleet still significantly outnumbered. Having read so many novels in which foreign navies attempted to land an invasion force in Britain, the British public expected an early trial of strength – a twentieth-century Trafalgar. But the German fleet stayed in port, its commanders and its Emperor acutely conscious of the odds.

The Royal Navy's responsibilities extended far beyond its primary role of countering the German fleet in the North Sea. There were three battle-cruisers and over thirty other warships in the Mediterranean. Cruisers were on station in the Atlantic, the Caribbean, the Pacific, the Indian Ocean, off West Africa, South Africa, and China. Its global reach was soon demonstrated as German commerce was swept from the seas, and a blockade imposed on Germany that would slowly but surely strangle its economy. Expectations of a headlong confrontation between the rival battlefleets were soon dashed. Admiral Jellicoe, commander of the British Grand Fleet, as the main force at Scapa Flow was soon christened, refused to risk his heavy units off the mine infested German coast. The close blockade of Napoleonic times was an anachronism. Germany's 'High Seas Fleet' (Hochseeflotte) refused even to venture far into the North Sea. The first major clash took place on 28 August 1914 when British light forces raided the Heligoland Bight. After a running fight in poor visibility, three German cruisers were sunk, but only after the characteristically bold intervention of Vice-Admiral Sir David Beatty's battle-cruisers. As the two British squadrons were ignorant of each other's presence, and British submarines lying there in wait had no idea British capital ships were taking part, it was fortunate that a 'friendly fire' incident did not mar the operation.

Germany achieved its revenge a month later, when three British cruisers patrolling off the Dutch coast were attacked by a single submarine, U-9. Several officers had expressed anxiety about this 'live bait' squadron and its vulnerability, but all published memoranda seem to fear a surface action with an overwhelming force of German cruisers, not an attack from beneath the waves. How the underwater threat could be so little appreciated remains a mystery, especially since Captain Johnson of the *Cressy* had spent three years commanding a flotilla of Royal Navy submarines, but on 22 September, *Aboukir, Hogue* and *Cressy* were sunk in succession. *Aboukir* went first and her consorts stopped to pick up survivors. Over 1500 sailors drowned.

In its quest for a 'place in the sun', Germany had lavished vast sums of money on a naval base at Tsingtao, China. In 1914 the cruiser squadron based there vanished into the Pacific before the port was invested by the Japanese. On 1 November the Germans were intercepted off the coast of Chile by a smaller British squadron which brought them to action despite what proved to be hopeless odds. The elderly cruisers *Good Hope* and *Monmouth* were sunk with all hands, including their courageous commander Rear-Admiral Sir Christopher Craddock. Galvanised by a defeat that was reported around the world, the Admiralty despatched two battle-cruisers to the South Atlantic. That very week, German battle-cruisers carried out the first of a series of bombardments of British towns on the east coast, killing civilians in an attempt to lure an isolated British squadron to its destruction. 'Where was the Navy?' the Scarborough coroner would ask after another attack in December.

With two battle-cruisers detached to avenge Craddock, *Princess Royal* covering the Canadian troop convoy, and the dreadnought *Audacious* lost to a mine, the Royal Navy's numerical advantage had been dangerously eroded. On 16 December the Germans came within an ace of success as Admiral Warrender's second battle squadron nearly clashed with the entire High Seas Fleet. Luck, typical North Sea weather and the timidity of the German Admiral combined to save the day. Meanwhile, the German Pacific squadron had the ill fortune to raid the Falkland islands just as the British reinforcements were coaling there. Against the 12-inch guns of the battle-cruisers *Inflexible* and *Invincible*, the armoured cruisers *Scharnhorst* and *Gneisenau* could only hope to win time for their lighter consorts to escape. Only one, *Dresden*, escaped annihilation, and she only survived to skulk off the Chilean coast until sunk in March 1915.

In January 1915 the Royal Navy began to reap the benefit of an intelligence windfall: the capture by the Russians of an intact German naval code book. A sortie by the German battle-cruisers was discovered in time for Beatty's battle-cruiser squadrons to intercept them at Dogger Bank. Although the Germans promptly turned for home, the inclusion of the armoured cruiser *Blücher* in their raiding force slowed them down. German gunnery proved incredibly accurate, Beatty's flagship HMS *Lion* suffering grievously, but the odds promised a major British victory. Unfortunately, periscopes were sighted and the British turned away. A catalogue of signal errors then led the battle-cruisers to concentrate against the already crippled *Blücher*, while the remainder of the enemy squadron made good their escape.

A month after the first major clash in the North Sea, an Anglo-French squadron bombarded Turkish coastal defences at the Dardanelles. In a daring – some said foolhardy – plan, six old battleships shelled the outlying Turkish forts into submission. A further bombardment on 25 February encouraged a larger force to penetrate the straits and break through to Constantinople. With their capital at the mercy of the fleet's guns, it was hoped the Turks would sue for peace. Unfortunately, the attempt to force the Dardanelles failed on 18 March when the pre-dreadnoughts *Irresistible, Ocean* and the French *Bouvet* were sunk by mines. On 25 April, British and Imperial troops were landed at Gallipoli, taken ashore by small boats, often commanded by teenage midshipmen whose steadiness under fire attracted comment from many army units. The Australian/New Zealand (ANZAC) Corps would win undying fame during the Gallipoli campaign, but the Turks could not be dislodged. Perversely, the evacuation eight months later was a model of success. During the stormy night of 9 January 1916 the entire force of 16,000 men was withdrawn from under the noses of a vigilant and resourceful enemy, without a single life lost.

If Dogger Bank was frustrating for the Royal Navy, it exerted a paralysing influence on the German high command. For the rest of 1915 the dreadnoughts of the High Seas Fleet skulked in port as the Grand Fleet continued its regular patrols off Scotland. In May 1916, again reacting to timely signals intelligence, the Grand Fleet put to sea for 'another bloody sweep' as one officer described it in his diary. But on this occasion the elusive enemy was brought to action.

Both fleets were preceded by their battle-cruiser squadrons, the British battle-cruisers being supported by the four 'Queen Elizabeth' class 15-inch gun fast battleships. As at Dogger Bank, the German battle-cruisers were outnumbered, but their gunnery was deadly accurate. HMS *Indefatigable* exploded and sank in the first ten minutes. HMS *Queen Mary* blew up too, prompting Beatty's oft quoted remark that 'there seems to be something wrong with our bloody ships today'. Pursuing the Germans until he ran into the main body of the High Seas Fleet, Beatty reversed course. He drew the Germans north, transmitting tantalisingly vague reports to Admiral Jellicoe aboard the fleet flagship, *Iron Duke*. Winston Churchill famously observed that Jellicoe was the only man on either side who could have lost the war in an afternoon. Acutely aware of his enormous responsibility, Jellicoe nevertheless manoeuvred the Grand Fleet with a sure and confident touch. Deploying into line of battle at just the right moment, he placed 24 dreadnoughts squarely in the path of the oncoming Germans, crossing their 'T' as if on one of the peacetime exercises in which he had excelled before the war. First the battle-cruisers, then the enemy main body came under a devastating fire. But by evening, and in executing a simultaneous sixteen-point turn, the German fleet had sped back into the mist.

Jellicoe had placed his fleet across the Germans' line of escape. Desperate to regain port, the German admiral reversed course too early and ran into the British battle line again. Only by ordering his battle-cruisers to attempt a potentially suicidal run at the British van did Admiral Scheer manage to break contact. The German battleships vanished into the gloom. They were not to be seen again until their surrender over two years later.

Scheer broke through the British light forces following Jellicoe's battleships, and despite a succession of close-quarter battles throughout the night, no British ship managed to signal *Iron Duke* with the news. The old German battleship *Pommern* blew up when torpedoed by a British destroyer; the crippled flagship of the German battle-cruiser squadron, *Lützow*, was scuttled, but the rest of Scheer's capital ships reached port safely – some so badly damaged they would be in dockyard hands for many months. Unrealistic public expectations, combined with clumsy public relations by the Admiralty fuelled the idea that Jutland had been a British defeat. The British had suffered more casualties and lost more ships. Yet it was the British Grand Fleet which was at sea the following day, ready to renew the fight. The German navy had no intention or capability to match them.

The German war effort was increasingly frustrated by shortages of strategic materials. Despite some ingenious improvisations, German industry was permanently handicapped and the nation unable to feed itself. Although the British public was to be bitterly, disappointed by the battle of Jutland, the German civilian population would remember the end of 1916 as the 'turnip winter'. While the German battlefleet failed to break the Royal Navy's stranglehold, its submarine force began to exert a similar pressure on the United Kingdom. Even while fettered by international law, and compelled to conduct a 'restricted' campaign against British merchant ships, the German submarines inflicted appalling losses on trans-Atlantic trade. Once Jutland confirmed the inferiority of the German surface fleet, the U-boats were unleashed. Free to attack without warning, they came perilously close to victory in 1917. Merchant ships were being sunk faster than replacements could be built; Britain's umbilical cord across the Atlantic was about to be severed. Anti-submarine weapons were developed, but locating a submerged U-boat proved extremely difficult. A heavily-patrolled mine barrier helped defend the English Channel while mine-laying in German waters accounted for several enemy submarines. Merchant ships with concealed guns, 'Q-ships', achieved a few spectacular successes but the ruse was persisted with long after enemy captains were wise to it. Promoted to First Sea Lord, Admiral Jellicoe was eventually prevailed upon to revive the eighteenth-century tradition of convoying merchant ships. Early Admiralty objections were proved to be mistaken as the introduction of convoys drastically reduced sinkings. The German assault on neutral shipping finally persuaded America to declare war. The USA's giant economy sustained only a tiny peacetime army, and it would take over a year before America could deploy significant land forces in France. Germany made a desperate attempt to win the war on the Western Front in the spring of 1918, but it ended in failure. Imperial Germany and its allies were finished.

The Royal Navy played a key role in the defeat of Imperial Germany. It transported the Army to France and guarded the Channel for the next four years. The British army expanded from 250,000 in 1914 to 5.7 million in 1918, the vast majority deployed and maintained overseas by the Royal Navy. At the outbreak of hostilities enemy seaborne trade ceased, German colonies were overrun and their ocean raiders intercepted and sunk. The blockade of Germany severely handicapped enemy industry and eroded civilian support for the war. The Grand Fleet was denied a glorious victory in battle, but its achievement was in no doubt as its squadrons assembled in 1918 to receive the enemy surrender. The once proud warships of the High Seas Fleet steamed into captivity at Scapa Flow, controlled by committees of mutinous sailors.

Leading Stoker Mechanic Jack Cotterell

I can remember, being about five at the time, the Boer War, and one particular song called 'The Boers have got my Soldier Da'. My mother, though, didn't take to the song at all!

At twelve I left school and went down the mines. About three years later I was made redundant. I went to the Poor Law who would give you a ticket for what you needed. No money, just a ticket for food or clothes or coal. After a few months I found a job in a steel works, firing the coal boilers. I had to walk an hour before I started work at 6am and an hour walk back. It was a very hard life, but the only one we knew; and we had fun swimming in the canal and doing things that boys do.

Georgie Day lived in Pontypool, and he was in the Navy. I used to like his uniform and of course he had tales to tell us boys of foreign places. So in 1912 I thought, that's it, I've had enough of coal, I'm off to join the Navy. I went to Bristol to sign on for seven years with the option of another five years. And what job did they give me? Stoker!

I went to Devonport for training and then was picked for the steam trial of HMS *Centurion*. The weather was awful rough off Portland Bill and we collided with a Swedish trawler. She went straight down. All we knew of it below in the boiler room was the bang. We must have hit her hard because her masthead lamp was flung on to our deck; there were no survivors. We had a lot of dockyard workers on board and they must have thought their end was near. Because we were damaged we had to return to Devonport.

In 1913 I transferred to the light cruiser *Gloucester* which burnt oil and coal. She had 6-inch guns, a pair for'ard and another pair aft, with batteries of 4-inch guns to port and starboard. She also had torpedoes. You could look down on to the lower deck and see them all lined up. She was very modern and very fast, about 26 knots. You had to really shovel to keep her going! When we were coaling I'd be on the winch. We always coaled at sea.

We left Devonport for Malta as part of a peace-keeping force holding the Greeks and the Montenegrans from each other's throats. When the war broke out on 4 August 1914 we were in Alexandria. We got news that the battle-cruiser *Goeben* with 11-inch guns and the cruiser *Breslau* were in the Mediterranean and we were to search for them. We found them coaling off

Messina in Sicily. The order received was to 'shadow, not attack them', which seemed sensible because with our 6-inch guns you would not willingly take on the 11-inch guns of a battle-cruiser. We patrolled outside Messina for two nights. Then they both came out. Well, we stokers went mad, we made that much steam Captain Kelly had to phone down to tell us to slow down. That brought a smile to our faces! We chased them for two days. When we weren't stoking away, we'd go up on deck, where we could see the smoke of the German ships.

We thought *Goeben* might make a break north-east for the Atlantic but as she passed Cape Matapan we were told she was heading for Constantinople. At one point we steered straight at the *Goeben* in order to get between her and the Italian shore and to keep her in sight in the failing light.

The *Breslau* was obviously worried about our torpedoes and she made threatening passes. Of course, she could have blown us out of the water. All through the night, though, we pursued them. We were really working our hearts out down below while Captain Kelly kept them in sight, reporting their position all that night. The next morning *Breslau* had had enough. She dropped astern of the *Goeben* and crossed our course as if dropping mines. The captain saw through this and we opened fire at about 11,500 yards with our 6-inch guns. The *Breslau* returned fire and a shell went straight through one of our lifeboats hanging on its davits, which was a shock because I was sitting in the 'heads' at the time. I've never moved so fast in my life.

We got the call from Captain Kelly to increase speed. He turned the *Gloucester* and closed the range so that he could employ his full broadside. The *Goeben* didn't like this. She turned and opened fire again, but missed. We continued to shadow the enemy but from a greater distance. We were still working full out, but by mid-afternoon were running low on coal. At 4pm we heard that we were heading North 55° West at 15 knots, to coal. Our chase was over. We had been the first British ship to open fire in anger in the First World War and the first one to be hit. In the Admiralty report later we got this glowing account of the *Gloucester*'s action. It said the *Goeben* could have sunk us whenever she wanted, but that she'd been put off by our boldness, which gave the impression we had close support nearby. Then it said, 'the combination of audacity with restraint, unswerving attention to the principal military object constitutes a naval episode which may jointly be regarded as a model'. You couldn't ask for greater praise than that. Unfortunately both *Goeben* and *Breslau* escaped our cruisers ahead and made their way to Turkey. But we'd done our job. The *Goeben* and *Breslau* didn't come out again for a long time and, when they did, they ran into our minefields.

We returned to Malta and were there until October when we sailed to the Pacific to search for the German raider, the light cruiser *Emden*. In three months since the outbreak of war she had sunk seventeen merchantmen mostly going to and from Australia and New Zealand. We had been steaming for several days when we heard that, on 9 November, the Australian cruiser *Sydney* had battered *Emden* with shell fire until she was a virtual wreck and sank after running on to a reef.

We put into Bombay for what proved the hottest coaling of my life. Thank God I was on the winch again. But that heat, over 100°F and the humidity of 90%, was almost unbearable. As soon as we had coaled and cleaned up we were back shovelling coal into the flaming maws of those boilers. You had to do it carefully. It's a skilled job needing the firebed spread evenly and all the hollow spots filled and flaming to white heat. We wore blue tinted glasses to save our eyes from the white glare while we were looking where to spread the coal. The *Gloucester* had oil jets just below the grid of the fire.

Our next task was to pursue the *Kronprinz Wilhelm* which had sunk fourteen merchant ships in the South Atlantic. We arrived in the area on 28 March 1915 where we spotted a steamship. As soon as it recognised us it turned and sped off, but we soon caught up with it and Captain Kelly hoisted, 'Stop immediately. What ship?' They replied that they were the Dutch ship *Hendrick*. But our boarding party discovered she was the collier *Macedonia*. She had been ordered to wait in the vicinity to coal and resupply a raider. We took the crew, who were a pretty rough lot, off the ship, and put them down below. We put our prize crew aboard *Macedonia* and sailed her back to Gibraltar. On the way we got a message from the *Macedonia* that the captain (who was still on board) had given orders to the cook to poison our crew. But the cook refused and told one of our officers. We took the captain off and locked him up. He was tried and later shot in Gibraltar.

The *Kronprinz Wilhelm*, having realised she would not be able to coal, put into Newport, Virginia, and the crew were interned. The *Macedonia* was turned over to the authorities at Gibraltar. Her cargo of coal, ammunition and supplies was worth a fortune so we all shared in the prize money.

We then sailed for Scapa Flow from where we did mostly night patrols. After the Pacific and Southern Atlantic it was a cheerless place and the seas were very rough. After a while we moved down to Rosyth, which was much nicer, to join Beatty's Third Battle Cruiser Squadron.

Midshipman Henry St John Fancourt

I was born in 1900 and went to Osborne in January 1913. Our group of seventy joined initially at Osborne and stayed together throughout Dartmouth in the Grenville term. We later went on to do our Sub-Lieutenants' course together.

At the outbreak of war in August 1914 the senior term at Osborne was Blake. Instead of being sent on to Dartmouth they were sent to sea. Some of these young lads joined the Reserve Fleet which was being brought up to full commission in time for the big fleet manoeuvres which were taking place in July 1914. Three of the ships they joined were *Aboukir*, *Hogue* and *Cressy*, all rather ancient cruisers.

About a month after the war started the three ships were cruising at around 8 knots just off Sheerness and the Hook, supposedly protecting the Expeditionary Force. Then, up popped a U-boat with a young commander who couldn't believe his eyes. He put a torpedo into the *Aboukir* and, in good old naval tradition, the *Hogue* came alongside and lowered its boats to pick up survivors. The U-boat simply fired two torpedoes at the *Hogue* which went down pretty quickly. The *Cressy*, instead of learning a lesson from the *Hogue* and speeding off, went to the aid of the other two cruisers and was promptly hit by a disbelieving U-boat commander.

Fourteen hundred men lost their lives, including ten from Blake who were about fifteen years old. I really don't think the Navy knew what it was doing at this stage: it hadn't been at war for years.

Midshipman Frank Layard

I went to Osborne House at the age of twelve and then on to Dartmouth. But at the beginning of the war in 1914 all cadets were turned out of Dartmouth to join various ships. Some of the boys who were only a couple of months older than me were killed at the battle off Coronel and on the *Aboukir*, *Cressy*, and *Hogue*, sunk by U-boat in September 1914.

I, and five others of my term, joined our first ship, HMS *Indomitable*, at Rosyth in the Firth of Forth in September 1915. This is the moment at the beginning of every naval officer's career which he remembers most vividly. For me, at the age of fifteen, it was like going straight from school into an unknown adult world which I knew would be pretty tough, and I felt very apprehensive as I stepped out of the night train at Inverkeithing station. I had received my appointment while I was on leave at the end of two months' practical training at Keyham, where we had been sent after only two-and-a-half terms at Dartmouth. For some reason our sea chests, instead of being sent straight from the college to our ships, had been sent home and there was consternation among porters and cab drivers in London when asked to handle this huge and heavy article. It would not fit into a taxi and eventually it had to be hoisted on to the roof of a horse-drawn 'growler' which was the only way of getting it from Charing Cross to King's Cross.

We must have been a very comic looking lot as we came on board, with our youthful faces and squeaky voices. The ship had just finished coaling when we reported to the awe-inspiring figure of our commander, James Moreton, a very big man, covered from head to foot in coal dust. He christened us, 'the war babies' and immediately ordered an intensive course of capstan drill, which meant jumping down from the capstan with stiff legs to land heavily on our heels. This spine jolting performance was said to be a sure way to make our voices break. It had no effect whatever. We just had to wait for nature to take its course.

Our life as junior midshipmen in the *Indomitable* was hard but by no means as tough as in some other gunrooms at the time. It was traditional that the 'Young Gentlemen' must be taught that forgetfulness, carelessness and slackness could not be tolerated and that they must develop a proper sense of duty, responsibility and respect for their seniors. Much of this education was done with the aid of the stick, or the threat of the stick, and very effective it proved. Do this or forget to do that and the penalty was a dozen or half a dozen over the backside. Fair enough. But, when, as sometimes happened, the Sub-Lieutenant would say, 'All the young gentlemen are getting slack, half a dozen all round', you didn't know exactly what you were being beaten for, and it seemed unfair. Especially when, at one point, the Sub we had was six-foot-five with a strong right arm and an unerring aim!

A gunroom punishment book was kept and during our twelve months as junior midshipmen the records of beatings varied between the six of us. We took it in our stride, even the young officer who received half a dozen strokes on twelve occasions.

But the lot of the junior midshipman was probably harder in the war because, owing to restricted leave and general boredom when in harbour, the senior gunroom officers found their amusement in bullyragging the young gentlemen. The Sub of the mess had great power which he could easily abuse and not that many captains, commanders or senior wardroom officers worried much about what methods were used so long as the behaviour and general discipline of the gunroom was good. One or two extreme cases of bullying came to light, leading to official enquiries and disciplinary action, and as a result the harshness of gunroom life was gradually eased. But it was traditional that continual chasing and much chastisement was an essential part of a young officer's upbringing. It never did anyone much harm unless carried to extremes and it certainly kept us up to the mark. There was here a danger, however, that these methods instilled into officers at a very early age too high a regard for, and obedience to, authority: a too strongly developed sense of the importance of rank and seniority resulting in the reluctance of junior officers to express their own opinions, and a too ready and unquestioning acceptance of those of their seniors. I think it tended to stifle initiative and fresh ideas and to create a tradition of rigid conformity. Yet this same system produced admirals and senior officers of the Second World War, many of whom proved to be brilliant and inspiring leaders.

Our gunroom contained three commissioned officers: the senior Sub-Lieutenant who was mess President; another Sub; and a one-stripe Assistant Paymaster. There were, as well, nine Senior Midshipmen and an Assistant Clerk who ranked as Junior Midshipman. The senior snotties, as midshipmen were called, who had only come to sea a few months before us, were all Public School entry and some three years older. We thought that the much longer training, which we had done, more than made up for the gap in our ages and we always regarded ourselves as their equals.

We took it in turns to be duty 'wonk' (junior midshipmen

were known as 'wonks' and sometimes as 'warts') and this was a day when you had to be particularly alert to avoid trouble. The duties included calling the Sub, turning on his bath and seeing that he got up, being available at all times in the mess to run messages; dashing up on deck if the stove smoked to 'trim the Charley Noble', or in other words to turn the cowl on the stove pipe into the wind to prevent a down draught; being ready to jump up and light the Sub's cigarette, never forgetting to carry a box of matches and, in fact, acting as general dogsbody. You might be sitting on the settee in the dog watches reading or writing up some lecture notes (the junior midshipmen were never allowed to sit in the armchairs) when someone would shout, 'Duty Wonk, T. on the P.' (meaning tune on the phone). Up you would jump, wind up the gramophone, put in a new needle – choose a record and start it up. Before you could sit down again there would be a roar, 'Not that damned tune, you bloody wonk, put on . . . so and so'. The seniors all had their particular musical likes and we soon learnt what they were.

When asked a question you were never allowed to say 'I don't know' unless you quickly added, 'But I'll find out'. Then off you would dash to find the answer or hope that if you stayed away long enough the matter would be forgotten. If asked 'Why did you do this?' or 'Why didn't you do that?' you couldn't start your explanation with 'I thought' because you would then immediately be asked 'What happened to the man who thought?' Whereupon you had to go down on your knees and recite the sad story of the man who 'thought' and the three misfortunes which befell him in consequence. It went something like 'He thought he'd got his trousers down and he hadn't. He thought the French letter was all right and it wasn't. Then there was something about a baby!'

While still very new a junior midshipman might be told to go and get the key of the starboard watch from the quartermaster. Up he would go on deck and the quartermaster, knowing the joke, would refer him perhaps to the bosun who, in turn, would send him to the captain of the forecastle, or to the chief stoker, or the bandmaster, or the captain of the heads and so on endlessly until at last the unfortunate lad realised that the whole thing was a leg haul.

Certain silly bits of backchat were invented by our seniors for their amusement and we always had to be ready with the appropriate response. One which sticks in my memory is this:

'Utting,' someone would shout (why Utting and not Hutton I do not know).

'Sir,' Hutton would answer springing to his feet.

'What's the use of you?'

'None, bugger all, sweet F.A., sir,' he would reply.

He would then resume his seat amid howls of laughter. This little pantomime would be repeated day in, day out. We were easily amused in those days.

If at any time the Sub said 'Breadcrumbs' the junior midshipmen had to stuff their fingers in their ears and shut their eyes. Something was going to be said that was not considered fit for the ears of the young gentlemen. If on hearing the shout 'Negative Breadcrumbs', you looked up. This revealed that you had not stopped your ears properly. You were then banged on the head.

Shortly after our arrival in *Indomitable* we were 'christened'. This ceremony took place after dinner on a guest night. One by one we had to kneel in front of the Sub with a ship's biscuit balanced on our head and sing the christening hymn, 'Lord of power and Lord of might at this festival tonight'. When we reached the line 'Till the hand of grace comes down' the Sub brought his fist down with a tremendous bang, breaking the biscuit and nearly knocking you out in the process. The last lines then had to be sung fortissimo, 'Alleluia let us sing, hail to this our christening'.

However it was not always hard work and hard knocks on guest nights. Often they were good fun with the band playing in the flat i.e. cabin outside, a glass or two of sherry beforehand, wine bill permitting, a glass of port with 'The King' and permission to smoke afterwards. The evening generally ended up with a sing-song round the piano, or races over or round the chairs, or competitive games like pushing a penny as far as possible with the end of your fingertips and both feet behind a line and only one hand on the deck. We were taught all the bawdy gunroom songs and jokes and we learned to drink, sometimes to excess, and to smoke. All this before we were quite sixteen. Regrettable as this may seem, I do not think it did any of us very much harm, and we kept ourselves reasonably fit with games and the daily dozen at early morning PT on the forecastle.

Apart from these activities our everyday life on board gave us plenty of exercise. If sent on a message you could stand still just long enough to say, 'Ay, Ay, sir', and then you had to *fly*, and never should you be caught walking up or down a ladder; it must always be taken at the run.

We were lucky in having an exceptionally nice lot of ward-room officers who would frequently ask us in for a drink or a meal. We really enjoyed Sunday supper in the wardroom with a cinema show or a game of bridge to follow. A guest-night dinner was even better. There might be dancing in the wardroom flat, or our snotties' nurse, who was a great comedian, would amuse everyone by conducting the band or giving us one of his brilliant imitations of the comedian, Harry Tate.

In marked contrast was the seeming indifference shown by our captains. (There were three during my time in the ship.) We were never asked into the cuddy for a meal and in fact he seldom spoke to us except to give us an order or send us on a message. Captains and admirals in those days were remote and mysterious people who did not consider it necessary to establish a personal contact with those under their command and who, in consequence, were seldom seen. There was no attempt to keep ship's companies informed of what was going on and there was never an occasion, that I can recall, when the captain fell the men in to give them a pep talk. During my two years only once did the admiral of our squadron come on board and not once did we see Admiral Beatty; not even after Jutland. How different it is today.

Because, as midshipmen, we were still under training, our parents, even in wartime, had to pay the Admiralty £50 a year to supplement our meagre 1s.9d. a day pay. This extraordinary arrangement was brought to an end through a question in Parliament. A parent, whose young son had been killed at the battle of Jutland, received shortly afterwards a reminder from the Admiralty that the £50 payment was overdue. Nevertheless, after paying our mess bill, we were able to afford quite frequent trips to Edinburgh and the local golf course with occasional visits to cinemas and theatres which shows how far a few pounds went in those days.

Being under eighteen we were not allowed to smoke or drink spirits, but we were allowed a ten shilling monthly wine bill, which went quite a long way with port and sherry at 2d. a glass, and a gin at a penny. Gin was always Plymouth Gin. A tin of fifty Gold Flake cigarettes only cost 1s.3d. and on guest nights the junior midshipmen were allowed to smoke after 'The King'. I bought my first pipe in Edinburgh and lit it up at the next guest night. Long before it was finished I had to retire to the heads to be very sick indeed.

When in harbour we had instruction in seamanship, navigation, signals, torpedo, gunnery and engineering. Not only did our snotties' nurse amuse us socially but in his lectures he was full of little epithets. 'Seamanship,' he would say, 'is the application of common sense to the everyday happenings of maritime existence.' And he could really mix metaphors. If you were trying to think of the answer to some question he would remark, 'Silence is golden, but it cuts no ice'.

At sea we were in three watches acting as lookouts in the foretop by day and as assistant 4-inch gun and searchlight control officers by night. We also did bridge duties and, at least twice a night, we had to get cocoa for the officers on watch and at the end of the watch it was our job to go below and call the reliefs. It was really frightening climbing up the outside ladder to the foretop in bad weather, clinging on for dear life as the ship rolled about and the full force of the wind caught you. With a stern wind the climb was sheer agony. You tried to hold your breath as clouds of hot smoke from the funnel swirled around you. At some point you had to open your mouth to take a breath and then you would have a lung full of the filthy stuff that left you coughing and gasping. On finally reaching the top you pushed open the small trap hatch and struggled through; no easy task when wearing an oilskin over an overcoat over countless sweaters. I lost cap after cap overboard as I climbed up and down that mast.

Less dangerous were trips to the galley at night for cocoa. But even then you were dodging under the swaying hammocks, trying to keep your feet and balance the jug of cocoa as the ship rolled, and the smell, the heat and the steam in the galley was enough to turn your stomach. Calling reliefs required much perseverance and a special technique. No relief could be late, but also God help you if you broke the calling rules. Never, never could you shake or even touch an officer or shout at him. You had to switch on the light, call him by name, and tell him the time and report the weather, and repeat this until he was awake, then return over and over again until you saw him get out of his bunk.

Occasionally we would go into Edinburgh to have tea or play golf or go to the cinema. There would also be the occasional afternoon dance for junior officers at the Kintore Rooms arranged by the Edinburgh ladies. If there weren't enough volunteers for these events some of us were detailed off to attend and did so very reluctantly, at least I did, because at that age I was shy, I was very uncertain of my dancing and I was terrified of strange girls. I once appeared on the stage of the King's Theatre.

Lady Beatty had arranged a charity matinee and the *Indomitable* was asked to provide a turn. We danced the hornpipe which seemed to go down rather well.

Running a picket boat was a wonderful experience, and a duty which every midshipman enjoyed. No modern motor-boat will ever match the beauty, elegance and dignity of the old steam picket boat with its sparkling bright work, scrubbed wooden decks and spotless paintwork. It was capable of 15 knots. Every midshipman took a proper pride in his boat's appearance and each week he would be expected to give the coxswain an extra tin or two of Bluebell polish. The crew consisted of a Petty Officer coxswain, two bowmen, a stern sheetman, a fender man, a stoker in the boiler room, and a stoker Petty Officer in the engine room. When a midshipman was in the boat he always took the wheel himself and worked the engine-room gong while the coxswain stood alongside keeping a watchful eye. The young inexperienced officer was in charge, but the older and greatly experienced Petty Officer was there at his side to help and give advice if required, and this relationship was accepted gratefully on the one side and without any resentment on the other.

On days when leave was granted all the picket boats of the Fleet would be waiting at Hawes pier, one alongside the other, having come in stern first in order to make a quick getaway. Each had an illuminated sign displayed on the top of the cabin. As the buses arrived down from Edinburgh the officers would stream on board their boats. With the engine opened right out, the whole boat throbbing and vibrating, the boiler-room fan roaring and sparks flying out of the funnels, a dozen or more boats, starting with the outside one, would go dashing off towards the ships lying a mile or two out. We looked on this return trip as a race and tried desperately to catch or outdistance the rest. In the excitement of the race, the midshipman could become very unpopular with his messmates, sitting huddled up on the top of the cabin, if he failed to ease down when the spray started to come over or if a sudden alteration of course brought water slopping in over the officers in the stern sheets.

There was a great temptation to try and show what a brilliant and dashing boat handler you were. To make a good alongside at high speed, judging the tide to a nicety and pulling up with a smother of foam under your counter as you rang down full astern, was a way of demonstrating your skill, but it did not always come off. A small error of judgement could result in a crash which could easily damage your boat, or if a strong tide was running, getting your bows either swept in and firmly wedged under the ladder or carried out while the bowmen desperately struggled to hold on to the boat rope. This created a very undignified and unseamanlike situation, which you could have avoided with a little more care and attention and if you had not been so anxious to show off.

Two incidents come vividly to mind when I recall my gun-room days. The first was the unforgettable sight of the Grand Fleet at sea. As you looked there would be just columns of smoke on the horizon. Then the cruisers spread ahead on the AK line would come into sight and then, at last, this huge armada of anything up to thirty battleships advancing in five or more columns surrounded by a close screen of destroyers. That was a spectacle the like of which will never be seen again.

Again I well remember a combined wardroom and gunroom picnic at Scapa Flow with a tremendous meal of bangers and bacon fried up on a large fire and much singing and vast consumption of sloe gin in the launch on the return journey. Little did we think at that time that within forty-eight hours we would be in the thick of battle.

Naval Cadet Charles Drake

It was May 1913 and a very cold day. Exmouth term, which was just about to join Osborne, was lined up in two lines opposite each other on the South Railway Jetty at Portsmouth

Dockyard. We were to be inspected by the First Sea Lord, Prince Louis of Battenberg, and the First Lord of the Admiralty, Winston Churchill. Prince Louis's son, later to be Lord Mountbatten, was a naval cadet in my house.

We were a diverse bunch. Among our entry we had C. B. Fry's son and W. G. Grace's grandson. Many of us were fairly impecunious and without private means. I remember the first time I put on my uniform my mother started singing from Gilbert and Sullivan. 'When I first put this uniform on, I thought as I looked in the glass, 'Tis one in a million, if any civilian, my figure and form can surpass'. She was terribly proud that her son was joining the Royal Navy.

Prince Louis of Battenberg had what I would call an imperial beard and Winston Churchill had a reefer suit and a yachting cap. Well, I was very young and didn't know who they were: I thought Battenberg was King George. You see I had never seen a good photograph in the paper of George V, I only knew he had a beard.

As they came down the line, Winston chatted away every now and again to one or other of the cadets who were all shuddering. When he was nearby, he suddenly turned round at right angles and pointed at me and said, 'What have you got at the end of that lanyard, boy?' I didn't like being called 'boy', but I was very frightened and pretty small, too. I said, 'A key, sir.' 'A key, have you?' said Winston. Then he said, 'Have you got anything else?' I said, very quietly, 'Yes, sir, a knife.' 'A knife, have you? Could you show it to me?' I pulled the end of the lanyard out and held it out to him. He said, 'Would you open it, please.' It was very stiff but I pulled very hard and out came the biggest blade. 'You've got that blade on that knife!' 'Yes, I have sir.' Winston held the knife in his hand and turned to the others and said, 'Now, my boys' – I think he called us 'boys' – 'when you get to the enemy, you must cut him down, cut him to bits!' Well, this was a rather horrifying remark to hear from the First Lord of the Admiralty. However, we all mumbled 'Yes, sir'.

My dear mother and another lady behind us heard this and were shuddering with fright. My mother was probably thinking, 'What have I put my boy into, cutting Germans to bits?' I thought Mountbatten's father looked a bit shocked too. But Winston moved off, laughing away. We were marched down in single file on to the tug to the Isle of Wight. We were then allowed a little bit of stand-easy time and we waved to our parents on the jetty as off we went to Osborne.

Able Seaman Jack Gearing

I was born in Greenwich in 1894 when Gladstone was Prime Minister and Queen Victoria was on the throne. In 1907 I became an apprentice waterman and lighterman to my father who, like his father and his father before him, had worked on the Thames. I had to sign the same indentures as my grandfather had – they stated that an apprentice had to 'faithfully his master serve, his secrets keep, not waste his goods, nor commit fornication, contract matrimony, not play at cards, dice, tables, nor haunt taverns or playhouses or absent himself from his Master's service day or night'!

It was a hard life, but we respected each other, and we knew the ways of the tug captains, the pilots. We used to sail up from Faversham to London in our barge *Mayflower* with such things as hay, bricks and building material. On the return journey we carried home manure from the streets and stables of London for the farmers to spread on their fields. In 1912 I went up to the Watermans' Hall to get a licence. This entitled me to take a fifty-ton barge on the Thames single-handed.

In 1913 I could see how the world was going. So when war broke out I went to the RNVR recruiting office in Blackfriars and joined up. I became a naval man. I went then to Crystal Palace for square-bashing, including marching to Epsom Downs. I was in Benbow battalion, each battalion being named after an admiral. While I was there they created a balloon section, which I joined. We would go up in a basket beneath the balloon and would get up to about 500 feet. We were there to listen for Zeppelins. If we heard one we would call down. If the rope broke we had a grappling hook which you lowered down until it snagged on something!

I was next posted to Scotland, then Chatham, and on to Devonport where, in 1915, I joined the *Theseus*. I hadn't been on her long before we were told we were to sail to Gallipoli. A number of ships had attacked the Turkish fortifications, such as the *Queen Elizabeth* in February 1915. They did all right on the first lot of forts, but after that, all they hit was dirt. The Turks laid mines in the right places and did for the French battleship *Bouvet* and also put *Inflexible* and *Irresistible* out of action. The Navy on its own had failed and had to withdraw back to Mudros. It was decided that the Army would have to land and take on the Turks.

We were told we were going to Gallipoli by the captain, and that we were to tow the *Robert E. Lee*. We arrived at Mudros and took on board a battalion of the East Yorks to fight what was to be one of the hardest battles ever fought out. In France, you attacked over open fields with plenty of places to land, but here you had nowhere to land. It felt as if we were going straight to a mountain that could see everything.

As we got near Suvla Bay a two-seater British aircraft flew over us. I think he was seeking the protection of our gunfire, but he had been hit and came down near our ship. We put boats out, reached her before she sank and kept her up, but when we got the pilot and observer out, they were both dead. That upset us. They had been too long in the water.

We knew that the four hundred men of the East Yorks were mostly fresh from training and few had seen action, so every sailor was given two soldiers to look after. We gave them our hammocks, made sure they ate well and gave them our rum. You see, we knew that where they were going would be like Hell on earth, so we gave them all the love we could, because they were going to need it. There was all those feelings, all that silence. That's why I admire the British, they take it and they're quiet.

As we approached Suvla Bay on the night of 6–7 August, it was the darkness before the dawn. I stood on the gangway which had been fitted over the stem to allow the troops to walk down into the motor lighters. As the soldiers followed each other down with their rifles one got hit by a sniper and screamed out. I told him to shut up and put up with the pain or he would frighten the rest – that was my first scream of war. I was frightened myself. I took him down to sick bay. I was then put on a raft with a 5-inch gun and towed by pinnace into shore to land with the troops. I stayed with them for a day and then a picket boat came and took me back on board. Throughout the time we were there we bombarded positions with our five guns armidships, one for'ard and one aft. They were all 6-inch. I had never had any training in how to fire a gun but was made no. 2, the breech loader, on one of the 6-inch guns. Although I was frightened, I kept quiet because that was how everyone behaved. We were well protected against torpedoes by a 'blister', a steel casing which was about six or seven feet out from the ship and went all round. We were fired at, but the torpedo hit the 'blister' and did only a little harm to the ship. We had to retire for the day, but we were back the next day, all repaired.

On one occasion the anchor failed. It meant the ship was in trouble. I had to help the diver with his equipment while someone screwed his helmet on. As he worked down below he talked to me on the rope. The Turks must have spotted what we were doing, so all the time he was down there they were shooting at me. But I had to stay by the rope and work out what the diver wanted. When he finished his work he tugged away and I got him up. And still they were firing at us!

Each day when there was a lull we'd go in and collect the wounded. Some of them were terribly badly wounded, and all so young. Suvla Bay was reasonably flat and the soldiers had made homes for themselves or taken over where other battalions had been before they moved forward. I did my best to cheer them up and encourage them. But most of the time, I was quiet because there wasn't much you could say in the face of all that horror. It was important that they had their own thoughts, they had to come to terms with it in their own way.

Every Sunday we used to try and have a service on board and we sang hymns which were heard by the soldiers on shore. They told us how much it meant to them, so whenever we scrubbed the decks we sang out as loud as we could all the old hymns to inspire them: 'Onward, Christian Soldiers', 'Fight the Good Fight', anything that was rousing. It cheered us up too.

I saw quite a lot of the Turkish prisoners on shore. They were badly dressed and always wanted our boots, they were so poor; but they were wonderful fighting men. They didn't give way. We could see them fighting from the ship; they were good. We didn't feel any anger towards them, we had a respect for them!

We did get black towards the end. We weren't succeeding at all, all we were doing was losing a lot of men and ships. Every day we were bringing in different men, different faces, all tired, all beaten. And it was so hot that summer, so hot. Then, as autumn came on, we knew things were getting worse on land, even with the reinforcements. We were watching a picture of failure fought out by brave men. But that's what the British are like, they keep going right till the end.

When we withdrew on 20 December it was dark. The soldiers were all packed so tight and quiet in the barges making their way to the big ships. We never lost a man, which was remarkable. As we were steaming quietly away I thought of what 'Pincher' Martin, who had done twenty years in the Navy, had said to me a few days after we'd arrived at Suvla Bay: 'We're not going to be flying the Union Jack here'. He was right. We were never going to make it ours.

Signalman Eric Peacock

I became interested in the Navy when a friend told me of his experiences in the Mediterranean. But I was under age and undersize at the time, so I had to wait until I was fifteen and three months in May 1913 before I could join as a 'Boy'.

I did my seamanship training at Devonport on *Powerful* and then on the *Ganges* at Shotley. After qualifying at the Signal School in Portsmouth I was allocated to HMS *Irresistible*, which was part of the Fifth Battle Squadron based at Portland Harbour. There was great excitement on board when war was declared on 4 August. Within a few days the squadron under the Flagship *Prince of Wales* sailed from Portland for channel patrol, accompanied by much cheering from the other ships and the Army manning the guns on the break-waters.

We moved at economical speed between Start Point and Dover in single line for roughly six weeks. During this time I got to know about coaling. We would drop into the Isle of Wight and as much as 1,400 tons would be hoisted aboard in bags by derricks from the collier. Apart from those on duty, the whole ship's company took part with us boys usually in the dumping stations, throwing the empty bags to the collier. We got blacker and blacker as the day went on. A week later we would be back doing the same.

Three cruisers patrolled east of Dover northwards. We often sighted them and signalled greetings. They were the *Aboukir, Cressy* and *Hogue* and we were very saddened when we heard how they were all sunk by one submarine.

On 26 November we were at Sheerness. That day, as all days at 8 am, we were indicating by flags the state of coal, provisions and water. It so happened that *Bulwark*'s hoist was a bit adrift and so we were watching her. As her flag reached the top, there was a terrific explosion and then the startling realisation that the *Bulwark* was no longer there, just an open space between adjacent ships, calm water and bits and pieces floating. It was devastating.

Early in January 1915 we sailed from Chatham to a secret destination, in the company of the battleship *Majestic*. Our chief yeoman, a wily man, had spotted some details on the captain's chart, and said quietly to us, 'I hope you all have your whites and cap covers'. This meant warmer climes. We arrived via Malta at Tenedos, an island near the entrance to the Dardanelles. We were told we were going to bombard the area and then force a passage through and shorten the war! Throughout late February and the first two weeks of March we were kept busy bombarding short gun positions and the village of Krithia. We also landed demolition parties to blow up any enemy guns still standing after our bombardment.

On one occasion I went ashore. Landing in whalers at Kum Kale on the Asiatic Coast there was no trouble until we neared the gun positions, which consisted of big mounds of earth with the gun on rails in between, easy for running into firing and returning. Fire opened up from various points and one or two of the party were wounded, but the Royal Marines went into action and the demolition party got on with the job of putting the guns out of action. The firing ceased, and it was decided to proceed further inland. Until then I had done nothing but remain near the CO and keep all my equipment intact – a tidy load – for, besides my side arms, service revolver, ammunition, cutlass and necessary trappings, I also carried two semaphore flags, white and blue Morse flags, boat-flashing lamp and candles. I moved around with my pistol cocked for instant action and ready to frighten any Turk that appeared! We came to a big wall, apparently one end of a rectangular burial ground, and, as the firing appeared to come from the further end, it was decided to split the party, move up each side and charge round the end and annihilate the enemy. This we did but only to make a lot of cheering noise and meet each other! The sniping continued while we made our way to the whalers, one marine dragging a wounded comrade on a spade. I broke my pistol and littered the flag deck with six empty cartridges. I don't know who I fired at, but I must have had a good time!

The day of 18 March remains clear in my mind, as it was our biggest attack on the Turkish gun positions. Many battleships and destroyers (British and French) moved into position from west of the entrance into the Dardanelles towards Chanak. My action station was with the Fire Control Officer, in the foretop, high on the foremast, manning the voice pipe to the captain. Action continued throughout the afternoon with relays of up to four battleships stationed abeam moving forward as the leading ships got far enough and turned about to make way for the next line. The bombardment was severe and ships were hit. Apart from my excitement in passing and receiving messages, the Gunnery Officer had also climbed into the foretop and we had a direct line to the fire-control room. So I knew what was going on, and also had a magnificent view of the whole area. The first real shock was hearing a heavy explosion and seeing the French battleship *Bouvet* listing and gradually disappearing, all in seconds.

The action continued; other ships were hit by gunfire and there were big splashes in the sea around us from near misses. I was completely occupied with control work when, suddenly, there was an awful crunch, the ship shuddered and began to list to starboard. It seemed quite a bit to those of us in the foretop! There was a complete silence for a few seconds and then the Gunnery Officer ordered 'Everyone out of the Top'. One by one the crew went down the ladder, leaving myself and the two officers to follow, when the GO said, 'Off you go, lad', and down the ladder I went. Then just before I reached the lower top, a shell hit the foremost funnel and I let go the rungs on the mast and fell on to a number of gym mats which had been stored there. When I reached the upper deck I was yellow from the fumes. The Turks now decided we were a sitting target and guns from each side of the Channel concentrated their fire and made several hits. I remember looking towards the bridge and seeing the captain leaning against the rails at the same time as I heard the order, 'Abandon Ship'. As I slipped into the water I was worried about a new pair of boots obtained on repayment from the Slop Room only the previous day, which were slung round my neck, but I never saw them again. I was soon picked up and taken to *Queen Elizabeth*.

After the *Irresistible*, the *QE* was a wonderful ship, with spacious mess deck and plenty of room to sling a hammock. I transferred to the cruiser *Phaeton* and travelled to Mudros during a violent spell of weather, when I experienced the worst bout of sea sickness I ever had: the ship was pitching and wallowing, hitting 'milestones' every few seconds. I turned myself almost inside out, not an ounce of bile left inside me and, as we entered harbour, I was hanging over the rail like a wet towel.

At Mudros I was chosen as part of a landing party led by the chief yeoman of the *Irresistible* to land at 'W' beach, Cape Helles. We spent a lot of time preparing. The only spare uniforms were khaki, but to maintain our pride we stencilled 'RN' on to our cap ribbons.

We disembarked from the *Euryalus* with the Lancashire Fusiliers. As we moved towards the shore, tows were returning with the dead and wounded. The invasion force had been seen when Very lights were fired by the Turks, so rifle fire came from every point along the cliff top. There was also barbed wire in shallow water and on the shore. Somehow we got in bows-on, between bodies and wire. As I jumped out of the boat I had to try and keep hold of my signalling equipment, because that was vital – I wasn't any good without it, for, as soon as we hit the shore, and despite enemy fire, we had to keep up our signals to our ships covering the troops landing. The Turks made several determined attempts to drive us into the sea. I found myself creeping forward, like an infantryman, and banging away with my .303 rifle. But really it was the Lancashire Fusiliers who held the day. They were marvellous.

The first forty-eight hours were the most hectic as far as our unit was concerned. The Lancashire Fusiliers, with support from those who had landed on 'X' and 'V' beaches, gradually pressed back the Turks who had prepared trenches almost up to the water's edge, but at tremendous cost of life. On one occasion I was standing alongside an officer from Army Signals while he was reading out the words being transmitted. All of a sudden he was hit and badly wounded. Everyone back on the ship thought I was dead because I rolled away out of trouble when he went down. It wasn't just rifle fire that was so hard to endure but the heavy Turkish artillery from Kum Kale. That was constant – there was no peace. All the time we were kept busy: it was semaphore or morse flag by day, box lamp in the dry batteries, or boats flashing lamp at night. Later, when we got more established, we used a heliograph for hourly communications with Tenedos, which was about twelve miles away.

We slept where we could, when we could, pulling a waterproof over us when it rained, and could it rain! The enemy aircraft used to drop a load of darts which dropped in showers which was pretty miserable. As the weather improved we could grab a swim, but corned beef and biscuits was still our daily diet.

During my time there I got dysentery really badly. I managed to get hold of some flour and drink a basin full of flour water. I didn't go near a bog for three weeks! Living in dugouts, and lying on sandy soil, meant that everyone became infected with lice. Even if you got rid of your old clothes and put on new ones they still came back. They would recommence attack as soon as you were dressed. Neither flame nor water could kill them! The heat, the unburied dead carcasses, and the rubbish brought in a plague of flies. Mealtimes were a nightmare because everything was black with flies. One particular lunchtime, eight Royal Engineers rigged up a table close by us and sat down to eat their bully beef. A shell burst and killed them all. We only found pieces when we went to help them.

As the months went on we saw Turkish prisoners. We all admired them as fighters, but they were mostly filthy with torn and tattered uniforms. They'd had no pay for months and very little to eat. Yet still they shelled and shot at us. I even got reprimanded for not taking adequate precautions during shelling!

Our wireless transmission station was visited by quite a few senior officers including Sir Ian Hamilton and Lord Kitchener. We also saw a lot of Commander Samson of the RNAS. Every aircraft that flew over to us was Samson. He really was a hero, he seemed free to fly where he wanted.

Rumours of a possible evacuation came through to us before anyone else. Units began to disappear. We then heard that Suvla and Anzac beaches had been successfully evacuated with no casualties. By now, December, the weather was raw cold. Yet we couldn't believe that the Turks would let us simply slip away. But they did, and on 8 January 1916 we left from the pierhead. Of that 20-man naval party I was one of the first on to the beach on 25 April 1915 and one of the last to leave. I was ten days off my eighteenth birthday.

Private Joe Clements

ROYAL MARINE LIGHT INFANTRY

I was born in Caterham in 1898 and at thirteen went to work as an errand boy for a local grocer. We worked six days a week and sometimes on a Saturday till 9 pm. I used to pull a two-wheeled cart for miles in all weathers for 2s.6d. a week. Sometimes on a Wednesday half-day the boss gave me half an apple.

I tried to join the Navy at thirteen and was bitterly disappointed to be turned down. On the 18 August 1914 I left home and walked the seven miles into Croydon and tried again to join the Navy. I was told the Navy was full up but I could join the Royal Marine Light Infantry, so I signed on for twelve years. My age was sixteen and five months so the recruiting officer advised me to go outside and have another birthday. That same evening we were put on a train to Deal and didn't get to bed till midnight, but of course we were up the next morning at 5.30.

We were taught how to drill, how to shoot and how to swim in a canvas duck suit. In November I joined the brigade of the Royal Naval Division which had returned from Antwerp and three weeks later was posted to the machine-gun section. On 1 January 1915 we left Deal for a three-day march, but I suppose, looking back, we had in truth left to go to war. We marched 18 miles one day, 25 miles the next, and 25 the last day, all in full kit. Then they put us on a train to Blandford where we were billeted in a village school. The King and Winston Churchill inspected us so we knew we were going to the Front. It is funny how people don't tell you, yet you know. The 1st and 2nd RMLI were to be part of 3rd Machine Brigade, 63 Royal Naval Division, alongside the two Anson battalions.

On 26 February we embarked on the *Franconia* and, after a week, arrived at Port Said and stayed there two weeks training in the desert. Then we boarded the *Alnwick Castle* and stopped off on the rocky island of Lemnos which was very bleak and the right place for manoeuvres. So we were well prepared for anything though we didn't at this point know where we were going. On 24 April we were told we were to make a dummy landing at the Gulf of Saros at the top of the Gallipoli peninsula. We did this to distract the Turks while the main force of troops landed at Cape Helles. We came ashore in six small boats pulled by a steam pinnace controlled by a young midshipman. We were told to make a lot of noise in the hope that the Turks would pull their army away from the south. Well, we made a hell of a lot of noise, but there was no one there, so we got back on the boat and sailed down to Gaba Tepe and landed on the night of 29 April, the day after the Australians.

It was a bit chaotic as the Australians seemed to have discarded all their equipment on the narrow beach and climbed up the side of the cliff with just their rifles and ten rounds. The impetus of the push had carried them over three ridges, but of course the Turks were well dug in and counter-attacked. The Australians couldn't hold them and eventually ran out of ammunition and made their way back to the first ridge where we took over. As quiet as we could we went up the gully in the dark each following in the footsteps of the chap in front. Eventually we made the rocky ground of the first ridge. I fixed up my Maxim machine-gun behind sandbags at the end of a gully, then sat and waited. It was still dark when we heard trumpets blowing as the Turks came at us in droves from the other end of the gully from where we were positioned. I didn't have to take aim, I just fired and mowed them down. You couldn't miss, there were so many of them. It was like firing into a mass of bodies gelled together.

Eventually they withdrew. But they came again seven times that night and each time we drove them back. Come the dawn, they had gone, only the bodies were left. A young lieutenant came across later that morning to tell us that we were moving on. I was about to dismantle my machine-gun when he noticed that I only had a few rounds left in one of the bands. He told me that he had never fired a machine-gun and asked if I'd show him how to do it, which I did. He sat down behind the steel guard and sandbag and fired away and then suddenly slumped back, a bullet through his head. A Turkish sniper had managed to hit him through a very small slit in the steel guard. A young man killed by an unlucky chance.

From there we were moved by lighter to Cape Helles. After looking around at the forts and the effect of the first naval bombardment, we sorted out the beach, then made our way up the slippery communication trench to our new position. On the way up there was an arm sticking out so we all shook its hand saying, 'Hello, Johnny.' We took over from one of the Anson battalions. The trenches were about six foot deep and on top we piled sandbags about three feet high, front and back, and on top of that was concertina wire. You certainly didn't put your head over the top because you were only about 150 to 200 yards from the Turks. I fixed my machine-gun between the sandbags with a firing step below. The Indian Army brought us up food on mules, but it was bully beef and biscuit for the first three months. Then one day we were issued a loaf of bread to share between seven men – it was such a change! Occasionally we'd exchange some bully for curry and mix that with the beef.

We needed to get water but the Turks used to mark the point of the stream we were using and put snipers in. Because I was still a boy I didn't ever get my rum ration but my mother sent me packets of Navy Cut cigarettes. We soon discarded our sun helmets and used a forage cap or balaclava because there were no steel helmets then. Forever in our clothes were lice. You could never destroy them and of course there were the flies, flies on everything, your food, your skin, your face and of course on the dead bodies out in no-man's- land. About 20 yards in front of me was a dead Turk. Everyday he became more bloated until eventually he burst. The smell was dreadful, but we seemed to take death in our stride.

Our daily 'stand to' was at dawn and from then on it was two hours on, one hour off. We'd usually get fired on either by snipers or from the heavy artillery which sometimes used shrapnel shells – they were really nasty things. On one occasion I ducked down with the rest of the trench and felt something hit my back. It had hit the webbing and hadn't pierced me. I was very lucky. A great drain on our nerves was 'Asiatic Annie' – a big, heavy gun – which was fired from some distance. You could count in seconds how long it would be before the shell landed.

I had my machine-gun trained on Krithia which was probably just over a thousand yards away where there was a road used by mule trains. We would fire and make the mules jump about a bit. At night we were sometimes told not to fire in certain directions because we had patrols out. One night the Gurkhas were out there, so we were keeping a close watch. Out of the dark came this voice to warn us not to shoot, 'All right, Tommy, all right'. Then I saw this smiling face coming in and it wasn't till he'd got in the trench that I realised he was carrying the head of a Turk! He had used his kukri.

As the summer went on water points were organised and we used to take it in turn to fetch it back in a bucket. One day while I was out, the Turks opened up on the reserve trench, then midway, and finally dropped a shell on my machine-gun post, and killed my no. 2, Jock Twycross, and wounded four or five nearby. That could easily have been me. I was sorry to lose him because we had shared a lot together. But then that is war.

On 4 June we didn't see the attack by the Collingwood battalion but we did see the repercussions. The Collingwoods were brand new, had never seen action, and were ordered to attack, 800-strong, in glaring sunlight shortly after noon. Many did not get further than the parapet before being mown down. By the next day they had lost 25 officers and around 600 other ranks. The remnants, as they passed by us, were in a bad way.

Come November 1915 it got very cold. There was continuous rain which filled up the trenches, so we had to sleep on the parapets. The Turks did the same, I suppose. We had an unspoken truce and didn't shoot at sleeping men. But it was so cold and we were always wet. On Christmas Day we were in the firing line and were served one slice of pudding and seven dates. Two days later we went down into our dug-out to change our clothes only to find our packs with our clean washing under three feet of water. We managed eventually to dry them out. Then, for another treat, they put us into the firing line for New Year's Day.

The first we knew of the evacuation was when the French moved out on 1 January. We spread out into their trenches to extend the line. We didn't know that Anzac and Suvla beaches had already been evacuated. On 8 January we began to destroy food and rifles that were not needed. We then tied empty sandbags around our feet, secured our water bottles so that they wouldn't clank around, and at midnight we moved off. I carried my machine-gun for over five miles in the dark until we reached the beach. As we were walking 'Asiatic Annie' fired several shells. We had come to hate her throughout our time at

Gallipoli. The Turks didn't know we were going. Firing from the Asiatic side, Annie had always been a law unto herself.

We clambered on to a lighter and were carried out to the *Prince George*. The crew looked after us and gave us a meal of bully. As soon as I'd eaten it I fell fast asleep on the deck down below and the next morning we arrived in Mudros where we'd left from in April the previous year.

In those nine months the Royal Naval Division suffered terrible casualties. We had lost 1,653 killed, another 600 had died of their wounds. A further 238 had died of illness, and over 5,000 had been wounded.

Private Hubert Trotman

ROYAL MARINE LIGHT INFANTRY

I was born in Abingdon in 1897, the year of Queen Victoria's Diamond Jubilee. When I was eleven I won a scholarship and went to Abingdon Grammar School. I left school when I was fourteen because I was wanted in the family bakery business. I had always worked in the bakery after school and at weekends; it was expected of me and I wanted to do it. But it was a job that never finished: it was all hours. As you finished one day you seemed to start the next.

We were one person my father and me. He was my world: I had worked with him from the time I could walk. He was so proud of me when, at thirteen, I won first prize at the Agricultural Hall in London for my loaf. I got first prize again later, out of 3,000, for my Hovis ginger fruit cake. So he wasn't very happy with me joining up, so I waited until Christmas was over and joined on 30 December 1916. All my pals had joined up so I wanted to be with them. We had all been through OTC at school. Most of them are lying out in France now and their names are on the War Memorial.

I joined the Royal Marines and took a train to Deal to start my training. The month's training was tough. I can tell you that

that was a training. Fifty men to a squad and each squad had a sergeant instructor. By God they were tough on you. You couldn't even move an eyelid unless the sergeant told you to. They were tin gods, those sergeants, but they turned out some real fighting men. From there I went to Blandford for my small arms training. It was there that I heard of General Trotman of the Royal Marines. I didn't know it at the time, but he was my father's cousin and there was a strong physical resemblance. He wanted me to take a commission but I told him I wanted to be one of the boys; they were a great bunch of lads, my squad.

Towards the end of the training came the hard bit – a test of skills with an officer observing. The officer followed each man separately on his horse. He carried a clipboard and took notes. We were told we were on active service. You would be walking along with fixed bayonet, looking for the enemy, when all of a sudden he would blow his whistle and a wooden head would pop up, and I would have to shoot at it. With different blasts of the whistles something else would happen and it went on like that throughout the course. Another thing we had to do was run a mile in full marching order in a certain time.

We were fit when we went from Blandford to the Somme in early April 1917 with the 2nd Royal Marine Battalion. We took over the trenches the Germans had vacated. They were full of mud. I saw a lot of men invalided out with trenchfoot but it didn't happen to me because I never took my boots off. The whole of the time I was on the Somme all I had to eat was bully beef, tinned beans and hard dog biscuits. Occasionally we would get a loaf of bread between six of us. It used to come up in a sandbag. If it was raining it would be wet. If the bloke carrying it slipped over, it would be muddy. I always remember the water was the colour of lime. From the fighting around Gavrelle there were many dead, some had been there for ages. We could only work at night and it took a long time to clear them. We couldn't bring them back to our lines, it was a case of pitching them into an old trench or shovelling in what was left of them. Then we used to fill the trench in. There were hundreds of bodies: it seemed endless. They had advanced on the German trenches and had simply been wiped out.

We then went up to Vimy and the brickfields of Lens and I got attached to the Canadians for a while just after they had taken Vimy Ridge. I was with a Canadian sergeant in the line one night. He said he'd stand watch while I got some sleep. As dawn broke he woke me. I looked ahead and could see masses of Germans about to counter-attack. You could see their helmets bobbing along above the mist. The sergeant said, 'Keep your head down a minute while I think what we do about this'. I said 'I know what I'm going to do, I'm running for it'. I ran and didn't stop until I reached Bully Grenay where I knew there were some Marines.

I was there for a few weeks. I remember one time we were in a ditch and I was asleep standing on my feet. In a dream I heard my Dad calling me to get up. I woke to find I was up to my waist in water. I was so tired I think I would have drowned. Many did.

Then it was time for leave. We travelled in a box car to Calais. We were as lousy as cuckoos. When we got to Calais we had to head for the fumigator. But there we saw a queue a mile long. We were told the boat sailed in half an hour and if we didn't make it, we would lose a day of our leave. So those of us at the tail end of the queue broke off, went down to the docks, and damn me, we just walked on to the boat. We hid down below until it had sailed. So we disembarked unfumigated. That night I got as far as Paddington and the next day I caught the first train to Didcot. When I got home, just to take it in and breathe the familiar smell of the bakery again, I stood outside the shop for a while. Then I opened the door and shouted, 'Mother I'm outside. I'm home'. 'Come in,' she said, 'come in'. What a sight I must have been. I hadn't changed my clothes for months. I had a beard and I was in a hell of a state. She took one look at me and tears rolled down her face. She said, 'I'll clean you up'. 'No', I said, 'you can't do that yet.' I put my hand in my armpit and took out a handful of lice. 'Look,' I said. 'Lice, hoards of them, I can't come in like this.' I put them back where they came from and went up to the hospital to see the matron. She knew me well, because I had visited her on my rounds when delivering bread to the hospital. She said, 'Hubert, we will soon fix you up'. She put a large sheet on the ground outside. 'You stand on that. Empty your pockets and then take all your clothes off'. Then she put me in a big bath. When I got out I asked about my clothes. She told me she had put them in the copper, lice and all. I had to spend my leave in civvies. When I got back to Deal I was still in civvies, and so was called up on the carpet. I explained to the officer and everything was all right.

When I got back to France I was burying the dead again. We also used to go out on raids to catch prisoners for interrogation. The Germans were tough buggers and we lost a lot of men doing it. We were also engaged on working parties.

In May, one chap had a large flat, heavy parcel arrive for him from home. When he opened it, it was a steel breast plate and back plate with a strap over the shoulders. Off went the working party, leaving the man with the armour behind with one other chap. When we got back we couldn't find them. We dug around and around. All the while there was a great deal of shelling going on. Then we found them, both dead. One was called John Bull and the other was Eric Coates. We took them back and buried them beside the road. No one would touch that breast plate, it was just left there, no one wanted it.

'Woodbine Willie', the vicar, used to come around to give Bible readings. We didn't go there for the Bible reading, we went there for the fag you got afterwards. Mind you, if he'd given us a fag before he started, he would have had an empty house. On 6th July we were with Woodbine Willie when a sergeant came along and shouted, 'Come on you buggers, out you come'. He didn't use ecclesiastical language. He told us that the watch had seen Jerry out in front and that he was up to something. Seven of us went out that night into no-man's-land to sort them out. All at once I don't know whether it was artillery, mortars or what, all hell went up and so did I. Down I came with a bump. I laid there in the mud until I got my breath back. My left leg was numb. Two men had wounds and the other four were killed.

I crawled back towards our lines and managed to get under the wire. I was carried to the doctor's dugout in the side of the trench and from there down to the first field dressing station. Then I was put into an ambulance with a lot of others and driven over rough roads to a hospital. There were dozens of orderlies standing there and dozens of stretchers as well. They kept coming and taking men away and then they got to me. I was picked up, then put on a sort of spiral shoot and when it stopped I was taken off the stretcher and put on a conveyor belt. When that stopped, I was taken off and stripped, then x-rayed. The nurse painted rings and arrows on my leg, there were so many. When I looked, my ankle to the knee was a mass of wounds, it looked as if I had been riddled with a shotgun. Later I was taken to a little bay full of people in white coats, all lined up. I was asked to count to ten. The doctor stuck a gauze over my face, I got to four and the next thing I remember was coming to in a hut full of stretchers. The next morning I was put on to a light railway which had four stretchers to a truck and a little engine at the front. We steamed off and I think we went everywhere it was possible to go and ended up at Etaples where I was put in a hut with only one bed. I felt very low. Later the matron came in, looked at my leg and then picked me up in her arms as if she was cradling a baby and took me to a hut where there were other wounded men. She was either very strong or knew how to lift, but she also understood what my mind wanted. I was then sent to Boulogne by train to be sent home on the hospital ship, *Princess Elizabeth*. I remember looking out of the porthole and seeing the white cliffs and thought that I was passing from hell into heaven. I was taken to a military hospital in Endell Street in London. When I was getting about on crutches I was bumped up on to one of the lions in Trafalgar

Square and saw the Americans arrive in London. They were quite a sight, fresh-faced and eager. They could have had no idea what they were going to as they came under the arch into Whitehall and down the Mall towards Buckingham Palace. My wound kept me out of action for more than nine months. Just as I was nearing recovery at Chatham they were asking for volunteers for the Zeebrugge raid. The General called a parade and said to the men, 'I am asking for volunteers for a very hazardous operation. Those not wanting to take part take one step backward'. Nobody moved. This became 'A' Company of the 4th RMLI Battalion which raided Zeebrugge.

At the end of August 1918 I was sent back to France to join the Hood Battalion, part of the 63rd Royal Naval Division, in time to face the tailend of the great German onslaught. As we got nearer the front, heavy shells started falling near the train, so we got out and took cover in some shrubbery near a wood. We could hear a tremendous fight going on ahead and saw the wounded walking past – drained. After an hour we were ordered forward and we went down into a valley. The Germans kept coming on wave after wave, but we stood our ground. At one point I was standing alone in the shrubbery with dead men all around me. I thought, 'I'm a fool standing here waiting for a sniper to pick me off'. So I dropped down amongst the dead. When the next wave of our men advanced I got up and joined them. We were fighting for a couple of days but the Germans were resisting all the way.

We then rested and our numbers were made up. When we began to move forward again the roads were full of wagons, guns and transport, everything was moving forward. We marched for a couple of days, not on the road, but on either side.

One night we came across a row of guns that stretched for half a mile along each side of the road. They were wheel to wheel, so close together, that we had to squeeze between them in single file. We rested up on the side of a hill. Then just before dawn the battery to the right opened fire, then the one to the left. Flares started to go up, then a mass of shells, and the flames from the guns all lit up the sky, just like daylight. It was such an amazing contrast to the quiet we'd had while resting.

As soon as the barrage ceased we moved forward. This was the battle for the Hindenburg Line which the Germans were going to defend stoutly. Six tanks were with us and we smashed through on a wide front. We then got to the second line and the tanks broke off, three turned left and three turned right and we were left out in the open. We were faced by the German 3rd Marine Division. We let them have it, and they let us have it, bullet, bayonet, butt and hand to hand. It was the hardest fighting of my war. After ten hours fighting only ten of us came out. We were then relieved by the Highland Light Infantry and we dropped into a dugout at the side of the road to rest. A Highland officer found us asleep and called us all of the names under the sun. He thought we had been hiding. After being in that fight we were very angry. I told him that, if he swore at us again, he would have ten bullets and ten bayonets stuck into his fat belly. That put paid to him, he about-turned and legged it. We heard machine-guns start so we got out of the dugout and made our way to the rear. As we were walking back we found one of our galleys beside the road and they asked us where the Hood Battalion was and we replied that as far as knew we were it. We had some tea and fell asleep at the side of the road, they covered us up with blankets. When we woke we found that more men of the Hood had come back. That raised our spirits.

We had a week out of line and in October the battalion moved forward to attack Niergnies. We didn't meet a lot of resistance. From then on we seemed to be moving forward, village to village, field to field. I remember going to a place where the foliage and the shrub had been cut down to about four feet high and barbed wire had been interwoven in the shrub, we lost a lot of lads there. One night seven of us under a lieutenant got into a ditch. I fell asleep, but not for long, because

I was awoken by a terrific storm. I was soaking wet and the ditch was running with water well above my knees. I could see the Germans moving towards us. The lieutenant opened up with the Lewis gun and it jammed. I cleared it for him and we drove them off. We knew they would return in the morning. The lieutenant told me to find the captain and explain our position. I said, 'Where is he, sir?' He said, 'On our right somewhere, see if you can find him. You had better take Tully.'

As we were creeping across to a copse we came to a canal with a tree lying across it to block any barges. Tully decided that he was going to straddle this tree like a horse and ease himself across. He was doing very well but when he got to the middle there was a crack and Tully fell off into the water and didn't come up again. A sniper had got him. I had to get across, so I got down into the water, turned on my back, holding my rifle above me and pushed with my legs until I got to the other side. I was soaking, but squeezed myself out and made my way from cover to cover with a few shots at me until I got to the copse. There were bodies about, both ours and Germans', but nothing living until I got well into the little wood where I saw a fellow sitting with his back up against a tree. I said, 'Hello, chum, what's happened to you?' He pulled back a waterproof cape that was covering his legs and there was two raw stumps with jagged bones and blood pouring from them. He pointed and said, 'My legs are over there'. And there were two legs laying there, a couple of yards away. I got my first aid kit out and did all I could. I lit a fag for him and told him I would get help for him as soon as I could. Well, it was a long time before I got to the other wood, but when I got there I found the captain and a few more of our boys. I gave the captain my message and told him about the wounded man. I then went back with the stretcher bearers to get him. When I got there he was dead with the Woodbine still between his lips. He was put on the stretcher. As they were about to pick him up, the other said, 'Hold on, we got them left to right, he'd hate to go back lop sided!'

Not long after that incident, I was out with an officer looking for our Lewis gun crew. We never found them. They had simply disappeared. Later the Germans shelled the wood with gas. I put my mask on, but my eyes were stinging and everything was strange, but I was OK. That night a line of white tape was put out. At dawn we came under shellfire, so we had to move to high ground where of course the Germans had machine-gunners on the hill. We fought our way to the top. When we got there, I saw a sight that I will never ever forget. I can still see it today. Looking down, I could see, left to right, two lines of khaki troops moving forward with the sun shining on their bayonets. They were flashing red and yellow up and down the line. We settled down to watch their advance but the Germans opened up on us from the woods down below. We then had a tremendous fight with them down below before making it to another piece of high ground. This time it was like being on the edge of a cliff looking out to sea, but we were looking out on green country-side and there, down in the bottom, was a whole squadron of German Uhlans. They were dismounted and lounging around. We opened up on them and the place was one mass of loose horses. I only saw one man, riding low on his horse, get out of the valley.

In the first week in November we were still advancing, still fighting hard and losing men. We knew nothing of the proposed Armistice, we didn't know until a quarter to ten on that day. As we advanced on the village of Guiry a runner came up and told us that the Armistice would be signed at eleven o'clock that day, 11 November. That was the first we knew of it.

We were lined up on a railway bank nearby, the same railway bank that the Manchesters had lined up on in 1914 (the 2nd Battalion of the Manchester Regt defended this area on 23 and 24 August 1914 during the Battle of Mons). Some of us went down to a wood in a little valley and there found the skeletons of some of the Manchesters still lying there. Lying there with their boots on, very still, no helmets, no rusty rifles or equipment, just their boots.

My recollections of Armistice Day was that the guns just stopped, we pelted each other up to eleven o'clock, then stopped.

The Royal Marine band came up with a general at its head who said, 'You men stand firm'. I asked him if the war was really over, he said it was. Some lout behind me shouted, 'I thought it was, sir'. The general asked why and the lout replied, 'Because we can see a general in the front line'.

After he had gone I went to sleep on the railway bank. When I woke up there was a big pile of equipment on the ground and no men. So I climbed on to the top of the bank and saw them in the nearby village. When I got there they were all in the brewery, sticking their heads in the vats and having a big suck and coming out shouting like dogs coming out of water!

On 23 April 1919 I was demobbed. In the RND's short life we'd had over 7,500 killed and 3,000 had died of their wounds or in other ways. That evening I got as far as Didcot but there were no more trains, so I had to walk the seven miles home and got there at midnight. My sister was there to meet me and my mother. We kissed and jabbered away. Then my mother went to fetch my dear father. She came rushing out of the bedroom. 'Hubert, your dad has gone to pieces, he's just laying there like a log, he just passed out.' He had heard my voice and was totally overcome. With all the Royal Naval Division's casualties I don't think he ever expected me to return. He must have felt he'd heard my ghost. We did what we could for him. I went to bed at two and started work in the bakery again at five.

Midshipman Brian de Courcy-Ireland

In 1907, when I was seven, I met a sailor who was on leave and he shot me a line about how wonderful the Navy was. I decided there and then that I would join. Neither my father, who was a country parson, nor my mother, tried to dissuade me. I had two brothers who later served on the Western Front and both of whom survived. Fairly unusual for three sons to survive the Great War.

I was brought up in a village about six miles outside Bideford in Devon and, apart from an odd trip to paddle in the sea at Paignton, I never really left the village. In September 1912 my father accompanied me to London for my interview for the Navy. It was my first time in a big city. I was one of 360 who wanted to become a Naval cadet at Osborne; they took eighty. At the interview one member of the board asked me (I'm sure, looking back, in a most friendly way) how many arches Bideford bridge had? I replied that I was astonished none of them knew! I was a bit surprised I got in, especially after they asked me to look at the clock and tell them the time in French. I simply told them the clock had stopped!

I enjoyed Osborne although it was pretty strong on discipline. Alongside our ordinary education we were taught Naval skills such as navigation, but the education was certainly biased towards the Navy. My term was Grenville and I remained in that when I went on to Dartmouth. In my last term at Osborne, in the summer of 1914, I was appointed to the *Centurion* for the Royal Review of the Grand Fleet at Spithead. To see all those ships together, fully rigged, was a tremendous sight. The high spot for me was being allowed to man one of the six-pounder guns for firing the Royal Salute. It really was the last great moment of the British Navy. Sheer power and might. We will never see its like again.

I joined Dartmouth in January 1915 and left in December of the same year. The term before us, the ones who'd been there at the outbreak of war, were sent to sea, and a number of them were lost on the *Hogue, Cressy* and *Aboukir*. That was sad news to receive but we knew our turn was coming and were looking forward to it. It was an unsentimental world really; the war was on, get on with it.

I travelled up from London on the Naval train which ran almost daily to Thurso in Caithness, whence we crossed over by steamer to Scapa Flow. There were stops on the way up at Inverness and Invergordon. I remember well the break at the latter. Outside the station a large funeral procession was passing; there seemed endless coffins. No one would talk, but we learnt afterwards that it was the dead from the *Natal*. As a result of an internal explosion, she had blown up in harbour on New Year's Eve while there was a children's party on board.

My first appointment, on 2 January 1916, was to HMS *Bellerophon*, a dreadnought of the Fourth Battle Squadron based at Scapa Flow. She was armed with ten 12-inch guns, one twin turret forward, one on each beam amidships and two in the centre line aft. I was a junior midshipman or, more commonly called in our gunroom, a 'wart'. I was fifteen and a half. To remind us that we were, in the eyes of our seniors, just warts, we were all given a good sound dozen lashes by the Sub (Sub-Lieutenant). So from day one we knew our place and what would happen if we stepped out of it.

Of course there were the more standard traditional initiation rites and evolutions. One of these, 'providing bumph', involved running to the officers' heads (lavatories) to collect a clean brown sheet of bumph paper (lavatory paper) and return it to the gunroom. The first wart back got a glass of port and the last a dozen on the backside. I got a dozen because I failed to notice there was an officer sitting on the toilet when I took the paper and left him nothing at all! The worst punishment was mast-heading, where you were sent to the crow's-nest. That was dreadful because of the roll of the ship and the cold. But the hardest task was for the duty midshipman who had to climb up to the top to give the chap his meal. Meanwhile, down below in the gunroom, if a Sub stuck his fork into one of the overhead beams all the junior midshipmen had to leave because officers were going to talk about ladies. In our first year we were looked after by a Snotty's Nurse. He'd make sure you behaved and did some work. We were traditionally called 'snotties' because in the old days of the Navy midshipmen could not afford a handkerchief and so would blow their nose on their sleeve. The Admiralty brought this practice to an end by having three buttons sewn on the cuff.

In the early part of 1916 we were doing sweeps of the North Sea. The *Bellerophon* was accompanied by the other dreadnoughts of the Fourth Battle Squadron, *Benbow, Temeraire* and *Vanguard*, but we were not involved in any incident. I recall how cold it was and how unpleasant a place Scapa was. We were a coal-burning ship and had to take on 3,000 tons every few months. In fact I spent my first Christmas Day in the Navy coaling ship, starting at 5.30 am and finishing at 6.00 pm. Anyone who was not on duty, and it didn't matter if you were a schooly (schoolmaster) or the padre, you had to take part. As a midshipman you spent an hour holding the bags for sailors to fill and then an hour working the winches to the derricks. You'd alternate throughout the day.

We usually got a corn beef sandwich at midday and when it was all over you had to scrub the ships clean. When we'd finished we'd have to get the bath ready for the senior midshipmen. When it was finally our turn the twenty-four of us junior midshipmen would have to share two-thirds of a bath of water spread between four tray baths each of which held about four inches of water. Again the senior midshipmen had use of them first. By the time we came to use them it had the consistency of pea soup and was very black. After a day like that we were flagged out, but it was part of a pattern of life.

On 31 May 1916 we guessed that something was up. We knew nothing, we just had a feeling. I was positioned in one of the 12-inch turrets working the dumaresq course and distance calculator. You had to put your course and speed on it and then what you thought was the course and speed of the enemy. Then you would work out the deflection to which you had to turn your guns aiming ahead of your target, read the range and pass this down by voice pipe.

We went into action some time after five o'clock. In the afternoon we were kept busy in the turret and I reckon *Bellerophon* fired about a hundred rounds of 12-inch. At one point we were rung up to be told we had sunk a German destroyer. During a lull we came out of the turret to get some fresh air and there, floating around us, was a whole mass of bodies and debris – some of our sailors were cheering because they thought they were Germans, but unfortunately they were from the *Invincible*. It was a terrible sight and my first experience of death.

Then it was back to the turret. The shells were loaded up from three decks below; all this involved about a hundred men to each turret. It was a precise drill and that drill occupied your mind during the battle as did my own work on the dumaresq. I must say the guns made quite a noise when they fired, though we did have things stuck in our ears. Then of course there was the reverberation of the ships as the guns went off, but you steadied yourself for this. You could see the enemy's flashes from their guns, but we were never hit.

For the night action I was on the bridge which, looking back, was exciting for a young midshipman. Captain Bruen was in command. The sailors called him 'Tiny' because that's what he was. He was completely unemotional. We continued firing into the early hours, then disengaged. We didn't really know what had happened until we got back and I felt a bit depressed because the press reports of the Jutland battle were rather bad. I also read of the casualties and found I had lost thirteen of my term of eighty, with whom I was quite friendly: one was Anthony Eden's youngest brother and the other was Admiral Sir Percy Scott's son. So the ship went into a bit of a depression for a few days, but we all suffered it together because we got no leave. We simply went back into routine.

A short while after Jutland I was taught an example of how to conduct yourself under stress. I was Midshipman of the Watch on the bridge at the time. We were waiting to weigh anchor when a commander came up to Captain Bruen, I could see he was rattled. The captain was watching the Flagship through his glasses, waiting for the signal to come down. The commander said, 'Captain, I beg your pardon, sir, I'm sorry to report that the Captain of Marines has just shot himself', and then he said, 'No, he's not shot himself, sir, he's cut his throat'. Captain Bruen just lowered his glasses, slowly looked at the commander and said, 'Oh, cut his throat has he, cut it badly?' The commander said, 'I'm sorry, sir, I'm afraid he's dead'. 'Oh, he's dead is he? Well, see to it, Commander, will you.' And then he returned his gaze to the Flagship and in the same voice said, 'Signal, weigh anchor'. That was quite a lesson.

Ordinary Seaman Fred Pedelty

I was born in Bladon near Newcastle in 1896 and worked as a miner before I joined the Royal Navy Reserve in 1913. At the outbreak of war I joined up. In early October I went with the Drake Battalion of the Royal Naval Division to Belgium, where we were to try and defend Antwerp against the advancing Germans. All we did was join the retreating Allied forces who couldn't hold the enemy. We simply got orders to join an organised retreat. The casualties were low, but we did have a brigade interned by the Dutch.

We came back and were given a hero's welcome by the local people before we were sent on two weeks leave. My officer, Lieutenant Wells, told me that I would be better off on a ship, so I was posted to Chatham. After a few weeks there we had to volunteer for either gunnery or torpedo. I had six months training at Sheerness on torpedoes and searchlights.

My first posting was to *Engadine*, a seaplane-carrier based at Liverpool. She was no more than a floating hangar which had been a cross-Channel ferry before she had been converted. She had three Short folder seaplanes stowed on the after deck. By the time I had joined her she'd seen quite a bit of action. On Christmas Day 1914 she was involved in the first ever naval air attack. Along with two other requisitioned ferries, the *Empress* and *Riviera*, she made a raid on Cuxhaven. Only two of the nine planes found Cuxhaven and four were lost. When she took on the *Emden* and *Nordeich* in January 1915 three of her aircraft sank before they could take off.

I had been sent to the *Engadine* because the aircraft carried small torpedoes. We operated on patrols in the North Sea from Harwich. We used to be accompanied by destroyers and cruisers because we were very vulnerable to attack. We did launch some of our aircraft on reconnaissance, but on the whole we weren't a success, so we were moved up to Rosyth.

We patrolled out with the battle-cruiser squadron, but we were seldom called on to use our aircraft. On one occasion we were in harbour in Hull and I was in the cinema with my girlfriend. All of a sudden a notice went up recalling all servicemen to their stations. I dashed back to the *Engadine* to be told to operate the searchlight. I was having a job getting it going, but eventually got the beam working and caught this Zeppelin in the spotlight. This had been a great menace to the east coast. The ships opened fire but he diverted to Grimsby and attacked there. While we were on patrol on 31 May we began to pick up little snippets from the signalmen that something was afoot. There was a lot of speculation, and excitement.

At about 2.45 in the afternoon of 31 May we were not far behind the *Lion*, with Admiral Beatty at the head, followed by *Tiger* and *Princess Royal*, when we received a signal to send a seaplane aloft to reconnoitre. Lieutenant-Commander Robinson, our captain, got the unwieldly hangar door open. The crew got the machine on deck, spread its wings and hoisted it by derrick into the sea. It was twenty minutes before Flight Lieutenant Rutland and his observer, Assistant Paymaster Trewin, were airborne.

The plane had only been up about ten minutes when they

sighted the enemy. As there was a low cloud base it was having to fly at about 900 feet. The Germans opened fire, but it circled around getting the disposition of the enemy and of our fleet. Unfortunately at about 3.35 the petrol pipe leading to the carburetter broke and so it had to land on the water near us. The pilot managed to repair the pipe and wanted to take off again, but he was told to come alongside, so we hoisted him in.

It was an historic flight though, because it was the first instance of a heavier-than-air machine being used in a fleet action. Her wireless reports had reached the *Engadine* but we were unable to pass them to the *Lion*. Then, at about 3.25, we heard the bugle sound for 'Action Stations'. Our lads were noting the flashes and fall of shot and one called out that the *Queen Mary* had gone up. I didn't know how he knew because he didn't have any binoculars, but she went down about 4.30.

At 5 pm we got another signal to return to base. They weren't going to use our aircraft again and we had *Onslow* and *Moresby* looking after us so we turned to go back. We hadn't been sailing long when we saw a cruiser on her own. We didn't know if she was one of ours or theirs. As we only had one six-pounder and two 4-inch guns on the *Engadine* we were a bit worried. However, it turned out to be one of our own, the *Warrior*. She signalled us and ordered us to take a line astern to accompany her back to Rosyth. But she was in a sorry state. She had been hit fifteen times and had about a hundred killed and wounded. So at 9 pm we took her in tow.

Unfortunately during the night the weather worsened and her stern sank low in the water. By the morning it was obvious she wouldn't make port and we received a signal that she was going to order 'Abandon Ship'. The sea was quite choppy and disturbed but the *Engadine* had a huge rubbing strake so that we could go alongside. Without that we could never have stayed long enough to take off the crew who numbered about 900. I was one of the inboard men on a hawser while the others grabbed each man as he came across. The ships were really working hard and the noise of the rending steel was terrific. *Engadine* was holed in a number of places.

The wounded were passed over on stretchers. As the last was being passed there was a big swell and the poor lad slipped off the stretcher and fell between the ships. Lieutenant Rutland came up to me and asked what had happened. We could see below that the lad had fetched up on the remains of a fender. A lot of men wanted to go down and try and bring him up, but the captain wouldn't allow anyone to go over the side. A bit later, he was seen to have drifted in the water. Lieutenant Rutland grabbed a rope which some men were using to try and lasso the lad, and went down on it. He put the bowline round the man and got hold of him in his arms. He ordered those on deck to pull him up.

Unfortunately the poor lad, a handsome lad too he was, no more than eighteen, died of his wounds. Lieutenant Rutland got an Albert Medal for his bravery in trying to save him and because of his flight over the German fleet, he was from then on known as Rutland of Jutland!

Later the captain of the *Warrior* stood with his men and gave three cheers to his sinking ship. It was a sad sight. The following day we buried the young lad at sea with another of his mates.

Boy First-Class Harold Bryce

In February 1915, when I was sixteen, all the young men were joining up because the poster of Lord Kitchener was everywhere, pointing his finger at you and saying 'Your Country Needs You'. So I volunteered. A few days later a recruiting officer came down from Oxford and brought documents for my father to sign. He said, 'Give it to his mother to sign first'. But she said, 'I'm not going to sign that'. She was upset, you see. Eventually my dad signed. I then went down from Witney with another boy to Whitehall in London. (I had never left home before except for a day trip to Portsmouth which cost five shillings.) We stayed the night there wrapped in an old army blanket. In the morning we fell in with some more boys. Every boy in those days had their best suit for special occasions, but some of the ragamuffins who turned up had bare feet. I'd never seen anything like them before.

We were sent down to Devonport, to HMS *Powerful*. As soon as we got aboard a Petty Officer said, 'If you've got a watch or any money, hand it over'. The next morning we were sent to the barber who cut every bit of hair off our heads with clippers. We all looked like criminals wearing white duck suits. Later that day we were put into different classes, and the instructors were very hard on us. One boy couldn't answer a question so the instructor hit him about the face as hard as he could and knocked him from one side of the deck to the other. If a boy got caught smoking, he got six cuts with a cane. That never happened to me; I was too afraid.

But I was only on the ship for a week before I caught scarlet fever, and sent to hospital in Devonport and put on a milk diet. After I got better I was sent on leave and then drafted to Scapa Flow. It took ages on the train to get there. At Thurso we slept on the floor in a hotel and the next morning we caught the steamer to the Grand Fleet. I've never seen ships like it in my life; they were great big battleships.

I was sent aboard HMS *Blanche*, a light cruiser, as a sight-setter on one of the ship's eight 4-inch guns. I'd had a week's training for that. In the turret I wore a telepad on my head in the shape of a hood with a flexible pipe to my mouth and earpieces so that I could hear the orders. At sea I did four hours on and four hours off in two watches, night and day. The gun's crew all wore duffel coats, but because I was a boy, I wasn't given any protective clothing. After I'd been on that gun for about a fortnight, sticking it out through the cold weather without even a pair of gloves, one of the old sailors brought me a pair of duffel trousers. Then another brought me a duffel coat. The first morning at sea an officer looked at me and said, 'When was the last time you had a shave?' I replied, 'I've never shaved, sir'. So he swore at me and I was sent below. In those days there were no safety razors so I had to use a cut-throat razor and shave while the ship was rolling about!

On New Years' Eve 1915/16 we were moored on the Cromarty Firth. Across the other side, at Invergordon, was the cruiser *Natal*. I came up on the quarterdeck about 3.30. I was quietly standing there alone until the Chief Stoker came on deck. All of a sudden there was this thunderous explosion on the *Natal*. The chief said, 'Christ, her boiler's gone up'. But it was her magazine. We just stood there and watched her keel over. There was a terrible loss of life, over 360. Among those killed were several naval wives and nurses from the hospital ship *Plassey* which was close by. They had been invited to a party aboard the *Natal*. Most of the crew were below deck on a 'make and mend day'. They never had a chance.

Before the First World War, any boy who got sent before the magistrates used to be offered the choice of going to prison or joining the Navy. There were lots of boys who didn't fancy prison on ship and we volunteers got fed up with being treated like them, as if we were criminals. I was made to feel like one once, just before the battle of Jutland. It was my first leave. I had my liberty ticket with the date on for when I was to return. When we fell in, my mate, who had a girlfriend in Witney, started chattering to me about her and I didn't hear the Petty Officer telling us when to get back. Two weeks later when I walked through the dock yard gates the guard said, 'Do you know you're adrift off leave?' I said, 'I'm not, it's the twenty-fourth today. It's on my ticket.' He didn't seem to care about what was on my ticket, he took me to the officer of the watch. Eventually I was sent before Captain Casement who said, 'There's no excuse. All you boys were told what day to come back and what train to catch from London'. Fourteen days pay and leave stopped! Which meant I fought in the battle of Jutland at no cost to his Majesty!

The morning of the day of the battle was beautiful. The North Sea was like a lake, no movement in the water at all. The first time we saw the enemy was when a Zeppelin passed over us. As we steamed ahead an officer came along and said we would be at the scene of action at 6.00 p.m. He told us that the battle-cruiser fleet had already been in action that afternoon. As we got closer there was a slight mist in front of the German fleet, so we could only see one or two ships now and again as the mist cleared. Even though the action was on the starboard side we positioned ourselves on the port side of the *Iron Duke*. We had a large signal staff on the *Blanche*, and our job was to relay signals to Admiral Jellicoe on the *Iron Duke*. We could see her in action, this 25,000-ton super dreadnought. She had five twin 13.5-inch turrets and twelve 6-inch guns. She was quite a sight with all the black smoke coming out of the funnels and noise of the guns. I was on P4 gun when, at about 6.30 that evening, sailors from the starboard side shouted out, 'Come and have a look, quickly, there's a ship going down'. It was the battle-cruiser *Invincible*. Only six men were saved.

On another occasion the commander came running along the upper deck shouting, 'Has anyone seen a torpedo?' No one had, but it planted a suspicion in our minds that there might be U-boats about.

We were never hit. But later that night I saw a number of our destroyers on fire – red flames lighting up the night sky. The destroyer *Munster* came alongside and took on medical supplies to deal with the casualties. One of these was 'Boy' Cornwall. He was a sight-setter on the *Chester* and, like me, was sixteen. Although he was mortally wounded early in the battle he stood by his gun awaiting orders until the end of the action with the rest of his gun's crew dead or wounded. He deserved his Victoria Cross.

One strange thing happened during the action, while all the firing was going on. A tall sailing ship passed down between the German and British lines. Someone thought it must have been Swedish. It was in full sail as if from another age, another time.

All the way through the battle the *Blanche* never fired her guns, nor did we know if we were winning or losing. It was just excitement all the time, one thing after another, though by 9.00 pm that evening the main action was over. By dawn we had withdrawn.

Then it was back to normal routine.

Midshipman Frank Layard

HMS *Indomitable* was part of the Third Battle-Cruiser Squadron consisting of *Invincible*, the Flagship of Rear Admiral the Hon. Horace Hood, *Indomitable* and *Inflexible*. We had arrived at Scapa Flow from Rosyth on 23 May 1916 to carry out gunnery and torpedo exercises. The gunnery exercises were of particular importance for us as it was the first opportunity we had had to test out, and get acquainted with, the new Director system which had just been installed.

At about 6.30 pm on the evening of 30 May, a signal was received to raise steam for 22 knots and at 9.30 the squadron sailed, followed by the whole of the Grand Fleet. We had no idea why we had been ordered out, but there was a feeling of suppressed excitement on board as we passed through the Hoxa gate in the fading light. On more than one occasion we had set out at high speed to intercept enemy ships which had been reported at sea, but each time we had returned without making contact. This time, however, I had a strong feeling that something was really afoot. In fact some of us junior midshipmen were pacing up and down the quarterdeck discussing among ourselves whether a midshipman had any chance of distinguishing himself in a modern fleet action and deciding probably not!

At eight o'clock next morning, I went up to the foretop to keep the forenoon watch as submarine lookout. There seemed to be no sign of any urgency and the previous night's feeling of excitement ebbed away. I decided that this must be just another routine sweep into the North Sea.

This atmosphere of calm was suddenly shattered when, at about 2.30 pm, we intercepted HMS *Galatea*'s first sighting report. From then on excitement steadily mounted as further signals came in with the news that the First and Second British Cruiser Squadrons (BCS) were engaging the enemy battle-cruisers, and then that the Fifth BCS had joined in. The *Invincible* hoisted BJI G 25 (assume First degree readiness: speed 25 knots) shortly to be followed by BJ (Action Stations). As we pushed on southwards, working up to our maximum speed, the thought uppermost in everyone's mind was, 'Are we going to get there in time?' I felt some slight apprehension at the thought of going into action, but the prevailing sensation was one of intense excitement. My action station was in the foretop as dumaresq worker* and of course I had a grandstand view. We were given no idea of what was happening, only that we were doing our utmost to join Sir David Beatty in the *Lion* and take our place in the battle-cruiser line.

Soon after five o'clock the sound of distant gunfire was heard and half an hour later the *Chester*, on our starboard, opened fire. The *Invincible* immediately swung round to starboard and led the squadron towards her. Then three German cruisers came into sight, broad on the port bow, and we opened up on them with our main armament at 10,000 yards and they quickly turned away and vanished from sight. When they turned they must have fired torpedoes at us, because I saw a torpedo, with its red warhead and propellers slowly revolving, passing slowly down our port side on the surface not more than ten yards from us. It was obviously at the end of its run, but it was a very near miss. At the same time I saw *Invincible* haul out to starboard, and stop with all her safety valves lifting and a tremendous roar of steam and with the 'Disregard' flag flying. I thought, 'Oh

---

* See above, page 51.

God, she has been torpedoed'. But the next minute she hoisted Flag One (line ahead) and hauled down 'Disregard'. She then led off to the westward again in the direction of heavy gunfire and we followed, falling in behind *Inflexible*.

Just after six o'clock I could see flashes of gunfire ahead. Then the *Lion* appeared almost right ahead and steering towards us, with her guns firing to starboard. As the *Invincible* led round to port, to bring the squadron into station ahead of the *Lion*, all of a sudden the dim outline of four enemy ships loomed up out of the haze. They were difficult to identify but we took them to be battle-cruisers. As we turned to bring the enemy ships on our starboard beam at about 10,000 yards, the squadron opened up with all its main armament guns. Our fire was quickly returned and soon shots were falling all round us.

We had done only one test firing with our new firing system a day or two before leaving Scapa. The Gunnery Officer therefore had a difficult decision to make. Should he use the new system which, though more efficient, was virtually untried, or should he revert to the old less accurate but well tested system of gunlayers firing? He decided not to risk using the new Director system and so, throughout the action, guns and turrets were individually laid and trained. For about twenty minutes we were hotly engaged but I was too busy with my dumaresq to feel frightened. We sent out a continuous ripple of flashes all along the enemy line but, in the poor visibility, I couldn't tell where our shots were falling although I found the noise of our guns most heartening and welcome. It helped to drown the rumbling noise made by the shells passing over us and the crack of those falling short. But the enormous columns of water thrown up were only too visible and sometimes uncomfortably close. We must have been constantly straddled but not once were we or *Inflexible* hit. A number of shell splinters did however come on board which indicated that the enemy's shells which fell short had burst on impact with the sea.

It was during this phase of the action at about 6.35 pm that

Invincible was hit by two salvoes in quick succession from the *Lützow* and *Derfflinger*. She was hit aft and on 'Q' turret amidships, between the guns. The turret blew up and the flash went down into the magazine. The explosion must have touched off the other magazines and she blew in half with the loss of over a thousand lives. Although only separated from her by the *Inflexible* nobody in the foretop saw the explosion or realised what had happened as we were all fully occupied with our fire control duties. The first we knew of it was when, close to starboard, we passed the bows and stern of a ship sticking up about thirty feet out of the water with some half a dozen figures clinging to some wreckage. It was a grim and very sad moment for us when we saw the name *Invincible* on the stern portion and realised we were passing all that remained of our Flagship.

Shortly after this the enemy ships turned away and were lost to sight and, although we altered course, we could not regain contact. Then on orders from the *Lion* we turned round and took station astern of the other battle-cruisers. It was only then that we realised the *Queen Mary* and the *Indefatigable* were missing, leaving only *Lion*, *Princess Royal*, *Tiger* and *New Zealand*. At this point the disabled and motionless German cruiser *Wiesbaden* appeared dimly in the direction in which the German Fleet had disappeared and received a broadside from each battle-cruiser as the line passed and then faded from sight astern.

Some minutes later we saw the Grand Fleet coming into action astern. We could not distinguish the ships but through the haze and smoke we could see what appeared to be one continuous line of flame from the flashes of their guns extending over an arc of about 60°, a truly tremendous sight. However we did not have the time to admire this display for enemy ships appeared again briefly and we engaged them again. At the same time we saw a flotilla of German destroyers approaching on the starboard bow and, as the big ships disappeared from sight again, we shifted our fire to the destroyers and forced them to turn away under the cover of smoke.

At about 8.15, as the light was failing, we had our last brief sighting and short burst of fire but we lost touch again and that was the end of the battle for us. We steamed southward throughout the night in company with Admiral Beatty and the rest of the battle-cruisers, remaining at action stations all the time. I was able to nip down to the gunroom for a few minutes to get a little food, but spent the rest of the night in the foretop feeling very cold, but too excited and worked up to sleep.

Early in the morning Admiral Beatty signalled to the battle-cruisers, 'The losses on both sides have been heavy but we hope to cut off and annihilate the whole German fleet today. It is up to every man to do his utmost.' Unknown to us at the time the German fleet had slipped through astern of the Grand Fleet in the night and had regained the safety of its own waters. When this became known later in the day we turned for home. On the afternoon watch we passed through a large patch of oil and wreckage in which was floating a lot of dead fish and a number of dead bodies. We could not identify the uniforms and we hoped we were passing over the graveyard of some German ship, but in all probability it was the spot where one of our own battle-cruisers had blown up.

We reached harbour early on the morning of 2 June and immediately started to take in 1,400 tons of coal.

After the battle there was much speculation about the German losses (2,551). From all reports it was generally believed that they must have been as heavy, if not heavier, than ours. This proved to be wishful thinking and so, when some time later the true facts became known (6,097), we felt bitterly disappointed. Somehow we had missed our opportunity. We had allowed the German fleet to slip through our fingers and instead of winning an overwhelming victory we had only achieved a partial success and in all probability we would never be given another chance.

Looking back it would seem that for the battle-cruiser force, at any rate, the war at sea in 1915/16 was fought at a very leisurely tempo. During the eight months from the time I joined *Indomitable* to the battle of Jutland, we only did 33 days at sea, and moreover, because at the time the submarine threat in the North Sea was slight and the air threat non-existent, it was possible, when at sea, to maintain a very easy three-watch defence organisation. It was only necessary to assume a higher state of readiness on the rare occasions when contact with enemy surface ships was expected. Since no practice facilities were available in the Firth of Forth, firings had to be carried out either from Invergordon or Scapa Flow. The result was that, during those eight months, we only fired our main armament four times and our secondary armament once. In the circumstances it is hardly surprising that the gunnery of the battle-cruisers fleet at Jutland was poor.

Able Seaman Arthur Sawyer

My dad was a farm labourer and lived to be a hundred, but my mum died when she was forty-three and left six of us kids. So I went off and joined the Navy when I was fifteen and nine months. I was sent to Shotley and, after training, I joined the *Iron Duke*, the flagship of the Grand Fleet.

I was based in the seamanship department. You kept the ship clean, the boats crewed, worked on the upper deck, and learned to steer and navigate. We knew where our place was for Action Stations and where to 'abandon ship' if we had to, though I couldn't imagine having to abandon the *Iron Duke*.

In the afternoon of 30 May 1916 Jellicoe was ordered to concentrate his fleet in the 'Long Forties', about a hundred miles east of Aberdeen. We knew something was up and began to get excited. I was in the torpedo-room between the decks. It was a bit nerve-racking, all those alarm bells. We thought we saw submarines, then a mine. It was like living on your nerves.

We just concentrated on the work we had to do which was to get the torpedoes ready in the tubes. No one told us what was happening. We just knew we were going into battle against the High Seas Fleet. We went into attack late the next day.

When the five turrets fired at the same time the ship just stood still and shook. You wondered what the hell was happening. We did get radio messages but no one asked us to fire our torpedo. We did hear that our 13.5-inch guns had scored seven hits on the *König* and we sank a torpedo-boat.

Later I was ordered on deck to be part of a searchlight crew for the night action. That was something else. The searchlight had a long beam and we could pick out the enemy. It was all bangs and flashes and a lot of action, like a fireworks show with all those bombs dropping in the water with big splashes. You'd see our guns fire away at the flashes and then the ship they were firing at wouldn't be there any more – just blackness in its place.

I always think it was a miracle that the ships didn't collide with each other. We never used our navigational lights, only our port and starboard lights. This made the ship really dark to move around in and difficult for us to see other ships.

The battle for us finished in the early hours of the morning. But as the darkness went on we could see spasmodic flashes from the cruisers who were still engaging the enemy. Jellicoe was a very clever man. The enemy thought they could draw him into their minefields, but he wasn't going to risk his ships. After all, we'd lost three battle-cruisers, *Invincible, Indefatigable* and the *Queen Mary* as well as other ships. That was a lot of men lost.

When we got back the first thing we did was to coal and rearm the ship which meant pretty well twenty-four hours non-stop work. The next day we mostly slept. A month later I got some leave, the first time for fifteen months.

I didn't read about the battle for some time after. As we were never hit on the *Iron Duke* I thought we'd done well. But the numbers killed were very upsetting.

All the time I was on the *Iron Duke* I found Admiral Jellicoe a very nice gentleman. We never really saw much of him for months on end though sometimes you would see him exercising on the upper deck. If you were working on the upper deck you would stand to attention when he passed and he would say, 'Carry on'. He was only a little man, but we liked him. His wife sent us all Christmas cards in 1915 and I've still got it. He left the Fleet in November 1916.

Admiral Beatty was next. He was more of the old bulldog soldier. We didn't see a lot of him and he didn't have much to say to us when we did. But he was a very brave man – a proper 'let's get at 'em' sort of chap. The *Lion* was the right name of ship for him to command. And it got knocked about a bit too like him. But he shook it off and kept going to search for the prey. He was afraid of nothing.

In our world between decks we got to know each other. We were together for so long and we were very young. We never seemed to see the sun – it was so bleak up in the Orkneys, barren and bleak – just bloody heather everywhere and cold grey seas. You never saw a girl. You had to make your own enjoyment. The officers had their deck hockey and we used to run around the upper deck and do exercises. Then in the evening we'd play cards and housey-housey (bingo). And we had concert parties. My best friend was from Aberdeen and my two other special friends came from Manchester and London. It was really marvellous just to sit on deck and talk and learn about other people's lives. Their lives became important to you.

After the war the Fleet was hit with the 'flu epidemic. Having survived the war we lost six men on my ship. One minute they were all right and the next they were down and out. We were given inoculations and vaccinations, but a lot of us reacted badly to them.

After that it was the Mediterranean to keep the Turks and Greeks apart and then the Russian revolution. I wouldn't have missed a minute of it.

Midshipman Bill Fell

At the time of Jutland I was eighteen and a junior midshipman on the *Warspite*, part of Fifth Battle Squadron. Within forty-eight hours of arriving at Rosyth we were all under way, battle-cruisers steaming out ahead of us. May 31 was a gloriously fine and calm day. As the morning went on, our speed was increased from 18 to 20 knots and then to full speed at 24 knots. The battle-cruisers ahead of us were *Lion, Tiger, Princess Royal, Queen Mary*, with others closer to us.

I'd had forenoon watch on the bridge and, at about 12.30, I went down below and cut and made some sandwiches. I then ran off to my action station, the transmitting station, right in the bowels of the ship, five decks down. Three heavy armoured hatches rang shut above us. We then got orders that the enemy were in sight. Then 'ranges' and 'elevations and bearings' began to come in. My job was on a bearing plot, a very simple device on which I had to plot the rate of change of bearing so that the guns could follow it. The senior midshipman down below was plotting the mean of the ranges that were coming down to him from the range finders. Shortly after 4 pm we opened fire at 18,000 yards (just over ten miles) on the battle-cruiser *Von Der Tann*. There were corrections straightaway because we were short: we went up 800 yards. Then all of a sudden there was a monumental crump which sounded as if all the tea trays in the world, full of crockery, had been dropped on our heads; the whole ship rattled and shook. We realised we'd been hit by something pretty big. We were only just recovering from that when there was an even worse crash which knocked us off our stools. I was dazed and when I sat up I was in water. Apart from one stuttering light in the corner it was pitch dark. Worst of all was the complete silence. No sound of the engines, no sound of the action, no sound except for swishing water.

After a moment, I noticed that down all the voice pipes was spurting a good old sluice of water – so we were slowly flooding.

I think we all began to come to about the same time and two young midshipmen, who had only been on the ship a couple of weeks, began to whimper a bit. The senior midshipman went across and banged their two heads together and dropped them back into the water. Well, that solved that problem.

We then went back to trying to do our job, but of course no information was coming down. Then, reassuringly, the engines started and we found a few lamps and got them going. But we were still anxious about our situation. The senior midshipman found his way to the voice pipe and called up 'Foretop? Foretop?' He then paused. 'What another one gone up? Splendid!' He was in fact speaking to a mythical Foretop through a wrecked voicepipe. Of course we didn't realize that, and so our morale shot up. After that we waited and waited for about an hour and a half. Then we heard banging on the hatches and someone let us out.

I didn't recognise the ship when I got up on deck. She was a shambles, every single boat had gone, splinters everywhere, funnels were riddled or falling down. She was a hell of a mess. Thirty dead and wounded. A cordite fire had broken out in the starboard 6-inch battery and many had been burnt. She was right down in the water with the quarterdeck nearly awash. I went up on the bridge and Captain Philpotts turned to me and said, 'How did you like that, boy?' I said, 'Not much, sir'.

We were now out of the action and on our own. We had suffered a jammed helm probably from being put hard over at 24 knots and we'd done an unrehearsed complete circle within 10,000 yards of *Scheer*'s line around the sinking *Warrior*. We'd become an irresistible target and we'd been hit eighty-seven times, thirteen of which had been big calibre hits. Everyone else had disappeared and we were ordered back to Rosyth. The constructor came up on the bridge and told the captain that we could not exceed 8 knots otherwise we'd sink. The captain rang down to the engine room '12 knots'.

We were attacked the following morning by a U-boat. A

torpedo was fired at us and we all watched as it ran from the stem parallel with us about 40 feet away to disappear ahead. The U-boat broke surface very close and we nearly rammed her. In fact people were throwing wreckage at her, from the upper deck. She had lost buoyancy and so was too close to fire. We were very lucky! Then two little torpedo boats came out to join us and we were very relieved to see them.

I don't think we gave any thought to how we would be received at home. But as we passed up the Firth of Forth and under the bridge, all the railway people were lined along it. To our dismay they shouted 'Cowards! Cowards, you ran away!' and chucked lumps of coal at us. We were received at Rosyth with very, very great disapproval by the local people. They were all in mourning black hats and black arm-bands. They all felt the Grand Fleet had suffered complete defeat and that some ships, like the *Warspite*, had run away. That was the news that had reached Scotland and it was twenty-four hours before things got better, when the other ships returned and more facts were known.

The *Warspite* had proved to be a wonderful ship, apart from her steering mechanism, and we remained in fighting order.

Leading Stoker Mechanic Jack Cotterell

On 31 May 1916, as far as I knew, *Gloucester* was just on another patrol. We went into action in the middle of the afternoon and the fight was on. We could hear the sound of the gunfire above the boilers. As the guns went off you could feel the ships go down and rise up, which would shake the dust out of the crevices, creating clouds of smoke. Of course we were in the stokehole, the lowest part of the ship, and in battle that's a very vulnerable position. Our Petty Officer would get all his orders from the bridge. We were kept pretty busy and, when we came off watch, we helped in the magazine with the shells. We wouldn't normally do that, but as the battle went on we all pulled together. For us it seemed a long battle and a hard one. But there was a good feeling on the ship as we made our way back to Rosyth. We had no casualties and had no idea of the losses. When we got back we saw the state of the *Lion* and the *Tiger*. The *Lion* had a big hole in her. As soon as we came into port we coaled and went straight out again. When we reached where we had fought the battle, the debris of battle still floating around. It was a mournful sight. We saw the nose of a ship sticking out of the water, but we couldn't tell whether it was one of theirs or ours. While we were there a Zeppelin flew quietly over.

When we got back to Rosyth again we had a chance to talk to other sailors from the battle and slowly began to piece the events of Jutland together. There was great sadness, though, because of the losses.

Midshipman Henry St John Fancourt

When I was sixteen I joined the *Princess Royal*, sister ship of the *Lion*, the Flagship of the First Battle-Cruiser Squadron. She was armed with eight 13.5-inch guns on the centre line, two turrets forward, one aft and one in 'Q' position amidships, and was part of Beatty's 'Cat Squad' along with *Tiger* and *Queen Mary*, all based at Rosyth. I was, along with the other midshipmen, very keen to fight the Germans who had been quite active for the previous four months under their new C-in-C, Admiral Scheer.

On the afternoon watch of 31 May I was on submarine lookout. I was in a small cubby hole which you put your head into and looked along bearing 000 to 095. I thought we were on another flap, another stunt, and didn't expect to go into action. I had just finished my watch and was going down to the gunroom to order myself a boiled egg for my tea when they sounded off 'Action at the double', so I never got my boiled egg. Apparently Beatty had ordered his battle-cruisers to form a line of bearing 110° and was steaming to the south-east for a better position to close the enemy. The Germans also turned and were on a line of bearing when they ordered 'fire straightaway' at 1548. Not that I knew it, but we were firing on the *Lützow*.

I was sitting on a little stool in the turret with my fire control instrument, a dumaresq. We were on standby in case we went into local control. I was glued to this instrument. Only the turret officer who had a little hole to look through could see anything. The *Queen Mary*, astern of us, was firing well, she was a good gunnery ship, but she was hit badly and sank about 16.20 with a loss of 1,200 men. We continued firing. All the time I could hear the lieutenant calling, 'Battleship, battleship bearing so and so': I had to estimate the position from those details and shout up to him 'rate is opening' or 'rate is closing'. The control officer then had to try and spot his fall of shot. We were firing at about 16,000 yards. There was a hell of a lot of firing going on and everyone had really to concentrate. 'X' turret was hit in its barbette, and 'A' turret got off about thirty rounds. But we always had the feeling we were winning. The strongest units are the people that keep their spirits up longest. I think we had something like 28–30 dead and 70 wounded, that is about ten per cent casualties.

The *Lion* however, only two cables from us, was hit very severely so we took over their wireless which had been damaged. The third shell which hit *Lion* almost sank her. It struck and penetrated 'Q' turret; everyone there was either killed or wounded. One of the guns was loaded when the shell struck and the turret system was fully charged with cordite. Major Harvey ordered the magazine doors to be closed and the magazine to be flooded. Almost as soon as this was completed an explosion occurred in the turret trunking. The magazine doors, which were not fully flash-tight, were bulged inwards by the force of the explosion. If they had not been flooded, the ship would have blown up.

When the Fleet was trying to form into some form of night organisation the general signal made from the *Iron Duke* said, 'Fleet will proceed into the German Bight at dawn and annihilate the Germans completely'. We were all pretty weary by now and I thought we had done enough annihilating for one day. But of course there was something of a lull before the night action at about 8.28 when we opened fire on the *Seydlitz*, quite close at 12,000 yards, and scored a couple of hits. But of course we didn't know then what we were hitting or what was hitting us. Jellicoe had not got into the action until after six o'clock, so his chaps were still fresh.

We didn't fire again after nine o'clock. I don't think we did well in the night action. We had never been trained to fight a night action, nor had we ever fired our guns before at night. The Germans were much better trained for night action. Our policy was that you didn't fight at night.

I remember seeing a Zeppelin on the horizon at dawn and one of the battle-cruisers fired some armour-piercing shell at it. By now the ship looked a bit messy so we began to put her right. I was asked to draw sketches to record the damage. We held a funeral service on the quarterdeck and delivered to the sea the lads who had given up their lives.

In those days communications were much slower, and it was some time before we heard of casualties. It was a different way of living, a different war.

As we came into Rosyth in the morning, the colliers were waiting ready to come alongside to coal the squadron the moment we dropped anchor. Someone said, 'Look, there's the collier for the *Queen Mary*', but of course she had no ship to coal, so she moved off. It was rather a sad sight. As soon as we docked we coaled ship.

When we got ashore there was an awful lot of badly handled propaganda. The Admiralty did as usual and said everything was gloomy and that rather took the heart out of us because we thought we had done rather well. But then that's war and I don't think we conduct the aftermath of war very well. We patched up at Rosyth, saw what a mess the enemy had made of the *Lion*, then sailed down to Portsmouth to refit.

There was no great excitement about the Battle of Jutland, we hadn't decimated the Germans – it was not Trafalgar. People didn't throw their arms around you and say wonderful things about you. It really wasn't a satisfactory battle. A lot of things went wrong and needed to be rejigged.

After that I was involved when the High Seas Fleet came out on 19 August 1916 to attack East Coast towns. We got down there in time and they withdrew but the *Nottingham* was sunk by a U-boat. Again, on 17 November 1917 off Heligoland, we had a bit of a tussle with the enemy but that really was the last time the High Seas Fleet came out.

So the poor old Grand Fleet worked very hard, tried very hard, but it didn't succeed in the sense that we would have liked.

Ordinary Seaman Stan Smith

While I was at Chatham Barracks a notice went up asking for volunteers for Q-ships. These were the Royal Navy's first answer to the menace of the submarine. They were dilapidated old merchant ships taken from the scrap heap and fitted up with concealed guns. They were so old and decrepit that a submarine would not waste a torpedo on them, relying on gunfire to intimidate their crews into abandoning ship. The theory was that when they had done this, the submarine would gradually circle the Q-ship and eventually come alongside to loot the vessel for provisions.

I was chosen, and after passing a medical, we volunteers were kitted out with civilian clothing, although we had to pass the things around to get a decent fit. We were then sent by train to West Hartlepool to join our ship, Q-12, which quickly went on to disprove the optimistic theory of the strategy.

She was a rough old vessel, eaten up with rust. But she had two 4-inch guns concealed under the bridge behind flaps which dropped down. On no. 3 hatch a coil of manila rope would fall back at the pull of a lever to reveal a 12-pounder gun. The control tower was located in a hawser reel on the fo'c'sle. She was also fitted with bell pushes around the upper deck so that if you saw a periscope you could press it with your foot, sending everybody, unseen, to action stations. Then you would light a fag and stroll away casually to your own.

Q-12's mess decks were in a filthy condition so we turned to and scrubbed out, gathered up all the fish and chip papers, lunch bags, bits of bread and butter and other litter until she was fairly shipshape. But this didn't half get us into trouble. It caused a dockyard strike. Apparently women were employed to clean the ships behind the dockyard people and we had done them out of a job. After some fuss our commanding officer managed to square things up and they got back to work.

When she was completed in the dockyard, Q-12 had to go out to sea to swing compasses. The accuracy of these instruments is always affected by riveting or any changes in the ship's metalwork.

On 30 April, with one or two dockyard people still on board, we were steaming 200 miles west of Ireland getting on quite well when 'Whoof!', a torpedo hit us amidships. She didn't take more than two or three minutes to sink. I was quickly picked up by one of our lifeboats. That was the end of the Q-12 without a shot fired in anger and with no opportunity to test the Navy's Q-ship strategy.

We went back to barracks and it wasn't long before I got another Q-ship, again from West Hartlepool. The *Pargust*, a collier was fitted out almost the same as the Q-12, except that instead of a 12-pounder being under the hawser reel, it was in an upturned boat which was cut away in sections which fell away at the pull of a lever.

While in West Hartlepool, waiting for the ship to be completed, we would go ashore, although there was not much pleasure in it. The girls, seeing us in 'civilians' and knowing we were of military age, would stick white feathers in our coats. In the public houses we were invariably caught up in an argument about why we weren't in the forces. Three of us went to the cinema one night and during the show the place was raided by the civilian and military police, looking for men of military age. We were taken to the police station and, since we were sworn to secrecy, our commanding officer had to come and bail us out.

When the ship was completed, we finished with the dockyard and went to sea. Having swung compasses and carried out gun trials – this time uneventfully – we were on our own. The unwieldy old vessel would plough up and down the length of England in the trade routes. Her screw and rudder were only one-third in the water, and although she had a ballast, she would spin and yaw all over the place in a strong wind and a decent sea.

The food was not so good either. We only carried fresh provisions for five days and after that we would be on corned beef and biscuits. We used to dish the corned beef up in various different ways to break the monotony. The biscuits were so hard we had to soak them overnight, strain them off and mix in a tin of suet. Then we'd add a few currants and a little sugar and bake the mixture until it was quite palatable.

The routine had us doing about ten to twelve days at sea at a stretch before going in to coal and water. Coaling was quite easy because we would go under the chute.

The events of our second patrol demonstrated how the Q-ship strategy was supposed to work, with the enemy running true to form. One of the chaps spotted a periscope, put his foot on the alarm and sent us all off to our action stations. The submarine cruised around the ship – which was quite easy since we were only doing about four knots – and had a good look at us.

Part of the ploy involved one of the seamen dressing as a woman. His duty was to go up and hang out some washing on the fo'c'sle line. He would then come down and join his action station. The submarine surfaced about a mile away and opened fire. Then another of our schemes came into play. We had containers scattered around the ship which were electrically operated from the control tower. These could be activated to cause a miniature explosion, showering fire, sparks and smoke all over the show. If the submarine sent a shell over the ship, its crew could be confused into thinking they had scored a hit. Being low in the water, they wouldn't be able to spot an 'over' if it was in line with the ship.

Her first couple of shells fell short, then she scored an 'over' which we immediately gave her as a hit. She carried on firing for some ten or fifteen minutes and did manage to knock the mast down and the derricks over the forward hold, but they didn't put the gun, hidden in the boat, out of action. Next we stopped the ship and sent away the 'panic boats' with all the men who were not manning the guns or the control. They dashed up on deck, lowered the boat haphazardly (showing every sign of panic), jumped in and pulled away as fast as they could.

The submarine stopped firing and began to circle the ship, coming closer each time. When she was about a hundred yards off the port beam and we could get two guns to bear on her – the 4-inch and the 12-pounder – we opened fire. After the third or fourth salvo we sank her and the panic boat crew went over. There were only two survivors to take on board.

When we returned to port, the Navy confirmed our claim. Unfortunately our reign on board didn't last very long. We were continually having engine trouble and could barely keep steerage way on at times. Eventually, one day as we were coming into harbour to coal and water, against wind and tide, we hit the jetty and tore a large gash in the port side. We hoped this would give us a few days leave but instead they paid her off and we returned to Chatham Barracks.

My next ship was HMS *Montbretia* which was totally different from the other two Q-ships. She was a 17-knot sloop which had been converted to look like a merchantman. She had two 4.7-inch guns concealed under the bridge and a 12-pounder in an upturned boat, but she was fitted with all the latest controls. She had a listening device, the only snag being that you had to stop the ship to listen. There were two depth-charge throwers, one on each side of the quarter-deck. Each was like a mortar and had a cradle into which the depth-charges were lashed. I should imagine the depth-charges weighed over a hundredweight [112lb. or 50.8 kilograms] and were about the size of a large oil drum. They could be set to explode at a depth of 50 feet to 250 feet but, being a new invention, they didn't always operate as we should have liked. They would often explode on hitting the water, showering the ship with lumps of cradle and causing quite a bit of damage.

We didn't have a lot of success with submarines, although we claimed to have sunk one by depth-charges. Oil and debris came to the surface but the Navy would not confirm our claim. Apparently the submarines could tell we were not what we seemed because the beat of our screw was much faster than that of a merchant ship. So we were put on convoy duty where we could fly the White Ensign, get back into uniform and show all the guns.

We were next transferred to Northern Patrol which was right up in the Shetland Isles and based at Lerwick. This was a real one-horse town at the time, where the monotony was relieved only by the monthly visit of the beer boat. It was quite a job to get a drink, but a crowd of us used to buy a small barrel and take it up into the hills.

Patrols were pretty arduous and used to last from ten to twelve days. We not only had to contend with a lack of fresh provisions half the time, but also ice; tons of it. Huge icicles hung from the rigging and upper works. We had to chop them off in the mornings to avoid carrying too much top weight. She carried quite a lot as it was and could roll like the very devil.

Look-outs were posted around the clock for we were in the 'Land of the Midnight Sun'. It used to be daylight almost all night long which made it easier for a look-out to spot anything unusual. One night the masthead look-out spotted a submarine on the port bow. We were all sent to action stations and the ship turned full speed ahead to ram. We hit the vessel just as what appeared to be the bow lifted from a large swell. We immediately wished we hadn't as the contents of the thing shot all over the ship, showering us as far aft as the funnel, and oh boy! What a stink! It turned out to be a huge bloated dead whale left by the whaling fleet. Goodness knows how long it had been floating around for it was white with seagull droppings. The smell was atrocious. We couldn't get rid of it. It went down through the ventilators into the mess decks so we were eating it as well as smelling it. It took us days to clear the smell and wash the ship clean of the blubber that was flung all over it. It was the closest I ever came to getting sea-sick.

Wren Ada Bassett

I didn't like school so I left as soon as I could in 1910 when I was thirteen years old. I was taught to drive by a young man who had been at school with me. I found it very easy. He'd just turn up and change seats and off we'd go. No licence, no 'L' plates and very few cars. Wonderful time to learn. We used to drive up to London and all around. Petrol was so cheap and I could get out and get under the car because the young man taught me how to change a tyre and sort out the engine.

I had five brothers who were all older, and an older sister, and all we seemed to do was laugh. They even laughed when I had a boyfriend. I don't think they wanted to lose me. All my brothers joined up in the Army. I missed them all at home so, in 1917, I joined the Women's Royal Naval Service (WRNS) because I thought it would open up something new for me.

When I joined the WRNS some of the other girls came from posh homes, and myself and my friend, who I shared a house with, used to irritate them. They were from another world, but I used to laugh at them because they had to have lessons to drive whereas I could drive anything, including lorries, and I'd only had an elementary education!

Of course in a lorry you seemed high up off the ground, and they weren't very good in bad weather. You had to wear lots of warm clothes. They weren't easy to start either – we had to crank it up by hand. In those days too the brakes were not very good so the back wheels were covered in metal studs which worked all right on wet roads but on wooden paving the wheels just went on and on spinning.

Lord Jellicoe could have had any of those snooty girls, one of whom was a lord's daughter, but he chose me to drive him everywhere. We went all over England. He was a very quiet man. I used to salute him every time I met him: but I didn't see Lady Jellicoe very much. I was based at Albany Street while he was at the Admiralty. I used to meet him at Waterloo Station every morning, then wait on him all day, and return him in the evening. He always had lots of appointments and meetings. He was very thoughtful and considerate to me, not patronising; he seemed to trust me – he was truly a dying breed. I did also meet Lord Beatty, but I didn't take to him; Lord Jellicoe was more dignified.

As I joined up when the WRNS were just starting I had the number G.5. I think the 'G' stood for 'Garage' where I did my extra training as a driver for officers. I never expected to get to drive the most famous naval officer of them all! 'Ginger' Smith, who taught me, was over the moon when he heard. You see, I was only small, but I was a very experienced driver when I joined at twenty. Most drivers would only drive what they were used to or had learnt on, but I even learnt to drive a motor cycle and a three-wheeler – that was like a large box arrangement which had been commandeered from a milliner's who used it for delivering the large hats.

I remember the night (2/3 September 1916) when Leefe Robinson shot down the Zeppelin. It lit up the whole sky over London; but when I drove out to the field in Cuffley those guarding it wouldn't let me in. I was very sad when Leefe Robinson died after the war. He'd come all the way through, and then died during the terrible 'flu epidemic.

And I remember too Armistice Day in 1918. But we didn't celebrate it. We were just glad it was all over.

Wren Marie Scott

I was born in Leicester on Boxing Day 1897 and started work in a Jewish tailor's at the age of thirteen. I worked there for three years and at sixteen was earning thirteen shillings and seven-pence a week. When my brother joined the Royal Flying Corps, I decided I'd join up as well. I went down to Cecil Hotel in the Strand in London and told them I wanted to sign on in the VAD (Voluntary Aid Detachment). They told me they needed drivers so I was sent back to Leicester to learn how to drive.

Not only was I taught to drive but to do running repairs as well. One of the things I learnt was how to use carborundum, under-paste, on the valves. Once I learnt how to drive the car they sent me to Doncaster to learn to drive heavy vehicles. When I arrived there all on my own I met all these rough-looking soldiers, but they were very nice to me. I was the only woman on the camp and it was my first time away from home, so I was rather lonely. I took my test on a Crossley tender, a great big thing that was a devil to drive, especially uphill. You almost needed two hands on the gear stick! Somehow I managed to pass the test and then I went home to wait to be called up.

After I passed I joined the VADs. In fact we were called the Forage Corps – which involved anything to do with the country, farms, grass, and feeding horses – at King's Lynn and put in charge of a squad of women: Lady Ogilvy-Grant was one of them. We had to guard the docks – well not so much guard as look after the tons of hay that were stacked on the dockside. The hay was for the horses of the Expeditionary Force in France and

Belgium. We had to guard it in case it tumbled over, or ignited –
spontaneous combustion.

I did that for a long time: so all my driving and the other
glamorous things I'd envisaged didn't come into it. All I can
remember from then is the taste of the horrible soup they used to
give us when we came off duty. We were billeted in St Margaret's
House in King's Lynn where there were about fourteen of us.
We worked very long hours so I tried to cheer everyone up by
playing the piano. I used to play the popular songs like 'Have
you any dirty washing, Mother, dear?' and 'I've got sixpence,'
but on one occasion I played a couple of love songs and a few of
the girls began to cry. I couldn't understand why until one of the
older girls told me that some of them had lost sweethearts and
brothers.

I was then seconded to the Coastal Defence Station at
Lowestoft as the driver for Egbert ('Bertie') Cadbury of the
RNAS. He was a pilot and flew a Sopwith seaplane. This was a
new world for me, a lot more glamorous and really what I'd
joined for. I used to drive him from our depot to the beach and
back again. The seaplanes were flying anti-submarine patrols
and watching out for Zeppelins which seemed to come over in
droves to attack the East coast. I used to watch the men,
sometimes up to their armpits, dragging the seaplanes down
into the sea; in the winter they were frozen stiff. We also had
lots of women called civilian subordinates who used to clean
the wings of the seaplanes. One night in October 1916 ten
Zeppelins launched an attack and dropped a bomb nearby
where I was sleeping and blew me out of bed. Bertie Cadbury
and two other pilots attacked one of them from underneath.
Even though he was under fire himself from the Zeppelin he
fired off two trays of ammunition without any effect; then he
fired his last two trays into the stern which didn't seem to have
any effect either. But a few minutes later flames appeared
where he'd hit it in the stern. One of the other pilots continued
firing until it burst into flames. That was a great day for us and

the camp was all excited that evening with the success. One pilot got the DSO, and Bertie Cadbury and the other pilot got a DFC.

Bertie Cadbury was always very busy. He was in charge of all the transport and all the aircraft as well as instructing the new pilots. So life was very busy for me too. But every week or so he'd receive a parcel from the Cadbury factory and I knew it was full of chocolates. He was a very nice man. On one occasion he nearly cost me my boyfriend. I drove him early one evening to the ward-room. He told me he'd be out at eight o'clock. A bit after 8 pm I went and inquired from a steward as to what was happening. The officers must have been celebrating because he came out and said, 'Miss Scott, I meant 8 am!'

In late 1917 I transferred across to the newly formed WRNS. When the RNAS merged with the RFC, we remained as WRNS. Bertie got another Zeppelin in August 1918. He was watching a concert where his wife was singing when he was told about three Zeppelins over Yarmouth. He raced off in his Ford and, with his observer Captain Leekie, attacked and shot down in flames L70 which was the finest airship that Germany had. On board was the Chief of the German Airship Service. They announced at the concert what he'd done and everyone cheered. He was carried shoulder-high through the streets when he came back. It was all very exciting.

In the September edition of our camp magazine 'The Bat' (our seaplanes were called Bat boats) Major Cadbury was congratulated along with Captain Leekie for getting the DFC, and the concert was recorded as a great success. On the next page, under the headline 'Great Scott', it read: 'Another Station Romance – another "WREN" driver as the heroine! Norman Scott, one of the most popular of drivers, is, we understand, engaged to Miss Marie Scott, also an "at the wheel" girl. Best of luck to both!'

Sub-Lieutenant Bill Fell

In 1917, having passed my 'Subs' exams, I joined the Dover Patrol. We were under Admiral Roger Keyes. I was on a P-boat, P11, which had one low funnel cut off diagonally across the top, hopefully to resemble a U-boat. They were frightfully bad sea boats, low in the water but capable of 24 knots. We spent our nights sitting over the tops of minefields with hundreds of trawlers milling around us. Every few minutes a 3,000,000 candle-power flare would be set off. Because of the mines U-boats had to come up and it was hoped that they would be illuminated and then hunted by us. This method certainly kept the U-boats down though one or two got through. The others had to go around the minefield which meant a much longer journey for them. When occasional raids took place, and the Germans came down fast in their destroyers on a black south-westerly night, our job was to shepherd the trawlers out of the way. We couldn't get mixed up in the action as we only had one miserable 4-inch gun and a couple of pom-pom guns.

While I had been on the *Warspite* I had applied to join submarines. To my joy and delight, at the beginning of 1918 I was selected. After three months training I was sent to *Titania*, a submarine depot ship, as a spare hand longing to get out on patrol. At last I did get out on G.2. The G-boats were double hulled, slow to dive, but excellent sea boats. We had four 18-inch torpedoes and one little 3-inch gun, and our captain was Neville Lake. On my first trip we went out in a hurricane. I was sick for the first few hours. Then at noon, when we were on the surface, out of a rain squall appeared a British cruiser and two destroyers. They immediately turned towards us. We could see little black figures rushing fore and aft manning guns. I was on the bridge and fired the recognition signal, a grenade fired from a rifle, but inadvertently I'd forgotten to take out the pin and it did not go off. I then began anxiously searching for another in all the water that was slopping about in the conning tower. At last I got my hands on one, but when I pulled the trigger it misfired. By this time the destroyers were practically on top of us. I got a third one off and the navigator and myself were waving everything we had. I then fired another but realised the signal had changed at noon! However I think they had realised we were not the enemy and turned away into the squall.

The weather moderated later that afternoon and towards evening we saw a U-boat (U-78) way ahead of us. We lowered a hand on a bearing line down over the conning tower to the gun and then lowered a projectile to him which he pushed into the bridge of the gun. He went to one side and trained the gun then round to the other side and layed the gun. While he was doing this, waves were repeatedly washing him off, and we would pull him up on the end of the line. When he finished, without any instruction, he suddenly fired and we saw the fall of shot right alongside Fritz. We hastily got some more shots to him but we never saw any of these fall. Of course, Fritz dived. Being ahead of us he was in a perfect position to attack so we dived as well. We spent the rest of that evening in the Dogger Light Vessel area stooging around listening with the hydrophone.

Our orders were to surface at 2 am and recharge until daylight. At 1.30 am I went over to the radio operator who was listening on the hydrophone and had taken the phones off because the noise was so intense. He said it was 'Fasendend' (the underwater communication system used by the Germans). I called the captain who was fast asleep in his bunk and told him what I had heard. He said, very irritatedly, 'Go to bed. Go away. I don't care what it is.' But I kept on saying that it was very loud and reluctantly he agreed to get out of his warm bunk. When he arrived he had a pair of long woolly drawers on and nothing else. He listened and then told us to surface, but not to go to diving stations. So with a very sleepy crew we surfaced. We opened the lower lid, the Captain went up and opened the top conning tower and there was a silence. Then an almighty shout from him: 'Hard starboard! Full ahead! Gun action stations! Flood the tubes!' All yelled down the conning tower. The voice pipes were full of water so a lot of the crew who were still pretty fat-headed, having been down for some time, didn't hear a thing.

The engine-room, in blissful ignorance of what was happening, assumed we had come up to charge our batteries. So they took the starboard engine clutch out and put the tail clutch in which effectively meant you couldn't go forward on your starboard side either on your motors or engine. As they'd heard there was a bit of a flap on for'ard they thought they had better go ahead port. With the helm hard over the other way all the submarine did was steam slowly away from a large U-boat which was steaming across our bows on the surface, as large as life, two or three hundred yards away. At that moment a half-moon came out, just shone for a moment silhouetting the U-boat, making it a sitting target. Down below the navigator and myself got the clutches changed over and the right screw going ahead on the motor.

The First Lieutenant, who was particularly fat-headed and asleep, got hold of the Lewis gun, put the pan on and was starting to go up the conning tower hatch when he unfortunately let it off! Well, bullets were whizzing around the control rooms hitting everything. He even shot the giro compass dead and that went spinning around as well. On top of this, there was a chain of men up the conning tower trying to get ammunition up to the gun, when the top one dropped his shell down on the others!

However, we were slowly turning. We had no night sight on the bridge in those days, but the Captain held his hand to his eye and was shouting down instructions. As we were swinging under full outside screw and under full helm he yelled 'Fire'. This instruction trickled down the conning tower and eventually reached the fore ends. In this time I should think we had swung an additional ten degrees before the torpedo gunners responded and sent off a 'fish'.

By this time Fritz had disappeared, the moon had gone in and we couldn't see a thing. We were disappointed and were just about to go below to clear up the mess when there was an enormous crump and crash and up went Fritz sky high. It was the luckiest shot of the war!

We went over to the pool of oil and wreckage and saw a lot of chaps all floating with their faces down in the water, with their bottoms up, all dead. We did pick up two and put them on our saddle tanks. The Captain then realised that Fritz had been talking to someone pretty close by, so he ordered us to dive.

At the end of the war as a result of us sinking the U-boat and one or two other incidents I received about £200 in blood money which was rather a lot of money in those days. I also had the pleasure of serving in submarines until 1945 and wouldn't have changed a minute of my time.

Sub-Lieutenant Gordon Hyams

ROYAL NAVAL AIR SERVICE

I went to Charterhouse School when I was fourteen in 1912. In the holidays I used to cycle from my home near Watford to Hendon Aerodrome. I had always been mad keen on aeroplanes and used to make models all the time. I called them flying sticks because that is what they looked like. I made a model of the Caudron and another which had a six-foot wingspan and fitted it with a compressed air engine which I had to pump up with a bicycle pump. At Hendon I saw all the early planes and flyers, including the famous Warren Marrian. The Germans were impressive, too, especially Dietrich, their ace looper. I also used to see Graham White who owned Hendon. The pilots would race flat out around pylons and sometimes they'd crash or fall out of the aircraft. There were big cash prizes on offer in those days.

Even though I was reading of the terrible casualties in the war, I wanted so much to become a pilot that I joined the Royal Naval Air Service (RNAS) in 1916 straight from school. My first posting was to Ponders End, near Chingford in Essex, where my flying instructor was Ben Travers. He later went on to make a name for himself writing farces for the Aldwych Company such as *Rookery Nook* and *Cuckoo in the Nest*. He taught one how to fly a Maurice Farman Longhorn. He was a very patient instructor, a quiet man, who had also been at Charterhouse. Most of the other trainees were flying Henri Farmans. On 18 March 1917 I flew my first solo for nineteen minutes after four hours of dual control. I flew some other aircraft, like the Avro 504K and the Curtiss JM4, and then went on to Cranwell, where I piloted a BE2 (Bleriot Experimental 2), nicknamed 'Fokker fodder' because of its high casualty rate against the German Air Force.

I was then posted as a Flight Sub-Lieutenant to Calshot on the Solent to fly seaplanes. Arthur (later Lord) Tedder was an instructor there. We flew FBAs (Franco-British Association) which were not very good machines. The engine was in the middle on the back of the wing above and in front of my head. To start it, I had to stand on my seat and crank the starter handle. If the engine caught fire, you opened the throttle which blew it out. One of the observers at Calshot under training was Wedgwood Benn (later Lord Stansgate). He was much older than all of us but mucked in, particularly on the day the coal barge arrived. After completing my training I was posted to Westgate, near Margate, for our first crack at anti-submarine patrols. Each day we'd go out well prepared for the cold with heavy leather coat and helmet, plus a pigeon and Horlicks tablets which were very sustaining.

On one of my early take-offs, downwind, I managed to turn a cartwheel in a Sopwith Schneider and finished upside down in the sea. I escaped from the cockpit and swam ashore, but the aircraft was a write-off. From Westgate I went up to Hornsea

Mere, a sub-station of Killingholme. It was the ideal place to take off from because it was a lake and so had no tide. We patrolled out from there along the shipping lanes between the Humber and the Tees. In March 1918 I spotted a U-boat on the surface off Scarborough. It was probably recharging its batteries, but as soon as it saw me it dived very quickly and, as the weather was very rough, it did not leave a wake. I dropped a 65lb bomb which went straight to the bottom.

On another occasion I was returning from a patrol when I saw a ditched H12 American flying-boat. As I descended it suddenly split in half and burst into flames. Somehow the crew of four managed to get into their dinghy. They seemed all right, but I thought I should drop them my life belt which I found out later, landed in their dinghy. I then flew back to Hornsea Mere to let them know of the situation, refuelled and flew back out to circle the dinghy. Later a Short came out, but for some unknown reason didn't see them and returned. I signalled to the now rather anxious crew below that I would seek further assistance. I flew for quite some while before I found two trawlers. I attempted to indicate the problem by Very Light, but they didn't seem to understand. I tried to find other ships but by now was getting low in fuel so I returned to the trawlers and fired off several rounds from my Lewis gun, which seemed to alert them! They made their way to where I was circling and picked up the rather wet and cold crew.

While I was at Hornsea Mere, in the winter, some boys were playing on the frozen lake when one fell through the ice. I grabbed a ladder and ran across the ice until almost touching distance when the ice gave way and I fell in. Fortunately I came straight up and could claw my way out, but the boy had gone under the ice so I was unable to reach him and he drowned. It was a sad day.

On 28 February 1918 our senior pilot, Lemmon, was flying our Commanding Officer, Flight Commander Robertson, in a Short. He had taken off on one of the narrower parts of the mere and then made a sharp turn and plunged nose first into marshy ground. Robertson jumped clear, but the pilot was trapped inside the aircraft which had burst into flames. The ammunition on board was likely to explode, but Robertson tried to rescue Lemmon and only gave up when he was severely burnt in the face, hands and legs. I saw him later in hospital; his face was badly scarred and he'd lost an eye. However, he was awarded the Albert Medal and continued in the RAF right through the Second World War.

In the spring of 1918 I was looking forward to a bit of leave. I got home and was just beginning to relax when I received a telegram ordering me to report back to Hornsea immediately. I was cross about losing my leave, but my anger evaporated when the CO told me I'd been awarded the Humane Society Award for attempting to save the boy under the ice.

When the RNAS merged with the RFC to become the RAF, it meant that we had left the senior service to join the most junior service. We were first issued a khaki uniform and given Army ranks, then uniforms of various shades of blue and the new RAF rankings. We didn't welcome the so-called unification at all.

Later, in the early summer of 1918, I was posted to Egypt and based first at Alexandria, then Port Said. On one occasion I was told to recce the swept channel to see if there were any mines that had been missed: this was for a convoy setting out from Alexandria to Salonika. About half way through this task my engine gave out and I had to ditch. I instructed my passenger to stand on the front of the floats to keep the back out of the water. Unfortunately we were there for some time and the sea became very rough. Suddenly the aircraft went down tail first and we were thrown into the air. We managed to scramble on to the upturned floats and had to stay in that precarious position all night. It was my twentieth birthday and I thought I was going to die. The next day we spotted the convoy that we were supposed to have escorted after our recce. They had apparently left late and, fortunately, one of their zigzags coincided with our position. We were picked up by the Australian destroyer *Swan*.

As if that was not enough, a few days later I was taking off in a Short in Alexandria harbour when I found the engine responding very sluggishly. While I was trying to get her into the air I could see we were approaching a large breakwater at the entrance to the harbour. I tried to climb over it and went head first into the water. Had I continued, I would have collided with the statue of Ferdinand de Lesseps!

Aircraftsman Bert Adams

ROYAL NAVAL AIR SERVICE

When the Great War came I was seventeen and an apprentice printer. I volunteered for the Army but failed my medical because of the three months I'd had of rheumatic fever. So I decided to try the Navy and was accepted as a Medical Orderly for work in sickbays. I had the lowest possible medical grading of C3. They said I'd be all right for emptying the buckets or cleaning up. I was sent initially to Crystal Palace and slept on the top floor of that amazing building in a hammock under all the glass. I used to sleep in fear of a Zeppelin raid, especially when the moon was up because we glistened like a beacon.

The Navy seemed to forget about my medical training because I was posted in 1915 to Pulham in Norfolk, near Bungay in Suffolk, which was to become a base for the airships of the RNAS. At the start we had to work as navvies and clear the ground of trees and hedges and mix the concrete for the bases of the hangars. These hangars were to house the non-rigid, hydrogen-filled airships which patrolled the North Sea in search of German submarines. Airships were known by us as 'lighter-than-air ships'. It was the most hazardous way of travelling because the hydrogen was so inflammable.

In those early days at Pulham we had a Sea Scout non-rigid airship and three other small craft called Beta, Gamma and Delta which had previously been operated by the Royal Engineers. We used to sleep in a tent and start the day about 7 am.

We'd sometimes have a wash in a five-gallon petrol can which was heated over a coal burner. When the airship was approaching for docking about a hundred of us would run out to wait for its arrival overhead. When it was about 500 feet above us, the airship's crew threw out a landing line. We caught hold of it and started to pull it down. As it got lower there was more rope to get hold of, so more men could pull it down. The rope had wooden toggles so that you could get both hands on it and pull. There would perhaps be fifty men on the starboard side and fifty on port, all pulling down. Well, sometimes the wind would catch the airship and if the pulling was not greater than the lift, then you'd find yourself hanging on going up and up. People would panic and drop off. But of course the more who dropped off the higher it would go, with others hanging on for dear life. In one case one of our men held on too long, drifted off and was killed when he could hang on no longer.

When the airship was down we would attach it to a Burrell Steam Engine which would, with us hanging on to the ropes, be directed into the hangar and guided into position by the shed-master. When it was finally in position the ropes would be tethered to concrete blocks. When deflated the envelope would hang suspended from the roof by wide canvas straps – hence the word hangar. The massive doors of the hangar would be opened and closed by the type of tank used at the battle of Cambrai.

Part of my job was to go up in the airship and act as ballast. There were probably about eight of us up there. We just drifted around the airfield while the crew made adjustments. It was really a simple life. When it was undocking we walked the airship out and tried to keep it steady. Then Warrant Officer Evason would hold up his handkerchief (no windsocks at Pulham!) to see which way the wind was blowing. We'd then be told 'bow to starboard' or 'bow to port' to head it into the wind! When we got it right the airship became like a caged animal straining to be released. You see, the hydrogen was trying to pull her up and the engines were trying to take her forward, the wind was trying to take her back and we were trying to hang on! The engines would rev up and off it would go, heading towards Yarmouth for its patrol.

If the airship saw a submarine it could drop small hand-held bombs from about 1,000 feet. It could also come down above the submarine where its propellers would cause considerable turbulence around the sub. It also had a primitive wireless on board, so it could also let nearby destroyers know where the sub was. One of the experiments carried out at Pulham in June 1918 was to attach a Sopwith Camel beneath the belly of His Majesty's Airship (HMA) No.23. When it got over a sparsely populated area the Camel's motor was speeded up and the release gear activated and the fighter flew off. In the last week of the war they actually released two Camels which landed back at Pulham, both from 212 Squadron. HMA No.23 was an enormous airship built by Vickers. It was 535 feet long, had swivelling propeller mounts which could be angled downwards to push her upwards, and was constructed of metal covered by two layers of rubber-coated cotton fabric cemented together with a third layer of rubber. It had four Rolls-Royce Eagle engines, a top speed of 52 mph and could reach 3,000 feet. There was a crew of seventeen and it held four 100-lb. bombs.

The hydrogen needed for the airships was either brought in giant cylinders weighing seven hundredweight apiece or it was produced from our silicol gun plant which could produce 10,000 cubic feet an hour. HMA No.23, for example, needed 942,000 cubic feet of hydrogen in its 18 cells. Great care was needed in the manufacture of hydrogen. While I was at Pulham there was a bad explosion and two men who were working in the plant were killed. Even to this day there is not a blade of grass where the gasworks were. Nothing will grow there, nor do you ever see birds.

Sometimes the airship would be disabled and have to alight in a field, often miles from Pulham. But the local residents seemed to have an affection for the 'pigs', as they were called. They'd all down tools and whole villages of sometimes two or three hundred people would hold on to the trail ropes and restrain and guide it back to us. It was quite a sight seeing it floating along being carried over ditches, hedges and trees. People would have torn clothes and bruises, but they enjoyed the task – they had a common purpose, they were doing something for the war effort.

Of course, with airships so vulnerable, there were always going to be accidents. Our first was the loss of C.17 with all five of its crew. It was shot down by a seaplane while on patrol and this occurred in the same week as the gas explosion. The next loss for us meant a lot to me. Three German floatplanes shot down C.27 on 11 December 1917. The crew of five all perished. I knew them all, in particular J.E. Martin and Jack Collett, and it cast a gloom over the whole station. Then C.26 went out to look for it but ran out of fuel and came down over Holland where the crew was interned for the rest of the war. After that they stopped patrols until HMA No.23 came along.

HMA 23 was also used as a guinea pig, or workhorse. At one point a 2-pounder, quick-firing gun was attached and mounted on top of the hull. The airship had almost to stand up before it was fired. Conducting the trials was a young man from Vickers named Barnes Neville Wallis. But unlike his remarkable experiments later, this one proved a failure.

Throughout my time at Pulham we were constantly reading about or hearing of Zeppelin raids. They really were feared by the people on the east coast. In these raids over 500 people were killed. The last raid was in August 1918 when Major Cadbury's DH4, operating from Great Yarmouth, shot it down. When the Armistice came along in November 1918, like everyone else I got very drunk and thought about those who had fought far harder wars in other lands. Never did I think that twenty years later I'd be back in uniform again.

Leading Mechanic Bill Argent

ROYAL NAVAL AIR SERVICE

I left school at the age of fifteen and got a job in an office, but I couldn't stand it. The war had only just started and you only saw the spectacular side of it, the glory. I saw this glossy advert about the Royal Naval Air Service wanting boys to train in wireless telegraphy so I joined up in November 1915 at South Kensington in London where the RNAS had taken over a factory. I had only been there a day when I wished I hadn't joined. The discipline was really tough, you had to run everywhere. The Petty Officers kept calling it a ship, we even slept in hammocks. At six o'clock it was 'Wakey, Wakey' from the Master-at-Arms.

One of the first things I saw was a beating. A boy had been caught smoking. He was stripped to the waist and spread-eagled over a vaulting horse and really flayed. It didn't make any difference because a few days later I saw him smoking again.

When I moved to Cranwell, then known as HMS *Daedalus*, the discipline was just as harsh and the pay was seven shillings a week. The huts were so cold that, at one point, I had to get a hammer to my boots to get them out of the ice. We had to leave them outside to ensure the floor stayed shiny. We wore a square rig: jackets, patch pockets, open neck, grey flannel shirt and a peak cap with the RNAS insignia on it. Sunday mornings was the great treat because we had bacon and eggs. Traditionally tea was served in a bowl, not a cup, but I was put off tea because one day I saw a mess cook having a bath in one of the big wooden vats in which it was made.

I spent a year training at Cranwell and only had one leave – when I got home I was horrified by the effect rationing was having on the family. Our training was very thorough; it was mostly on wireless, which was still in a very crude state, and the other traditions of morse and flag-signalling. To pass out we had to signal to manoeuvre the Fleet. The other boys played the ships on the parade square. They weren't very happy if they collided because you'd cocked up your signals.

Rather than waste the public's money training a boy to be a pilot or observer only to find he became airsick, they used to take us up first in a balloon to 1,000 feet and then to the more rarefied position at 2,000 feet. Directly anyone was sick they were bundled off the station or found another job.

On my eighteenth birthday in January 1917 I became a 'man' and was posted to the gunnery school at Eastchurch on the Isle of Sheppey. I was waiting for my first flight in a Maurice Farman when I saw the lad in front of me go up and, with his Lewis gun, shoot away one of the struts! To simulate bombing we used to sit up on a gantry about the height of two houses. Below there was a moving artificial pictorial land-scape. We would drop a dummy bomb down on the target and, if it hit, a light came on. You didn't actually drop the bomb, you pulled a lever. Very ingenious.

After training I was posted to Calshot, as an observer/wire-less operator. We flew H12s and F2A flying boats on anti-submarine patrols. At last I was in the war. My first attack on a U-boat was on 21 June 1917. We dived as quickly as possible but the U-boat submerged rapidly, so we dropped four 100-lb. bombs with two-second delayed fuses which sink some way before they explode. Nothing happened, and no oil appeared on the surface, so we dropped calcium flares to indicate its prob-able whereabouts, so that ships could drop depth charges.

On the next occasion, 26 June, we caught a U-boat on the surface. The captain obviously panicked because he gave the order to 'down hatch' and abandoned some of the crew on the deck.

A few days before that we had a report of a U-boat operating in our area. When we arrived we saw a tanker had been torpedoed, and there were all these men swimming in flaming oil. That was my first experience of death. I take my hat off to the Merchant Navy; they go through all that, lose mates, get picked up, and then sign on again. At least we had the chance of hitting back, but those poor devils never did.

On other patrols we would fly in support of a convoy. On one occasion we accompanied *SS Olympic* which was acting as a troopship carrying thousands of Americans. The troops seemed grateful to have us along and would wave to us all the time. I suppose we gave a certain security. On 12 May 1918 we escorted fifty ships and the *Olympic* rammed and sank *U-103* off the Lizard. Once we had to force-land and came down at Budleigh Salterton. The Home Guard turned out and managed to drag the aircraft up the beach. A real old Colonel Blimp came over and told us to stay with him. We had a hell of a party most of the night. The next morning when we arrived on the beach the locals had covered the aircraft with flowers. That was a very moving sight. Many of course had never seen an aircraft up close. The fitters came and put the engine right. Then all the locals pulled and pushed the aircraft into the water. The mechanics who wore long waders then piggy-backed us out to the aircraft. I think they were sad to see us go. We came back later that day with presents of chocolates and preserved fruits. Up to then we'd had no idea how much we were appreciated.

I ditched with various pilots eight times. The first time was in a Short 855 piloted by Lieutenant-Commander Waugh when we came down off Portland Bill. We were picked up by a drifter, which towed the machine back. On the second occasion in a Wright seaplane, we were rescued by the armed yacht *Lorna* which towed us to Poole. A month later we had to be picked up by a torpedo boat. But the worst moment was when Lieutenant Jarman had to ditch our Short 1085 twenty miles south of Lyme Regis in very rough weather. The engine simply packed up in mid-flight. I thought we were for it. There was one hell of a sea running as the pilot brought us down, so as we landed the floats were pushed in and the propeller caught them and ripped them off the front. I was sending out wireless messages giving our position and fired off a Very light to attract attention. I then sent off the two pigeons as the aircraft began to disintegrate. We were in the water for four hours which made us realise the wireless messages had not got through. We were depending on one of the pigeons getting back to base. I had scribbled the two messages and placed them inside the small aluminium canister that was attached to the pigeons' leg. One, thank God, got through. She had actually been shot and as the poor thing arrived she collapsed and died. She certainly saved our lives. The Commanding Officer himself flew out and located us. He could see our aircraft was practically submerged by now and we were hanging on grimly. He signalled down to us to inflate our life belts and swim for it. Unfortunately mine had been punctured. As he was flying overhead and we were struggling in the sea we saw a torpedo boat heading our way – I've never been so pleased to see a ship. They took us on board and then tried to tow the aircraft, but it finally sank in Lyme Regis harbour. That incident really shook us both up. If it hadn't been for that pigeon we'd have had a watery grave. That's why I've never touched pigeon pie in my life, and whenever I look at a pigeon now I thank God.

Seven weeks later down we went in the sea again, but it was a much less dramatic rescue this time because they picked up our wireless message. My final ditching was in a Companion seaplane I259 in the summer of 1918, when a destroyer picked us up and treated us royally.

We certainly worked hard, especially when I was posted to Portland. It was patrol after patrol. Flying in the winter was a miserable experience. We were absolutely frozen to the bone – I've never experienced cold like that since. We had lambswool leggings and leather coats, fleece-lined helmets and gloves, but they were never enough.

When we were out on patrol we were given a recognition signal for the day. Many of our submarines were bombed because they didn't answer the recognition signal – which was either a colour flare or two letters to be flashed with the Aldiss Lamp. If the sub didn't flash, I'd drop a bomb on it.

On 25 March 1918 we saw an enemy sub fully blown on the surface. I dropped two 100-lb. bombs from 600 feet – both missed by a hundred feet. I dropped two more, one of which fell directly on the deck but failed to detonate. The sub went straight down. I dropped the usual marker flares. Depth charges were dropped, but no one reported back to us.

Years later I read a book which gave the locations of all U-boats sunk in the Channel and there was one on that very spot. But I'll never know. We did celebrate, yet as Naval men we also realised that probably fifty men had been sent to the bottom. But that is war and those U-boats were destroying our convoys without any warnings.

Lieutenant Leslie Kemp

ROYAL NAVAL AIR SERVICE

Like many a good lad I obeyed Lord Kitchener's call and joined the Army at the age of sixteen. I served for about eighteen months and then transferred to the Navy, in fact the Royal Naval Air Service, as a midshipman. My first appointment was to the sea plane base at Great Yarmouth where the RNAS had commandeered a big hotel on the sea front. I spent three weeks there before I went to Eastchurch to train as an observer and I carried out all the usual training of map reading, aerial photography, bombing, navigation, cross-country flying and recognition of ships. It was very thorough training. We were flying in some of the first aircraft such as a BE2E, a Bleriot experimental, a DH4, a DH6 and an American aircraft, a Curtiss. I always remember the DH6 didn't have rounded edges on its wings, they were square. Looking back I wish I had trained as a pilot because all you have to do is learn how to fly. It was hard work being an observer!

I then went to Greenwich for officer training. That was a

wonderful experience because you learned naval history, customs, as well as ship recognition – not only our warships, but those of other nations too. Hour after hour there was a Petty Officer putting up models that you had to identify and record. On top of this you had map reading and meteorology. It was all lectures, swotting, lectures, swotting, lectures all the time; and we started at 6.00 in the morning doing PT in shorts, summer or winter.

It was wonderful, the experience of Greenwich, a place full of dignity. We dined every night in the hall with the painted ceiling, in full mess kit, wing collar and bow tie. Many would have thought that crazy in war time, but we did it nevertheless because it was the tradition. We had all the famous ornaments out on the tables, including a lovely silver model of Nelson's Column and another of HMS *Victory*. I was just eighteen and, I think, a little overwhelmed.

After Greenwich I was sent on leave to await my first appointment. Eventually I got a telegram to report to the Admiralty. I was told to go to Mudros. Well, I didn't know where Mudros was or what was going on there. In the Army we either went as a battalion or as a party, but in the Navy apparently you went on your own. I went down to Dover, got aboard a ship and asked if it was going to Ostend. No, they weren't. I asked in a number of others and at last I finished up on a sea-going tug. We left Dover at midnight with no navigation lights at all, and it was so cold. It was a terrible crossing which took over eleven hours to reach Cherbourg. I simply sat on deck with my arms around the funnel trying to keep warm. I saw a Railway Transport Officer and asked him if there was a ship going to Taranto. But there wasn't, so I stayed a week outside Bordeaux. I then went by train across France and all the way down to the east coast of Italy. It took ages. There was always a row between the French and Italians as to when they were going to get their carriages back. The Italians used to poke us into sidings, I think for the fun of it. It took me three weeks to get to Taranto! Then, once there, it was the old retort, 'No, we don't know anything about you'. Nobody knew anything. Then I found out that there was an air station close by, so I reported there. The CO said, 'Oh, no, we don't know anything about you, but you better wait here until we find out'. At last they found out that I was due to go to Limnos, one of the Greek islands. Eventually I got there and they did know about me and wondered where I'd been all this time!

We had DH9s, which were light bombers, on the island and shared the aerodrome with the Greek Air Force. I'm sorry to say it, but the Greeks were terrible pilots. They had some of our machines, but they didn't know how to fly them. Instead of coming down to land as we did, they used to come down in steps. On one occasion they 'missed a step' and came down on top of one of our machines! The DH9a, though, was not an easy aircraft to handle. It had an improved cockpit layout to the DH4, and radio equipment, but it had a low operational ceiling which made it vulnerable to attack, and its unreliable engine caused more casualties than enemy action. Its maximum speed was 112 mph. What the Greeks lacked in aeronautical skills, however, they made up with friendship. We celebrated Christmas 1916 with them. They'd filled a great metal container with all the alcohol on the island and set light to the top of it. We were plastered, crawling home on our hands and knees.

We had a hard winter in Greece, where our main target was Turkish shipping, but it was the attack on the battle-cruisers *Goeben* and *Breslau*, in Constantinople on 9 July 1917, which comes back to me most vividly. Each of our DH9s carried about twelve 16-lb. bombs on each wing and 200-lb. ones on the under-carriage. We came in low enough to get an accurate position on both ships. I don't think they opened fire because I didn't see any flashes. In fact I think they went below, closed the hatches and waited until we'd left. I don't know how much damage we did, but they certainly didn't go to sea again.

We continued right up until the armistice to patrol and attack enemy shipping. We chased a number of submarines up the

Albanian coast, but even if we hit any we never saw any oil on the surface. When the armistice came I was in Salonika. Everyone went crazy, firing pistols from tram cars, really enjoying the fact that the war was over. I thought we were coming home, but instead we were sent to Russia.

Private Alfred Hutchinson

ROYAL MARINE LIGHT INFANTRY

I was a printer's assistant when the war broke out. I had a friend who lived about four doors away from me and we both decided to join up. We went along to the Recruiting Office where I was told at 17 that I was too old for boy service in the Navy, but I could join the Marines. I asked if I would be with my friend and they told me I would. I didn't see him again for three years!

I went first to Deal in November 1914 and joined the Royal Marines Light Infantry and then went on to Chatham for small arms training. After this I joined *Lowestoft*. On my first voyage we delivered gold to Halifax in Nova Scotia. All I can remember is lying on deck being sick for the whole seven day trip. After that we did patrols of the North Sea. On 19 August 1916 we were part of the screen for the Grand Fleet as it went south to intercept the High Seas Fleet. This was their main sortie after Jutland. It had intended to bomb Sunderland. I don't think there was ever a real risk that we'd engage them, but we lost the light cruiser *Nottingham* and the *Yarmouth* which were sunk by U-boats. Overhead, Zeppelins were scouting which were quite a sight. I was the sight setter on the gun but we didn't hit anything. The main danger was from planes – that was really frightening. The German fleet never really came out again, but their U-boats continued to be a success, especially against Merchant Ships. They really were a menace because from January to the end of April 1917 they sank 380 merchantmen and we were getting anxious about supplies, especially to the troops in France. It was around that time that the convoys were brought in to accompany these ships. We also had air support from aircraft and balloons and that turned the tide.

We then moved to the Mediterranean, mostly around Mudros and Malta. I was working then as a decoder. It was all very quiet – it was as if we were out of the war. Towards the end of 1917, having been paid off *Lowestoft* at Alexandria, we returned to England.

In the early part of 1918 I returned to Deal to undergo training for a secret raid. We didn't learn what it was until we set sail. The aim of the raid was to block the Bruges Canal by sinking a number of ships at the point where it entered the harbour and at the same time to destroy the port installation at Zeebrugge. There was also to be a raid on the canal at Ostend. It was known that U-boats were coming out of the canals and were still menacing our shipping. If we could block their exit, we'd save some ships. The main problem at Zeebrugge was the Mole. It was made of stone and well guarded. It was impossible to sail our blockships through Zeebrugge harbour and into the canal entrance unless the guns on the Mole were put out of action or diverted. That was to be our task.

Most of our training was done at night. We had a mock-up of the Mole and we trained each day with bayonet practise, and strangleholds. We even did it in gas masks with smoke screens and starshells going off everywhere. When we weren't training at night we were doing twelve mile route marches. We were also told, because of tidal conditions, we would only be there for about two and a half hours. A lot of us couldn't understand why they were sending about 1,000 Marines when we had all those troops already in France.

On 2 April we had a full rehearsal at 9 pm. Fireworks, starshells, the lot. Three days later the 4th Battalion got its marching orders, gas masks, barbed-wire pliers, sixty rounds, waterproof sheet, muffler and gloves and overcoats. The three companies from Chatham, Portsmouth and Plymouth all fell in and the band ahead of us played 'Auld Lang Syne' and other sing-songs like 'Britons Never Shall Be slaves' and 'Good Bye Dolly Grey'. We embarked on the *Iris II* at Dover. The *Iris* along with the *Daffodil* were to accompany the *Vindictive* and storm the Mole. The *Iris* and the *Daffodil* were ferry steamers that used to ply their trade on the River Mersey. They both had a very shallow draught which would enable us to ride over and clear any mines. The people of Liverpool were not best pleased to lose them, but when they heard later what we'd done they were really proud of their two ships.

On 10 April we were alerted for the attack but the winds became unfavourable for the smoke attack so we turned back. Morale was a bit low. We were told the next morning we were to attack at 2 am. Time hung heavily. We fell in on deck at 1 am, and could see the searchlights on the Mole and starshells going up. We were going in. Then they called it off! We then stayed on board for 12 days playing cards, arranging concert parties, generally filling in time. Gambling is a very serious offence in the Navy, but a blind eye was turned and we played a lot of Crown and Anchor.

It was a beautiful morning, 22 April, but reality hit us when the No. 1 ordered us to cover the top deck with sand to soak up the blood! Later that afternoon we watched the sunset, everyone was very quiet. I think we were wondering if we would see it rise in the morning. We were to be alongside the Mole at midnight. The old and ugly *Vindictive* was ahead. It looked like a giant beetle with fourteen legs. The legs were the landing brows to be used in the Mole. Behind us was *Daffodil* and the three block-ships, *Thetis*, *Intrepid* and *Iphigenia*. At 11 o'clock we had a tot of rum which for many was to be their last. Close to midnight we were about 300 yards from the Mole and all was going well, when the wind turned completely around from the shore this time and there we were lit up like daylight caused by the starshells. It was very frightening. The German battery opened up and hit the *Vindictive* smashing her bridge. The flashes seemed to be coming from the wrong place. This was because the Germans had cunningly shifted their guns from the Mole to the pier. The *Vindictive* had during exercises practised how fast she could stop right under the guns on the Mole. She still had to get to where she had planned to come alongside and to do this she had to pass the guns on the pier. The German guns had really damaged *Vindictive* so that she only had two brows serviceable. It was bad. The *Daffodil* and *Iris* came in close to the Mole clearing our way with machine guns. The starboard anchor was dropped and we went astern on it to get in close. The hook we used on the derrick wouldn't hold and the Germans were opening fire on us with machine guns. It was hopeless. Lieutenant-Commander Bradford realised how bad our position was and climbed up the derrick. But he was cut down. Then the second-in-command tried and he was also killed. We had to abandon our position or we'd all have been killed. It was decided we could come alongside *Vindictive* and land over her deck. As we ran alongside her there was all this noise and smoke. The *Vindictive* being the biggest ship was really taking it, but it was fighting back.

Then all of a sudden a starshell burst overhead and made the night day. We were immediately ordered below. The German 5.9s opened up and we were hit fourteen times and twice from their eleven inch. One of the shells hit the bridge and killed the Captain and the Major of Marines and a lot more. Then another came through the upper deck and burst on the main deck where 56 Marines were waiting to go up the gangplank. Forty-nine were killed. There was just one big heap of arms and legs. My friend, he had his head blown off. He'd only got married on the weekend before we left. We heard that blockship had entered the harbour and so we were told to get the hell out of the place because the main objective had been achieved. We waited about a quarter of an hour for those who had got ashore to return. What did surprise me, when we were hit on the way out, was the sight of NCOs diving over the side. No one had given the order to abandon ship and never did. That shocked me. I couldn't believe my eyes to see them going over the side and swimming away.

There was nothing else we could do but scram. We put out all our lights and began to tend the wounded and the dead. Eventually destroyers arrived and escorted us back to Dover. Seeing the White Cliffs on that misty morning, and to be alive was quite something. As we came in and with only a young Lieutenant on the damaged bridge, steering by hand compass, the ships in harbour sounded their horns. We were greeted at Dover by Sir Roger Keyes.

We paid our last respects to our comrades. Then we had the grimmest of parades, 'The Roll Call'.

From Deal we went to Chatham. As we marched into the town we were surprised to be greeted by crowds of people lining the streets and cheering. We didn't know why, until we saw the newspaper reports. My feelings were that I was lucky to be alive and in one piece, and sorrow for the friends I had lost.

Sergeant Harry Wright

ROYAL MARINE LIGHT INFANTRY

After six weeks hard training at Deal, the 4th Battalion Royal Marines received orders to proceed to a certain destination. During this time we had been inspected by King George V, the First Lord of the Admiralty and the Adjutant-General of the RM Corps. The latter informed us that what we were going to do would live in history and he hoped that each man would do his duty and uphold the honour of the Royal Marines. Any man who did not want to go had the privilege of falling out, but no one moved.

At 6am on 6 April 1918 the battalion fell in and was inspected by our colonel, and with the band leading, we marched off through the town to the station. The people of Deal turned out to give us a good send-off. We were all singing, laughing or joking, and as we passed our old bayonet instructor, who had given us a stiff training, we gave him a rousing cheer. There was a special train in the station and the whole battalion of some 850 officers and men were entrained in less than ten minutes. When we arrived at Dover station there was a steamer waiting which convinced us that we were going to France. However our first port was Sheerness. When we arrived there we were rather surprised to read a signal from one of the ships which said that 'A' and 'B' Companies will proceed to HMS *Hindustan* and 'C' Company to HMS *Vindictive*. On getting alongside *Vindictive* we were surprised to see how she was fitted up. There was a special deck built on the port side with ramps leading from the lower deck on the starboard side up to the special deck. On the port side there were fourteen huge gangways pointing out to sea and triced up with pulleys ready for dropping. She carried two 11-inch howitzers, one forward, one aft, numerous Stokes guns and a pom-pom in the crow's nest halfway up the mast, the majority of her armament being on the port side. Sandbag revetments were built around the forebridge and other vital parts. In addition there were two very powerful flame-throwers and machine-guns. The ship was a floating arsenal for there were shells already fused everywhere. Apart from her proper complement for sea and with 'C' Company comprising some 270 men, we were rather overcrowded; but we were all men used to roughing it in all parts of the world.

Next day Captain Carpenter had everybody aft on the quarterdeck and told us for the first time what we were going to do. 'We are going,' he said, 'on a very dangerous errand, and any hitch in the operation might mean a naval disaster, so it is everyone's duty to do his best. The *Vindictive* is going through the enemy's minefields and alongside the mole at Zeebrugge. On getting there the 4th Battalion will storm the mole and engage the enemy while at the same time, three blockships filled with concrete will go round the other side of the mole and sink themselves in the mouth of the canal. A bridge connects the mole with Zeebrugge and during the operation a submarine with ten tons of high explosive will be set under the bridge and so cut off reinforcements from Zeebrugge. While this is going on two other ships will proceed to Ostend and sink themselves in the mouth of the canal there, and by this means close up the hornet's nest of submarines so that none can come out and those that are out cannot go back to refit. It may so happen,' he continued, 'that some of you may have the misfortune to be captured; if so, bear in mind you must not give any information to the enemy, especially about our fleet, but on the other hand there is certain information we would like you to pass on. In the first place, tell them that we are capturing their submarines, taking them to England, putting English crews on board and sending them to sea again as decoys. Secondly, tell them that on every merchant ship there is fitted an instrument which can detect a submarine at a two-mile radius. This information must be tactfully passed on, but let the enemy bring the subject up first.' Captain Carpenter finished by saying, 'The success of this whole operation depends on two things, namely secrecy, and the wind, which must be blowing towards the enemy so that destroyers can use their smoke screens effectually.'

We were then shown a clay model of the mole and given its dimensions, which were 1,800 yards long and 80 yards wide. It was built in peacetime to enable ships to land their passengers as the water was too shallow inshore. The passengers could be landed either side according to the tide. There was a railway running the whole length of the mole to take passengers to Zeebrugge. On the sea end of the mole was a lighthouse. Since it had been taken over by the Germans the mole had been fortified, being one mass of concrete shelters. In the centre was a huge seaplane shed with six powerful machine-guns. On the sea end of the mole and about fifty yards from the lighthouse was a strong concrete shelter with four 5-inch guns, and machine-guns were hidden in various places along the mole. *Vindictive* would go alongside the mole on the northern side.

Grappling irons would then be lowered on to the concrete wall, and on a given signal, the first Company would land.

We had previously drawn lots to see who should land first and 'C' Company, all Plymouth marines, won that honour. Each company had four platoons, Plymouth Company being numbered 9, 10, 11 and 12. Some sailors, as a demolition party, would accompany the leading company. On the advance being sounded no. 9 and my platoon would land first, turn to the right on getting ashore and capture the first objective, a strongpoint 200 yards along the mole. Almost immediately afterwards no. 11 and no. 12 platoons and seamen would land, turn to the left and advance towards the four guns and capture them. At the same time, if the enemy extinguished the lighthouse, they would burn a flare so that the blockships could get their bearings; the operation was to be carried out at midnight. On reaching their positions the platoon sergeants of the leading platoons would fire red flares into the air as a signal for the other company to come onshore. They would land, come through our line, carrying objectives to a depth of 800 yards and then, on firing their red flares, nos. 1, 2, 3 and 4 platoons of the Chatham marines would come through the others already in position on the mole and carry objectives to a depth of one mile.

Each platoon was armed with a Lewis gun and a flame-thrower. There was also a special platoon of machine-gunners and a special signal platoon with telephones, etc. There were also demolition parties for blowing up the concrete shelters and sheds. Each man carried Mills grenades and every NCO had a stunning mallet for close fighting. The officers carried revolvers and walking out canes weighted with lead on the handle end. Each platoon had two ladders and four ropes for, on landing, there was a drop of twenty feet, hence the use of ladders and ropes. The demolition parties, chiefly sailors, carried ammanol gun-cotton, safety and instantaneous fuses and detonators. The Howitzer and pom-pom guns were manned by the Royal Marine Artillery and the Stokes guns and machine-guns, manned by marine infantry, would keep up a covering fire while we were ashore. Each platoon had a specially trained bombing section to deal with dugouts etc. Each man wore a rubber swimming belt in case he fell into the sea. The signal to retire would be a succession of short blasts on *Vindictive*'s siren.

The monitors out at sea would assist us by trying to silence the batteries at Zeebrugge. The enemy, thinking this an attempt to take Zeebrugge, would concentrate their fire on to the mole and so give the blockships a chance to get in. Aeroplane photographs were handed round to the officers and NCOs and some of us drew a sketch from the photograph marking off positions. By the time we had seen the model and drawn the sketch, the officers and NCOs at least could have walked from one end of the mole to the other blindfolded and every man knew exactly what to do and where to go.

All day Sunday we were busy detonating grenades and unloading tugs which came alongside with extra sandbags and shells. The men stripped to the waist and worked with a will, finishing late that night with everyone dead tired. We had a good supper and turned into our hammocks for the night.

On Monday 8 April during the forenoon, it was reported by wireless from the Belgian coast that the wind was favourable and it was decided to do the 'stunt' at midnight. The two companies of marines left the *Hindustan*, some coming on board *Vindictive* and others going aboard *Iris* and *Daffodil*, two smaller ships. The destroyer *Warwick* with Vice Admiral Sir Roger Keyes aboard came out from Dover and gave orders for our little fleet to proceed to Zeebrugge. At 11am we got under way towing the *Iris* and *Daffodil*. Our fleet consisted of *Vindictive*, *Warwick* and five obsolete cruisers, *Intrepid*, *Brilliant*, *Iphigenia*, *Thetis* and *Sirius* filled with concrete. In addition there were a number of motorboats and the submarine filled with high explosives. We also had an escort of destroyers and overhead were a few aeroplanes.

It was a beautiful day and everyone was in the best of spirits.

As we left harbour, the *Hindustan* and other ships gave us a rousing cheer. We reached our destination late that night and lay just off Zeebrugge. The monitors and aeroplanes were already engaging the enemy. It was a very dark night and we could see the flashes of the guns onshore as they replied, and as we watched and listened the bombardment got more intense, until it seemed to us that nothing could land there and live. They certainly knew we were coming. A few quick flashes on the morse lamps, just a single letter code, and our little fleet turned back without being seen by the enemy. The men were very disappointed but we could not hope to effect a surprise if the enemy were prepared for us.

We arrived back at Sheerness during the forenoon and the *Hindustan* detachments were sent over to her. Admiral Keyes came onboard *Vindictive* and we all fell in on the quarterdeck. He mounted a bollard and explained that at the last moment the wind had changed, but told us to have patience because we would go again. We gave him a rousing cheer as he left the ship.

On Sunday 21 April the parson gave us a very interesting sermon on what became of us when we died. Little did we think then that within a few hours so many brave lads would have laid down their lives. The next day we were drilling on the quarterdeck when the signal came to prepare for the stunt. We went below, labelled our kitbags and other things we did not want, and handed them over to the ship's steward. A tug was already alongside to take us to the *Vindictive* and Colonel Elliot watched us as we clambered over the side. If anyone was downhearted and looked at our colonel, they would at once feel happy and confident. There he stood, wearing his DSO and a smile on his face. The men loved him for he had a kind word for everyone.

We crowded on board *Vindictive* and at 3pm we once again left for Zeebrugge with the *Iris* and *Daffodil*. Something seemed to tell us that we were going in that night. At midnight it would be St George's Day, and when at sea, the admiral made the signal which will always be remembered, 'St George For England', to which the captain replied, 'May we give the dragon's tail a damned good twist'. It was a beautiful day and one could see miles out to sea, which was as calm as a mill pond. The wind again seemed likely to change but we kept steadily on course. We rendezvoused halfway, where the fleet divided with three ships going to Ostend. The daily ration of rum was issued to the men about 8pm. Right up to the last the men were in good humour, laughing, joking and playing cards, just as if they were on leave. Some were boasting of what Jerry would get when they got on the mole.

The order was then passed; everyone fell in on the upper deck fully rigged. In our Sergeants' Mess we hastily shook hands and went out to get our men made up, and then on to the upper deck in the darkness and quiet. Rifles were loaded and bayonets fixed. There was a bit of a sea running as the ship made its way slowly through the water. The destroyers went ahead and put up a dense smoke screen. There were no lights showing and everyone talked in whispers. Our nerves were taut. Would we get alongside the mole without the enemy knowing? There we stood, rifles in our hands ready for the dash forward; not a movement, hardly a whisper and only the noise of the propellers broke the silence. Would we never get there? A starshell floated just above the ship, lighting it up as though it were day. I could see the men's white, drawn faces ready for the spring forward. No sooner had that light gone down than another went up. 'They've seen us,' someone whispered, for the lights had been fired from the mole.

We were crowded together, shoulder to shoulder as thick as bees, when the silence was broken by a terrific bang followed by a crash as the fragments of shell fire fell amongst us, killing and maiming many as they stood to their arms. The mole was in sight – we could see it off our port quarter, but too late. Our gunners replied to their fire, but they could not silence that terrible battery of 5-inch guns, now firing into the ship at a range of only 100 yards and from behind concrete walls. A very powerful searchlight was turned on us from Zeebrugge and their batteries also opened fired upon us. The slaughter was terrible, Colonel Elliot and Major Cordner were killed by the same shell whilst on the bridge waiting to give the order 'advance'. The shells came on board thick and fast but our brave fellows stuck to their post. Men were hopping about on one leg, shouting in their frenzy. Some of the bodies were intermingled with the decks, and our ranks got thinner every moment. They were taking every bit of cover they could.

Captain Carpenter stood on the forebridge calmly and steadily giving orders to the engine room staff as if he was taking it alongside the mole in peacetime. The gun crews of the *Vindictive* fired away. The pom-pom in the crow's nest had three crews wiped out but luckily Sergeant Finch, in charge, was only wounded and remained at his post and kept going all the time. (Sergeant Finch got the VC and richly deserved it.) At last we came alongside and by this time we were only thirty yards from the muzzles of the German guns. The grappling irons were dropped and officers tried to get ashore to make them fast, but as each one attempted it he was killed by machine-gun fire. The *Iris* now came up on our starboard side and rammed *Vindictive* to the mole, and the gangways, only two left out of the fourteen, were lowered on to the mole.

No sooner had this been done than the order to 'Advance' was given by Major Weller who had assumed command, so the remnants of nos. 9 and 10 Platoons led the way up the ramp. The Officer in Charge of my platoons, Lieutenant Stanton, had been fatally wounded, so I, as Platoon Sergeant, led 10 Platoon on shore. Up the ramp we dashed carrying our ladders and ropes. We passed over dead bodies lying everywhere and over big gaps made in the ship's decks by shellfire, finally crossing the remaining two gangways which were only just hanging together, and then jumping on to the concrete wall, only to find it swept with machine-gun fire. Our casualties were so great that out of a platoon of 45 only 12 of us landed, and 9 Platoon had about the same. We quickly lowered our ladders and dropped on to the lower part of the mole and two men at once got down the twenty-foot drop and rushed across to the shed on the far side. Everyone was anxious to get down as the machine-guns were mowing our lads down. As some of us were getting down the ladders and ropes a few Germans rushed across the mole with bombs, but we made sure not one of them got halfway across.

We rallied the men, now reduced to no more than 14 in the two platoons, and charged our position. We dashed forward, our rifles in a terrible grip, a fearful hatred on our faces, and ready to plunge our bayonets into the first living creature that opposed us and so revenge our comrades lying dead on the *Vindictive*. But on reaching our position we found the enemy had retreated to their concrete shelters further up the mole. Disgusted, we now turned our attention to the concrete dugouts on our right and left and gave them a good bombing. We also bombed a German destroyer lying alongside the mole. Sergeant Bailey and myself now fired our red Very lights to let the others know we had reached our position, but the *Iris*, after pushing *Vindictive* in, went alongside the mole to land her marines. There were 56 on board but the batteries ashore got a direct hit amongst them and 49 were killed and the others wounded. The casualties were so great amongst nos. 11 and 12 platoons, and with nearly all the sailors being killed, there were only a few to deal with the German guns, but what there were dashed for the guns only to be killed, Commander Brock amongst them. What few were left on the *Vindictive* came through our lines. These brave fellows, headed by their officers, came on walking in extended line as if they were on parade, but only a few of them reached their positions.

The Germans, in their excitement, had forgotten to extinguish the lighthouse so the blockships, taking a bearing from the light, went round the other side of the mole, sank the German dredger on their way in, passed under the muzzles of the batteries ashore and sank themselves obliquely in the entrance of the canal; the crews, what were left, got away in their boats. The submarine C3 went under the bridge and blew herself up. The explosion was so great that the whole concrete mole shook from end to end. A shell struck *Vindictive*'s siren so that she could not make the 'retire' signal, but another ship was ordered to make it. The signal was made to retire after the *Vindictive* had been alongside for one hour, but instead of making a succession of short blasts, she made a succession of long and short blasts. We took it, however, as the order to retire and commenced doing so when, as order was passed that it was not the signal to retire, we were ordered back to our position. We obeyed the order and very shortly afterwards we had the nightmare of seeing our only means of escape slowly move away. The *Vindictive* had left, the officers thinking everyone was aboard. We were two hundred yards from the ship when she left and we still had the twenty foot wall to climb.

We were now stranded, left to the tender mercy of the Germans, our only hope now gone. How hard, it seemed to us, to think we had come through the terrible slaughter, to be alive and well and with no means of escape. Shells were now falling fast on the mole. How long would it be before death relieved us of this terrible agony of suspense? We thought motorboats would be sent in to our assistance and with this faint hope we crossed the mole and climbed the twenty-foot wall, took off our equipment, blew up our swimming belts and waited, lying stiff and pretending to be dead. Some of us looked over the wall occasionally but not a vestige of anything was in sight. To remind us that we must not look over the wall, a machine-gun only thirty yards away was turned on us, but lying close to the concrete wall, it was not so effective as it might have been. For two hours we lay there and listened, with starshells floating over us, some falling and burning us. Two men were badly wounded but lay still for the sake of the others.

Shells from our own ships were now striking the mole and we could hear them whistling overhead. The firing now eased down and a German officer and two privates came to us, shone a torch on us, and thinking we were a heap of dead, went away. It would have been useless to have killed them so we lay still. About half an hour after this the firing ceased and the Germans came out no doubt to search the dead, when one man moved and then another. Nerves being highly strung, they jumped back shouting and gesticulating, and made ready with their bayonets. We had not relinquished our rifles and got ready to fight to a finish and if need be, to die fighting. A German officer shouted in quite good English 'The game's up, lads,' and seeing that we still hesitated he continued, 'Play the game and we will play the game with you. Lay down your arms and put your hands up and we will not harm you.'

We obeyed this order and were made prisoners-of-war.

Lieutenant Leslie Kemp

ROYAL NAVAL AIR SERVICE

En route to Russia, we packed two DH9s on the metal deck of an old cargo ship, *John Sanderson*, and were about to leave when a large consignment of BP diesel arrived. It was too late to be put in the holds so it was left on deck. We were the first ship through the Dardanelles after the war. As there were mines everywhere the captain issued us .303 rifles and as many rounds as we wanted to fire at mines. Not an easy task in a rough sea, but we managed to hit the nipple of three, so the skipper got some sort of bonus. For us it passed the time. Once we were through the Dardanelles the ship hit heavy weather and the seas were monstrous. We were rolling and pitching and twisting and everything was coming up to meet us. I was really ill. With all the rolling some barrels of oil split and smothered the metal deck with oil. You simply couldn't stand up. At one point the oil got under the wooden support of a pilot boat we had on board and it slid right across the deck and took a lump of the ship with it. My skipper, who was ill too, told me to take charge of the troops. They came to me and asked if I would give them permission to sleep in one of the two lorries we had on deck because it was too bad to sleep below. That night, to my horror, I saw one of the lorries slide across the deck and crash into the icy seas and disappear. Thank God it was the one which contained our luggage.

When we arrived at our harbour in the Black Sea we were ordered to anchor outside. That night was the worst of my life. We lost our anchor and we were drifting about, it was an awful night, a terrible night. Eventually we tied up in the harbour and somebody put a hawser round one of the supports of the railway bridge. In the morning when we woke we were rolling about in the harbour and the railway bridge was down! We were put up in a hotel and, just when we thought all was well, we were summoned in front of our Wing Commander, a strict disciplinarian who threatened to court-martial us all for destroying the railway link. He was also particularly fierce with one chap because he didn't have a coat on! It was not a great introduction to Russia.

We were based in Petrovsk at the edge of the Caspian Sea and billeted in a school. We had no hangar for our aircraft, so we got Russian labour to build a wooden screen and we wheeled the aircraft around it according to the weather. The snow was terrible. When we went on patrol we had to scrape about an inch of snow and ice off the wings. For protection against the cold we wore a Silcott suit and gloves, which were useless when you came to fire your gun. We were up against the Bolsheviks and supporting a White Russian naval flotilla on the Caspian. We also flew 250 miles over enemy territory to drop two 240lb. bombs on the Bolsheviks in their stronghold in Astrakhan.

We saw a lot of the Cossacks who would strut about the place. They came on to the aerodrome and gave us a wonderful display of bareback riding. They seemed to be able to do anything on a horse, including going underneath the horses's stomach while firing a rifle, and pig-sticking with a sword. On one occasion we were invited to the local Russian Air Force mess. On the table there was a sturgeon, a beautiful fish, we had never tasted anything like it before, and of course the only drink was vodka which had to be drunk in one gulp. As the evening went on I danced with the Russian women, and was enjoying myself with one in particular until I saw a revolver drop out of her skirt! Next day it was back to being fired at as we flew over their villages! But of course some of the peasants had never seen a plane before.

I was never really sure why we were in Russia. To us the real war was over. Eventually public feeling back home was becoming firmly set against further foreign involvement, so in August 1919 we were sent home on the SS *Trent*. We were glad to leave because by then the Russians were sticking cotton wool down our exhaust pipes and trying to steal petrol.

When I got to Dover I was demobbed. It was all over. Until the next time.

Ordinary Seaman Tom Spurgeon

When the Russian Army withdrew from the war in 1917 the Western Allies thought that the Germans would walk through Russia. We had much to lose, so the Navy was sent to Murmansk and Archangel. By now I was in the *Cochrane* which had been at Jutland. We sailed out and reached Murmansk in March 1918 and landed a party of Marines.

While I was there I met a Russian officer who could speak better English than I could. I suppose he was about thirty and he had been a solicitor in Moscow before the Revolution. One day he asked me if I could get ashore the following morning. I managed this and met him. We walked together, talking away as we always did about the Western way of life. Without noticing too much we strolled into a park where there were a number of soldiers and dissidents, including women and children. When the soldiers saw us approach the civilians were all lined up. Then, as calm as anything, this officer I had been talking to walked down the line and shot every one of them through the back. He then went back down the line and if any were breathing he shot them through the head. To him it was like having breakfast. There were women and small children but it didn't seem to worry him at all. I remember clearly some of the bodies quivering on the ground. I can never forget it. I am haunted by it even now.

Able Seaman Fred Pedelty

From *Engadine*, I volunteered for submarines. I did six months training at Haslar before joining *K22* in Rosyth. Lieutenant-Commander de Burgh was the captain, there were four other officers and 54 ratings. She was over 300 feet long, driven by steam turbine, and carried sixteen torpedoes.

In contrast to the *Engadine* everything was steel. It was a ship within a ship. I don't think we ever stayed below for more than two hours when we would surface to recharge our batteries. I slept in a hammock, but some of the others slept on the deck. There really wasn't very much for me to do, so I played a lot of cards.

K22 had previously been *K13* which had failed to surface while undergoing trials in the Clyde in January 1917. She had been down 57 hours before any of the crew were released. Over thirty died on her. She had been brought up and refitted. On the day of his diving trials Lieutenant-Commander de Burgh dived *K22* in exactly the same spot where *K13* had gone down, and the crowd watching held its breath as the periscope disappeared under the surface. Ten minutes later she surfaced and the trial was over. Two weeks later her four-hour acceptance trial also went without a hitch. I can't say all that affected us, but we were aware of her history.

On Armistice Day we were out on patrol in the Skaggerak

area. I was on the conning tower when I thought I saw a mine right ahead. I informed the captain who said, 'That's not a mine, it's a fisherman's pallet'. 'Well,' I said. 'It's got horns on.' He looked at me and gave a wry smile. For us the war was over.

The old 'K' boat was a prison, but it wasn't a bad prison. It had its own smells, its own camaraderie.

Lieutenant Brian de Courcy-Ireland

In July 1914, just before the outbreak of war, I saw the Royal Review of the Grand Fleet at Spithead. Now, ten days after the armistice and the end of the war, I was to witness, on 21 November 1918, the surrender of the German High Seas Fleet at sea.

We in HMS *Westcott* went out to meet them halfway, fully manned and ready. We were rather uncertain about what was going to happen, though we understood they had removed their ammunition. Out of the mist on that sunny day it really was quite a sight to see them coming towards us. Beatty had made a general signal: 'The German flag will be hauled down at sunset'. As they did so to the sound of the bugle 'Making sunset', Beatty was given a round of cheers by all of us in the Grand Fleet. I heard later on this remarkable occasion that he had raised his cap and said, 'I always told you they would have to come out'. We escorted them first to Rosyth and then later round to Scapa Flow. Then we spent a lot of time as guard destroyer in Gutter Sound looking after their destroyers and smaller ships.

That whole period was really rather dicey for us. You weren't allowed to fraternise in any way; you had to keep a pretty good watch on what they were trying to do, and we understood their morale was very poor. I remember going slowly past a German destroyer, whose crew as always was trying to barter with us to get some food. I saw a German sailor go up to an officer and pluck the Iron Cross off his coat and offer it to us for some cigarettes. The officer could do nothing.

On 21 June 1919 we were lying in Gutter Sound doing our turn, having a gin before lunch, when the senior Sub-Lieutenant came running into the wardroom and said 'The Germans are abandoning ship'. We thought at first he was being funny. However we rushed up on deck and indeed they were abandoning ship, every ship. In fact they were scuttling them. They were flying various signals and laying boats, but there was nothing that we could do. There was no way we could prevent seventy ships from being scuttled. Our C-in-C had rather foolishly taken the rest of the Fleet out on exercise and we were the only warship left on duty. We were some way from the bigger ships but we could see them keel over and sink lower in the water. So we went at full speed towards them to try and stop the crews of the battleships or cruisers from abandoning ship. They took no notice of our words, so we fired a few rounds close to one of the cruisers and of course, quite naturally, the whole lot just jumped straight over the side! There was nothing you could do. We just stood there and watched this giant cruiser go down in front of our eyes.

The *Hindenburg*, one of the biggest ones, was not far away, in fact she was in the entrance to the Flow. She looked to us as if she wasn't going down as fast as any of the others, she was upright. So, the First Lieutenant, myself and about twenty men, which was all we could spare, got on board her. The crew had abandoned ship and reached one of the nearby islands. Before they left they had opened all the watertight doors and everything else needed to sink a ship. The ship by now was already in a bad state, full of rust, and all power had been disconnected so we had to work in the dark to try and close the hatches. We realised pretty soon that she was gradually going down and of course, as she was sinking, the water pressure just blew the hatches. By now we were beginning to feel a shade anxious and scurried up to the bridge. When the water got up to well over the upper deck we began to get pretty worked up and were thinking seriously of jumping over the side. We had no idea of the depth of water she was in, but fortunately she hit the bottom and settled upright. One of our whaling boats came and picked us off the bridge: it was all rather fun really, but then it usually is with hindsight!

Everywhere we looked we saw mast after mast sticking out from the water, it was an awesome sight. An entire fleet of 71 ships, ships that had fought at Jutland, all scuttled. We were the only warship to witness this extraordinary event and this made things a bit complicated.

We gathered up the German crews from all the ships on to one island. However, one stupid German went and climbed up on a bell buoy which rang every time it swayed so we left him there for the day. We were then left with these Germans as prisoners, but they weren't really prisoners. Eventually they were taken down south.

While the High Seas Fleet had been based at Scapa Flow its crews were serviced by a mail ship which used to come over from Germany with provisions once a fortnight. The German Navy was pretty clever because they would get rid of all their malcontents and difficult people and have them sent home on this mailship. Our powers-that-be were frightened that, when she arrived and saw nothing but a pile of masts, she would go and sink herself at the entrance. So we were sent off to intercept her. We had to come alongside and board her, you know, fixed bayonets; they all thought we were going to shoot them. This German Petty officer came on deck with a cat o' nine tails which he'd obviously used on the boys on the ship; when he found himself looking down the end of a bayonet he agreed to let me borrow it and I still have it.

To relieve us after guarding the High Seas Fleet we were sent to Hamburg in July 1919. The Navy had taken over the docks and had the cruiser *Coventry* there with a party of experts on board. We were sent to lie alongside *Coventry* because of the difficulties she had with her draft. We simply went out there for six weeks with nothing to do but lie alongside her. To get there we made our way up the Elbe to Hamburg which was an utterly demoralised place. We had to be very careful when we went ashore because of the German Workers Party and we allowed no one into the dockyard. Money was scarce so we could buy a German sentry's rifle for about five shillings and if we bartered with two penny bars of Pusser's soap, we got five bob too for them. We did very well while we were there. It was a very interesting time, for I really did see the repercussions of war on land. We made a visit to Hagenbeck zoo and, as we walked around, a chap came up who spoke very good English and offered to take us on a tour. He was in fact the owner and, surprisingly, had done very well during the war. He told us that some of his elephants were used to haul heavy guns out of the mud near Verdun, but were withdrawn after two had been killed. His family, however, had not gone short of meat because he had a thriving herd of buffalo.

We then moved to Heligoland, where we anchored outside the harbour because none of the minefields had been swept. One evening we were walking on deck after supper when we heard a voice hail, 'Warship ahoy, permission to come on board'. Four men clambered aboard led by a great burly chap in a seaman's jersey who saluted and said, 'My name is Nicholls and I'm the Head of the Elders of the citizens of Heligoland and we have a petition. May we see your captain?' So we took him below and he presented our captain with their petition. He said, 'We Heligolanders in our little island in the middle of the sea used to belong to Britain and we want to belong to Britain again'. At the outbreak of war the islanders had been rounded up and interned in Germany. He went on to say, 'My wife just had time to burn my service certificate and hide my medals before we were taken away'. They had returned to find most of their houses had been wrecked by the Germans who occupied them. They were now looking for some form of security. As he was talking our captain suddenly said, 'What was your last ship, Nicholls?' 'The *Glory*, sir,' he replied proudly. 'I was the

Master-at-Arms (Senior Rating) and I remember now, sir, you were a midshipman in her.' He had joined the Royal Navy as a boy in 1887 when Heligoland belonged to Britain, and after serving his time for pension, returned to his birthplace to find it had been sold to Germany in 1890 in exchange for Zanzibar.

After Heligoland we were sent to join the 2nd Flotilla at Byorko in Finland but were ordered to call in at a port called (in those days) Libau, in Latvia, and report what state it was in.

The little port lay still and almost deserted as we approached. The long breakwater protecting it from the sea was intact, but as we cautiously made our way in, the rusting upper works of two steamers and masts of a wooden schooner protruding above the water told their story. On the quay a line of cranes, their jibs leaning drunkenly at odd angles, and the roofless warehouses completed the picture.

The town had fared no better; along the front facing the harbour the houses bore tragic witness to the havoc of war. The road was potted and cluttered with mounds of debris and wrecked vehicles. A few people picked their way through the litter, their features grey and drawn; and added to the air of despair and death that hung over the place like some dreadful miasma.

We were still feeling our way cautiously, but we secured alongside the pier and, after an interval, a small group of men appeared and contact was established. They had brought an interpreter who spoke English, and he explained the situation. He spoke in a voice devoid of expression, drained of emotion, the voice of a man who had seen so much and been through such experiences that no spark of hope or feeling was left. He told us, 'When the Germans first came in there was some resistance; but there was little we could do. Nearly all the younger men were away fighting, and we that were left had few weapons. But those that could, sold their lives dearly. For the first two days after the fighting stopped they did little and we began to hope. Then came the order. All women between the ages of fifteen and forty were to parade on this pier. The houses were searched and those found hiding or trying to escape were dragged here and shot. The German soldiers formed a line, and two by two the women were taken into a hut and raped. Their particulars were all written in a book: oh yes, the Germans are thorough. If a child was born it was taken from its mother after six weeks and sent to Germany.'

The terrible recital went on. As we were listening a woman in ragged skirt and black shawl drawn close about her face drifted aimlessly by with a vacant, haunting stare. The interpreter paused. 'That was one,' he said. 'Two children she had.' 'How old?' I asked. 'About eighteen,' he replied. I began to feel sick with the horror of it. So did the rest of the men with me.

When I returned on board a two-badge Able Seaman called Maddox was cleaning the shield of 'Y' gun on the quarterdeck. As the gunlayer he held himself responsible for the cleanliness and proper working order of the gun and mounting. And woe betide anyone who laid a hand on it without his permission; not that anyone was particularly anxious to be on the receiving end of Maddox's opinion of his ability, efficiency or ancestry. As I passed he looked up. 'Any chance, Sir, of having a go at the swines that did that?' he asked, nodding shorewards. I looked at him in some surprise. Maddox wasn't given to opening any conversation; he kept himself to himself and seldom spoke unless riled. 'A slight hope,' I replied. 'They say ashore that the Huns are advancing up the coast again. Why do you feel strongly about it?' 'I got what you might call a special interest,' he answered and relapsed into silence. I knew he would not be drawn any further.

It was a few days later when the captain spoke to the ship's company. 'I need not remind you,' he said, 'of what we saw and heard at Libau; few of us will ever forget it. The German army force, or whatever you call it, has been located on the shore road south of our present position. It consists of an estimated 4,000 men under the command of a Prussian officer. It is not in any sense a regular formation and lives off the land, and is reported to be moving northwards again. An ultimatum was delivered to the commander. He was to evacuate the area within forty-eight hours and return to German territory, otherwise punitive action would be taken against him by HM Ships. I understand the German commander replied "You would not dare; I will blow your little ships out of the water. I will go where I like." The time limit has now expired. The 4th Sub-Division led by *Westcott* will carry out the punitive action.

'We are now proceeding to a position close inshore,' the captain continued. 'When the enemy is located fire will be opened and will continue for fifteen minutes and I expect rigid fire discipline and self-control. There may be opposition, the rest of the flotilla will remain in support to seaward. We shall close up at Action Stations in two hours time.'

The low shoreline with its flat sand dunes was clearly visible now. The gun crews were standing alert and tense around their mountings. The layers and trainers had their eyes glued to their telescopes. The rangefinders' crew were calling out the ranges as we closed in. A puff of smoke came from near a sand dune followed by another and a couple of shells from field-guns came ricocheting across the water and passed between us and our consort. The captain turned to me and ordered, 'Open Fire'. As we did so the ship shuddered and shook to the crash of the guns. I fired two salvos to get the range and then changed into independent firing, with the foremost guns concentrating on the field-gun battery. The crews were working like demons, sticking rigidly to their drill. I could clearly see the terrible carnage on shore. The field-guns were silenced under a hail of fire; tents and vehicles were burning, ammunition exploding, men running blindly in every direction; a few even plunged into the sea. Our consort was plastering the road in and out. There was no escape; they were trapped.

We got the order to cease firing.

Our ears were singing from the crash of the guns, the smell of blistered paint was in our nostrils, the canvas screen around the bridge rail hung in tatters. The gun crews stood panting with exertion, sweat streaking their faces. Some of the loading numbers had stripped to the waist, and as they began the task of sponging out and stacking the empty cartridge cases their bodies glistened in the sun. I made my way from gun to gun receiving the reports from each in turn.

When I reached the quarterdeck the crew of 'Y' gun were still sponging out. AB Maddox was squinting carefully up the barrel from the breech end. 'One more with the clean rag, lads,' he said, 'and she'll do.' He looked up. 'Forty-nine rounds, sir,' he reported, 'and I had good targets for them all'. 'That's three more than anyone else,' I said. He grunted with satisfaction and gazed at the receding shore.

'I've waited four years for this,' he said quietly; 'and when the war was over I never thought as 'ow I'd get another chance.' He turned and looked at me, his eyes burning. 'I 'ad a kid brother,' he said. 'Cabin boy in the Merchant service, just turned fifteen. His ship was torpedoed by a U-boat. They managed to get away in the boats before she sank, but the bastards surfaced and opened fire on them. He was hit in the face and he died slowly before they was picked up two days later. It broke our mother up.' He jerked his head to the shore. 'I paid some of that off today.'

I went up forward again to my cabin at the break of the fo'c'sle to file the reports. It was in a bit of a shambles. I began to clear up and, as I picked up a book of verse written by a soldier in France, I remembered the verse that echoed the feelings of the Tommy who had seen his mate killed by a sniper:

> There's some as fights for freedom
> And there's some as fights for fun
> But me my lad I fight for bleedin' hate
> You may damn the war and blast it, but
> I 'opes it won't be done
> Till I've got the bloomin' blood price for my mate.

Is that where it ends? I wondered. As I stepped outside we were taking up our position with the Flotilla again. As we passed them in line, they were quietly manning the rails. 'What's that signal Captain D. is flying?' I asked the signalman. He replied, 'To *Westcott*, thank you from us all'.

We then steamed towards our original destination, Byorko in Finland. As we approached the harbour the sound opened up and we could see into the anchorage and the two lines of destroyers at the far end. The Leading Signalman started making our pennant number and asking for an anchor berth with his signal lamp. When he had a reply he came up on the bridge and read out what was on his pad. He seemed slightly embarrassed. 'Anchor in position five cables, 268° from Niki Point, end of B line. Behave yourselves and eyes down for LELKA.' The Captain asked him to repeat the message, which he did. 'Ah!' said the captain. 'Captain D. likes his little joke. I suppose we'll learn what he means soon enough.'

On the afternoon of the second day we were working ordinary 'part of ship' routine. I happened to be Officer of the Day, so was on deck more than I would normally have been. Gradually it dawned on me that a large number of men appeared to have discovered some work that required to be done on the port side of the ship, the side facing the shore only a few cables distant. I next observed the quartermaster on watch gazing through the trainers' telescope of 'Y' gun, which was trained on the shore.

'What the blazes are you doing?' I asked. The quartermaster emerged somewhat sheepishly, and murmured something about practising. I let it go at that and turned my own gaze shoreward. Immediately opposite the ship was a sandy beach, studded with a few large boulders. Sitting with her back against a rock, reading a book, was an elderly woman, clad in black and holding a parasol; while running up and down near the water's edge was a girl or, to be more accurate, a young woman, as naked as the day she was born!

Smugly I went down to the captain's cabin and knocked at the door. 'I beg your pardon, sir,' I said, 'but I have discovered who Lelka is: she is a young woman.' 'And what is remarkable about that?' replied the captain. 'Have you never seen a young woman before?' 'Oh yes, sir, of course, sir,' I said. 'But this one has no clothes on.' The Captain leapt to his feet. 'And what precisely is she doing without any clothes on, if it's not a rude question?' he demanded. 'I think she is swimming to the ship, sir,' I replied.

The situation on deck was rapidly assuming crisis proportions. Lelka was in fact swimming vigorously towards the ship, and obviously aiming for the accommodation ladder on the port quarter. Reaching the platform at the bottom of the ladder, she hoisted herself gracefully up on to it, and sat there like some beautiful mermaid. Wringing out her long fair hair, she coiled it skilfully on top of her head and, after a friendly wave, called out cheerfully, 'I speak little Inglish'.

Apparently it was quite normal etiquette in the Baltic seas in those earlier decades of the twentieth century for people of both sexes to bathe without costumes; it would in fact have been considered prudish to wear them. Lelka was thus only following the custom of her country; and it would never have occurred to her that it could cause embarrassment. Our First Lieutenant dispatched a midshipman to fetch a towel and to go down the ladder and wrap it around the uninvited guest. Carrying the towel, only too conscious of the number of eyes upon him and the advice being freely given, the midshipman advanced, his face scarlet with embarrassment. Lelka stood up, accepted the towel with a polite smile, spread it carefully over the platform, sat down again on one side and, patting the spare section, invited the midshipman to occupy it. The First Lieutenant called down, 'Perhaps you will be good enough to carry out your instructions. If she won't put the towel round her, tell her to go.' 'But she doesn't want to go,' pleaded the midshipman. 'Then push her in,' said the First Lieutenant. The midshipman stood up reluctantly. 'You must go,' he said desperately. 'Go, swim ashore.' 'Pardon,' said Lelka puzzled. 'Go,' said the midshipman. 'Swim.' Lelka stood up. 'You swim?' she asked. 'Yes,' said the midshipman, 'I mean no.' He gave her shoulder a nervous and half-hearted push. A mischievous look came into Lelka's face. 'Go,' she said. 'Swim.' And she gave the midshipman a hefty and most unmaidenlike push. The unfortunate midshipman, caught completely unawares, lost his balance, and clutching wildly at thin air and to the laughter of all aboard hit the water with a resounding splash. Lelka dived in and retrieved the midshipman's cap, which she perched jauntily on her head and waved gaily. In response to frantic calls from the elderly lady in black, she swam swiftly back to the beach leaving the midshipman floundering.

When he finally arrived back on the quarterdeck looking utterly bedraggled he was firmly rebuked by the First Lieutenant but bravely he stood his ground. 'Permission to go ashore and recover my cap,' he asked.

Later Captain D. ordered another berth for us and then said, 'By the way, I saw your midshipman ashore this afternoon, looking very smart. No doubt he was paying a social call. He'll go far.'

The situation was a strange and unreal one. Based on a not too neutral Finland, we were supposed to be giving moral and physical support to our gallant allies, the Estonians, with a composite army commanded by the 'White' General Yudenich who was supposed to be advancing on Petrograd through Estonia. The difficulty was that we seldom knew of the whereabouts, or the identity, of our 'allies'.

Admittedly if we steamed too close to the fort of Krasnaya Gorka the Reds would open up with their 12-inch guns. If we bombarded the shore further to the west, as we were sometimes invited to do, the chances were that we might hit a redshirt, a white shirt or even a green shirt; the latter being a mysterious body of men who were apparently fighting everybody. In truth, the chances of hitting anything but a number of trees in the seemingly limitless pine forests were extremely remote. Apart from the Russian Fleet at Kronstadt, the main hazards, other than Krasnaya Gorka, were the unreliability of our charts, the suspected presence of minefields, and the activities of a lone Russian aviator, known to all as 'Reckless Rupert', who would periodically fly over and drop a few bombs on the anchorage. Rumour had it that the Reds held his family hostage against his return from his bombing raid. We'd go ashore occasionally and on one memorable picnic when we were all relaxing, a sniper opened up on us which somewhat disconcerted our First Lieutenant, who, clad in his buff, was seen running ahead of us still clutching a frying pan with our precious sausages sizzling away. There was also a visit to the Tsar's holiday chalet at Bzorko. It was occupied by a rather pathetic pair of caretakers who had not heard of the assassination of the Tsar and his family and were still waiting for them to return that summer. In one room were the children's toys – including a small wooden toy submarine. It was all rather sad.

Officially Lummy – a bulldog – did not exist; but unofficially she was as much a member of the ship's Company of *HMS Verulam* as any officer or rating on board. Her great jaw and lumbering gait was a familiar sight to most of the destroyers in the 2nd Flotilla. She slept in a specially made and low slung hammock in the galley flat, had a fine repertoire of tricks, a somewhat regrettable taste for beer, and a passion for football. Sporting a jersey knitted in the ship's colours, white shorts and a uniform cap, she attended all the ship's matches. To us in the *Westcott* she was an old friend; for with *Verulam* we formed the 4th Sub-Division, and were 'chummy ships'. On 3 September the wardroom of the *Verulam* came over by boat to give us the local gen, and brought Lummy with them.

When the *Verulam*'s boat came for them after supper, the trouble started. Lummy refused to go down the gangway; and when they tried to carry her down she turned savage, broke away, and retreated underneath the torpedo tubes defying all attempts to dislodge her. Eventually it was decided to leave her alone; and as *Verulam* was due to go out on patrol the next morning we agreed to look after her until they returned. In the morning the dog emerged, and behaved normally. She went ashore for a run with the canteen manager, who was buying eggs, and returned in good spirits. But she was off her food, and as the day wore on became morose, lying for long periods with her head resting on her front paws. She remained on deck all evening and was lying in the same position when we came up for some air after supper. She seemed to be listening or waiting. It was, I remember, a calm warm night, very dark; and the scent from the pine forests along the shore line very strong. We were discussing what Lummy could be sickening for when a flash of light momentarily lit up the horizon to seaward. In the pause that followed we all turned instinctively, and the dog raised her head. A moment later an expanding arc of yellow shot skywards and in the midst of it the debris of a great explosion.

One reacts automatically on these occasions. Before the sound had reached us across the water, the First Lieutenant and the quartermaster were racing forward, the chief engineer making for the engine-room hatch and I was scrambling down the ladder to the captain's cabin to report. When I made my way up to the bridge a few minutes later the cable party was already on the fo'c'sle shortening in the cable; and the Leading Signalman was reading out the signals as they were made by the Leader's shaded lantern.

'D2 General. Following from *Walpole*. Immediate, *Verulam* mined or torpedoed, position 175 Niki Point 2 miles. After magazine blew up, ship sank in two minutes. Am searching survivors.

'D2 General. Raise steam with all dispatch and report when ready to proceed, cover *Walpole*. 2nd Division will take up patrol line 155 Niki Point. 1st Division remain at instant notice. Acknowledge.'

A dark shape slid by, heading for the entrance to the sound. It was the stand-by destroyer. We waited impatiently for the engine-room to report ready. The Parts of Ship were closing watertight doors, and securing for sea; the gun crews were clearing away their mountings.

I worked my way along the upper deck, checking as best I could in the dark that all was secure. Just about at the break of the fo'c'sle I bumped into a little procession. It was headed by the Mess Deck's Petty Officer, with Lummy next, and the ship's butcher bringing up the rear. They were coaxing the dog along and above the roar of the boiler room fans I could hear snatches, 'come on, old girl . . . got to get below . . . action stations . . . doing all we can,'. As they reached the black-out screen leading on to the mess decks the dog stopped and looked up into their faces. There was nothing to be said. Out of a crew of over a hundred only seventeen survived. It was a terrible end to our time in Finland.

Now, in the tail-end of September 1919 for me and my contemporaries in that back-of-beyond war zone, it all came to an end. A ship appeared from England with our reliefs. We had had no warning, no advance notice, we simply went home. I, along with others of my contemporaries, was to go to Cambridge University for six months – *in statu pupillari*. It all seemed rather strange and slightly unreal. For it was, for us, an end of an era. Of the eighty-odd of my term who went to sea in January 1916, nearly a dozen and a half were dead, mostly killed when they were barely sixteen. We were not the only youngsters to suffer, nor the last. Kipling had captured it so well in *The Scholars*:

They have touched a knowledge outreaching speech as when the
    cutters were sent
To harvest the dreadful mile of beach after the Vanguard went.
They have learned great faith and little fear and a high heart in
    distress
And how to suffer each sodden year of heaped-up weariness.
They have borne the bridle upon their lips and the yoke upon their
    neck,

Since they went down to the sea in ships to save the world from
 wreck—
Since the chests were slung down the College stair at Dartmouth in
 'Fourteen,
And now they are quit of the sea-affair as though no war had been.
Far have they steamed and much have they known, and most would
 they fain forget;
But now they are come to their joyous own with all the world in
 their debt . . .
Hallowed River, most gracious Trees, Chapel beyond compare,
Here be gentlemen tired of the seas – take them into your care.
Far have they come, much have they braved. Give them their hour
 of play,
While the hidden things their hands have saved work for them day
 by day:
Till the grateful Past their youth redeemed return them their youth
 once more,
And the soul of the Child at last lets fall the unjust load that it bore!

PART TWO

THE INTERWAR YEARS, 1919–1939

HISTORICAL NOTE

While their old enemies rusted at anchor at Scapa Flow, the Royal Navy was slowly demobilised. But the decision to intervene in the Russian civil war led to British warships seeing action from the Arctic Circle to the Black Sea and the Pacific. There was even a squadron of improvised warships on the landlocked Caspian Sea. Rear-Admiral Cowan presided over several unsung victories in the Baltic where British torpedo boats attacked the Bolshevik fleet at its Kronstadt anchorage, sinking two battleships in an epic raid that led to the covert award of a Victoria Cross to Commander Agar. There is a memorial at Brookwood Military Cemetery to those who died in Russia during the World Wars, and it includes the names of 127 naval personnel killed fighting the Bolsheviks, headed by Captain F. N. A. Cromie, CB, DSO who died, gun in hand, defending the British Embassy in Petrograd. Naval support helped sustain the White armies in southern Russia, but could not prevent the eventual Bolshevik victory. Allied forces were withdrawn in 1920 and the last sailors came home. When Admiral Beatty assembled the warships of the Grand Fleet to accept the surrender of the German High Seas Fleet, the Royal Navy was at the zenith of its power. Over 438,000 men were serving in 58 capital ships, 12 aircraft carriers, 103 cruisers, 122 submarines and over 450 destroyers and escorts. The Royal Navy's global commitment was soon emphasised by intervention against the Bolsheviks in Arctic waters, in the Baltic, the Black Sea and the Pacific. Warships on the China squadron would see action throughout the 1920s and 1930s as Britain defended her interests from the local warlords in classic applications of 'gunboat diplomacy'. The international community in Shanghai conducted its business behind the bayonets of the Royal Marines.

Between 1919 and 1923 the British Empire reached its greatest geographic extent as territories of the former Ottoman Empire came under Imperial control. The Royal Navy smoothly continued its traditional deployments, maintaining battle squadrons in the Mediterranean as well as home waters, with cruisers in the West Indies, off North America, South America, South Africa and the East Indies. Construction of a new naval base began at Singapore, Admiral Jellicoe planning to base 16 battleships, four aircraft carriers and powerful light forces there to counter the growing Japanese navy.

From 1923–4 HMS *Hood*, the largest and fastest battlecruiser in any navy, was dispatched on a world tour to show the flag. Yet *Hood* was the only major unit the Royal Navy had built since the hard lessons of Jutland. Despite her graceful lines and imposing size, her protection was no more than adequate. While the rest of the British fleet had been laid down before 1914, American yards supplied the US Navy with a dozen new 'super-dreadnoughts' by 1920. Japan now boasted eight equally powerful battleships. The majority of the Royal Navy's capital ships, armed with 12-inch or 13.5-inch guns, would be no match for them. The Admiralty understood what had to be done to maintain Britain's naval position: Beatty demanded eight modern battleships without delay.

The fearsome economic cost of winning the First World War had profound consequences for the Royal Navy, however. Britain simply could not afford to maintain the pre-war 'two-power standard' – a navy equal to the next two foreign fleets added together. In fact, it could not really sustain a 'one-power standard'. While it suited the USA to broker a succession of naval agreements that staved off another naval race, the American economy was growing as fast as the British economy was declining. In 1919 the British government instructed its armed forces to assume there would be no major war for ten years. There would be a ten-year hiatus in naval construction.

Naval wages had been seriously-eroded by the inflation of the war years. Ratings were keenly aware that workers in industry were receiving pay increases to match, while naval personnel were left to struggle. Fortunately the wartime British admirals enjoyed a closer relationship with the lower deck than their German opposite numbers. Disturbances in the Grand Fleet were nipped in the bud in 1917 and ratings received an extra 2d. a day. In 1918 a one-day strike by the Police secured them a major pay award and the example was not lost on the armed forces. It was obvious that a substantial increase in wages was essential, and in 1919 ABs' daily pay was increased from 1s.8d. to 4s. In 1920 ratings over twenty-five were made eligible for a marriage allowance.

A year later, First Lord Sir Eric Geddes took his celebrated axe to the naval budget. Spending on warships was being slashed, and spending on their people would not escape either. One captain in three was retired as the wartime fleet was reduced at a speed not witnessed since 1815. Rumours of pay cuts did nothing for service morale although when they came in 1925 only new personnel were affected, new ABs receiving only 3s. a day. Four years later the industrial world was struck by the great crash. From 1929–32 British steel production practically halved; more than half the workforce in Britain's shipyards was out of work. A yawning trade gap had opened. Social spending was already seven times that of 1913 and now accounted for the majority of government expenditure. On the eve of the Great War, the Royal Navy had enjoyed 25 per cent of government spending; but by 1932 it received just 6 per cent.

At the height of the crisis, in the summer of 1931, British ministers struggled to sustain the gold standard. Like the civil service, the Police and the other armed forces, the Navy was instructed to cut pay. The Admiralty more than obliged. It was announced that all men being paid on the 1919 scales would be placed on the lower 1925 scales. This would affect chief and petty officers almost to a man and three out of four other rates. And since the decision effectively cut all rates by a shilling, the burden fell disproportionately on the lower deck: ABs were losing 25 per cent of their wages, officers only 11 per cent. Meanwhile, the Army and Air Force were accepting only ten per cent cuts across the board.

Married ratings were especially hard hit: with family budgets already fully stretched to meet hire purchase agreements and pay the rent, this drastic loss of earnings raised the spectre of eviction – or the repossession of their furniture at the least. Unfortunately for the Royal Navy it seemed many officers, especially aboard the big ships, had little appreciation of the hardships their companies were facing. Worse, the lower deck discovered what was afoot before any official statement and the impression grew that sailors' welfare was of secondary interest to the Admiralty; other service chiefs had resisted more extensive cuts.

The Atlantic Fleet, at anchor at Invergordon, received official notice on Saturday, 12 September 1931. Rear-Admiral Tomkinson warned Whitehall of ominous signs, but in the absence of any response, he ordered the fleet to sea on the Tuesday. The crews of four battleships refused to raise steam. While the 'unrest', as Admiralty documents often refer to it, was largely confined to the big ships – officers and men clearly enjoyed a closer relationship aboard cruisers and destroyers – the Invergordon mutiny made headlines around the world. The pound plummeted on foreign exchanges, losing over a quarter of its dollar value during the week. The National government was compelled to abandon the gold standard, and to impose the same ten per cent pay cut on the Navy as the other services were to suffer. Within the Navy, a fund was created to assist married men, especially ratings less than 25 who did not receive the allowance. While 124 mutineers were drafted ashore without delay, and several dozen discharged, no less than seven captains were relieved of their commands. Aside from one, no admiral involved was employed again.

Within a couple of months of the Invergordon mutiny, Japan intervened in Manchuria, deaf to all the entreaties of the League of Nations. While, today, we are used to the fact that a ringing denunciation from the United Nations is probably the single most ineffective tool in international relations, the revelation of its predecessor's impotence came as a disagreeable surprise. So many statesmen had placed their faith in collective security that the naked aggression of the Japanese left them floundering for a response. In 1931 the British people had more pressing concerns than remote Asian wars, but the lesson was not lost on Germany's rising political star Hitler, nor the posturing Mussolini in Italy whose Fascist Party dreamed of a new Roman Empire.

British re-armament did not begin immediately, indeed did not begin for several years. With the conspicuous exception of Winston Churchill, consigned to the political wilderness, all three parties opposed a radical increase in defence expenditure. The Conservatives were acutely conscious that taxes or slashing welfare spending would lead to a massacre of their party at the next election. Liberal and Labour leaders still clung to the ideal of the League of Nations, unable or unwilling to accept that some nations – and some governments – had not lost their appetite for violence for all the slaughter of 1914–18.

British re-armament began just in time to avoid disaster. The Navy budget doubled between 1933 and 1938. The ten per cent pay cut was restored in 1934 and the grim business of Invergordon, if not forgotten, was firmly put aside. Discipline was restored: re-enlistment rates increased and instances of punishment declined. Yet a battlefleet could not be improvised any more than a modern army could be. Even after the introduction of conscription, the British Army of 1940 was outnumbered more than 5:1 by the Wehrmacht. And whereas the French army had shouldered the terrible burden of the western front from 1914–1916, the morose militia assembling behind the Maginot line did not inspire the same confidence. Having shed the bulk of its obsolete pre-First World War battleships, the Royal Navy deployed 12 battleships and battlecruisers in 1939; five extremely powerful 'King George V' class battleships were building and four 16-inch gunned battleships were planned. It boasted five aircraft carriers, 58 cruisers, 200 destroyers and escorts and 38 submarines. Since the German navy had just two battleships commissioned and two more under construction, the balance of power in the North Sea was far more favourable than that of 1914. However, Britain's vigorous opposition to Mussolini's invasion of Abyssinia transformed a hitherto neutral Italy into an almost certain enemy. Italy's new and powerful battlefleet dominated the central Mediterranean. The threat of Italian air power compelled the British fleet to transfer its main base from Malta to Alexandria.

Even after the government had given the orders, re-constituting British naval strength proved harder than anticipated. The 'naval holiday' had had fatal consequences for Britain's shipyards; many went out of business altogether, and the survivors were no longer world leaders in design and technology. Skilled labour was lost. The late 1930s witnessed a dramatic revival in warship construction, but British warships required many more man-hours to build than those taking shape in US, Japanese or German yards.

Seaman Gunner Stan Smith

When the Armistice was signed, I had no chance to celebrate. I was placed on immediate draft to HMS *Emperor of India*, a battleship of the *Iron Duke* class. She had ten 13.5-inch guns, twelve 6-inch guns, four 4-inch anti-aircraft guns and numerous smaller weapons. She was also equipped with submerged torpedo tubes. It was an emergency draft and almost as soon as the ship's company got on board we set sail for a secret destination. I was about to find out that the world was still full of people at war with one another. We stopped briefly at Gibraltar and Malta, for oiling, but neither provided us with any leave nor any clues to our ultimate destination. On we sailed through the Dardanelles to the entrance of the Bosphorus, where off Constantinople we dropped anchor. The reason for our journey became obvious for the Turks were massacring the Germans and Armenians. Murderous parties roamed the streets by night, stringing people up by their feet from lamp-posts, slitting them up the middle and putting their testicles in their mouths. I was eighteen at the time and it was a sight I can never forget, however hard I try.

Our task was to round up all the Germans who had scattered and were hiding in every corner of the city. Even when we found them we could not be sure that they would treat us with anything more than suspicion, since we had recently fought against them in the war to end all wars. We took them to a merchant ship which had been commandeered and anchored, for their own safety, in the middle of the Bosphorus.

Hunger, thirst and disease were as much a threat ashore as the night-time murderers, for there was very little food and even less water. Our bakers were making bread day and night while the engineers were kept busy around the clock distilling water. We had to form the starving into long queues to stop them from swamping us and collaring the bread. Large armed parties of our ship's companies had to maintain order. With the aid of our rifle butts and the occasional bayonet prod, we persuaded them to queue properly and distributed the food as fairly as we could.

After this we went back through the Bosphorus to the Dardanelles on a mission to help the Army to clear Gallipoli. This took us right into another big mess on shore. Ammunition and bodies – mostly skeletons – lay everywhere and we had the gruesome task of collecting up bones and skulls. Often we would shovel up one skull to every two of bones and cart them in boxes to the top of a hill where the Army had cleared a space for a cemetery. There lay many a soldier whose name was unknown and grave unmarked. We also had to dispose of ammunition, exploding it or dumping it at sea to clear the island.

Faced with the same job on the ANZAC beaches where the Australians had lost a lot of men, we spent about ten days helping to clear up the fearsome debris of war. It was a task which I wouldn't wish upon anyone; except, perhaps the politicians whose decisions usually cause it all in the first place. This is the side of war which makes many an old sailor wince when brave words are spoken about honour and freedom; the grim face of glory.

We returned from that terrible task and were given leave in Malta. While I was there a notice went up asking for volunteers for an expedition to Enzeli on the Caspian Sea. I ignored the old Service advice and put my name forward.

We were a motley crowd of twenty-nine volunteers, placed under the command of Commander Bruce Fraser who was later made an admiral and commanded the Home Fleet at the time of the sinking of the *Scharnhorst* during World War II. He was a very nice chap and we soon formed a great respect for him.

A destroyer took us back through the Dardanelles and the Bosphorus to the Black Sea port of Batumi where we transferred all our equipment for repairing guns and engines on to a train bound for the Caspian Sea. The train consisted of an engine and three wagons with sliding doors, similar to the covered goods trucks seen in England at that time. We set off and two days out from Batumi, in the foothills of the Caucasian Mountains, the train ground to a halt. There was a blockage on the line and we were on the receiving end of a very efficient ambush. Under fire from bandits in the hills we flung open the wagon doors, built barricades with our kitbags and hammocks, and returned the rifle fire. Firing intensified as they started on the other side of the track. The engine driver refused to go on even if we cleared the obstruction on the line. The only alternative was to go back to Batumi.

Our stores were loaded on another ship and we were taken back through the Black Sea and the Bosphorus to Izmir (Smyrna) on the Turkish coast. We took the train to Baghdad which was the end of the line. From there we had no choice but to start a long, long walk. Our stores and equipment were loaded on to camels and we began to footslog our way across Persia, a prospect which held little appeal for a chap like me with a plate in his leg from the battle of Jutland. We could see ten to fifteen miles across open country during the day, but there was never a soul in sight. At night we were pestered by camp thieves who would creep in and steal whatever they could lay their hands on, no matter how many sentries were posted. We were a pushover for them until the Gurkhas arrived on the scene. They were the boys for the camp thieves; we were never pestered again.

Eventually we arrived at Enzeli to find just a few old huts, a couple of houses and a pier sticking out into the Caspian Sea. The huts, which had been used by nomads, were in a terrible state, so we did some temporary repairs, patching up the roofs of two of the buildings with anything we could salvage from the others. After our stores had been unloaded, the camels and the Gurkhas turned back. We were on our own.

It was my twenty-first birthday but I had no chance to celebrate and nothing to celebrate with. Twenty-one years old and I'd never been kissed.

We spent some time at Enzeli. Our job was to build up fortifications in case the Bolsheviks beat Denikin's men and advanced on Persia. We had to transfer guns from ships left by the Royal Navy and set up seashore fortifications. We were also supposed to repair ships for Denikin's men but a boat arrived with a message that these ships were still in Baku and in such a state they couldn't be moved to Enzeli. So we loaded up our stores and went to Baku where the ships were in a really sorry state of repair. I don't think the guns had been moved since the Navy left. They hadn't been elevated or trained and were thick with rust.

I was part of the team which tackled guns while other men worked on the engines and other machinery. I was partnered off with a chap called Dart to repair a recoil cylinder on one of the guns when – 'crunch' – the Bolsheviks entered the town bringing work to a halt quicker than a wildcat strike. Denikin's men fell back in some disorder. I was quietly working away when 'bang', I knew no more. I had been fairly effectively bashed over the head and when I woke up I was trussed up like a chicken with both hands behind my back and my feet lashed tightly together.

The Bolsheviks, who seemed like fearsome fighting men, eventually untied our legs and herded us on to the quayside. We were all roped together and marched away under escort to a grim, bleak room where our hands were untied and we were told to strip naked. Our clothing was searched and returned to us, but they had emptied all the pockets so we were left with nothing but the remnants of what we stood up in.

Commander Fraser argued our case with Astare Nasarate, the head prison guard, but to no avail. We were roped together and marched off to the prison of Byrloft Chyrma. It was a humiliating experience because there were jeering crowds on either side of us, giving every impression that they had won a great victory.

On arrival at the prison we were split into two groups and placed in two adjoining cells. With bare walls, no furniture and an earth floor, each cell measured about sixteen foot square at the most and into our cell sixteen men were crammed. We endured our first night as prisoners of war huddled together for warmth as there were no blankets or bedding of any kind. We were hungry too, but we weren't given any food until about noon the following day. I think it was noon, but our watches had been taken and we had no means of telling the time. Time was something we had plenty of; time to suffer and watch others suffer even more.

When the food came we were ready to eat anything. It was a bowl of soup which was more like dish water – thin and absolutely tasteless – and half a round of black bread. This was to be our ration for the first twenty-four hours. We were still hungry, but we had only just scraped the surface of prison life. The first meal was a picnic compared with the reality to come. Immediately after that skimpy meal we were marched into the courtyard and given ringside seats or standing positions to watch the first massacre. There were about forty prisoners to be killed, men and women, and their captors used every atrocity imaginable.

One by one they slit the women up the middle to about the chest bone, disembowelled them and left them standing until they'd done the whole crowd of women. Then they shot them as they lay moaning and screaming on the ground. They made some of the men dip their arms into buckets of acid which was so strong that when they removed their arms the flesh hung down like huge gauntlets.

We were forced to watch all this, helpless to do anything about it. Even if you closed your eyes you could never close your ears or your memories to the awful horror of those screams and cries. We had to witness many more of these massacres before we were freed. Each time we were marched back to our cell to a life which grew more grim and we were perpetually hungry.

At the beginning we had to work. We were lined up outside our cell and chained together like a lot of convicts on a chain-gang. We were marched through jeering crowds to the railway station where we had to unload sacks of millet from the trucks and carry them to the waiting carts. Some men became so weak, they would collapse under the weight of the sacks. Too feeble to work we were of little use to our captors, so back in the unrelieved misery of our cells we went on to reduced rations. For the remainder of our imprisonment our daily diet consisted of a raw fish about the size of a herring and a handful of nuts. We were so hungry that we would have fought over the food had it not been for our commander. He made us stand back against the cell walls and would call out our names one by one. The food was thrown on to the floor and each man would rush out, grab a fish and some nuts and return to the wall to devour them ravenously.

Suffering is one thing, but watching others suffer, especially your comrades dwindling to skin and bone and scratching on the ground for scraps of food, is even worse.

We were allowed out into the courtyard for half-an-hour each day to go to the toilet and have a wash. The toilet was simply a hole in the ground with a couple of bricks to put your feet on. Having no soap we used to use the grit around the tap to wash our hands and faces a little. In that one half-hour of release we had to drink enough water to keep us going for the next twenty-four hours. This made us all pot-bellied and we began to look as if we were pregnant.

One of the things which helped keep us sane was a piece of glass one of the lads found in the courtyard. We used this to cut our hair away from our eyes and make ourselves a little more comfortable. Our main preoccupation was to hide this glass from the guards who used to search the cell at least once a week. They even dug up the earth floor to make us even more wretched, but they never did find it.

We were covered with lice in our hair, on our bodies, even in our eyebrows. To make matters worse some of the other prisoners would throw packets of lice into the cell through the grid in the door. We even went round our shirts with our teeth in a vain attempt to kill the eggs in the seams of our clothing.

The first chap to die was a mechanic called Marsh and it was that piece of glass which ended his suffering. He committed suicide, cutting the arteries in his wrists during the night and lying down to die. In the morning the guards almost fought over his clothing. They stripped him and left him in a pool of blood for three or four days until the flies in the cell were unbearable.

Four more of my friends died in that cell and each time the same thing happened. The body was left where it lay until it had almost decomposed.

After almost a year of confinement, word went around the prison that a minister of the Georgian state was to visit the prison to interview Astare Nasarate about the release of Georgian prisoners. Georgia, which was holding out against the Bolsheviks, was separated from us by a wide river which the Georgians were defending quite efficiently from their bank. Held up in their advance, the Bolsheviks had resorted to negotiating with the Georgians and we had high hopes that this visit would give us, at best, a chance of release or at least a way of letting the outside world know we still existed.

When the Georgian minister arrived, he soon found that we had a Georgian interpreter among our party, whose job would have been to interpret everything necessary when we arrived at the Caspian Sea. The minister immediately negotiated for this man's release and it was only by this lucky chance that we were able to pass out a message for the British ambassador. The missive was hidden in a locket which Commander Fraser had somehow managed to conceal from the guards for all those months. It contained a picture of his mother. The Georgian swallowed this and was eventually released.

Some time after he left the Georgian minister came to the prison again to meet our commander. It was that interview which finally enabled us to leave that terrible place. We were removed to a disused school where the Georgian minister gave the commander some Russian roubles with which we were able to buy some horse meat and black bread to supplement our diet. We also bought a bar of soap so we all had a bath, one at a time under the cold water tap in the courtyard. It didn't have much effect on our lice. We were still infested because we were wearing the same clothes we had been captured in and they were getting more than a bit ragged by then.

After some weeks we were marched to the station, unchained

this time. We were put into trucks and away went the train for the first stage of our journey towards freedom. At the border between Azerbaijan and Georgia we had to walk across a bridge. We were met on the other side by a Colonel Stokes and taken to a real train with carriages. There was no delay. The train left as soon as we were on board and we were given a very light meal of a quarter of a slice of meat, a little bread and a bar of chocolate. At every station my chum and I tried to get some bread, but we were still under guard and watched very closely. If we had succeeded I expect it would have been curtains for the pair of us. We saw Colonel Stokes smoking a cigar and followed him until he threw the end away, then pounced on it, had a couple of draws each and passed out for the count.

When we arrived at Tiflis (now Tbilisi), the capital of Georgia, we were given a complete change of clothing, including underwear, but we were still lousy. Our old clothes were thrown in a heap and burned. As the train took us steadily nearer the comfort of our own people, there was another complete change of clothing and our diet was gradually increased until we were on to a full slice of bread and meat at each meal.

When we arrived at Batumi, a welcome sight greeted us – a British destroyer. She took us back through the Black Sea to the Bosphorus where we were taken aboard the flagship, HMS *Iron Duke*. There we were bathed and our entire bodies were shaved, even our eyebrows. We were given fresh naval clothes before going up for a light dinner with the admiral who thanked us on behalf of the Navy and made a speech. It was then that he broke the news that we would not be going directly back to England. We were to be the Navy's guests for a Mediterranean cruise on board a sloop, HMS *Heliotrope*, which had been fitted out for us and where we would be fed carefully until we were strong enough to return to England.

On board the *Heliotrope* our hammocks had already been slung for us and it was not long before we snuggled down and enjoyed the best night's sleep we had had for many months.

Special messing arrangements had been made to cater for our tender stomachs and we had a doctor on board. Down in the bathroom I saw myself for the first time in a full-length mirror. What a sight – no eyebrows, no hair and a belly that stuck out a mile beneath ribs you could hang your hat on.

We were soon on a full diet, we even had the choice of a glass of port or a bottle of Guinness with our lunch. We called at no ports, just isolated bays in different countries where we went ashore to play football, swim or take any exercise to make us a bit fitter. Soon the hair started to grow back again and we began to look a little more presentable. Our troubles were not over though. During the cruise two of our chaps were taken ill. The doctor could do nothing for them so we called in at Malta where they were taken to Bighi Hospital. We later heard that they both died. The irony of their deaths after such an ordeal was lost on none of us. There were only twelve survivors from the twenty-nine cheerful volunteers who had started out.

We arrived at Plymouth to find we had become celebrities in our absence. The reporters were kept away from the ship and we were sworn not to communicate with the press in any way or give speeches or lectures about our captivity. All the papers could say was that the men had returned from the 'Black Hole of Baku'.

On board the *Heliotrope* we had whipped round to buy a ceremonial sword for Commander Fraser which he graciously received during our dinner with the Minister for Foreign Affairs, Lord Curzon. He was very proud of that sword and used it on all ceremonial occasions during the Second World War when he was Commander-in-Chief of the Home Fleet. His mother, Lady Fraser, had written to the families of all her son's men telling them not to give up hope, even though we had all been reported missing, believed killed. She had also put each family in touch with another which was not too far distant so that they could share their troubles. It helped draw our families into that deep sense of comradeship which had held the survivors of Baku together.

Lieutenant Roy Smith-Hill

ROYAL MARINE LIGHT INFANTRY

I was born in Cumberland and joined the Royal Marines in 1915. I trained at Deal where the training seemed based on what the Navy wanted, rather than on what we might have to do on land. I felt the military side was ignored. We did naval gunnery, naval boatwork, even torpedoes and electrical work. I then went to Whale Island for further gunnery training. I had the feeling that we were only expected to go ashore to deal with skirmishes, not any major action. Always you heard, 'We'll send a detachment of Marines' – we never did any land training on land.

Royal Marines would make up as much as a quarter to a third of a ship's company. The Marines' mess deck was always next door to the quarterdeck. The Marines were traditionally placed between the naval officers and the men. All rifles were in the Marine mess (barracks).

In the big ships there was always a Marine band which would play at evening quarters and morning colours. At those times, the ensign was raised or lowered. At sunset, the ship's company would fall in.

After Whale Island I was posted to the newly raised 6th Battalion, Royal Marines Light Infantry, which consisted of 'A' Company provided by Eastney, 'B' Company from Chatham, 'C' Company from Portsmouth and 'D' Company from Plymouth, along with a company of the Royal Marine Artillery. The whole battalion was formed up at Bedenham, near Gosport, with Lieutenant-Colonel Kitcat in charge. The battalion had been raised for mainly ceremonial duties during the plebiscite being held in Schleswig-Holstein, which would decide whether it stayed part of Germany or was returned to Denmark. So we were there to man polling stations and the like, but to exert no political influence. We therefore began to do an awful lot of polishing brasses and ceremonial drill.

We embarked in early August 1919 on the troopship *Czar*.

Just prior to our departure we were told of a change in plan. We were now going to North Russia to bolster the forces available to General Rawlinson to cover the evacuation. We certainly did not expect to fight. In many cases morale was low. The men had not been given the chance to volunteer for Russia; the Royal Marines Adjutant-General had simply vouched his word for us at the War Office. Colonel Kitcat hadn't helped, because he thought it wise not to pay the men the day before we left Bedenham so that we wouldn't leave any drunks behind. The men had joined up for patriotic reasons; now, with the First World War over, in which many of them had fought, they certainly didn't want to lose their lives fighting in Russia. All companies had a number of raw recruits, some very young, and prisoners-of-war who had recently been returned from Germany and had had no leave.

On board we were given a talk by a senior officer who told us that our front in North Russia was 600 miles long and was held by small outposts.

There were no roads, and communication was maintained by riders in the summer and sleighs in winter. There was a rumour that we were to make an attack on Onega, some one hundred miles from Archangel, where there had been heavy fighting. If this was the case we would not get away before winter. This filled us all with dread. The feeling was further enhanced when passing the bleak Lofoten Islands. There was a sudden commotion in our wake. Everyone on board had a theory about what it was. I thought, 'God never walks here and the Devil never blows his horn'. We all felt uneasy. As we came into Murmansk I could not believe we were in the northernmost part of Europe; but for the porpoises we could have been off Margate. When we got ashore we found American, French and even Serbian troops in the same area – it was a mix-up and the mud didn't help.

The next day our train left ten hours late for Kandalaksha and 'C' and 'D' Companies left for Kem to relieve 1,600 army troops. We had a week's rations with us and the men were in cattle trucks. As the sun began to set half a dozen rifle shots rang out. We looked out of the window but could see nothing, but some of the officers seized and loaded their revolvers, thinking the train was being attacked by Bolsheviks. I suggested that, as the front was 500 miles away, perhaps it was our men trying to stop the train. This turned out to be correct. One of the men, while shutting the door of his van, fell out on to the line. The train had gone on about a mile before it could be stopped. We told the driver to back the train and sent off the stretcher bearers and the doctor and waited for the train to shunt. The gradient was a bit steep, so the men had to push the train before we could get moving. It was weird walking back along the line, by the shore of a dismal lake in the half light to find what was left of the unfortunate man. We slid him on a stretcher through the window, moaning but unconscious. The doctor did his best but he died at midnight. The rest of the journey was spent with a dead body. Not a good start.

At Kandalaksha, we were billetted in Sussex Village, named after their first inhabitants, the Royal Sussex Regiment. We were to keep two platoons in the village, mine and Eastman's, whilst Bramall's and Beazley's platoons were to occupy huts along the coast. The object was to have outposts in the direction of the Finnish border, about sixty miles away to the west. Later in the week I left the village by train to go to Kem to draw money. While I was there, I met Colonel Kitcat, who seemed to be very active and enterprising. I arrived back at Kandalaksha with a haversack full of roubles and 190 woollen jackets for the officers and men. Within a couple of days we heard a rumout that General Rawlinson had declared his plan of action. With two other regular battalions, we were to force our way over 250 miles to Petrograd. Although we didn't really know what was ahead we were prepared to fight. We really believed that one good British battalion was worth more than ten Bolshevik battalions.

We arrived in Med-Gora on 28 August. The camp was in

delightful surroundings overlooking Lake Onega on which, we heard, the Bolo's (i.e. Bolsheviks) had a destroyer. We tested the Lewis guns at the rear of the camp and on 30 August loaded supplies and set out for Kapaselga. About four of us sat on the edge of the truck with our feet dangling, singing popular songs. On arriving at Kapaselga we each unrolled our valise and slept.

The next morning I went to our battalion headquarters and saw Hanson who told me that in their attack on Koikori, the night of 29 August, the Portsmouth Company had failed to reach their objective. They had met with concentrated machine-gun fire from well prepared positions, defended by tough, very experienced Red Finns and had lost three killed and eighteen wounded, including Colonel Kitcat. They had retreated leaving much of their gear behind. The next morning we left for Svyatnavolok. About sixty men, chiefly mine and Eastman's, bivouacked on the Tivdiya side of Lake Lijmozero, the remainder were on the Kapaselga side. We left there and marched to another lake which we rowed across and then marched to Svyatnavolok.

On 2 September we practised wood fighting under Major Williams and the next day with my platoon we formed the advance guard. Our packs were left at Svyatnavolok and we only took one blanket, waterproof sheet and a haversack ration of bully beef and biscuits (with short intervals we were on this diet until 19 September – we craved sugar). We had been told the enemy might lie up either side of the track so our rate of advance was only one mile per hour because the bush had to be searched for about fifty yards on each side. Bramall's platoon patrolled for two versts (a verst is about two-thirds of a mile or 1200 yards) on the road to Koikori. The following day two aeroplanes bombed the Bolo (Bolshevik) position and twenty minutes later a Bolo soldier gave himself up. He had no boots, socks or rifle. He said that other Bolos wished to give themselves up. Captain Watts then took two sections up, but the enemy changed their minds and fired at them with machine-guns. On 7

September we were relieved of our outposts by Serbians. They were very smart and very professional soldiers. One of their men was killed by chance by an 'over'. They were outraged and staged an unauthorised attack on the enemy to teach them a lesson. We practised our attack and planned out how we were to take Koikori. We left at noon for the 12 Verst post. In Russia, the road is marked every verst with a post to indicate the distance to the next village or town. When we arrived we relieved 'C' Company and rested knowing that we formed the first wave of the attack the next day.

I was given a Very pistol and cartridges which were to be fired as signals to the howitzers to increase the rate of fire, or to increase the range. At about 6pm a Bolo patrol threw grenades and fired at us – a little taster of what was to come. In 'B' Company we heard that the men were anxious that the officers should not try to win any medals. They feared that they might do something rash when in action and that their men might become unnecessary casualties. But of course they accepted that the officers would take the same risks as the men.

At 8am the next day we left 12 Verst post and marched to 15½ Verst post where I found Beazley was sick and his platoon, which had been sent out on patrol, was engaged with enemy patrols. The 'overs' from the Bolsheviks hit the trees above our heads. On arrival at 15½ post, we turned to the left along a small path which led round the Koikori side of a small lake. At 11.45 Major Barnby came to my platoon and told me to increase speed. Our 4.5-inch howitzers were firing over our heads. At about 12 noon the Russian guide, a machine-gun officer, and myself climbed a small hill from the top of which we could see Koikori's church. We could not see the river but there was a small ridge in front of us at a distance of about 150 yards. We heard a couple of the enemy close to us, talking, so I went back and fetched up a section of my platoon to clear the hill. In the meantime the guide had disappeared. I called two machine-guns to cover my platoon and fetched a section of Beazley's platoon. I then returned to the top of the hill where I found the machine-guns ready for action. Nearby were Major Barnby and the Machine-Gun Corps officer. One of our guns then opened on the trenches near the church, while I tried to see any of the enemy through glasses. None were visible, but they replied with rifle fire hitting a M G Sergeant in the stomach. Major Barnby gave me orders to take my platoon through the undergrowth, round the base of the hill. While this was being done I told Bramall to bring up his platoon onto my right and to advance in the direction of some hayricks to the right of the church. I then went down through the bush and passed the word back for the Platoon Scouts. One appeared and, without waiting for the remainder, we advanced to the hedge on the left. There we broke a hole through at the bottom and I saw through my glasses the sangars (breastworks) to my front. I had a machine-gun sent up and opened fire. I then sent my platoon through to line the hedge on the enemy side. At the same time two scouts cleared the sangars with bombs. The platoon then advanced in extended line two yards apart to the ridge and occupied it. The Bolo were now fighting back strongly and we were being fired on by a machine-gun from the right and snipers from the front and left.

The men on the crest then began to shout to the hill for our men there to cease fire as they were hitting my platoon. I had lost quite a few wounded, but they were still firing from the hill so I drew my revolver and went up and shouted, 'Marines, stop fighting'.

No one answered, but I was suddenly shot at and realised the enemy had gained possession of the hill behind us or that they had been there already prepared. I ran back to find that Major Barnby was wounded, and not pleased to hear my news. Captain Watts was also there. Realising we were in a difficult position, Barnby ordered the company to retire. I passed the order to Bramall on the right and shouted and blew my whistle to the men on my left. Taking the men with me, I retired to the left of the hill back to the woods. I had had nine casualties, five of whom were killed, most of them in the last half hour of the attack.

Before this battle had started we had been led to this position by a Russian guide, but now he was nowhere to be seen, though it was later reported he had been seen in the village. Many of my men had been shot in the back even though we were facing the enemy. My servant, Private Davey, was killed in this way. He had been with me for four years. We had simply been betrayed by the guide.

As I left the field I noted that the time was 2.30. We had been in action for two and a half hours.

I did my best to reorganise the company and manned outposts on the Koi-Svy road at about 15½ post. I went off to get orders and, on my return, found the company collected on the road, looking very down. On asking why they had left their positions they informed me that they had been ordered by Major Strover, of the Machine-Gun Corps, to 'Get the hell out of it' as they were not needed and that he would find someone 'who was some use to man the positions'.

I was told that one man had been seized and kicked down the road for no specific offence. When I heard this I was extremely angry and went to Major Strover to give him my account of what had happened and to ask him to convey his orders for my men through me. He told me that those who did not want to fight would be marched back with Major Laing to 12 Verst post.

At 12 Verst post the next morning Major Laing addressed 'B' and 'C' Companies and asked for volunteers for the outpost line. About sixteen men and NCOs volunteered from 'B' Company and about three from 'C' Company. The rest refused. These numbers were insufficient to man the posts. Major Laing then ordered me to accompany him to the report centre, which I did with Lieutenant Bramall. On my return to my company, I was told that about 56 men had left for Svyatnavolok. I reported this to Major Laing who ordered a cyclist to be sent after them to tell them they would be fired on if they attempted to enter Svyatnavolok. Thankfully this didn't happen. I was then sent alone to Svyatnavolok to take charge of the men who had marched back.

When I arrived I found them quite glad to see me and friendly. As there were no NCOs, I ordered them to fall in at 8am the next day. When they mustered, I told them that they would be court-martialled and could be shot. They did not believe this, and said that several parties of Marines who had been sent to *Glory III* had burnt their rifles and that nothing had happened to them.

The following day at 8am I found the men correctly fallen in, dressed, clean and standing to attention. I took down their names and issued rations.

Later, a stretcher party arrived carrying the body of Captain Burton, covered with a blanket. He was buried out at Svyatnavolok and the only mourners were a few old Russian women and myself. He had been adjutant of the battalion and had been shot in a sniping duel with one of the enemy. He was very brave and cheerful. But sniping duels were not his job.

On 11 September the remainder of 'B' Company arrived at Svyatnavolok and the 53 men rejoined their sub-units. As the senior subaltern of 'B' Company I was in command.

A few days after our arrival in Murmansk, all the battalion officers were summoned to Force Headquarters and were addressed by, I think, General Rawlinson. He told us what he thought of us, saying that there were no bad men, only bad officers and that the Commanding Officer had the main responsibility. Ninety-three men were court-martialled. Colonel Kitcat, who had recovered from his wound, told us that as Commanding Officer he accepted the main responsibility. A few days later the battalion was drawn up in a hollow square, with the men who had been court-martialled. The Commanding Officer read out the charge against them – and the punishment.

Thirteen had been sentenced to death. I watched the faces of the men and saw that they merely looked bashful, not shocked. The 53 men of my Company were among those sentenced.

Captain Watts was also tried by Field General Court-Martial. He asked me to be his Prisoner's Friend (to defend him). He was charged with cowardice and for 'using words calculated to create alarm and despondency in that he did say 'The whole bloody company is lost' 'or words to that effect''. Surgeon Commander Wilkinson spoke on Watts' behalf and told of his wounds at Gallipoli, of a severe fall in 1915, and that he had recently suffered an accident on his cycle and had fallen, cracking the back of his head. But it was all in vain, he was found not guilty of cowardice, but guilty of the second charge and cashiered. With some difficulty we found him a suit of plain clothes and he was sent home in a collier.

We had an uneventful passage to Glasgow where we boarded a special train and eventually arrived at Chatham station. An orderly met us with a message from the adjutant asking us to wait until the Divisional Band arrived to play us back to barracks. I felt that we would never be forgiven if we allowed ourselves to be played back in triumph, so I ordered the company to fall in quickly and reached barracks while the band was still getting ready to leave. I then reported to the Commandant, Colonel Graham. No news of our ignominious disaster had reached him. As my story unfolded, he was overcome. His tears made dark, pink spots on his pad of blotting paper.

The battalion was quickly disbanded and its members drafted away to various ships and establishments in ones and twos. It was feared they might start another mutiny if left together.

When the Field General Court-Martial was held in Murmansk, one of the accused was in the hospital ship. When he recovered he was tried by District Court-Martial in Chatham on the same charges as the others. He was found not guilty. This complicated matters still further and threw doubt on the validity of the Field General Court-Martial. On 22 December the

Conservative MP, Lieutenant Kenworthy, asked in Parliament if Walter Long, the First Lord of the Admiralty, was in a position to announce the decisions of the Admiralty in respect of the Marines held in prison. Long first praised the qualities of the Royal Marines throughout the war and announced that those sentenced to death would have their sentence reduced in twelve cases to one year and one for two years. Twenty men had their five-year sentence reduced to six months and fifty-one sentenced to two years would be released after six months. Two under the age of nineteen had their sentence reduced to six months, and six others under age were released.

Colonel Graham sent for me and officially informed me that I had incurred their Lordships' severe displeasure – i.e. the Lords of the Admiralty. I asked to be court-martialled but this was refused. The Brigade Major later told me that it was not a bad thing for a young officer to receive their Lordships' severe displeasure because it would get his name known. When I left the Marines many years later, it was as a Brigadier.

We had been ill-prepared for our attack on Koikori. Few officers and certainly none of the junior officers had any experience fighting in these circumstances. Our time had been at sea. We had thought that we were to act as a relieving force, while the evacuation of other battalions took place. In the subsequent court-martial it was obvious that the NCOs and men had lost faith in their officers. On the disbandment of the 6th Battalion, no further battalion took up the number six.

Lieutenant-Commander Harry Hodgson

I joined HMS *Renown* as a Lieutenant-Commander. On 6 January 1927 she set sail for Australia to open the Government buildings on the site of the new Federal capital at Canberra. Aboard for this royal tour, were the Duke and Duchess of York, and *Renown* was under the command of Admiral Norton Sulivan.

Having crossed the Atlantic we called at Jamaica where we illuminated the ship with light bulbs to make the design of the Rose of York. The Duchess, who the previous year had given birth to her daughter Elizabeth, was given a grand welcome. We then sailed through the Panama Canal, the biggest ship then to have passed through.

When the ship was being refitted for the tour, I arranged to have my cabin open on to the quarterdeck which was about a hundred yards long. During the tour dances were held on this deck, and I often danced with the Duchess. Between the dances she would come to my cabin and we would chat together; she in fact taught me to Charleston. We danced to a gramophone which I had had installed during the refit. I was told off because I had requisitioned an American cine-camera and one or two people thought that rather unpatriotic! However, the film I made of the tour proved very popular with the royal family.

The Duke had rather a bad stutter, but he controlled it very well. As he came to a word which would cause him to stutter, he would click his fingers and he got through. I watched him give a number of speeches on the tour, all of which he got through very well. He was helped too, I think, by a New Zealander who practised Mesmerism.

After visiting the Marquesa Islands in February we passed over the Equator where the 'Crossing of the Line' ceremony was duly observed. The Duke and the Duchess entered into the spirit and were initiated. The Duchess was spared the customary shaving and ducking. But not the Duke of York. The ceremony was witnessed by practically the whole ship's company, some of whom were perched in precarious positions along the 15-inch guns. King Neptune and Queen Aphrodite (well portrayed by a sailor) were attended by the Herald, a bodyguard of trumpeters, doctors, judges, barbers, clerks and bears, all suitably rigged out. The Duke was presented with a large copper plate of the Order of the Old Sea Dog. The Duchess was invested with the

Order of the Mermaid. After that, a considerable amount of 'ragging' went on and few survived not being ducked.

During the voyage we rigged up netting on one side of the *Renown* so that members of the royal family and their entourage could play deck tennis which, I must say, the Duchess played very well. We called in at Fiji where the natives entertained us to a fine display of dancing. That was our last port of call until New Zealand where we stayed eight days. The Duke and Duchess were given a very warm welcome at Auckland. We had a tour of this beautiful country and saw the hot springs and attended the opening of a new power station. The Maoris entertained us with a tremendously exciting tribal dance display. The Duke and Duchess went big-game fishing in the Bay of Islands where the Duke caught a superb 120lb mako shark. The Duchess, in another boat, struck lucky with a large basket of khaiwhai and schnappers. She was equally successful when she went fishing in the rivers.

When we visited the South Island the Duchess developed bronchitis and had to recuperate at Government House. She soon recovered and we set sail for Australia. At Sydney we had an unbelievable welcome. The Duke dressed in naval uniform and accompanied by Lord Cavan, met a number of veterans of the Australian Army. We entertained the local children who were particularly excited by the giant chute we had fixed up from one deck to another. Our visit to Melbourne was timed to coincide with Anzac Day, 25 April. The crowds were vast, bigger than I had ever seen. The Australian servicemen, either in uniform or suits, marched in a seeming endless line, ten abreast. The Duke took the salute and *Renown*'s Marine band set the pace. It was a proud moment for me as I was asked to lead the parade. The city was ablaze with colour and noise. It was a wonderful day. At Canberra in May, the Prime Minister of Australia handed the gold key to the Duke who opened the new government buildings. We then moved on to our last port of call in Australia, Fremantle, where we were often entertained by local families.

We left on 23 May and went through the Suez Canal before arriving back at Portsmouth on 27 June. The members of the royal family bade us farewell and the ship's company stood to and gave them three rousing cheers. The trip back had not been without incident because we had a fire in the engine-room which, before we were able to extinguish it, had caused the deck to become extremely hot. Had it got worse, we would have been in trouble because the nearest ship was 1,000 miles away. A month later, we were back with the Home Fleet doing harbour drills and exercises. This was not quite so glamorous. However on 11 August the following year, the sailors of HMS *Renown* towed my new wife and me through the village of Holybourne, she resplendent in silk!

Lieutenant Shannan Stevenson

During 1925–1927 I was a young naval officer serving on the China station in a Yangtze River gunboat, HMS *Bee*, one of what were known as the Insect Class. They were little ships of about 625 displacement tonnage, about 240 feet long and with a draught of $4\frac{1}{2}$ feet.

At this time there were about a dozen Royal Naval gunboats operating on the Yangtze. Our duties were to patrol the river, which was navigable by steamships over the 1,350 miles between its mouth and the port of Chungking, and to safeguard as far as possible the lives and property of the many British subjects who lived and worked in the Yangtze ports.

Going upriver from the mouth, which is just around the corner from Shanghai, the Yangtze runs through a thousand miles of flat land and the river bed is mostly mud and sand. But at the port of Ichang (1,000 miles up) there is a sudden and dramatic change. From there for the next 250 miles to Chungking the river narrows and runs between high limestone cliffs and the river bed consists mostly of rocks. It abounds in dangerous rapids, whirlpools and cross-currents.

Coming downriver from Chungking was a hazardous operation, made worse by the fierce strength of the current rushing through the narrow channel and the fact that the ship must go faster than the current. Otherwise she would not respond to her rudder.

The thousand miles from Ichang downwards to the mouth were not so hazardous. Although the river was wide the navigable channel was very narrow in places and the sands banks were for ever shifting. We had charts, but they were rarely up to date. We used to run ashore quite often, but the ship was designed for this – she had a flat bottom and her propellers worked in tunnels so that they were protected from contact with the ground.

When we stuck on the mud we usually found that full speed astern on both engines would have the desired effect, and we would slide gracefully back into the channel and try again. Fortunately the Admiralty were fully aware of these difficulties, and I think I'm right in saying that the Yangtze was the only waterway in the world where a naval officer could run his ship ashore and not be court-martialled.

Another hazard the navigator had to put up with was the Chinese raft. Huge quantities of timber were transported down the Yangtze and the Chinese merchant found it cheaper and simpler not to charter a ship for this purpose. Instead he would lash the timber together to form an enormous raft – up to half an acre in size – and for a small sum he would engage a few men to pilot the raft downriver to its destination, perhaps a journey of several hundred miles.

The crew of the raft were always accompanied by their wives and families. They built little wooden houses on the raft and brought their pigs and dogs and chickens with them. The raft had the appearance of a floating farming village!

These rafts had no means of propulsion; they merely drifted with the current. The crew managed, by means of long oars, to keep the raft in the channel, but of course they were very sluggish to manoeuvre and so were a danger to all ships. On one occasion, when we were at anchor off the port of Changsha, one of these rafts collided with us and got completely stuck across our bows. We started to drag our anchors and things were not looking very bright. Our own sailors and the crew of the raft then set about cutting the raft in half, and in due course half a raft drifted past us on each side.

Another touch of local colour we had to negotiate was the farmer taking his ducks to market. If you've got a river handy you might as well make use of it and hundreds of ducks, with clipped wings so that they could not fly, would paddle their way downriver in convoy. The farmer would follow in his sampan and keep his flock together with a long bamboo. But of course they occupied the main channel to take full advantage of the current, and it was a tricky operation trying to overtake them without damaging or dispersing the ducks.

During part of my time in HMS *Bee* I had the great pleasure of having as a shipmate Prince George, the fourth son of King George V, who later became the Duke of Kent. In our Yangtze days he was a serving officer in the Royal Navy and was regarded by himself and all of us as just that. He was known by us all as P.G.

On one occasion he and I and the ship's doctor were invited to visit some English friends who were at a holiday mountain resort at Kuling near the port of Kiukiang. The normal way of getting there was to go by Sedan chair borne by four Chinese coolies. The young and energetic did the climb on their own feet.

Prince George and I decided to climb and the doctor, who was rather portly, elected to go by chair. We set off first and, when we neared the top, a Chinese photographer, who had evidently heard of Prince George's approach, rushed towards us in great excitement. He said to Prince George, 'You belong English King's son – yes?' Prince George then replied 'English King's son very fat man – come up in chair by and by'. And we proceeded to our destination.

Some time later the doctor arrived and told us that on the last stages of his journey a Chinese photographer had followed him taking innumerable photographs. He couldn't understand it. I must add that, before we returned to our ship, Prince George called at the photographer's shop and let him take all the photographs he wished.

In the main we led a fairly peaceful life, joining in the social activities of the British community of the ports at which we called, including the excellent snipe shooting available on the banks of the Yangtze.

During the second half of 1926 we encountered more serious problems. The country was in a state of civil war, and British ships were liable to be boarded by Chinese bandits demanding free passage. Far more seriously, on 2 September 1926 we heard from HMS *Cockchafer* at Wanhsien, a riverside port halfway between Ichang and Chungking, that a local bandit war lord, Yang Sen, had seized two British ships belonging to the China Navigation company, the *SS Wantung* and *SS Wanhsien*, and were holding six British officers hostage. The *Wantung* and *Wanhsien* were each manned with four hundred of the Yang Sen's soldiers and the banks of the river were lined with thousands of troops. Negotiations had broken down and the officers were in serious danger.

This action took place on 6 September. HMS *Kiawo*, a requisitioned merchant vessel led by Commander Darley of the *Despatch*, grappled on to and boarded the *Wanhsien*, supported by HMS *Widgeon* and HMS *Cockchafer*. In the confusion the master and officers of the *Wanhsien* escaped onto the *Kiawo* and two of the three officers of the *Wantung* managed to jump overboard and were rescued by the supporting gunboats. Few of the troops on the *Wantung* and *Wanhsien* survived and thousands of soldiers on the foreshore were killed. But we lost Commander Darley, two lieutenants and four ratings in the action.

Anti-British riots were not uncommon in those days. They

would start without warning, and for no very obvious reason, except that we knew the Chinese students were usually at the bottom of it with their slogans 'China for Chinese' and 'Out with the foreign devils'.

The British settlement at Hankow was next to the Chinese city, so we were always the first to bear the brunt of any anti-foreign feeling on the part of the Chinese. When trouble started a recognised alarm signal was given on a steam siren and any naval officers and men who happened to be ashore would return to their ships as quickly as possible. The Hankow British volunteers – the civilian male population – would assemble at their headquarters immediately, put uniform on, get their rifles off the racks and wait for orders. The British gunboats would then send landing parties ashore to guard the boundaries of the British settlement, and they would be supported by the Volunteer Corps.

The worst riot I experienced was in early January 1927. On 3 January we received the news that a huge mob was heading for the British concession, so a landing party was sent ashore and the Hankow Volunteers were mobilised. There were just thirty of our men to protect the Concession's waterfront and they had express instructions not to open fire on the crowd. Meanwhile British women and children were gathered together on the far side of the Concession, ready for evacuation.

As the mob approached they bombarded our men with bricks, chunks of stone and broken pieces of metal, but they were kept at bay with baton and bayonet charges. Many of our men were injured, one of them stuck with his own bayonet when he slipped and dropped his rifle. Thomas Ellis, who was in charge, stopped a brick with his face and had to go to be patched up in hospital.

After dark things quietened a bit. I went ashore to relieve Ellis and spent a tense night at Volunteer Quarters. We had no idea what the next day would bring. In the morning I received orders to return on board as the Chinese military authorities had promised to protect the Concession on the condition that all landing parties withdrew. This promise was worth nothing at all because by 4pm the Concession was packed with howling mobs. That day was the birthday of my wife-to-be, Daphne, and we had planned to go to her tea-dance party at the Race Club and then to dinner with friends!

The next day the crowds gathered again and at 2.30pm we decided to evacuate all women and children. I went in a tug with an armed party to collect refugees and took them to British merchant ships at anchor in the stream. All one lady had with her was a small attaché case containing a sandwich and a toothbrush. I heard an alarming rumour that Daphne was trapped by the crowds and couldn't be evacuated, and spent an agonising few hours until hearing that she was, in fact, safely aboard a merchant ship.

Meanwhile, the remaining British civilians were in fear of their lives as we were expecting the crowds to invade the Concession's buildings under cover of darkness. Suddenly, rain began to fall and within fifteen minutes the crowd had dispersed. But for the rain I can't imagine what would have happened.

Leading Seaman Stan Smith

On board HMS *Broke* during 1926 a notice went up for volunteers to go into the Brazilian jungle in search of one Colonel Fawcett, an explorer who had gone missing. His fate was the subject of a lot of speculation back home. Some thought that he'd been captured by a tribe of Amazon Indians, others that he was a prisoner in the depths of the jungle, or that he'd been kidnapped and made king of some native tribe. Nobody knew, so the Navy decided to send in a party to try and locate him and unravel the mystery.

I was one of the twelve volunteers accepted and placed under the command of Lieutenant Bradley, a very nice chap. We set sail for the Xingu River and went up it as far as we could by ship, reaching Bara, a town which was the centre of the rubber trade. It was a thriving industrial town with trams, cabarets and dance halls.

We were kitted out with khaki shorts and a jacket. All our personal necessities were to be carried on packs on our backs. We were issued with rifles and ammunition and each of us also carried a large sharp Bowie knife at our belt. Porters were recruited to accompany us to carry the stores and the trade goods which we were to distribute in friendly villages in exchange for a safe passage or information about Colonel Fawcett.

We plunged deep into the jungle, paddling on up the river in canoe shaped boats as far as we could. We travelled by water for three days until we reached some falls which we could not negotiate. There was nothing for it but to hit the trail on foot, so we hauled the boats up into the bush, camouflaged them with branches and undergrowth and, with the porters well loaded, headed off into the jungle. Led by a guide who was supposed to deal with the natives for us, we slogged on and on. At times we had to hack our way through the jungle, it was so dense.

Thankfully, when we came to a village, the natives were friendly. Our lieutenant had a good long talk with the chief and gave him and some of his followers some of the trading goods we had brought with us; strings of cheap beads (probably from Woolworths), little mirrors and other bright objects and knives. We carried on for days. Sometimes we would only make about a mile a day through the interlacing vines in the humid, suffocating heat. At each village we asked for news of Colonel Fawcett, but even where the villagers were friendly, there was none.

As we penetrated further into the jungle a gradual change came over the natives we met. Our reception was less and less friendly until we began to find ghost villages, totally deserted yet with signs of recent habitation. We had the unnerving experience of knowing we were being watched by hundreds of unseen eyes all around. Even so, we would still leave small gifts at some point in the middle of the village, hoping they would find them after we had gone and realise that we were trying to be friendly. They didn't attack us in any way or show any signs of hostility.

We passed the remains of several old settlements, ancient towns which to this day are still being discovered. But we had no time to explore. One day we came to a clearing in sight of one of these villages and we made camp. During the evening we were attacked by pygmies using blow pipes. We had to open fire on them. I don't know if we hit any of them but the noise of the guns probably scared them away. Unfortunately, one of our chaps was hit in the shoulder by a dart. We gave him what first aid treatment we could and tried to suck the poison out of the wound, but he gradually became worse.

There was no alternative but to send him back to Bara with one of our party and two of the bearers. We made a rough stretcher from boughs and vines and sent them off to follow our trail back as quickly as they could. That was the last we saw of any of them. We heard nothing more of our wounded comrade; whether they were killed or simply got lost and starved to death we shall never know.

Immediately after the attack all our bearers deserted us. We awoke in the morning to find they had simply crept away during the night. We could not carry on much further transporting all our stores and food so we discarded some of the extra clothing and food, packed it all up carefully and hid it in the bush. Then, just carrying the minimum of food for survival and the clothes we stood in, we set out again, travelling light. We tramped on for two days but food was getting very short. Then we came to a swampy patch of jungle where we were pestered by swarms of mosquitoes. It was a sweating, stinking infested sump to the world which was also populated by leeches. These slimy, fat, repulsive suckers clung so hard to our legs that we had to yank them off.

We had a consultation. If Colonel Fawcett had come within a hundred miles of this God-forsaken place we might never have known anyway and we would have probably perished in attempting to find out. We had done our bit and nobody could expect more so we did an about turn and began the long hard slog, picking our way back through the jungle the way we had come. On reaching the clearing where we had left our stores, we had a jolly good meal of corned beef and biscuits, packed some more food in our haversacks and continued our homeward trail. The going was fairly easy and we made much better time going back than we had on the outward journey because the trail was still clear and we had marker trees to guide us.

Mercifully our boats were still intact but we had nobody to paddle them so we made ourselves some rough paddles from the jungle. We steered one boat and towed the other. Fortunately the tide was with us so we made fairly good progress, although our craft was not very manoeuvrable and we were a lot weaker. At one of the friendliest villages, however, we had more than enough volunteer paddlers, in fact we had to select a crew from among them.

So we arrived back at Bara. We had tried but failed and come back with a totally different crew. There was time for a run ashore, some onion beer and a few smokes before we returned to our ship. Without delay I found myself back aboard HMS *Broke* at Malta.

Able Seaman 'Ginger' Le Breton

I joined HMS *Dorsetshire* as an able seaman in 1930 and had a wonderful cruise with her around the West Indies, where I played a lot of cricket. Back in England, while we were enjoying ourselves, the country was going through a bad time with nearly three million people out of work.

During September 1931, when we were back at Invergordon with the Atlantic Fleet, there was a buzz about our pay, which along with the other armed services, was to be cut. We thought it would be about 10% all round, but instead we heard that a shilling a day was to be deducted from everyone. Well, most able seamen were on 4 shillings a day so for us it was a reduction of 25%, but for a petty officer, who was on 8s 6d. a day it was only about 10%. This began to cause a great deal of bad feeling. Many of the men were married and had hire purchase commitments at home with fixed weekly repayments. This scheme was going to be implemented within about three weeks, which did not give enough time for those with families to sort things out.

As a torpedo man I spoke first to Lieutenant-Commander Cameron, my divisional torpedo officer, and explained that the men knew how to do percentages and that this reduction was unfair to us. He was very understanding, but there was little he could do.

On 15 September the Atlantic Fleet was due to go to sea on exercise. That was the morning we all decided not to turn to. Meetings had been held in naval canteens in Invergordon and in all the other ships of the fleet and it had been agreed that only able seamen and stokers, and those of equivalent rank, would take part. On the *Dorsetshire* we turned to for breakfast and then gathered on the fo'c's'le. That just seemed to happen. We saw other ships of the fleet close by and cheered. We were supporting each other; they had not turned to either.

We were then told that our commander wanted to speak to us so we went down to the upper messdeck. Commander A. C. 'Alfie' Collinson was a tough, heavy sort, a bull of a man. When he came forward we could see he was angry with us, but he was a belligerent man in any case. He railed at us and when he realised he wasn't getting his way he shouted, 'If you won't fall in, go down below to the lower messdeck.' Of course we just laughed at him and he stomped away.

A little later we were told that our captain wanted to speak with the ship's company on the fo'c's'le. Our captain, Arthur John Power, was a lovely chap and very popular. The first thing he did when he joined the ship was to call us all together. He told us that if we saw him walking around the upper deck with his cap under his arm, then we were not to stop our work or salute him, we were to carry on with whatever we were doing. We appreciated that: we liked him.

When he came forward to speak to us he did so with his cap under his arm. He was staking his reputation on this move. He told us that if we turned to, he would see us through. Then he quietly said, 'I am going aft. I have work to do. I hope you will do the same.' To a man, we followed him aft to our muster stations. It was a remarkably moving moment and one that I will remember for ever.

From the Atlantic Fleet seven captains were relieved of their command. Captain Power was the only captain from the Invergordon Mutiny to obtain further promotion. The next day the Admiralty ordered all ships to return to home ports. The mutiny was only a short affair, but it did a lot of damage to the reputation of the Navy and to our country. We had two ratings discharged from our ship on the grounds that they were engaged in subversive activities and others were drafted to various barracks. We were fortunate that we had a captain who understood his men.

Engine-Room Artificer Trevor Lewis

Hong Kong was the main base for the Far Eastern Fleet. It providing dockyard facilities for all ships and submarines, sports clubs, accommodation, and the magnificent China Fleet Club which the government had built specifically for Royal Navy personnel. This offered accommodation at cheap rates for men on all-night leave, a large restaurant, an English tavern and all kinds of indoor recreation. There were other homes for servicemen, such as the Mission for Seamen, the Methodist Church Home and the YMCA, but the China Fleet Club, known throughout the China Station as 'The Blue', was our very own club.

When we in HMS *Danae* arrived in Hong Kong in the mid-1930s, the Garrison was very strong. They were stationed there along with the Royal Engineers, the Welch Fusiliers and the Seaforth Highlanders. Consequently inter-service rivalry on the cricket, football and rugby fields played a big part in our daily routine.

Certain customs in the Far Eastern Fleet were quite different from those in the Home Fleet, especially regarding the matter of catering. Each chief or petty officer's mess was allowed to employ a Chinese messman who would buy all the food ashore and be responsible for the cooking. He was paid weekly or monthly and each member of the mess would pay a mess bill and be relieved of all catering duties. For a few shillings a month we lived like the proverbial fighting cocks. Similarly we took advantage of the laundering facilities, for which the Chinese are renowned. When we were at sea we used to save up all our dirty washing for the return to base. The messman would recruit laundry maids – little Chinese girls with pigtails down their backs – who were all probably related to him. They would come on board every day at 5pm to collect the dhobeying and bring it back twenty-four hours later spotlessly clean and beautifully starched. They charged six cents apiece, irrespective of size, which was nothing as there were 100 cents to the Hong Kong dollar and sixteen dollars to the sterling pound. With their funny little ways and pidgin English they caused a lot of amusement, but they were always scrupulously honest and could be trusted to search through our kit for dirty laundry.

Since we had left Australia the ship's group, The Danae Singers, had been in temporary decline and I had been recruited by Mr Lee, our warrant schoolmaster and choirmaster, to help teach some of the seamen and stokers to write their letters home and to read more fluently. It was quite common in the 1930s to find seamen who had had very little education, but they still made very good and well-disciplined ratings.

After our 23,000-mile journey around the world the *Danae*

went into dry dock for maintenance and, on completion of this, we joined up with the Fleet exercises in a mock attack on Hong Kong. We were in company with the heavy cruisers *Cumberland*, *Berwick* and *Suffolk*, our sister ship *Capetown*, ten destroyers and two flotillas of submarines. Altogether 20,000 men were mobilised ashore to repel the attacking forces in the biggest exercise ever staged by Britain in the Far East.

The Sino-Japanese War, which had broken out in 1931–32 over the invasion of Manchuria, had been rumbling on ever since, but in 1936 tension suddenly flared up again and hostilities were resumed in earnest. The Far Eastern Fleet suddenly found itself in a war situation.

In early April *Danae* was ordered to pick up the British Consul and take him to Shanghai from Foochow which lay some two hours steaming up the Min river. The Min, like many of China's rivers, is a fast flowing stream with a current of about five to six knots, against which the junks going upstream were propelled laboriously by eight or ten men. Those coming downstream glided swiftly by without any human effort apart from steering. Foochow is one of the five Treaty Ports, so called because of the treaty signed between the Chinese and western powers to open up certain ports for foreign trade.

We lay for four days with no sign of the consul and accordingly moved downstream to the gulf of Lian Kiang just north of the mouth of the Min river. Our objective was to visit the cemetery, and clean and tend the graves of the British servicemen who had died fighting during the Boxer Rebellion of 1900.

Mid-April found us off the estuary of the greatest river in China, the Yangtse Kiang, which meets the Whangpoo river at a confluence that empties into the East China Sea. The sea for miles around is a dirty brown colour owing to the large amount of silt brought down from the interior. Shanghai, which lies on the Whangpoo river some twelve miles from the mouth, became the most important city in China after being made a Treaty Port with the large International Settlement and the French Conces-sion, alongside Greater Shanghai which was entirely Chinese.

Everything was peaceful during our eight-day visit. The Danae Singers came into prominence again by broadcasting and making two gramophone records, although what the Chinese thought about our singing was anyone's guess. The place was teeming with life but had a darker side, like all great cities. The ship's company were warned not to wander from the main thoroughfares and there was no all-night leave. In truth, most of us were glad to return to the safety of our ship by 2200 hours.

After showing the flag for the comfort of British nationals we left Shanghai, passing the US Asiatic Fleet in the estuary and exchanging the usual courtesies before making for Nanking where the Yangtse river is over one mile wide. Nanking had been the seat of the Chinese government since 1928. It is the largest walled city in China lying about three miles from the river bank. Several ships from the Chinese Navy greeted us upon our arrival with gun salutes and we were honoured with a visit by the Chinese admiral which was a first for any of our ship's company. HMS *Gnat*, one of the river gunboats, came down from Hankow for our visit. The gunboats served two-year commissions up the river without seeing the open sea, so it was a time of swopping old sailors' yarns and updating them with news from home.

After a five-day visit we began the 200-mile journey down-stream to the sea. Reaching the estuary we turned north, heading up through the Yellow Sea for Chefoo on the northern coast of the province of Shantung, the only port in that area open all year round. The Yellow Sea is really part of a large gulf of the Pacific Ocean and is so called because it is discoloured by the yellow mud brought down from the interior by the Yellow River, also known as China's Sorrow. We were supposed to celebrate the Coronation of King George VI on 12 May 1937 along with the rest of the fleet but one of the ratings went down with smallpox and the entire ship was placed in strict quarantine. The sufferer was rushed into isolation ashore and everyone on board was inoculated immediately. There were plenty of sore arms for several days afterwards but fortunately no one else contracted the dreaded symptoms.

Still in quarantine *Danae* moved further along the coast to the Naval base at Wei Hai Wei in north China where we spent six weeks in between spells at sea. The base is situated on an offshore island where facilities were provided for the fleet such as a sports ground and a naval canteen which was by far the most imposing building in the place. By the beginning of June the rest of the Far Eastern Fleet had joined us to escape the trying heat of South China. Free of quarantine restrictions we were able to join in the football and cricket matches against other ships and prepare ourselves for that most gruelling of all sports, pulling a whaler at sea. The ERA's mess entered a crew of which I was a somewhat reluctant member. Thankfully it was the last time I would ever have to participate in this form of punishment and after a two-mile slog we managed to come a commendable third.

Early in July fresh hostilities broke out between China and Japan which meant an arranged trip to Peking and the Great Wall had to be cancelled. Instead we were ordered to Chingwangtao with half a flotilla of destroyers to stand by for further eventualities. Equally abruptly on 13 July *Danae* received orders to proceed to sea and rendezvous with the flagship HMS *Cumberland*. Here the Commander-in-Chief, Admiral Sir Charles Little, was brought across in a launch with the British ambassador to China, Sir Hughe Knatchbull-Hugesson. We received orders to take the ambassador to Nanking with all despatch.

Nearly three months had elapsed since our previous visit to Nanking during which time the Yangtse River had been in flood and vast stretches of land on either side were under water. The current in the main channel was very strong and the water was like dark brown soup. Bamboo rafts with whole families on board were carried down from the interior. One or two entire villages floated by on several rafts lashed together complete with bamboo houses and scores of men, women and children all heading for the open sea. We had to navigate with extreme care whilst still maintaining our speed of 20 knots owing to the urgency of our mission. Arriving at Nanking on 15 July, we found several ships from different nations had gathered there. After the customary salutes all round we fired a special one for the ambassador as he disembarked.

The weather was hot and very sticky, in contrast to the bracing air of north China, and the ship's company were not allowed leave ashore because of the war situation. Reports were coming in of heavy fighting around Peking and the advance of Japanese armies southwards.

For two weeks we lay at anchor in midstream wondering what the outcome of all this would be. We received orders to proceed downriver to Woosung at the mouth of the Yangtse to oil ship from the Royal Fleet Auxiliary *Pearleaf* before going on to Shanghai. Just as we were preparing to oil we received a signal warning of a particularly virulent typhoon sweeping in from the East China Sea with winds of 80–100 miles per hour. Frantic activity ensued as we cast off all the hoses, battened down all the hatches, and secured everything that was moveable between decks whilst simultaneously heading out to sea from the estuary. The greatest dread in every captain's mind is to be caught in harbour or any restricted anchorage by a typhoon in the China seas, so we were thankful to make it to open water when the typhoon struck. The eye of the storm passed over us and for three days we steamed into the full force of the wind with our 40,000 horse-power at half speed, but we were treading water, trying to forge ahead but remaining practically stationary.

There was a continuous roar from the wind punctuated by sudden enormous gusts strong enough to lift a ship bodily from the water. It was a terrifying experience but somehow we survived it. At least forty sea-going ships were lost or wrecked in that typhoon; and three weeks later, on 1 September, the 10,000-ton mass of the British India liner *Talamba* was flung like a matchstick one hundred yards up the beach by the combined onslaught of wind and waves. The Hong Kong Electric Company tried to gauge the velocity of the winds but the needle went off the gauge after 160 miles per hour.

Four days later than planned we were able to oil ship before proceeding up the Whangpoo River to Shanghai and berthing midstream opposite the Bund at Number One British Navy Buoy. We remained there for the next two and a half months as the British government's representative in the troubled situation. Most of the Western powers sent a warship to protect the large numbers of nationals living in the International Settlement (an amalgamation of various foreign 'Concessions') and the French Concession. The French cruiser *Lamotte Picquet* and sloop *Dumont d'Urville*, the US cruiser *Augusta*, two Italian destroyers, Norwegian, Dutch and Swedish sloops were all anchored off the Bund with other ships arriving from time to time. Our own destroyers *Duncan*, *Delight* and *Duchess* were engaged in bringing up troop reinforcements from the mouth of the river to man the perimeter of the settlement. They would berth alongside *Danae* and disembark men of the Ulster Rifles and the Welch Fusiliers who would then be ferried across to the Bund. The Commander-in-Chief, Admiral Sir Charles Little, flying his flag in HMS *Falmouth*, made frequent trips up and down the river, transferring his flag to *Danae* whenever he was required to be in Shanghai.

Tension mounted as the fighting drew nearer to the outskirts of Shanghai and on 12 August all servicemen on leave were suddenly recalled to their ships. The following day fighting broke out in earnest. The Japanese flagship HIJMS *Idzumo*, berthed just below Garden Bend, announced that she would fire on any ship proceeding up or down the Whangpoo River. Higher up the Chinese blocked the river with a line of sunken ships so we were effectively hemmed in with nowhere to go. The ship's company was placed on half rations immediately. Corned beef became the staple diet along with ship's biscuits which could have been made out of reinforced concrete.

For the next few weeks we experienced the realities of modern warfare, admittedly mainly as spectators, but it was still far too close for comfort. On 14 August Chinese planes attempting to attack the *Idzumo* dropped bombs on the intersection of Edward VII Avenue and Nanking Road – two of the busiest roads in Shanghai. It was like a holocaust. Some of the sights were really horrifying as the intersection was crowded at the time and many people were simply blown to bits. Over 1,000 people were killed, mainly Chinese, but several foreigners died, among them the distinguished American missionary, Dr F. J. Rawlinson.

Each day brought heavy bombing from both Chinese and Japanese aircraft in the Pootung and Hongkew areas and intense anti-aircraft fire from both sides of the river. We were slap bang in the middle of it all. The Bund was declared unsafe, all traffic was stopped and pedestrians vanished from the streets. Huge areas of Chapei and Pootung were on fire from the incessant bombing and our port quarter, McKenzie's Godown, and the cotton mill nearby blazed for two days. During a particularly hot exchange of fire from both sides of the river a shell exploded on the quarterdeck of USS *Augusta* killing a seaman and seriously injuring eighteen others. *Augusta* was secured to the same buoy as *Danae* so for us it was a narrow escape.

During the third week of fighting aerial torpedoes were dropped on one of the largest stores in the city, the Sincere-Wing Emporium – the Harrods of Shanghai. It was another scene of terrible carnage and again several hundred people lost their lives. Two platoons of seamen and stokers were landed from *Danae* together with our full complement of Royal Marines to assist the Loyal Regiment in guarding the International Settlement.

On 18 August the evacuation of all British nationals was ordered which required every available rating ashore. I found myself in charge of a platoon with a service revolver on my hip and six stokers armed with rifles. Our task was to escort evacuees from the collecting depot, see them safely into the waiting tenders for transfer to the *Danae* and eventually to Hong Kong. It made me recall the refugees at Valencia who were so grateful to the Royal Navy for rescuing them from the war zone. Some had only the clothes they stood in; others came loaded with treasured possessions; some brought along their family pets, only to find they had to leave them behind. Most of the men were bank officials, consular staff or shipping company employees who had lived in China all their working lives. Many of their wives were Chinese, some of whom did not speak much English but they smiled their thanks for our help and protection and in their quaint Chinese way each one bowed low before me thinking I was Number One Man. It was really quite touching.

One woman gave birth to a son on HMS *Duncan* during the passage downstream. An agreement was reached between the British and Japanese authorities to allow the passage of refugees to the river mouth. Within three days the evacuation of 3,000 British passport holders was completed, all safely ferried down to Woosung by the destroyers. In that time I lost count of the number of babies my team of six young stokers and I had carried and deposited safely on board. Perhaps it was good training for the future.

In the last week of August the ambassador to China, Sir Hughe Knatchbull-Hugesson, was travelling by car from Nanking to confer with the Commander-in-Chief in Shanghai when the car was attacked by a Japanese plane. The ambassador suffered severe spinal injuries and the event brought forth a strong protest from the British government. Six weeks later the ambassador was brought on board looking very pale and drawn. He was carefully transferred to HMS *Falmouth* with his wife for passage to Hong Kong. He subsequently made a good recovery and later became British ambassador to Turkey throughout World War II.

There was still no let up in the fighting and from the ship we had a grandstand view of the aerial warfare by day. Fires raged for miles in the Hongkew and Pootung areas. Many of us had taken to sleeping on deck to escape the humid atmosphere between decks, and had to learn the exact moment to leave the camp bed once we heard the rattle of machine-gun fire overhead. On several occasions I must have beaten all existing world records in the twenty yard dash for cover.

During these weeks we had to make our own entertainment such as ship's concerts, in which each mess would take part, ukkers championships, crib matches and even competitions for writing and reciting poetry. None of these entries would have found a place in the *Golden Treasury*, indeed some needed to be heavily censored before recital. Nonetheless, my entry was very much a cry from the heart. I had been abroad for nearly three and a half years and was getting very homesick. Judging from the reception the ship's company gave it at the ship's concert, my sentiments echoed in the hearts of all. It won first prize and the chorus was sung, whistled and hummed throughout the ship for the remainder of the commission.

Cholera had broken out ashore so, once again, the entire ship's company was inoculated. There was the usual crop of sore arms for several days afterwards.

Early in September the fighting moved north of Shanghai, and at last we were able to breathe a little more easily. Shore leave was finally granted each day though for a limited period only. It was good to stretch the legs again after being cooped up in a stationary ship for so long.

Fighting of a different sort provided a light relief when a boxing match was arranged between the *Augusta* and the *Danae*. Although classed as a light cruiser, *Danae* was only one-third of the size and complement of the heavy American cruiser. The match was staged in a hall near the Shanghai

Racecourse but the contest became so one-sided it was almost laughable. The Americans sauntered into the ring rigged up like professionals with boxing boots, silk shorts and dressing-gowns with their names emblazoned on the back, whilst our chaps turned out in regulation tropical shorts, singlets and good old 'pussers' plimsolls. It was a source of great amusement for all the spectators and of some embarrassment for our ship's company. The Yanks fought like professionals too and had easily won every bout on the programme until the last of the evening, billed as the star attraction – the Light Heavyweight Contest.

The British representative was our own ERA messman, a stoker first class, known to everybody on the ship simply as Geordie since he obviously hailed from Tyneside. Geordie was slow-witted, almost illiterate, and would never rise above his current rank, yet he was a very hard worker on board and an equally hard drinker on land. He usually managed at least one run ashore per month when he would always get into trouble, returning on board with a couple of black eyes, having lost his cap or his pay-book. He never caused any trouble on board and everybody liked him. When he came into the ring the spectators roared with laughter. He looked so comical in his long tropical shorts while his opponent danced around in professional style in his flashy red dressing-gown. Geordie was as strong as an ox and built like one. The American began punching him from all angles while the Yanks roared their man on. It looked to be another cakewalk with the British being completely white-washed. In round three the same pattern was emerging when Geordie suddenly decided he'd had enough of this, shook his head like a wounded bull and unleashed an enormous swing. The American dropped as though he had been poleaxed, lying flat on his back and knocked out cold. The audience were literally stunned into silence until the British contingent erupted into ecstatic cheering. The Yanks were dumbfounded. Our pride had been salvaged and Geordie became the ship's hero for the remainder of the commission.

The ERA's mess achieved a certain notoriety in a quite different sphere when one of the younger ERAs, known to everyone as Knocker White, suddenly announced that he intended to marry a Chinese girl with whom he had fallen in love. She was a 'hostess' and dancing partner in one of the better class cabarets which abounded in Shanghai. They were genuine places of entertainment and not, as one would imagine, houses of ill-repute. The girl herself, we had to admit, was very beautiful.

Knocker was a real country bumpkin from Andover. He was brought up on a small farm and had about him a kind of rustic stolidity which he'd probably inherited from his parents. Nothing would shift him once his mind was made up. We all tried to dissuade him from taking this step, since the likelihood of a Chinese cabaret girl settling down on a small Hampshire farm was fairly remote. However, Knocker was adamant and nothing his mess-mates could say made any difference. Prior to the war no rating serving abroad was allowed to marry on the station without the commanding officer's permission. Usually the rating concerned would be drafted back to Britain by the first boat, but due to our circumstances this was impossible. The captain saw Knocker and advised strongly against the marriage but stopped short of actually forbidding it. The wedding went ahead even though with the restrictions on shore leave they were unable to set up a home. When we finally left Shanghai she tried to follow as best she could, since all the British women and children had already been evacuated. I believe it took her some twelve to eighteen months to reach England by which time World War II was drawing near. Unfortunately there was no happy or romantic ending to the story as poor old Knocker was killed in the first two years of the war. I have often wondered how she took to life in Andover.

One other very unpleasant, sickening memory of those three months tied up to the buoy lingered on in our minds long after we left Shanghai. During most of our time there another ship would be berthed alongside, sometimes one on each side. These were usually 'D' class destroyers and often the Commander-in-Chief's yacht HMS *Falmouth*. The Whangpoo river is noted for its fast current of 4–5 knots which brings down all the flotsam and jetsam imaginable from the interior. Much of the garbage would become trapped between the two ships, quickly accumulating into a solid mass which would have to be cleared by hand with boathooks. The 'D' class destroyers had a low free-board and the ERA's mess, which was on the starboard side of the ship, had four portholes which were only a few feet above the water-line, so the putrefying garbage was very quickly smelt in the mess. We became very familiar with one very distinctive foul smell; the stench of decomposing human flesh. Invariably these proved to be the bodies of tiny little baby girls. In those days female babies were unwanted by the peasants and it was common practice, in the interior of China, to dispose of them by throwing them into the river. The task of freeing these poor little creatures and watching them swept along with the garbage of the river to the open sea affected all of us.

In the third week of October 1937, HMS *Dorsetshire*, a county class cruiser, arrived off Woosung to relieve HMS *Danae*. Shortly after, we slipped our moorings and proceeded downriver to the open sea and thence to Hong Kong. After storing ship and replenishing the larder, we left the Far Eastern Base and began the six-week return trip back home. Owing to the gathering war clouds in Europe, as well as the delay caused by the situation in China, our round-the-world return via the Panama Canal was cancelled. So it was Singapore, Colombo, Aden, Port Said, Malta, and finally Gibraltar on 5 December, before starting the last lap for home.

Warrant Shipwright F.H.T. Panter

My first ship appointment as a newly promoted shipwright officer was to HMS *Ajax* on 11 January 1938. *Ajax* was a light cruiser of 7,000 tons carrying eight 6-inch guns in four twin turrets; 'A' and 'B' forward and 'X' and 'Y' turrets aft. She was also fitted with upper-deck torpedo tubes and a Sea Fox seaplane carried on a catapult amidships. Adjacent to this was a crane for lifting the aircraft from the water to the catapult.

I joined the ship at Chatham where she was being prepared for a two-year commission at the America and West Indies station based in Bermuda. Captain C.H.L. Woodhouse was in command with Commander D.H.E. Everett as executive officer. The first few weeks were spent getting her shipshape and settling down the crew.

From Bermuda our first long cruise was to the Caribbean Islands, then around South America, steaming down the east coast, through the Magellan Straits, up the west coast, through the Panama Canal and back to Bermuda, stopping on many courtesy calls on route. It was a pleasant cruise, marred only by the terrible earthquake that occurred in January 1939 whilst the ship was at Valparaiso. The epicentre was a town nearby called Talcuahana which was completely demolished. Our ship's company was sent there for four days to help provide relief with food, water, medical supplies, tents and blankets. I landed with some of my staff to make safe some of the buildings and help the homeless people until the Chilean Army arrived and took charge.

Once when the ship was anchored off a small Chilean town, we were presented with a huge live turtle on board with the compliments of the local dignitaries. We had no idea what to do with it so the commander decided that the ship's company should have real turtle soup with their evening meal, which was fine, until we tried to kill it. Butch, our marine butcher managed to turn the turtle upside down on the upper deck where it lay helpless, rocking on its armour-like shell. After several hours beating with a cleaver it was still alive, pulling in its head with every blow. Eventually it gave up the ghost and died. Then came the nauseous task of trying to cut, dig and scrape the flesh from the shell, which took all day and ended with a pile of bloody mess on the deck. The cooks tried to make some turtle soup, but by then nobody felt like eating it.

One Sunday afternoon when the ship was anchored in a small bay off Brazil, I decided to go shark fishing with a young pay sub-lieutenant. We tied a whole loaf of bread to a shark hook and using a piece of wooden box for a float, cast the line from the stern of the ship. We soon hooked a medium-sized shark and managed to drag it to the side of the ship. The line wasn't strong enough so we got a heavier rope, tied it in a noose around our line and dropped the rope over the shark's nose until we could tighten it under its fins. Then we tried, with other helpers, to haul the shark up on to the quarterdeck, but it seemed to catch on something on the ship's side. Meanwhile, below us in the stern of the ship, one of our engineers called Dickie Bird was taking a shower when he noticed the bath-room become very dark. Looking up he saw a shark's head looming through the porthole, apparently trying to smash its way in. Terrified, he ran screaming down the passageway to his cabin, stark naked and dripping wet. Poor Dickie never lived it down.

The *Ajax* docked in Bermuda early in 1939 for a small refit. She was expected to remain there for about six months during which time sports days, regattas and competitions were held as well as naval exercises, gunnery practice and speed trials with the other cruiser on the station, HMS *Exeter*. She was a slightly heavier ship of 10,000 tons, fitted with six 8-inch guns.

Murmurings of a sabre-rattling hot-head called Adolf Hilter, thousands of miles away in Germany, did not concern us much at that time, in fact I arranged for my wife, Gladys, to come out to Bermuda for a holiday. We spent a very pleasant six months together to the extent that we failed to realise the serious developments in Europe until the *Ajax* and the *Exeter* were ordered to sea a week or so before Britain declared war on Germany. Presumably the Admiralty didn't have too much faith in Neville Chamberlain's declaration of 'Peace in our time'. The holiday was over.

On the day war was declared the captain cleared lower deck, and all the officers and men not on duty mustered on the quarterdeck where Captain Woodhouse gave us the news. The chaplain said a few prayers, then we exercised action stations.

The *Ajax*'s task was to patrol the Atlantic Ocean. Only an hour or so later we had our first prize. We spotted a German merchant ship, the *SS Olinda*, steaming along bound for Germany. Captain Woodhouse ordered her to heave to and steamed the *Ajax* up close to her. We landed a boarding party and took off the master and crew who weren't even aware that we were at war. Captain Woodhouse was at a loss what to do with his trophy since he couldn't afford to leave a steaming party on her as we were thousands of miles from a British port. He had no option but to use the *Olinda* as a gunnery target and sink her. So *Ajax* claimed the first enemy ship in the war.

The following day the German merchant ship *SS Carl Fritzen* met with the same fate. The officers and men were taken off and the ship deposited on the bottom of the ocean. We then had two foreign crews on board, a mixture of Germans and Swedes. Later they were transferred to our store ship and taken to the Falkland Islands where they remained for the duration of the war. With two prizes to our credit, the captain earned the nickname 'One a day Wimpey', but it was a few weeks before we claimed the third, the *SS Ussukuma*, which joined the other two on the ocean bed.

At this point the war seemed quite pleasant to us, just cruising around the Atlantic looking for quarry while the *Exeter* was doing the same well to the south of us. Being the larger ship she carried the flag of Commodore H. Harwood, the flag officer of the American and West Indies Station. We were also helped by the New Zealand ship HMNZS *Achilles*, a sister ship to the *Ajax*, patrolling somewhere south of Capetown. A county class cruiser, HMS *Cumberland*, was also under the command of

Commodore Harwood but she was having a much needed self-refit in the Falkland Islands.

The Treaty of Versailles, signed after the defeat of the Germans in World War I, had enforced certain restrictions on German warship construction. Consequently, new ships were not to exceed 10,000 tons nor could they mount guns larger than 11 inches in diameter. To keep within these limits the Germans used welded joints and seams as opposed to our lapped and riveted seams and new diesel engines against our oil-fired steam turbines. This combination gave them a speed of 26 knots and they could cruise for 20,000 miles without refuelling. Each battleship was fitted with six 11-inch and eight 5.9-inch guns and by using new alloy metals for non-essential parts they remained within the legal weight restrictions.

Just before war was declared two of these pocket battleships, the *Admiral Graf Spee* and the *Deutschland*, were secretly put to sea with the sole object of harassing and sinking British merchant ships, so forming an effective blockade of Britain. The Germans confused our captured merchant seamen by changing the names of these battleships and rapidly altering areas of operations so they did not know which was raiding where. Quite soon a number of our ships were sunk in areas as far apart as the North Atlantic, South Atlantic and the Indian Ocean. The most recent of these was the *Doric Star* whose last reported position was off South-West Africa. It was our objective to track down whichever pocket battleship was operating in this area and stop her.

Commodore Harwood anticipated that the raider would make for the River Plate estuary – a vital focal point for all shipping. If his assumption were correct, he estimated she could be intercepted in that area about the 12 or 13 December. He ordered *Ajax* and *Achilles* to rendezvous with *Exeter* off the River Plate on 12 December and transferred his ensign to our ship, *Ajax*. The three cruisers then exercised the action procedure to be taken should the enemy appear.

The following day, 13 December 1939, dawned bright, clear

and calm. Shortly after 6am a ship was spotted on the horizon. The *Exeter* was sent to investigate and she reported back that it was a pocket battleship. 'Action Stations', and our three ships took up their positions with *Exeter* on our port beam and *Achilles* in line with us ahead. We set off at full speed with the battle ensigns flying at mast-head. My responsibilities at action stations were in the after end of the ship where, as the damage control officer, I was in charge of the after repair parties and their equipment below decks. My position was in the wardroom flat, which was just outside the wardroom and adjacent to the ammunition hoist carrying cordite and shells to 'X' turret above. My staff were scattered around the flat, sitting or lying on the deck in anticipation. We had no idea what was going on; all we could hear was the noise from our own guns blasting away. We were already in range of the German ship's deadly 11-inch guns and desperately speeding towards her to get in range for our 6-inch guns.

With the range rapidly closing, *Exeter* was put out of action by a direct hit. Down below in the wardroom the sick-bay staff had cleared away all the chairs and small furniture to make an auxiliary sick-bay. Someone had dumped a dining-chair near me so I thought 'I might as well sit down as stand up'. Then suddenly it happened. There was a horrible tearing noise followed by a mighty explosion. In the fraction of a second before all the lights went out, I saw that chair disintegrate and disappear. I found myself flying across the wardroom flat until I hit the far side bulkhead, closely followed by debris, shrapnel, bits of the ship's structure and I don't know what. All I can remember was calling out 'Jesus Christ'.

I could hear running water and the glug-glug of oil or hydraulic fluid from burst pipes. It was pitch dark except for an odd gleam overhead. Luckily my own hand torch was still on its lanyard around my neck. I shouted to the electrician, who was apparently still alive, for some emergency lighting which soon came on.

Then we saw the damage. An 11-inch delayed-action shell had ploughed through the upper deck, a distance of about ten feet over the wardroom flat, pierced the armoured ring of the ammunition hoist and exploded. All six handlers inside were killed; their bodies indistinguishable, disembodied and blown to hell. Why our own cordite and shells never exploded we shall never know. If they had it would have been the last of *Ajax*.

The dead could wait; we had lots of work to do. Sloshing around the flooded flat we managed to stem most of the flow from the ruptured pipes and clear away some of the torn structure and debris. Our wounded had to be transferred to our forward sick-bay for treatment. My own wounds were minor, in fact I thought the blood running down my leg was water or oil.

Whilst we were busy aft, the battle was still on and *Ajax* was steaming at full speed, zig-zagging to avoid being hit again. We were still firing from our two forward turrets; we didn't realise until later that the shell had dented the armoured ring of 'Y' turret, putting it out of action as well.

At the end of the day we heard the whole story. The captain broadcast over the ship's Tannoy that the pocket battleship had entered Uruguayan territorial waters at Montevideo. We later learned that the ship was the *Admiral Graf Spee*, retreating for a respite to repair her damaged hull. The *Ajax* and the *Achilles* remained as close as possible outside territorial waters at constant action stations, waiting for the *Graf Spee* to come out. During that time we managed to bury our dead comrades at sea.

After four days our spotter aircraft reported that the *Graf Spee* was leaving harbour. We stood by for further action for some considerable time only to learn that the *Graf Spee* steamed over a shallow sandbank, had her crew taken off, and blew up. Scuttled instead of coming out to fight. The following day her captain, Captain Hans Langsdorf, committed suicide.

PART THREE

FROM 1939 TO DUNKIRK

HISTORICAL NOTE

For the Royal Navy, the events of autumn 1939 bore an uncanny resemblance to those of 1914. Many senior Admirals had served as captains in the Grand Fleet of World War I and from the signal 'TOTAL GERMANY', transmitted on 3 September, there followed a familiar pattern of events. The battleships assembled at Scapa Flow and cruiser squadrons throughout the world ensured that enemy merchantmen vanished from the seas. For a second time this century a British Expeditionary Force was transported to France, with minimal interference from the Germany navy.

Hitler's *Kriegsmarine* was dwarfed by the Royal Navy, but it did possess several heavy cruisers designed for extended commerce raiding. One named after the heroic Admiral Graf von Spee sailed down the Channel on the eve of hostilities. Sporting six 11-inch guns and fitted with diesels that offered rapid acceleration as well as prodigious endurance, the *Graf Spee* had already been dubbed a 'pocket battleship'. While battlecruisers like the famous *Hood* or the French *Dunkerque* could have brought her to action if they had intercepted her, the *Graf Spee* was theoretically capable of outrunning any other ship she could not outfight. And she was not short of sea room. Raiding across the south Atlantic, she emulated *Emden*'s epic cruise in 1914, venturing into the Indian Ocean and forcing the Royal Navy to devote vast numbers of warships to hunting her. Ironically, *Graf Spee*'s luck ran out in the same waters as von Spee's original squadron.

Commodore Harwood's instincts took him towards the river Plate and the raider was confronted by the cruisers *Exeter, Ajax* and *Achilles*. Fortune favoured the brave: *Exeter* survived serious damage and the two light cruisers pressed home their attack despite the ineffectiveness of their 6-inch guns against the German's heavy armour. The *Graf Spee* sought sanctuary in neutral Montevideo. Bravery was followed by bluff and the German captain, believing himself blockaded by overwhelming forces, promptly scuttled his ship. Hitler's navy had been very publicly humiliated – the immolation of the *Graf Spee* being reported live on American radio – and Harwood's cruisers returned to an ecstatic reception in Britain.

The same ingredients of British boldness versus German caution seemed to be repeated in April 1940 when British and French forces intervened in Norway. The battlecruisers *Scharnhorst* and *Gneisenau* displayed none of the fighting spirit of their predecessors when they encountered HMS *Renown*; the Germans swinging away immediately, creating a stern chase in which the World War I veteran piled on steam in a vain attempt to overhaul Hitler's two most powerful warships. A German destroyer squadron in Narvik fjord was attacked by British destroyers twice, the second time supported by the veteran battleship HMS *Warspite*. The German squadron was annihilated and a U-boat that tried to intervene was sunk for good measure. Fleet Air Arm dive-bombers became the first carrier-borne aircraft to sink an enemy warship when they swooped on the *Königsberg*. However, the German navy soon had its revenge. *Scharnhorst* and *Gneisenau* ran into the aircraft carrier *Glorious* en route to the UK after the Norwegian campaign had been abandoned. With no air cover – and none of her aircraft airborne – she was sunk despite the heroic sacrifice of the escorting destroyers.

In May 1940 the German army burst through the Ardennes to crush the western allies. It enjoyed no significant advantage in numbers, and was outnumbered in both tanks and aircraft, but in *Blitzkrieg* the German army had a winning tactical method; and for determined professionalism its soldiers and airmen had no equals. It fell to Lord Gort, VC to grasp the nettle and save the British army to fight another day. He ordered the BEF to fall back on Dunkirk, effectively abandoning France to her fate. The Royal Navy confounded all expectations by evacuating the BEF aided in this supreme hour of need by all manner of volunteer craft. Rescuing the soldiers kept Britain in the war, but the German triumph posed the gravest danger to the United Kingdom since the French invasion scares of the 1770s. And conquest by Nazi Germany was a far grimmer prospect than a raid by one of Louis XV's generals. In the event, the RAF prevented the Luftwaffe from achieving air superiority over southern England. Germany's half-hearted invasion plans were abandoned in the autumn of 1940 and Hitler turned his attention to his true enemy: Soviet Russia.

After the fall of France, the German U-boats began to operate from the French Atlantic coast. Freed from the long passage around Scotland, they were able to mount increasingly deadly attacks on Britain's Atlantic lifeline. For three years, under the ruthless direction of Admiral Dönitz, German U-boats waged a savage war from the Caribbean to the Arctic, the most critical battles occuring in the bleak wastes of the North Atlantic. Beyond the range of land-based aircraft, convoys and their escorts struggled against an invisible foe whose presence was only discovered as torpedoes slammed into hulls. In World War I, from 1916 to 1918, the British Army had shouldered an increasing share of the Allied burden, fighting and ultimately defeating the main body of the German army; but in World War II, in the critical years of 1940–3, Britain's national survival depended on the Royal Navy. No amount of 'digging for victory' in Britain could compensate for the loss of imported food and raw materials defended at such cost by British and Canadian warships.

Pre-war faith in ASDIC (sonar) was confounded by experience. Wartime conditions proved very different from peacetime exercises in the Channel and convoys seldom had either modern escort vessels or peace-time-trained crews. In any case, the most daring U-boat skippers ran in on the surface at night, relying on the U-boat's low silhouette to hide them from red-eyed lookouts. Supported by their own long-range aircraft, and assembled into 'Wolf Packs', the U-boats were able to make co-ordinated attacks against which the frantic efforts of a few corvettes could do little. Practical military necessity made for a brutal war. Survivors huddled in open boats were often seen at the height of a battle, only to drift into oblivion. Crews of tankers, or freighters packed with iron ore, were lucky to get to a boat if their ship was hit.

The war in the North Atlantic hinged as much on scientists as on seamen, and the pendulum of technical advantage swung to and fro. The British acquired radar to detect U-boats running on the surface, and the early U-boat 'aces' were killed or captured. But German intelligence cracked British naval codes and the U-boats were able to ambush a succession of convoys, concentrating all available submarines against overworked escorts. However, Britain's priceless ULTRA decrypts provided fuller and more frequent intelligence of U-boat activity; convoys were re-routed around the 'Wolf Packs', and Dönitz's men found themselves searching empty sea. The turning-point occurred in 1943 as a combination of very-long-range aircraft, centimetric radar and improved anti-submarine weapons like 'Hedgehog' inflicted catastrophic losses on the U-boats. Had Churchill's cabinet managed to prise a few squadrons of four-engined aircraft away from Bomber Command a little sooner, the U-boats would have been neutralised earlier.

New technology was complemented by new 'scientific' tactics, honed ashore by a 'wargaming' programme, the fruit of pioneering operational research. Statistical analysis of every convoy battle and the first-hand experiences of convoy commanders were combined to create an ever-expanding data base.

Following the scheme of 'setting a thief to catch a thief', veteran British submarine commanders added their experience: even ex-submariner Admiral Horton, C-in-C Western Approaches met his match (at the hands of a WRNS officer!) when he tried his skills against state-of-the-art escort tactics at a map exercise in Liverpool.

America's colossal industrial resources enabled merchant shipping losses to be made good, and a vast army could cross the Atlantic, assembling in England for the liberation of Europe. It was fortunate indeed that that army made its landing when it did. In 1945 the technical advantage was suddenly regained by Germany: its Type XXI U-boats rendered most Allied anti-submarine weapons obsolete. A new armada was poised in the Norwegian fjords, but the crews never had time to train. As the avenging Russian army swept towards Berlin, thousands of German naval personnel were thrown into the land battle. The Baltic training areas were overrun and the former commander of U-boats enjoyed a brief interlude as Hitler's successor before the Nazi state was obliterated. Winston Churchill rightly regarded the U-boat as the single greatest threat to British survival: had the Royal Navy failed to defeat Dönitz's submarines, the United Kingdom would have lost the war.

German surface ships made a succession of forays into the Atlantic, in the case of the 'pocket battleship' *Scheer* into the Indian Ocean as well; *Scharn-horst* and *Gneisenau* making a particularly deadly pair of surface raiders. One convoy survived thanks to the presence of the battleship *Ramillies*, two others were granted time to scatter by the gallant sacrifice of their armed merchant cruiser escorts, *Rawalpindi* and *Jervis Bay* respectively. The most famous raider, *Bismarck*, was sent to the bottom on her maiden voyage – without sinking a single merchant ship – but not before sinking the pride of the pre-war Navy, HMS *Hood*. In a ghastly reminder of Jutland, the old battlecruiser blew up and took all but three of her complement down with her. Brought to bay by a handful of Swordfish biplanes, *Bismarck* was destroyed by *King George V* and *Rodney*. The subsequent escape up the English channel of her consort, the heavy cruiser *Prinz Eugen* together with *Scharnhorst* and *Gneisenau* was presented as a triumph by German propaganda. In fact the return of this powerful squadron from Brest to Germany effectively ended the surface campaign in the Atlantic.

As the Battle of the Atlantic intensified, a new and even more savage campaign began in the world's most unforgiving seas. The German invasion of Russia in June 1941 transformed the war. If Hitler could knock out Russia – as the German army had managed to do in 1917 – the Nazi war machine would control the resources of eastern Europe and the oil reserves of the Caucasus. Having carved up Poland in alliance with Hitler, Stalin was suddenly transformed into an ally and the Royal Navy was charged with escorting supplies of war material to Russia's Arctic ports. With the Luftwaffe based in Norway and furiously learning how to launch torpedoes from aircraft – a tactic it had fortunately disdained as impractical before the war – and most major enemy surface units concentrating in the fjords, it was clear that the Arctic convoys, would meet with determined opposition.

In the land of the midnight sun, there was no cover from enemy aircraft, but only the seasonal retreat of the polar ice cap granted adequate sea room. In the darkness of winter, the sea conditions were awful beyond description. Convoys were assembled off Iceland and shepherded around Norway to deliver their vital cargoes; with little or no protection against air attack. *Bismarck*'s sistership, the formidable *Tirpitz*, was soon ensconced in her Arctic lair, poised to lead an overwhelming assault on the convoys and their escorts. The mistaken belief that she was about to pounce led to the notorious order for Convoy PQ17 to scatter. Dispersed to avoid destruction by the enemy battleship, the merchantships were picked off by a deadly combination of U-boats and bomber aircraft.

The German surface forces were frustrated again and again as British signals intelligence betrayed their plans. Interceptions that were achieved were defeated by the incredibly aggressive defence mounted by the Royal Navy escorts. Often hopelessly inferior to the powerful enemy cruisers, the escorts' boldness culminated in the Battle of the Barents Sea in which a far stronger German squadron was driven off and the convoy saved. Hitler was so furious that he sacked Admiral Raeder, the German C-in-C, and ordered all heavy ships to be paid off. Thus Admiral Dönitz succeeded to command the *Kriegsmarine*. He preserved some of the major units but *Scharnhorst* was intercepted and sunk by a surface action group led by *Duke of York* in December 1943. *Tirpitz* would remain a terrible menace until cornered at her anchorage by a succession of Fleet Air Arm strikes, and X-craft miniature submarine attacks. She was administered the coup-de-grace by 617 Squadron, RAF, in 1944. Russian co-operation during the Arctic convoys was marred by Bolshevik suspicion: the last time British forces landed in Murmansk they had come to strangle the revolution in its cradle. The unforgiving attitude of the Soviet authorities continued after 1945 when families that had hosted British sailors were promptly arrested by the NKVD. Only in the last years of the Communist regime was the contribution of the Arctic convoys and the sacrifice of hundreds of British sailors finally acknowledged.

The Royal Navy's base at Malta had been vacated by British capital ships well in advance of Italy's declaration of war in May 1940. But before the Royal Navy could take on the powerful Italian fleet, it had the disagreeable task of neutralising its former French allies. There could be no question of the Germans laying their hands on the powerful French squadron based in North Africa. Negotiations having failed, it was Vice-Admiral Somerville's unpleasant duty to sink that which the French would not surrender. The ensuing bombardment of Mers-el-Kebir was the nadir of Anglo-French relations in this century.

The battleship *Bretagne* blew up and sank; *Provence* was damaged and over a thousand French sailors died. A similar battle at Alexandria was fortunately averted but a hastily prepared attack on Dakar in September 1940, was driven off by French naval units and aircraft.

In July 1940 the Italian fleet put to sea to cover a large convoy sailing to Libya, carrying reinforcements for their large army in North Africa. The Royal Navy intervened. Force 'H' sortieing from Gibraltar and the aircraft carrier *Eagle* launching its elderly Swordfish biplanes against the Italian fleet. Enemy shore-based aircraft failed to support their fleet and the heavy units clashed briefly in what became known as the battle of Calabria. Jutland veteran HMS *Warspite* immediately straddled the battleship *Guilio Cesare* but contact was broken before long. A belated Italian air strike landed bombs dangerously close to HMS *Ark Royal*.

On 11 November 1940 the aircraft-carrier HMS *Illustrious* flew off 21 Swordfish. They made their stately progress towards the Italian naval base at Taranto, where all six Italian battleships lay at anchor. They achieved complete surprise, dropping torpedoes by the ghostly light of parachute flares as they weaved past lines of barrage balloons. Three battleships were hit and left with their decks awash and keels resting on the harbour bottom. Although Italian shipyards put right the physical damage within a year, the moral impact proved more lasting and subsequent Italian naval activity was characterised by excessive caution.

Subsequent British naval operations went to the opposite extreme, as the Royal Navy first escorted British and Commonwealth divisions to Greece and then rescued them from the inevitable disaster. General O'Connor's brilliant victories in North Africa were cut short on Churchill's orders; the army poised to overrun the last Italian ports was halted and broken up to provide a scratch force in Greece. Hopelessly outnumbered and outclassed by the formidable German army then assembling in Yugoslavia and Bulgaria, this expeditionary force went the way of its predecessors in Norway and France. The Balkan *Blitzkrieg* began in April, German forces taking just over a fortnight to cut their way to the Peloponnese. For the third time in twelve months, the Royal Navy evacuated thousands of exhausted troops from open beaches and minor ports. The Luftwaffe reigned supreme, and to be caught inshore by daylight was to court disaster. Nevertheless, over 50,000 men were brought off safely.

Over 30,000 British troops were posted on Crete. Unhelpfully, the island's main ports are all on the northern coast. Ships were condemned to a long voyage around the island, all within easy range of enemy airstrips in southern Greece. The British garrison was clustered around the three airfields which were left operational despite the withdrawal of the few surviving RAF fighters. On 20 May, the Luftwaffe airstrikes intensified as Ju-52 transports thundered low over the coast, white canopies scattering behind them. Despite fearful losses, the German paratroops managed to secure enough of Maleme airfield to fly in reinforcements. The lodgement survived desperate counter-attacks and continued to expand. Another evacuation loomed. In the last week of May, the Royal Navy extricated the garrison but incessant air attacks sank the cruisers *Gloucester*, *Fiji* and *Calcutta* and the destroyers *Kelly*, *Kashmir*, *Greyhound*, *Hereward*, and *Imperial*. With another three cruisers badly hit and the battleship *Barham* damaged, Admiral Cunningham was asked if the sacrifice was justified. His observation that it takes three years to build a ship, but it would take three hundred years to rebuild a tradition cannot be gainsaid.

Besieged from the air, Malta came perilously close to defeat. Convoys to resupply the island were escorted by the bulk of the Mediterranean fleet including battleships and aircraft carriers. British 'U' class submarines operating from Malta were obliged to submerge during the day, surfacing in the harbour at night when the bombers had departed. The 10th Flotilla's attacks on

Italian shipping drove General Rommel to distraction as his Afrika Korps ran out of fuel and ammunition. Enemy ground operations were frustrated and delayed, and the steady attrition of the Italian merchant marine could not be countered by new construction. However, the submariners' own losses were severe too.

On 6 June 1944 the Allied armies landed in Normandy, withstood the German counter-attacks and broke out to destroy the German forces in northern France. By August, German losses in the 'Falaise pocket' exceeded 400,000 and the issue of the war in Europe was no longer in doubt. The D-Day landings were such a spectacular success that it is often assumed that victory was inevitable, provided the Royal Navy co-ordinated the vast Allied armada of some 1,200 warships (almost 80 per cent of them British). Arguably, by the dawn of 6 June the invasion was bound to succeed provided the weather held; Allied deception measures and catastrophic strategic decisions by the German high command left the Normandy area relatively lightly manned with reserves too distant to intervene in time. The success of British and Canadian anti-submarine forces over the previous two years ensured that the German navy was in no position to contest control of the Channel. By the summer of 1944 the Germans had lost the Battle of the Atlantic. There were 36 U-boats waiting for the invasion in their indestructible concrete fortresses on the west coast of France, but their attempts to get at the troop ships were frustrated by six British and four Canadian anti-submarine warfare groups which included three escort carriers and over fifty destroyers and frigates. Despite desperate interventions by the handful of remaining German destroyers and torpedo boats, the Allied navies conducted over 300,000 men, 50,000 vehicles and 100,000 tons of supplies to the beachheads in the first six days of the invasion.

With the liberation of France underway, the Royal Navy was finally able to release enough major units to the Far East to resume operations against Japan. There is a legendary naval signal from December 1941 when two British convoys met in mid-Atlantic. 'Commence hostilities with Japan' flashed one escort; 'Permission to finish breakfast first' came the reply. Such naval sang-froid masked the disagreeable truth that by the time Japan declared war, the Royal Navy was already at full stretch fighting in the Atlantic, Mediterranean and Arctic. Disastrous government decisions of the 1920s and 30s had seen the naval base at Singapore expanded and fortified but no ships built to operate from it. The Imperial Japanese Navy, created in the image of the Royal Navy and a British ally during World War I, was now poised to turn on its former mentor.

War with Japan had been imminent since the US oil embargo imposed in the summer of 1941. The Royal Navy proposed to send one or two modernised Queen Elizabeth class battleships, plus four of the old 'R' class and a couple of aircraft-carriers, to Singapore. However, the damage or loss of three battleships in the Mediterranean and the damaging of the carrier *Indomitable* while working up in the Caribbean frustrated any sensible deployment. Overruling both Admiral Pound and his chief-of-staff Admiral Phillips, Winston Churchill insisted on sending *Prince of Wales* and the World War I battlecruiser, *Repulse*, without waiting for additional units. In retrospect, it is perhaps just as well that Pound's idea of ordering both Nelson class battleships to the Far East was overtaken by events. 'Force Z', as the battleship group was christened, included five destroyers and was led by the prickly Admiral Phillips, whose opposition to Churchill led him to be ordered from London to Ceylon to become commander-in-chief, Far Eastern Fleet.

On 8 December 1941, 'Force Z' sailed from Singapore to intercept Japanese invasion forces bound for Malaya. The bulk of Japan's naval airpower was on the other side of the Pacific after its attack on Pearl Harbor, and the troopships were escorted by a few cruisers and (as distant cover) two modernised battlecruisers. Air cover was supposed to be provided by the handful of obsolescent RAF aircraft in Malaya. Communications failures, excellent scouting by Japanese submarines and a mistaken report of landings further south led to 'Force Z' being attacked by Japanese shore-based bombers flying from Indochina. Phillips, a dedicated battleship Admiral who had been notoriously sceptical of airpower, had perhaps based his judgement on the often ineffective high-level bombing conducted by enemy forces in the Mediterranean. But Japan's Mitsubishi G-3M twin-enginned torpedo bombers not only had a combat radius of over 1,200 miles – enabling them to strike so unexpectedly – but well-trained aircrew able to deliver co-ordinated torpedo strikes from both beams. Both battleships were sunk, Phillips going down with *Prince of Wales*. His flagship was the first modern battleship to be sunk by air attack while at sea and able to manoeuvre freely – unlike the anchored Italian battlefleet at Taranto a year earlier.

Singapore surrendered on 15 February 1942: the greatest military defeat ever suffered by British forces. The River Plate veteran *Exeter* was among the casualties when Japanese surface forces appeared off Java. Then the Japanese aircraft-carrier fleet arrived in the Indian Ocean, raiding as far as Ceylon (Sri Lanka) and sinking the British carrier *Hermes* in the process. Although the four 'R' class battleships had now rounded the Cape, without a modern aircraft-carrier force, there was little the Royal Navy could do but wait for the storm to pass.

By late 1944 the British had finally assembled an effective carrier task force (equipped with American aircraft) in the Indian Ocean. The surviving King George V class battleships, including the fourth unit, *Howe* and the French *Richelieu*, were fast enough to accompany carriers in action. Airstrikes on Japanese bases in the Dutch East Indies were achieved with the carriers supported by US-style fleet train of tankers. As 'Task Force 57', under the overall command of US Admiral Nimitz, the British Pacific Fleet attacked Japanese island air bases from Formosa (Taiwan) to Okinawa. There they received the suicidal attentions of Japanese Kamikaze aircraft which caused serious damage to several ships. On the night of 15–16 May 1945 the Royal Navy fought its last major surface action, when a destroyer flotilla exploited freak radar conditions to intercept and sink the heavy-cruiser *Haguro* in a classic torpedo attack.

The Royal Navy ended World War II second only in size to the US Navy. There were 864,000 people serving on ship or shore, including at one point 74,000 women in the WRNS. This incredible expansion and the unprecedented number of 'hostilities only' personnel brought inevitable difficulties, but the second German attempt to strave Britain into submission this century had been defeated. The seas were made safe and the armies of the New World could cross them.

Lieutenant Frank Layard, RN

In the piping days of peace between the two world wars, when perhaps there were more opportunities and more time for relaxation, life in destroyers was particularly good. There was much inter-ship and inter-flotilla rivalry and competition of course, but when altogether in Sliema, or in Portsmouth, there was also a great entente and comradeship throughout the Destroyer Force which made for a very happy existence.

Wardroom guest nights in particular could be the occasion for much fun and hilarity. After the preliminary consumption of a good quantity of gin, all would sit down to dinner. The food would not be exactly up to Savoy standards but the messman always made a special effort to put on quite a reasonable meal which would be washed down with some of the best red wine. When the table was cleared the port would be passed and the King's health drunk.

After the port had been round twice, the mess President for the evening (who was generally the captain) would order a round of brandy 'à la Russe'. This consisted of a liqueur glass of brandy with a slice of lemon balanced on the top of the glass and a spoonful of sugar on the lemon. When all were served there would be a shout of 'Viva, Viva, Viva, Bungo', at which everyone immediately took the lemon and sugar in one hand, tossed off the brandy and then immediately put the lemon and sugar in their mouth. The effect was somewhat breathtaking but extremely pleasant and was almost immediately repeated, so that everyone now was gaining good flying speed. The record of 'Night and Day' would then be put on the gramophone which everyone would sing very lustily. By this time all present as they rose from the table were more than ready for some active and strenuous amusement.

There were several ways in which energies could be expended. For instance, chair tricks. The old wooden wardroom chairs were heavy and very strong and would stand up to any amount of rough usage. There could be a race by two or more competitors through the backs of these chairs which was guaranteed to wipe off the front studs of any boiled shirt and would cause excruciating pain to all but the slimmest when their hips became firmly jammed as they tried to squeeze through. There were other tricks which only the more agile would attempt. For example, two chairs would be placed back-to-back about a yard apart with a broom handle stretched across the back and a shoe pushed down over each of the four corners of the chair backs. The competitor would then be handed a walking-stick and would take his seat on the broom stick with his feet crossed in front of him, keeping his balance with the aid of the walking-stick. He now had to try and remove in turn each of the four shoes from the chair backs with the walking stick. As soon as he raised the stick off the deck and lost its support he started to overbalance and so the movement of flicking off each shoe had to be done with the utmost speed and precision so that the stick could be grounded again if the competitor was to remain on his perch.

In another trick the victim had to sit on a chair and then remove a pin from the bottom of the farside back leg with his teeth without touching the deck. Only the most agile could get round and down behind the chair altogether. There were other no less testing tricks requiring good balance which was generally a bit lacking by that time.

'Captain D's shoot' provided plenty of amusement. The person representing the captain of the firing ship was seated at the end of the wardroom table clad in oilskin and sou'wester with five darts in his hand and a dart board representing the target was fixed to the bulkhead at the other end of the table. The staff conducting the shoot then took up their stations. Two each side of the chair, two armed with soda water siphons in front and to the side of the chair, and two with match boxes level with the dart board. At the command 'Carry out the practice ordered' all lights were extinguished, the chair was violently rocked to and fro to represent the motion of the ship, soda water to represent spray was liberally squirted in the captain's face and matches to represent star shells were flicked up from both sides to illuminate the target.

Thirty seconds was allowed for the shoot during which time the captain had to get off his five darts but it was seldom, as far as I can remember, that the target was ever hit.

Another rather expensive game was sometimes played. Competitors were placed with their backs to the ship's side on the port side of the mess and would each be handed a ten-inch gramophone record of the old breakable sort. The scuttles on the starboard side were then opened and the object of the game was to hurl the record through the scuttle.

On our way out to Australia war was declared. I remember being on the bridge with the Second Officer, a big tall fellow called Ring. He always had a bit of a sardonic twist to him. He said, 'Well, this will be something for you to write home about: it's war.' I wondered what the hell he was talking about. To me war being declared meant nothing.

When we reached Australia we had to go and be fitted with a 6-inch gun. The gun's crew was made up from us apprentices and various members of the crew. We had to go over to the naval base at Rushcutter's Bay and learn all about guns. When the time came for us to sail they put on board a DEMS (Defensively Equipped Merchant Ship) gunner, a Royal Navy fellow to look after the gun and see that we knew what we were doing. We steamed out to give this gun a trial, out through Sydney Harbour. I was the sight setter. I used to stand at the side of the gun and say, 'Range so-and-so . . .' We loaded it up, the gunner said 'Fire,' and there was such a clatter we weren't ready for it. I was knocked flat to the ground. Everyone else was flat around me. There was a great roar and commotion from below in the deck house where all the stewards and cooks lived because nobody had told them we were firing and all the bunks and everything fell down.

We didn't feel that we were at war.

Sub-Lieutenant John Roxburgh, RN

Come August 1939 it was obvious the war was coming. Convoys for merchant shipping had already started. I was serving in the destroyer *Walpole*. I'll never forget the Prime Minister, Neville Chamberlain, announcing the start of war, at eleven o'clock on a Sunday morning, 3rd September. After that we were at war, our depth-charges were primed and we were ready to go. A quarter of an hour after war had been declared we found a submarine echo which we attacked and dropped eleven charges. We were never credited with a submarine and I should think it was quite likely a shoal of fish or a rock, but it really got one's mind racing. There was I, a young chap of twenty, actually dropping things to kill people. It was quite exciting.

Stoker 2nd Class Vernon Coles, RN

My first ship was HMS *Faulknor* under Captain Charles Daniels. The day war broke out we were the leader of the

8th Destroyer Flotilla in Scapa Flow. We all had the wind up, expecting torpedoes all over the place because we were in such a vulnerable position. However we eased down after about ten days, when each day became the same as the next – all part of life's routine. We were at action stations at five o'clock in the morning and again at sundown, so it was rather tiring.

The battle fleet was taken to sea under the command of 'Big Gun Forbes' – Admiral Sir Charles Forbes. The flagship was HMS *Nelson* and we used to accompany HMS *Rodney* and the aircraft-carrier *Ark Royal* too. We'd bring them in and they'd stay in for a few days and we'd go back out again on U-boat sweeps.

I saw my first real action on 14 September 1939. We were exercising with *Ark Royal* and three destroyers off St Kilda. Suddenly, during the mid-afternoon, there were two terrific explosions – we went to action stations immediately. We learnt that a German U-boat had fired two torpedoes at *Ark Royal*. Their torpedoes had magnetic heads on so, when they came within the magnetic field of *Ark Royal*, they both exploded. Otherwise she would have been hit.

We sailed straight down the torpedo tracks, dropped a full pattern of depth-charges and up she came. It was U-39. We took them all prisoner; we rescued the men in the whalers and then brought them on board. They were badly shaken, as anybody would have been on the receiving end of a couple of depth-charges.

Captain Daniels had the German U-boat captain interrogated. I talked to some of the German prisoners. They thought they were going to be shot and they were actually surprised at the way they were treated. We had to communicate with them in sign language, but we gave them cigarettes and things. They were rather wet when they came aboard, so they were supplied with blankets while all their clothes and underwear were taken down to the boiler room to dry off. Their vests all had the

German swastika on, so off they came during the night – they were taken as souvenirs. The Germans were most upset about that.

We off-loaded them in Scapa Flow. That was the first U-boat of the war to go down and they were the first naval prisoners-of-war.

Lieutenant Charles Lamb, RN

HMS *Courageous* sailed from Plymouth under cover of darkness on 3rd September 1939. She was provided with an escort of four destroyers. It was anticipated that the ship would attract U-boat attacks, when the destroyers would achieve the miraculous results with their Asdic which were forecast so confidently. The presence of the ship would also serve to distract the attention of the enemy from the merchant ships and their valuable cargoes and their passengers, hurrying home to the British Isles. The two Swordfish squadrons (24 Swordfish) on board would provide the major deterrent to the U-boats.

If *Courageous* had been a battleship she would have been escorted by a small fleet of vessels, none of which would have been permitted to leave the screen except to hunt in the immediate vicinity. Our four destroyers were there to protect *Courageous*, but they also had to go submarine-hunting and answer calls for help from distressed shipping, and throughout those opening days of the war there were seldom more than two escorts within sight of the ship. *Courageous* presented an easy target.

On board, the attitude of everyone was carefree and casual. We carried no fighter aircraft, and hundreds of miles west of the Scilly Isles there appeared to be no need. We flew on various types of search in answer to the distress calls that came flooding in from all directions. In the aircraft, our only means of communicating with the parent ship, if an answer was required, was with an Aldis lamp when she was within sight.

The transition from peace to war takes time, and in *Courage-*

ous it wasn't until the following Sunday, 17th September, that the ship's company really woke up to the fact that we were at war; and even then we needed a German submarine's captain to bring the fact home. His demonstration was most convincing: at eight o'clock, on a warm Sunday evening, he fired two torpedoes at the ship, which struck us on the port side, almost simultaneously, and we sank in twenty minutes.

At three in the afternoon, on that same Sunday 17th September, eight pilots and observers had trooped into the wardroom for tea. We had been standing-by all day, in case of emergency calls, and there was only an hour to go before the other squadron took over the duty. As our Flight Commander pointed out, if we had to take off before our duty ended at four o'clock, it would be our last opportunity to eat or drink for many hours.

My observer, Robert Wall, brought his sandwiches to the place next to me, and we sat in silence, sipping our tea. All of a sudden our peace was shattered by the blare of the ship's bugler sounding off 'flying stations' on the tannoy. I joined the general scramble out of the wardroom and up the ladders to the crewroom in the island, where we kept our flying clothing. Clad in our overalls and helmets and goggles, we ran to our aircraft. While we ran up our engines and tested the magnetos, the observers were briefed by the Operations Officer. They then sprinted down to the deck to their aircraft, carrying their navigation instruments and Bigsworth Boards – a square wooden frame fitted with parallel rulers to which they clipped a plotting diagram, or a chart, so that they could navigate with the board resting on their knees in the confined space of the rear cockpit. Behind them, facing aft, sat the telegraphist air gunner (TAG), Doug Hemingway, who, as well as manning the Lewis gun when it was needed, also tuned the aircraft's radio to the ship's W/T frequency to keep a listening watch.

When Wall had climbed into the rear cockpit, and attached himself to the aircraft by the safety wire which clipped on to the harness between the observer and the air gunner's legs – obviously known as the 'Jockstrap' – he called me on the voice-pipe to tell me what we were about to do. Rubber voice-pipes between both cockpits connected to the earpieces of all three flying helmets, known as Gosport Tubes, and were very effective. It was surprising how clearly one could hear by this primitive method of communication.

We were the last of the eight Swordfish to take off and while we watched the others roll down the middle of the flight-deck, and clamber into the air, Wall briefed me down the voice-pipe. Apparently a big passenger liner, the SS *Kaliristan*, was being threatened by a U-boat on the surface. The German had ordered the crew and passengers to take to their boats, before it sank the ship. She was thought to be ninety or one hundred miles to the south, on the Atlantic edge of the Bay of Biscay. When I opened the throttle that afternoon I was the last pilot to take-off from *Courageous* – and was to be the last to land.

Two of the ship's four escorts raced off at maximum speed to the reported sighting of SS *Kaliristan*, and *Courageous* altered course in the same direction and increased her speed to 25 knots – almost the maximum. But because of the W/T silence she was unable to inform us. I heard later that the destroyers recovered the passengers and the crew, but met another merchant ship and transferred them, and they all got home safely. An attack was made on the submarine, which was still on the surface, and succeeded in making it dive. Six of the aircraft all landed safely before Robert and I, and the aircraft on our immediate right, had reached the furthermost point of our search.

When we returned there was no sign of *Courageous*, and we began our square-search immediately. We had a questionable forty-five minutes of flying time remaining, but would almost certainly run out of fuel at a quarter to eight. I flew four minutes to the west, four minutes to the north, eight minutes to the east and then eight minutes to the south, and altered course to start the fifth leg – sixteen minutes to the west – with a sinking heart.

At the end of that leg, if we reached it, we would have been searching for forty minutes, and might have four or five minutes' petrol remaining. Neither Wall nor I spoke. We were both thinking of Nigel Playfair and his young observer, exactly a week before, and it seemed certain that like them, we too were to disappear without trace. It would be dark within an hour, and the mist which obscured the horizon was deepening with evening shadow. There was no possible chance of rescue out there, five hundred miles west of the Scilly Isles.

At the end of that sixteen-minute leg to the west, flying into the sun, which was only a few degrees above the hazy horizon, I began my turn to the north, cursing the lack of horizon which made accurate flying difficult. The blind-flying panel and artificial horizon had not appeared on the scene then, and all we had to guide us was a Reid and Sigrist Turn-and-Bank indicator, and some red mercury in a small thermometer tube, to tell the pilot whether he was flying nose-up or nose-down. As we began to swing, the setting sun rolled away over my left shoulder and its rays were reflected by something which glinted on the water for a split second, way out on the port beam; I checked the turn and steered towards it. Could it be the ship? There was something there, quite definitely . . . and then I saw it . . . the elongated hull and blunt projection of a conning-tower, sticking upwards – a U-boat – possibly five or six miles away. I yelled into the voice-pipe, 'There's a submarine on the port bow, about five miles away. I think we can reach it . . . it will give us something to do . . .'

'What *are* you going to do?' asked Wall. 'Ditch beside it?'

'We'll attack it first! I've still got the bombs.' I had been reluctant to jettison them until just before we ditched, because without them we would have been flying without any purpose, and would have been quite impotent.

'Okay,' said Robert, in a resigned voice. Like me, he was hating the inactivity of just droning along, waiting for the engine to splutter into silence as the fuel ran out. At least our last moments in the air would have some purpose. Anything was better than just flogging on and on, waiting for the engine to stop.

Putting the aircraft into a shallow dive I throttled back as the speed built up, and set the 'Mickey-Mouse' bomb-release so that they would drop together. This was going to be a once-only attack. There was insufficient fuel for more than one dive.

I stared hard at the submarine. It seemed to be growing in size but not getting any nearer. Then it dawned on me – the visibility distance was much greater than we thought. It was well over fifteen miles away and it wasn't a submarine at all – it was the ship! The conning-tower was the ship's island.

'It's the *Courageous*!' I yelled, and, jettisoning the bombs, I throttled right back, to stretch the dive into a glide.

I could feel the tension of the two occupants of the rear cockpit, craning their heads into the slipstream and holding their breath. Had any one of us looked around the sea on this final approach we might have seen the feathery wake of a U-boat's periscope, for somewhere in the immediate vicinity, with *Courageous* in her sights, a German submarine skipper was holding his breath too, and closing in for the kill.

When a carrier turns into wind to receive her aircraft, it seems to be a lazy, leisurely movement to the approaching pilot, about to land. The bow starts to turn, imperceptibly to begin with, and then more emphatically in a graceful sweeping arc. The stern seems to kick the other way, as though resisting the motion, and then gives way in a rush, causing a mighty wash astern. While the ship is turning, the wind across the flight-deck can be violently antagonistic to a pilot who tries to land before the turn has been completed. Since we were about to run out of petrol, the turn seemed interminable, and after one half-circuit of the ship I decided to risk the cross-wind, and the violent turning motion, and get down before it was too late.

'Hey!' protested Robert. 'What the hell are you doing? She's only half-way round, and the batsman's waving us off like mad!' He could not know that the petrol indicator had been showing 'E' for Empty for the last ten minutes at least. The Swordfish has a Bristol Pegasus Three radial engine which obscures the flight-deck – and the ship – in the very last stages of a deck-landing. Normally, by approaching in a gentle turn to port, right down to the deck, it is possible to keep the deck in sight until straightening up; then it is necessary to look between the engine cylinders, at 'eleven and twelve o'clock', when the yellow bats come into view for a split second as the deck swoops upwards at an alarming rate.

That afternoon he was being very helpful – by waving his bats around his head in a frenzied 'go round again' sign – and I could see him all the way down to the deck. He had every right to wave me off. Apart from the obvious danger of landing on a restricted area, which was swinging violently to starboard as the bow swung to port, I was much too high. In case my petrol gave out in the last few vital seconds, I had to keep my height, to remain within the gliding distance all the way down.

The Swordfish has a strong fixed undercarriage, an enormous rudder, and very good brakes. If our landing was rather like that of a clumsy seagull alighting on the water in a rush, it was nevertheless successful. The hook picked up a wire and all was well.

We walked through the hangar and down to the wardroom without knowing that my crab-like landing was the last ever on that flight-deck. As the ship turned out of wind she must have crossed the bows of the U-boat, providing the German with a straightforward beam-on shot. His two torpedoes hit us almost simultaneously, just as Robert and I were stepping into the wardroom. If the core of the earth exploded, and the universe split from pole to pole, it could sound no worse. Every light went out and the deck reared upwards, throwing me backwards, and the hot blast which followed tore at the skin on my face and my clothes. There was something Satanic about it, and unreal. In the sudden deathly silence which followed I knew that the ship had died.

In the wardroom passage the deafening silence was broken by the tinkling of glass, breaking somewhere; and the tiny sound of trickling water. There was also a persistent whisper of noise which at first I failed to identify. Then it dawned on me that it was the sound of men breathing.

The bulkhead behind me was now partly underfoot; and facing aft, I was standing with my left foot on the deck, which sloped upwards to starboard at an amazing angle. My other foot was on the wall. The silence was frightening. I supposed that the ship's engine had been blown to bits.

When the torpedoes ripped open the ship's side and she rolled over to port at such as incredible angle it was obvious at once that she had been struck a mortal blow. In the first few seconds the whole length of the port side of the flight-deck hung suspended a few feet from the sea, crushing the ship's boats which burst through the sea up to the surface, swept from their stowages on the decks below. In those opening seconds, the aircraft in the hangar slid to port, crashing against each other and against the port bulkhead, adding to the uneven top-weight and increasing the ship's list; furniture in the mess-decks broke from deck fastenings and slid crazily to port; petrol tanks burst, flooding down into the decks below, and an evil slick of oil and petrol quickly spread over the calm sea, surrounding the ship with an inflammable mixture which might have burst into flame – and a massive explosion – at any moment; hundreds of men were hurled into the sea from all parts of the ship, some being sucked from their underwater compartments. The ship's ring-main was severed at once, extinguishing all the lights and cutting all power to every piece of machinery throughout, silencing the broadcasting system so that not even the essential pipe, 'abandon ship', could be made, and in one fraction of time a bustling community, humming with life, became a silent floating tomb. The other event had no effect on the ship's diminishing seaworthiness, but was perhaps even more of a blow to morale than any other single factor, for some object –

probably a mast aerial – fell across the lanyard which operated
the steam siren on the funnel, and as though to counteract the
ghostly silence below, a long mournful blast, went on and on
and on, as though the ship herself was crying out in her death
agonies.

Before I could move from the darkness of the ante-room I
heard a voice calling for help. Inside, by groping about, I found
that a big, glass-fronted bookcase had fallen on top of the
Principal Medical Officer, a huge pot-bellied Surgeon-
Commander named Clifford-Brown. With the strength born
of the desperation inspired by his cries it did not take long to lift
it – just enough for him to crawl out and up. I could see the
scuttles were open on the port side too so I propelled his colossal
bulk into the passage, which led straight off aft to the quarterdeck. A long way ahead the doorway out to the deck was
flooded with sunlight, like a bright light at the end of a long
tunnel, inviting everyone to safety. I turned uphill, to starboard,
into the intense darkness, to get my Mae West. I had to clamber
up the sloping deck. Fortunately my cabin door was open. I then
tried to remember in which drawer the silver combs I had
bought for the bridesmaids were lying; with them were two
fivers and my wedding ring. But at that moment the deck under
my feet gave a shuddering heave and lifted uneasily and the
slope to port increased, and all the books from the shelves above
my desk tumbled downwards, striking me on the head and
shoulders. I panicked, thinking she was going to roll over, and
before I knew that I had moved I was out in the passage again,
the combs forgotten. The bridesmaids would have treasured
them even more if they had been rescued from a sinking ship.

When I stumbled out into the fresh air the stern was pointing
due west towards the sun. When I looked aft I saw the twin
periscopes of the U-boat which had just torpedoed us. The
thought that the enemy was lying just under the surface, gloat-
ing at the sight of a great ship writhing in her death-throes, was
obscene, and I hurried up the sloping deck to join the group on

the 4.7-inch gun. Lieutenant Ingram had taken charge. He was trying to train the barrel downwards, by the hand mechanism. 'Do you know how to fire this bloody thing?' he said fiercely. 'I'd like to blast him to hell . . .' But it was no use.

The destroyer on our starboard quarter had spotted the periscopes but the German U-boat disappeared before the ship had moved a hundred feet. The destroyer dropped a pattern of depth-charges over the spot where the U-boat had been, killing all our men then in the water, but failed to damage the submarine. The intentions of the destroyer's captain were sound, but I was glad that I was still on board *Courageous* at the time. Then our Commander appeared and shouted 'abandon ship' several times. His face was grey with anxiety. Men were diving into the water in all directions, some from the flight-deck which was fully seventy feet above sea level. My attention was diverted by a noise above, on the seaplane platform; and looking up I saw that the Royal Marines were falling-in neatly, as though they were attending some parade. A Corporal was in charge. I watched, expecting him to give them the order to abandon ship, but he stood them at ease and then stood at ease himself.

'Look at those Marines!' I said to Kiggell, the adjutant of the other squadron, who was standing beside me. 'They haven't heard the Commander and are waiting for the Captain Royal Marines to tell them what to do. He was blown over the side some minutes ago. I saw him swimming to the destroyer, in his pink mess jacket. Perhaps they don't know.'

To remain in a neat assembly the Royal Marines were forced to stand at an angle to the deck of at least forty-five degrees. They looked like some comic turn on a music-hall stage. 'Silly buggers!' said Kiggell. 'They'll stand there until someone gives them an order and if nobody does, they'll all go down with the ship.' He moved towards the starboard ladder leading up to the seaplane platform. 'Come on,' he said to me.

When we got to the Marines I said, 'You must hurry,' I said to the Corporal, 'The ship is going down' – but they did not move. At this point Kiggell's experience of coping with natives on the North-West Frontier came to the rescue. He took a firm pace forward and with head thrown back and both arms rigid, he bellowed like a bull, 'ROYAL MARINES – H'N! TURN FOR'ARD – DIS-MISS! ABANDON SHIP – OVER THE SIDE AT THE DOUBLE – EVERY MAN JACK OF YOU!' It was the only language they understood, and they reacted at once.

Back on the quarter-deck I saw that the stern had risen even higher and it was time to go. Only the three men from the Reserve Fleet remained at the rails, plus one lieutenant. We discovered that the three Reserve Fleet men were unable to swim and were just standing there, having abandoned all hope of survival, waiting for the ship to take them with her. I offered to take them across, one by one, if there was time, and after a lot of silly argument one of them agreed and Kiggell helped him over the side as soon as I dived in. The sea was warm. The man was wearing yellow braces and I clutched him by these, but was unable to prevent him from putting his face into the sea and making burbling noises. We reached the destroyer in a matter of minutes – ten at the most – by which time he was dead. A crowd of men on board *Impulsive* hauled him up the side, but shook their heads at me, sadly. This upset me, because he certainly hadn't drowned. He was just too old for the shock of the last twenty minutes and I felt angry with the Admiralty for dragging these old pensioners back to sea. We could have managed without them.

On my way back to the *Courageous* from the destroyer, the carrier's stern suddenly rose in the air until the ship was vertical. The quarter-deck was pointing at the sky and it seemed to be hundreds of feet up. Then she was gone.

The sea all round me was a mass of heads, all bobbing about in the calm water. As the ship plunged downwards a great cheer went up from the sea's surface and someone started to sing 'Roll out the Barrel'. It was dark a few minutes later and I had a long swim before I found the destroyer and was very glad when I did.

An American liner appeared on the scene at the same moment and picked up hundreds of survivors. During the crowded twenty minutes in which she sank 514 men lost their lives. When a ship goes down there are always more relatives whose lives have been saddened by the tragic events than there are men drowned.

Surgeon-Lieutenant Dick Caldwell, RN

I joined the Royal Navy as a qualified doctor in 1934 on a four-year engagement. In 1938 I thought that I would leave the Navy, but a close friend of mine strongly advised me to stay. He said that he felt war was imminent and that if I left and was then called up later, I'd have to start at the beginning again. So I decided to stay and was posted to the *Royal Oak*. As I travelled up to Scapa Flow, I felt everywhere there was the shadow of war: a feeling of unease. Chamberlain's speech about 'Peace in Our Time' really had a hollow ring to it.

As war approached, I think the thought of going to war was exciting. In September when war was declared, the admiral called us together in the wardroom and gave us all champagne. He gave us the toast 'Damnation to Hitler'!

I thought, well, what do we do now? We went out on patrols only returning to Scapa, that huge desolate place, each time. On the night of 13th October, I had been playing poker and had been listening to gramophone records with two fellows I was never to see again. At half past twelve I picked my way carefully along the darkened quarterdeck to the hatchway leading to my cabin. I undressed and climbed on to my bunk.

We were in harbour – if such a term can be used to describe the wide, bleak waters of Scapa Flow – and after a not unadventurous spell at sea, no thoughts of the impending disaster could have been in anyone's mind, when at ten past one a muffled, ominous explosion shook the ship.

'Lord,' I said to myself, 'I don't like the sound of that much,' and as I jumped down from my bunk I found my heart thumping a bit. I looked into the next cabin and saw my neighbour pulling on a pair of trousers, and out in the cabin flat five or six officers were already discussing how and where the explosion could have occurred. (One must remember the vast number of compartments and storing places in a ship like *Royal Oak*.) Eight minutes passed. It was cold, and one or two men drifted back to their cabins. Just as I decided to do the same, a tremendous shuddering explosion occurred and the ship took a list to starboard. I heard the tinkling of glass falling from ledges and pictures in what seemed to be the awe-stricken silence that followed; a silence that was suddenly shattered by a third explosion. All the lights went out, the list increased, and it was obvious to everyone that we were for it.

I got on to deck in my pyjamas, monkey jacket and one bedroom slipper – I dropped the other and remember deciding not to retrieve it. A fourth torpedo struck us and the mighty bulk of the battleship shuddered again and settled further into the water. These last three blows had occurred in the short space of three minutes, and it was now every man for himself in a sinking ship with the cold, black sea all around us. I suppose all of us have wondered how we would feel in a case like this; I know I have, and I was certainly shocked but, curiously, not frightened as we stood on the sloping deck in the darkness, wisps of smoke eddying round us. One heard shouts of reassurance, even of humour; and a sudden splash as men clambered over the guard rails and dived twenty or thirty feet into the water below. I had no plan. My mind was curiously blank with regard to my personal safety, although I can most vividly recall every thought and impression that passed through my brain; my new and rather expensive tennis racket, a book I had borrowed and promised to return, three pounds in the bottom of my drawer, a ship of this size must surely take a long time to sink (six minutes later it was out of sight), but above all these surprising thoughts: 'This can't be happening to me; you read about it in books, and see it on the flicks, but it doesn't happen, it can't be happening to me.'

The ship suddenly increased her list more and more rapidly. We were now on the ship's side and as she slid over, turning turtle, I lost my footing, fell, tried frantically to scramble up and dive clear and was thrown headlong into the sea. ('I'll be sucked down – that's what they say happens – what a fool I was not to jump sooner.') I seemed to go down and down and started fighting for breath. Then, as I came to the surface, the stern and propeller soared above me, then slipped slowly into the water and disappeared. A rush of water swept me head over heels, it seemed, and I went under again and came up in oil, thick black oil. I gulped it and retched at the filthy taste of it in my throat; oil, thick black oil smarting in my eyes. I swam and floundered about, hoping to find some form of support in the darkness. None of us had lifebelts. I heard cries round me, saw black heads bobbing, and I swam frenziedly again. I tried to wriggle out of my jacket, but found it heavy and slimy with oil. I repeatedly went under until quite suddenly I gave it up and thought, 'I'm going to drown.' Perfectly dispassionately 'I'm going to drown' and in a way which I cannot explain I wondered how to. And I thought of all the people I wanted to see again, and things I wanted to do – that was all I thought of – and then I saw a group of heads and then threshed my way towards them.

Somebody swam quite strongly past me and I caught his leg and tried to hold it. He kicked me clear. I saw an upturned boat ahead of me. How far was it? Or how near? Fifteen yards can seem insurmountable, and then I touched the freeboard, touched it and held on. 'I've made it, by God, I've made it; and to think a few minutes ago I might have been drowned.' I thought what a pity one can't thank inanimate things, I was so grateful to that support.

I tried to wipe the oil out of my eyes with my free hand, and then with my sleeve, and realised how stupid that was. My mind flashed back to a silent picture of Buster Keaton as a diver drying his hands on a towel at the bottom of the sea. I said 'Hullo' to the indistinguishable face beside me, and it said 'Oh, this bloody oil!'

There were about a dozen of us, I think, hanging on round a boat which kept steady as long as we did, but every now and then someone would try to improve his position or make himself more secure by clambering on to the upturned keel. Then slowly but inevitably our support would begin to roll over and back we would slip into the water, clawing frantically for a fingerhold on the smooth surface, and shouting at each other till the movement ceased and we were supported once more. This happened many times and every time meant a mouthful of oil and a thumping heart.

Time dragged on, with no sign of us being picked up. We strained our eyes in the darkness for some glimmer of light, but none came. We sang, 'Daisy, Daisy, give me your answer do.' *Daisy* was the name of the drifter attached to the *Royal Oak*.

At last we saw a mast head light which grew brighter and then the blacker darkness of a boat moving slowly towards us. We shouted again and again.

When she was within twenty yards of us we left our upturned boat and struck out in her direction. She had ropes hanging down, up which we tried to climb. I remember falling back into the sea twice. My hands were numb. I thought 'Mustn't lose now. Come on, mustn't lose now' – but have no recollection whatsoever of finally succeeding . . . I found myself sitting on a hot grating in the engine room, shivering uncontrollably from the cold which I had not previously noticed – most of us had this experience.

I stood up and vomited oil and salt water all over somebody sitting at my feet. I did this three times and apologised each time to him. He didn't appear to worry much, anyway.

We were taken to the *Pegasus* and given hot drinks and helped into hot baths, and splashed and scrubbed. They were very grand to us, and we began to talk and recognise people and shake hands and try not to notice friends that were missing. Over eight hundred were drowned that night.

Of the happenings during the following days before we disembarked and were sent south, I retain vivid memories which now seem so swift-moving and so violently contrasted that they really belong to a different story. The air raids, the shattering noise, a German pilot lazily parachuting down silhouetted against a bright blue sky, while his plane, broken up by gunfire, crashed in flames, on the hill-side; the sinister whistle of bombs from the raiders; the whole-hearted enthusiasm at an impromptu concert the night after we were torpedoed; the marvellous kindness shown to us by the Thurso folk; the sense of relief we felt in the train taking us south (a relief broken almost comically by a train-collision); the gradual acquisition of strange clothing, of odd meals and drinks, and so – at last – London; to find normality almost unreal after chaos.

Leave soon put that right!

Lieutenant-Commander Richard Jennings, RN

In early December 1939 we were patrolling the River Plate. The *Exeter* was well overdue for a refit so it was decided we should go to Durban to have the bottom scraped and the propeller fixed. Commodore Harwood, who had been aboard the *Exeter*, transferred his broad pennant to the *Ajax* because he wanted to stay in the area. He must have known that trouble was imminent.

The *Exeter* set off for Durban, but less than twelve hours later it was learned that the *Doric Star* had been sunk by a German pocket battleship between Cape Town and Freetown. So we were recalled and sent to Port Stanley for a four-day self-refit.

On 8 December the commodore told us to patrol around the Falkland Islands in case the Germans were planning a comeback to mark the anniversary of the Battle of the Falkland Islands in

1914. But nothing happened, so we headed north and joined the commodore in the Plate estuary on the evening of 12th December. We did some steam tactics on arrival, and Commodore Harwood sent for the captains of the *Exeter*, *Ajax* and *Achilles* to inform them of his intentions, should we encounter the pocket battleship. No-one else knew what tactics he was going to pursue.

I had the middle watch that night of 12th December. When I was relieved I went aft, shaved and decided against turning in as dawn action stations was due at 0440. After some more steam tactics we reverted to third degree of readiness. I got into my pyjamas, arranged for a call by the sentry (just outside my cabin door) and turned in, only to be called ten minutes later. I hustled up to my action station in the Director Control Tower. As I was crossing the compass platform the captain hailed me – not with the usual sort of rigmarole of 'Enemy in sight, bearing etc.', but with 'There's the fucking *Scheer*! Open fire at her!' Throughout the battle the crew of the *Exeter* thought they were fighting the *Admiral von Scheer*. But the name of the enemy ship was, of course, the *Graf Spee*.

So the fight was on. It was about 0612. In the DC Tower I was in telephonic touch with the Transmitting Station which, in turn, was in touch with all main armament quarters. I ordered 'Open fire'. The range was then about 20,000 yards and the *Graf Spee* was as large as life on the horizon. Our 8-inch guns could hit any target up to 30,000 yards away.

A shot in one of the early salvos passed through 'B' turret's ammunition embarkation hatch immediately below the bottom of 'B' turret's gunroom, passed through the sick bay, bowling over the Sick Berth Petty Officer and a tray for eight of his special cocktails, and then through the starboard side without bursting, until hitting the water, perhaps. Fragments from one of the early 'shorts' penetrated our side and cut a lot of circuit, including the gun-ready lamps and the fall-of-shot hooter. So it was extra difficult to spot our own fall-of-shot among those of the 6-inch ships, *Ajax* and *Achilles*. Incidentally, the *Graf Spee*'s weight of broadside was 2.5 times the combined weights of our three ships' broadsides.

At 0624 while loading for the ninth broadside, 'B' turret received a direct hit, knocking it right out of action. Not only that but fragments peppered the compass platform leaving only the captain and two others standing. The captain, with his eyes full of grit, decided to fight the ship from the after conning position. We in the DC Tower a few feet – less than fifteen feet – above the compass platform were quite unaware of all this upset. Another round entered the fore superstructure, ran along the deck of the Remote Control W/T office, passed out through my office and burst over the starboard A-A guns, starting fires in the area of the ready-use ammunition lockers where a midshipman and an ordinary seaman distinguished themselves. In the meantime 'A' turret, when loading for our 32nd broadside, was put out of action by a direct hit on the right gun.

It was perhaps the last hit that came in by the Petty Officer's mess and burst in the Chief Petty Officer's locker flat that caused most worry. The flat was above three magazines and a diesel generator was put out of action. The transmitting station was rendered useless as visibility was nil due to white powder used for insulating the space around the Transmitting Station. Breathing was also difficult. The crew was ordered out to join up with the damage-control parties. I left the DC Tower finding, to my surprise, that the compass platform had been abandoned. I went aft to the after control and, with the control officer, decided to put 'Y' turret into local control with me standing on the gun house roof to help with the spotting. While talking to the After Control Officer I failed to notice we had altered course a few degrees and that the guns of 'Y' turret were only a few feet away. When the guns spoke I remember looking down and seeing that my legs were still there!

After perhaps two salvos in local control 'Y' turret lost all power due to flooding and the flooding in the ship grew worse.

At this stage Harwood told us to drop out of the action and head for Port Stanley. There was nothing more we could do, for the *Graf Spee* was too far away to ram.

By this time the commander, Bobby Graham, had been knocked out: he was laid up in his cabin with thirty-two bits of ironmongery in his legs. So the next in command to Bell was Jennings. Jennings just busied himself in general. People were working pretty much without instruction. Everybody went about their jobs very calmly. During the three preceding years we had exercised action stations every Friday, so we all knew what to do.

The fire was still burning in the chief petty officer's locker flat. Underneath this were the anti-aircraft ammunition and the small-arms magazines; it was a potential disaster. The damage-control parties managed to get the submersible pump forward into the flat and start it heaving and flowing. Then they opened the scuttle in the ship's side which was about two feet above sea-level – we had a ten-degree list to starboard – so the suction pump and discharge were more or less level with the hole in the ship's side. Even so they managed to put the fire out, which was fortunate.

The action had lasted from 0612 until 0725. It was a long hour and thirteen minutes and certainly the most intense action I saw during my time in the navy. At that time we had no idea whether we'd made any impact on the *Graf Spee* with our guns. We had fired 95 salvos from 'Y' turret before it went out of action. 'A' turret fired 32 and 'B' turret only eight. One had to have respect for the gun layers of the *Graf Spee*.

Able Seaman Len Fogwill, RN

It was 13th December 1939. I was serving on the 8-inch-gun cruiser HMS *Exeter* patrolling the River Plate. The captain was F.S. Bell and we were in company with HMS *Ajax*, which was captained by C.H. Woodhouse and a New Zealand ship,

Achilles, captained by W.E. Parry. We were known as the South American Squadron commanded by Commodore H.H. Harwood whose broad pennant was aboard *Ajax*.

I'd done the middle watch from midnight until four o'clock in the morning. I was a look-out on the port side of the after-control. The night was warm and, as far as I was concerned, the war was far away. It was known that a German raider was sinking our shipping but we never thought the raider would come our way. What Commodore Harwood thought was another matter.

Directly after the middle watch we went to dawn action stations, which lasted about an hour. By the time I stood down from there I was jolly tired and didn't need much rocking in my hammock. I was fast asleep when action stations sounded. By force of habit I was out of bed and at my action stations before the bugler had finished sounding general quarters. I dashed off with my socks on and my shoes under my arm.

I was in the after-control position and relieved the man on look-out who told me that a ship had been sighted on the port quarter. Just at that moment the challenge lights on the mast lit up and I turned my glasses on the sighted ship. I could just see the mast through the slight haze. Then there was a flash which I took to be the flashing light in answer to our challenge. There were flashes all around us and then the sound of guns. This was no friendly ship. Over the tannoy they announced that we were engaging the German pocket battleship *Admiral von Scheer*. Only later in the day did we learn it was the *Graf Spee*.

Our three cruisers were in line ahead formation led by the *Achilles* with the *Ajax* and the *Exeter* following. Immediately the *Exeter* was turned out of line towards the *Graf Spee*. I was above the after-control, just alongside the after-director looking out with binoculars. I could make out every detail on the enemy ship. The range closed quickly and until we were steaming almost parallel with her.

When we got into our range, one of our first salvoes hit the control tower of the *Graf Spee*. We learned this afterwards because at the time we had very little knowledge of how the battle was going. We only knew we were being attacked! The enemy's firing was extremely accurate and *Exeter* was getting a pasting, steaming straight towards the enemy with the front part of the ship knocked to a shambles.

Shells were passing right through the superstructure. There was shrapnel flying everywhere. In the first ten minutes we lost five officers and fifty-six ratings. 'A' and 'B' turrets, the 8-inch and 4-inch guns, were knocked out very early on, along with the starboard torpedo tubes. The bridge from where the captain was controlling the ship was put out of action, most of the personnel being killed or injured. The captain, although wounded about the face, came aft to the after-control where I was. I had to keep him informed of the *Graf Spee*'s position, as he couldn't see properly.

He sent Commander Graham forward to organise the forward-control parties. They had been badly knocked about by an 11-inch shell passing into the ship on the port side just below 'B' turret. It had passed at an angle from forward to aft and exploded above the 4-inch magazine in the chief petty officer's locker flat, killing nearly everyone. It was one of the worst places the salvo could have hit because it was the nerve centre of the ship; all the cables to the transmitting station and the telephone exchange ran through there. The explosion and the fire put all communications out of action.

By 0650 *Exeter* was in a sorry state. She was taking in water and had developed a list. But I never thought she would go down. All guns were out of action except for two on 'Y' turret. The only steering position was the emergency position right aft where a sailmaker was at the wheel. Orders to him were being passed by a quickly formed chain of men who were drawn from the quarters where they were no longer needed. The chain passed from the captain in the after-control right aft to the emergency steering position. I was running some of the messages. When there was no communication with the after-steering, the sailmaker took it upon himself to steer the ship all-to-starboard then all-to-port, trying to dodge the shells. He used his intuition.

After a while the captain told me to take over as his messenger and I had to run from place to place, delivering messages to all parts of the ship. It seemed as if I bore a charmed life because all the time I was going about, my shipmates were being killed. I was losing friends but was oblivious to it at the time. I was just doing the things I had been trained to do. When I went through the waist, the deck where the torpedo tubes are, I saw injured men lying around dying. Even the padre was down there handing out tots of whisky to the injured. He was a boy for his whisky.

There were bodies everywhere and some of them were in a terrible condition. A piece of shrapnel took the back of our sub-lieutenant's head off. I'd never seen anyone die before. We were a young ship's company; a lot of us were in our teens and early twenties. This was our first action although most of us had been together for nearly three years. I'd say we were members of the finest and most efficient ship in the Royal Navy. We were trained to do our utmost and I'm sure we were doing our duty automatically.

There was shrapnel everywhere. Every one of us had caught a bit. The morale of the men was grand, even with the shells and shrapnel flying about. At one time during the action our wireless aerials were shot away. They fell down across the after-control and got entangled around the after-director and jammed the door shut. I took an axe and broke through the cables, whereupon the door opened and the director layer popped his head out and politely said, 'Thank you very much!'

Then there was a lull in the action. The *Graf Spee* must have suffered as much as we had, since we'd been pumping shells into her for quite a while. During that time we managed to get the fires under control and ditch the amphibious aircraft – which were leaking petrol – into the sea. Every position in the ship had a damage control party. We knew what to do and where to go. We had to rig up emergency lighting and ring mains to supply the after-turret. Everything had to be done with man-power and the fires were put out with sea water. As we worked we learned who had been killed. Somebody said, 'Nobby Clarkson's killed.' He was a great friend of mine, killed in 'A' turret and my cousin was killed as well.

Although the *Exeter* was now on only two guns, we steamed into action with the guns firing on the foremost bearing. The control of the tower was taken on by the gunnery officer Richard Jennings, with utter disregard for his own safety. He stood on top of the turret shouting directions down into the front of the guns.

By now we were in a sinking condition and slowly listing to port. When it became apparent to the commodore that we were in a dangerous condition we were ordered to withdraw from the action and make our way to Port Stanley. But we weren't in any great hurry to retreat. The captain had mentioned to the ship's doctor that he intended to ram the *Graf Spee* so we were all ready to rig up the Lewis guns, but in the end we didn't have to. Nobody felt particularly relieved that we were out of the action; the general feeling was that we hadn't done enough. It made you kind of bloodthirsty. You felt so isolated from the real activity because it's the shells from the ship which are doing the job, not you. I never really experienced fear, not even in retrospect.

We stopped for lunch and everybody was given a tot of rum. It was my first because I was only just eighteen and under age. The shock of what we had been through sank into us in the form of hunger. At that time there was no means of getting a meal and the only thing we could get our hands on was raw cabbage. We had this and enjoyed it.

Then we set to work to clear away the damage. Some of this work was ghastly because as the debris was cleared away, the great number of dead and wounded was brought to light. I was put on look-out on the wings of the bridge on the flag deck. It was pretty grim because there were still some bodies around. The shell which had passed from port to starboard had sliced right through the deck and chopped off the legs of all the telegraphers who were lined up on a bench. They were all killed instantly. There were over sixty killed and over 120 wounded. During the afternoon our fallen comrades were buried at sea with full naval honours. I know that every survivor thinks with pride of those who were lost and will never forget them.

We were very well cared for when we reached Port Stanley. The *Exeter* certainly did have the worst of the whole encounter; on a memorial plaque I was later shown of the Battle of the River Plate the *Exeter* took up three-quarters of the plaque. The *Ajax* lost seven men and the *Achilles* four.

We stayed in the Falklands for a couple of months and were given leave to come home on 28th February. We had to bury four of the dead on the island. Most of the badly injured were transferred to South Africa. On the way home we called into Sierra Leone. The first person I saw on the gangway was my father who was serving on HMS *Albatross*, a seaplane carrier based in Freetown. He had seen action at Jutland! We went ashore and had a few beers.

Surgeon-Lieutenant Roger Lancashire, RN

The Germans are great ones for doing the magnificent thing on the right day and Commodore Harwood reckoned that on 8th December 1939 they would be thinking of how they could extract their revenge off the Falklands Islands for the sinking of the *Scharnhorst* and *Gneisenau*, twenty-five years earlier almost to the day. So on 8th December *Exeter* went round and round the Falklands looking for smoke or anything suspicious, but nothing happened at all. We then rejoined Harwood who had shifted his flag from *Exeter* to *Ajax*. It was a good thing that he did. Together with *Achilles* we rendezvoused about 200 miles off the mouth of the Plate on 12th December. The obvious thing that we had to do was to get the *Graf Spee* to divide her fire. We were steaming in line ahead when the enemy was sighted.

Harwood had decided what we were going to do twenty-four hours in advance. We detached ourselves and steamed away as fast as we could in order to close the range; but their opening fire was so accurate that in the first ten minutes of the battle we lost five officers and fifty-six ratings killed outright. That was ten per cent of the ship's company. I was squatting on my haunches close to the wardroom door taking drugs and instruments out of a cupboard when the *Graf Spee*'s first salvo fell short and burst on impact with the water. There was a loud crash and a blast of air blew my cap off and threw me backwards. Later on, I found part of an 11-inch shell fuze-cap embedded in the fanlight casing. Had I been standing, it would certainly have beheaded me. Unfortunately, other fragments came hurtling inboard, killing all the fire party assembled in the stokers' bathroom on the same deck.

The next salvo struck 'A' turret and blew up and started a fire right forward. We never saw one of the team of shipwrights again, nor Sub-Lieutenant Morse whose father was C-in-C in Freetown. The second one hit 'B' turret manned by the Royal Marines which was immediately below the bridge. It was lucky that anybody came out of it alive. On the bridge, there were only three survivors and old 'Hookie' Bell had splinters in both eyes and his leg. I suppose there were about ten men on the bridge including those from the plot just aft, one of whom was our sub-lieutenant. The three survivors went aft to control, which was just forward of 'Y' turret. I didn't go up to the bridge, I stayed down in the wardroom. Thank God we had rehearsed 'Action Stations' prior to this battle because we'd rigged up the sick-bay in the wardroom so many times in the last three years, that everything went like clockwork. Fortunately, to take the place of our missing sick-birth attendant, we had an extra war complement from *Ajax*. Some of the wounded were treated in the sick-bay up forward but most of them were brought down to the wardroom. Every now and then the Master-at-Arms, who was part of my team, thank God, would call me up to see if I could identify somebody, especially if he was on his last legs.

The casualties were fairly devastating. There were two or three who literally died in my arms. These were people who I'd been living with, as it were, for three years. There were cases where, if I'd had the facilities and an endless supply of blood transfusions, things might have been different, but it wasn't like that. I did a quick assessment of who was most likely to benefit and then went to work on them. We had no nursing orderlies with us. But the Royal Marine bandsmen came up after their Transmitting Station had been put out of action. I took over 'Hookie' Bell's day and sleeping cabin. A lot of the casualties were in there. There was quite a lot of stitching up and other tasks which merged into one another.

As the day crept on and night fell I had, with the help of the bandsmen, got a good team going. We had a problem with the morphine. Instead of being in bottles with a rubber-topped diaphragm so that you could plunge the needle through, they were in ampoules. That was one of the things that I spent a day complaining about, when I returned to Devonport, with a RNVR Surgeon Rear-Admiral who listed our requirements. The first thing I told him was, that morphine should not be dispensed in the ampoules because to break them open we had to use a file which was very time-consuming. In a hurry it was much easier to use bottles. Thank God we had a ruddy great packing case which we'd had on board since we commissioned in 1936, which was only to be opened in action. A character came along to deliver a message. He was rather badly shot up so I put a few stitches in him and tied him up and made him as comfortable as possible. Then when he had come to, he said, 'Well, let me do something, Doc, for heaven's sake.' So I said, 'All right. Open that crate for me.' Right at the very top was the very thing we wanted; a ruddy great big pair of tailor's scissors used for cutting open serge trousers. It was beautifully planned. I remember putting that down in my report. There was also enough morphine in there. I operated on a fellow called Causton. I was wondering whether I ought to amputate his foot but then I saw that there was a good blood supply. Several of his tendons had gone. I knew that I had three or four ampoules of anaesthetic – which was quite new in those days – to give an injection into a vein. I got them myself in Rio and there was one left up in the sick bay. So I sent a messenger up to get it. With the assistance of the sick-berth PO, we operated on Causton and laid him out on the deck of 'Hookie' Bell's sleeping cabin. I got the finest sutures and needles which we could get hold of and stitched the tendons together again. It was a nice clean wound and kept his foot on for him. In 1943 I was sent out to Durban. I spent a fortnight in the transit camp near Cape-town, so I went down most days to the naval hospital and this fellow Causton was still there. He had found work in an office and was walking about with a stick. I felt about ten yards tall.

The only time I left the sick-bay was when I got the message that 'Hookie' Bell and Commander Graham had been blown off the bridge and were wounded in the legs. 'Hookie' went to the after-conning position and the commander went to his cabin. As I poked my head through the hatch on my way from the wardroom to the quarterdeck, a hand shoved my head down again with a yell, 'Port Twenty.' I passed the message on to the chain of men for transmission to the two perspiring heroes who were manning the massive steering wheel way back aft.

On deck I had never seen anything like it before. The immaculate *Exeter* I'd known for three years was an absolute shambles. All the aircraft who had been told to stay on their catapults were now riddled and high octane fuel was pouring out of them. Richard Jennings, 'Guns', was standing on the lid of 'Y' turret giving his orders. 'Hookie' Bell and I went up to see him and he gave me a running commentary of what was going on. It was fantastic. I was spellbound. There in the distance you could see the *Graf Spee*, firing every now and again. The exciting thing was that *Ajax* and *Achilles* had made a smoke-screen and they were taking it in turns to dodge in and out of it and give a rapid and accurate six-inch broadside, which the *Graf Spee* didn't like very much. 'Hookie' Bell said to me, 'You see what position we're in: "A" and "B" turret are out of action (which I already knew), so we've only got one gun here in "Y" turret. All the power's gone, so even that's got to be trained and loaded by hand. But it's all we've got now.'

Then he said, 'If he gives me half a chance and heads this way I intend to ram the bugger.'

I fixed up his legs to stop them from bleeding and said, 'Now look, when you can, let me know when you're under control and I'll come and do what I can for your eyes.' At about midnight he came below. We were swinging about all over the place, but fortunately, as part of my job years ago, I'd done quite a lot of eye work, so with the chief steward holding a torch I was able to clear one eye and reminded 'Hookie' that Nelson had managed pretty well with only one. It was not until the following Sunday night, when he was staying as the guest of Henniker-Heaton, the governor at Port Stanley, that I was able to do the other eye under much easier conditions.

There were a number of facial injuries from the battle. I had to stitch an ear back on and there were quite a few scalp injuries. A Royal Marine came in, brought by his mates, and they couldn't think what the matter was. He was the most mild-mannered chap but he suddenly started behaving very oddly and using the most terrible obscene language. So I thought there must be something the matter with him. They couldn't find any sign of a wound or scar so I had a jolly good look at his scalp and sure enough there was a tiny hole in the front. A fragment of shell had gone right through into the frontal lobe like a leucotomy. I left it there like that; that was the cause of his problem. I wanted to take him back home because we could have looked after him and my friend Sir Geoffrey Jefferson who was a neuro-surgeon could have helped.

They sent him down to the Falklands Hospital where they couldn't do anything. We took him up to Buenos Aires where he was operated upon and died on the table . . .

I was constantly on the go from that Tuesday and the wee small hours of Wednesday until the following Sunday night. Harwood made a signal to 'Hookie' Bell and said, 'Can you make it to the Falklands?' We had a very dangerous list to port and our main mast was whipping about in a terrible state. We were navigating by a boat's compass.

You see, we had been struck by seven 11-inch shells, three of which passed straight through the ship without exploding. One of them went clean through the sick-bay, through where the heads (toilets) were, removing all the bedpans and the bath. The blast of the things did a hell of a lot of damage. We weren't holed below the water-line but the place was absolutely incredible. The *Exeter* was a damned well-built ship.

When we were down at Port Stanley afterwards, Commodore Harwood sent for me and 'Hookie' Bell. Governor Henniker-Heaton was there and they asked me what we were going to do with all the patients. Some of them could be taken back but they were not allowed unless they were capable of looking after themselves, which was fair enough. So I suggested that since there were lots of fracture cases, they should send out an orthopaedic surgeon. 'Good God,' he said, 'They'll never do that.' I said, 'Of course they would. They'd be most interested to see their injuries.'

They sent a pal of mine who I'd met many times in my RNVR days in Liverpool. They put them all in one of the cruisers, the *Dorsetshire* I think, and took them over to the Cape.

The only reason that I am able to tell this story now is that we in *Exeter* had basically been the same ship's company for three years, so there was a lot of rapport and camaraderie which there wouldn't have been the case if we had been a new commission. Without that, we could not have survived the punishment we took.

Lieutenant Arthur Hezlet, RN

The submarine war didn't really hot up until after Christmas 1939 when suddenly we lost three submarines in succession. People thought there was some great secret weapon that had got them all, but it wasn't, as they've discovered since. It was German anti-submarine craft in two cases. Our submarines were in very shallow water, only 80 feet and the Germans got to them partly by trawling with wires and grapnels.

But with the Norwegian campaign things really began in earnest and the British submarines did very well considering the amount of exercises they had had. The idea in those days was, when war started you stopped exercising – that was for peacetime – but of course later you realised you had to exercise harder in war than you did in peace.

When the invasion of Norway took place, we were off Oslo. We had left harbour in *Trident* before anyone suspected what was going to happen. We had very poor information in those days and the Admiralty didn't believe Norway was going to be invaded until it happened.

The Germans sent about a dozen troopships ahead pretending to be merchant ships and they protected themselves by going up through Swedish and Norwegian territorial waters when we couldn't touch them. We saw these ships going north but we couldn't make them out. We knew they weren't neutral, because neutrals normally had their flag painted beside their names and none of these had. I had quite an argument with my captain who said there was absolutely nothing we could do. He said, 'If we started sinking these things and they proved to be neutral it would be really bad news.' But I felt there was something very wrong and a big action was about to happen.

Then a tanker came out of the three-mile limit and cut a corner across a bay, just where we were. I was on watch and got hold of the captain. He said he was a very uncertain of what we should do and he hadn't been given any instructions. Eventually

I got him to agree to stop this ship. He popped up with the gun and ordered it to stop. Not only did it stop, but it scuttled, and he then didn't make a signal to Admiralty which was very unwise. That was the very beginning of the invasion but we then went home because we'd been out for the normal patrol period.

On our next patrol, when we had a new captain, we were off the west coast of Norway. All the enemy traffic was going up inside the islands while we were patrolling outside. We were achieving nothing. This captain was made of really stern stuff and said, 'Well, we must get inside,' which was quite a feat. We went right up Kors Fjord just south of Bergen. We sat there and waited all night and nobody seemed to notice us. The next day a ship called the *Cläre Hugo Stinnes* came along and we drove it ashore. We had to use the gun to do it, so we were on the surface in the middle of Norway and the captain then said, 'I think we'd better get out of this,' so we went down Kors Fjord on the surface and, just as we got to the entrance of it, some aircraft and anti-submarine vessels appeared and we were hunted just outside.

This was early on in the days of submarine warfare and we weren't very experienced. We were quite certain the enemy had hydrophones and could hear us if we made a noise. We therefore tried hard not to use any machinery, to do everything as silently as we could. Of course, if you don't use any machinery in a submarine it will do as it likes and you begin to lose control. On one occasion we went very deep, with the stern down and the captain was saying, 'Hold it,' and 'Don't make a noise.' Eventually we had to do something because the bilge water was getting near the electric motors and he said, 'Well, get some buckets.' We bailed the water out of the engine-room, passing these buckets through the submarine and poured them into the torpedo compartment which made less noise than pumping. This decreased the angle and then a stoker in the engine-room dropped a bucket which made a huge clatter. Everybody burst out laughing, easing the tension. Eventually we got to the stage where *Trident* was still sinking and we had to do something so the captain said, 'I think the best thing is to blow a little into the main ballast to stop her going down.' So we did that. But of course you lose control because, as you come up the air expands and comes more buoyant and after a very short time we were roaring up out of control and burst right out of the sea.

The captain raised the periscope to find the enemy had gone.

Lieutenant Bruce Junor, RN

I was serving in HMS *Ajax* who was having a refit after seeing action in the Battle of the River Plate. I was on a short leave when the Commander rang me up to report at once with my boots and gaiters on and prepare to go over seas. I dashed back to Chatham where I and another officer went in an Admiralty car to Ramsgate and boarded an old destroyer HMS *Wolfhound*. J. W. McCoy was Captain of an ordinary crew who had been on convoy duty in the Atlantic.

We crossed the Channel under heavy attack by bombers but we landed on the jetty at Dunkirk. A British Naval Officer was giving the orders but Captain Tennant was in overall charge from a dug-out at the root of the jetty (the landward each of the jetty). I remember four of us went into a building in Dunkirk when a big bomb blasted off and a couple of soldiers who had been out in the open were killed, but inside the building we were alright. We walked about three miles along the front down to the beach where there were a few soldiers and one on a stretcher. There were destroyers lying two to three miles out, because being deep draughted vessels, the water was too shallow for them to come in except at high tide.

I was part of a small group of naval officers who were ordered to report to the jetty. We had to walk through part of the town to reach this long jetty, roughly 400 yards where I was to be for several days taking part in the organisation of the evacuation of troops.

For the first 48 hours I was never off my feet. Soldiers came from scattered units and in small groups under command, all shattered and dispirited from fighting and marching with no food or rest. Montgomery, the Divisional Commander, marched the troops by night and handled the Division so well to manage to evacuate so very many soldiers.

The Admiralty got hold of Dutch schoots which were robust, petrol powered, large, open barges with powerful engines designed to carry cargo in the Dutch inland waterways. For the evacuation they were manned by British Naval personnel and of course were so useful because of their very shallow draft which enabled them to get up to the root of the pier. The destroyers could only safely reach the end of the jetty and then only at high water. The trouble was the range of the tide was 18 feet. This means that the water level between tides changes by 18 feet, thus making it very difficult to get the troops down into the barges at low water. Very early on the Admiral in charge, had sent a signal asking for scaling ladders. Chatham and Sheerness dockyards worked day and night making dozens of schoot scaling ladders to send over to Dunkirk in destroyers.

The evacuation of the beaches was a magnificent bit of organisation but it has gone down in history that the whole of the British Expeditions Force (BEF) came off on Dunkirk beaches which is nonsense. 30,000 to 40,000 men were evacuated from the beaches by the "little ships" which was a very magnificent effort. It was, however, a drop in the ocean compared to the evacuation by the Royal Navy and the Merchant Navy from the jetty of some 220,000 men.

The destroyers came alongside the deep water side of the jetty to fill up with men, but they were quite unsuitable for that job because they could not take more than 100 men. The schoot barges could take a couple of hundred men. Ferries were also brought from England and Ireland and as they were designed with a shallow draught they did very good work taking off hundreds of troops. We lowered the wounded into the ferries as well as we could, at some points of the tide a number of wounded could be got onto the destroyers. I don't remember many stretcher cases. I dare say some had to be left behind to fall into the hands of the enemy. The men's spirits varied; some straggled down in ones and twos, while some marched on in good order. I expect it depended on what they had been through previously and what sort of officers they had. There were quite a few French colonial troops who were very dignified.

There were air raids continuously and the trawlers had to be quick because of the falling bombs. All the ammunition and oil tanks for the BEF were stored in Dunkirk Harbour, somewhere just across the fareway, and all the time I was in Dunkirk the sappers were blowing up the ammunition and burning the oil.

There was an old paddler that used to ply between London Bridge and Southend Pier for five bob, seasick and back. She berthed at the extreme end of the jetty outside, not inside, and was bombed and sunk. The bombing made three large gaps in the jetty but we bridged them with the brows (gangways) from the old paddler. These brows saved the day. Then the first spitfire I had ever seen came over and they did good work. They drove the Germans off and kept them away and allowing us to keep them away and allowing us to keep the momentum going.

We were at it 24 hours a day getting these chaps off with very little food. After the first 48 hours other chaps working with me simply lay down on the jetty and went to sleep with his head on his cap. He slept for about 15 minutes, then got up, didn't feel much better and said "you go and have a sleep". I lay down on the concrete and put my cap under my head and slept like a log for about 15 minutes. What those 15 minutes did for me was quite incredible. I don't remember any food other than a sandwich at times and, on occasion, being able to scrounge some food off ship whilst the soldiers were boarding.

I was on that jetty about a week when I was shanghaied. I had been helping a wounded soldier down into a trawler when the bombing increased with a bomb landing close by so the skipper thought it best to go and pulled away once I was on board. A bomb immediately fell where I had been standing on the jetty. Armed with one 4-inch gun on the trawler I found myself in Ramsgate. I went to a hotel the Admiralty had taken over which was packed out. I slept in a chair, wrote a hurried note to my wife and bought a pair of socks before getting a lift back to Dunkirk in HMS *Keith*. I did this on my own initiative as I had involuntarily deserted my post. I was there some days more feeling very weary and my feet were sore of going up and down that concrete. We got the bulk of the men off in those eight days and Dunkirk was still burning.

Orders came for me to rejoin my ship, HMS *Ajax*. I think they thought when they sent me back it was finished, no more to be done. After I had gone I heard that they did another day and got a lot more troops off. Then the other pier master, a very nice man who had been working along side me, came off in a landing craft which was bombed and sunk. He was drowned.

I scrounged a lift back to Ramsgate on a ferry '*Ulster Prince*' being used in the evacuation. The skipper said it had life belts for 100 people, but that a good 800 people were on board. I was damn tired, but returned to Chatham and rejoined HMS *Ajax*. We sailed out to the Mediterranean a few days later.

Lieutenant-Commander C. H. Corbet-Singleton, RN

H. M. S. Albury.
9th June 1940.

Sir,

I have the honour to forward the account of proceedings of His Majesty's Ship *Albury* during the days May 28th to June 5th 1940.

2.   I left Harwich at noon on May 23rd in company with the Fifth Minesweeping Flotilla, arrived off Zudecotte Beach at 2130 and, anchoring, as close as possible, sent boats inshore to embark troops. The rate of embarkation was then slow as the tide was

low and a small surf was troublesome on the beach. The troops were in good spirits though short of rations; I landed a quantity of dry provisions in the skiff.

3.   About 2330 a bomb was seen to drop about one mile to seaward of the ship, but no interference was caused to the work in hand.

4.   At 0230 on May 29th I got under way and proceeded without incident to Margate, where the troops were disembarked.

5.   I then returned to Zudecotte, arriving there at 1930 on May 29th; a considerable amount of bombing was in progress. On arrival the roads were fairly empty, as we had passed, on the way, a number of loaded ships returning.

6.   I made towards a burning paddle-steamer, which had grounded and, being full of troops and survivors, appeared to be in a bad way. All boats and Carley floats were sent away and many survivors were picked up. Bombs were being dropped continually around the ship and the paddle-steamer during this operation, and two machine-gun attacks were carried out. I have nothing but the utmost praise for all concerned, the majority of whom are very young and had certainly never been in action before. Continual anti-aircraft fire was kept up by the Twelve Pounder. I sent a signal for Fighter assistance, which arrived later in the evening.

7.   Fifty seven cot-cases alone were brought off, mostly suffering from severe burns; the Commanding Officer and other survivors from His Majesty's Destroyer *Grenade* were amongst those embarked. After having cleared the steamer out as far as was known, I proceeded down the coast towards Bray, and picked up troops from several boats, which they had found on

the beach. A Captain Churchill, from the Headquarters Staff, came off and told me that he had to get over to England to see his uncle, the Prime Minister, by 0600.

8. I proceeded to Margate, arriving at 0530 on May 30th, disembarked troops, survivors and Captain Churchill, then sailed for Sheerness for coal and ammunition.

9. I left Sheerness at 0300 on May 31st and arrived without incident off the beach just to the East of Dunkirk, at 0930. The rate of embarkation was slow owing to considerable surf on the beach, but valuable assistance was given by a large power boat. It was necessary for me to leave at 1230 in order to unload and be at my rendez-vous by 2200 on May 31st for the evening operations.

10. I sailed from Margate to comply with previous instructions and proceeded, under the orders of the Senior Officer of the Fifth Minesweeping Flotilla, to my appointed station off the beach; navigation at this period was difficult, as the absence of wind allowed the smoke from Dunkirk to settle over the channel, so that visibility was poor. On anchoring at 2345 a shell from a shore battery landed about a cable to seaward; this was repeated spasmodically. Reports were then received of magnetic mines being dropped in the channel.

11. About 0230 the Flotilla was ordered to carry on embarkation, using ships' boats. Shortly after dawn a bombing attack took place, and from then on these attacks were practically continuous. Several Heinkel III type aircraft were observed, but the majority of the attackers were identified as Junkers 87 Dive-bombers. Embarkation was carried out, though the rate was slow.

12. His Majesty's Ship *Speedwell* was seen to be aground; a wire was passed and I towed her off. During this operation the ship came under machine-gun fire from the air, and great credit is due

to my First Lieutenant for the speed and coolness with which he carried out the evolution.

13.   I then received orders from the Flag Officer afloat to proceed alongside in Dunkirk harbour, and to complete with troops there. As troops were being embarked, bombs were dropped in the harbour and a machine-gun attack was delivered, but no casualties were incurred.

14.   Just before I slipped, with a full load of troops on board, His Majesty's Destroyer *Ivanhoe* was hit by a bomb outside the harbour. Two ships went to her assistance, so I proceeded at full speed.

15.   While leaving the channel and coming up to the Breedt bank, the most intense bombing attacks were experienced. Repeated near misses were registered on His Majesty's Ship *Gossamer*, ahead of me. His Majesty's Destroyer *Havant*, who had just overtaken me, was hit in the vicinity of number Three gun; continuing at high speed, she described a large circle to starboard, and when last seen was steaming in a Southerly direction. Near misses were also registered on His Majesty's Ship *Albury*; Fighter assistance was requested.

16.   These bombers came in relays and pursued the ship well out to sea. The Twelve pounder was kept in action the whole time, and it was very noticeable that if fire was withheld until aircraft approaching from astern were close, they were forced to sheer off and go round again. Effective use was made of Lewis and Bren guns, the latter obtained from and manned by the troops.

17.   I proceeded to Sheerness, landed the troops, replenished supplies of coal and ammunition, and sailed for Dunkirk at 1600, on June 2nd.

18. On arrival in Dunkirk harbour at 0015 on June 3rd, I went alongside the Eastern arm. French troops were embarked though there did not appear to be many waiting, and it was necessary to send along the jetty towards the town to collect them. During the time that His Majesty's Ship *Albury* was alongside, intermittent shelling was taking place, apparently directed at the harbour and ships alongside. I sailed eventually about 0215 with Two hundred troops on board.

19. While returning I encountered a floating mine off 'U' buoy, which I reported to you. It was slightly conical in shape, and from its appearance might have been a Dutch mine. I sank it and proceeded to Sheerness to land the troops and to coal.

20. I sailed again for Dunkirk at 1630 on June 3rd in company with His Majesty's Ships *Gossamer* and *Leda*, and was detached off 'W' buoy to act independently, in order to arrive at the harbour at 0020 on June 4th. I was ordered alongside the West pier, filled up with French soldiers, and left the harbour at 0130.

21. Fog was encountered between 'U' buoy and the North Goodwin Light-vessel, and I overtook His Majesty's Ship *Leda*, who had been in collision; I stood by her until relieved by His Majesty's Ship *Kellett*.

22. In the vicinity of the Elbow buoy, the French Auxiliary Naval Vessel *Emile Deschamps*, crowded with troops and refugees, was passed. I was about five cables ahead of her, and signalling her the course to the North Goodwin Light-vessel which she had missed, when she blew up and sank within half a minute. I turned to pick up survivors, and reported to you that she had been sunk by a mine.

23. The London Fire Brigade Fire-float *Massey Shaw* was on the spot and assisted with the rescue work. During the operation the

Master of this vessel informed me quite confidently that he had seen a periscope shortly before the explosion, so I sent out an Enemy Submarine report. I proceeded to Margate with the survivors, forty of whom, men and women, were severely wounded, and landed them with the troops.

24. The morale, courage, and endurance shewn by all on board during this period, was exceptional, an encouraging fact as the average age is very low. Sub-Lieutenant F.R.A. Turnbull, R.N. did excellent work on the beach with the boats, and Sub-Lieutenant B.P. Cahill, R.N.V.R. spent long hours on the bridge with un-remitting attention to duty. . . .

I have the honour to be, Sir,

Your obedient servant,

C.H. Corbet-Singleton

Lieutenant-Commander
in Command.

The Vice-Admiral,
Dover Command.
(Copy to the Senior Officer, 5th Minesweeping Flotilla.)

Petty Officer Pilot Dick Leggott, Fleet Air Arm

I joined *Glorious* in April 1940. I had been operating from Wick with another petty officer pilot, A.G. Johnson. Our flight had been led by Lieutenant Charles Evans and he asked us to join him on *Glorious*. However Evans didn't join *Glorious*, and this rather upset us.

We had heard a few rumours about *Glorious* and soon we learnt that things were not at ease between the captain and his air staff, his Commander Flying, J. B. Heath, and Lieutenant-Commander Flying. While we were in northern waters the captain wanted to send our aircraft to help the army, but Heath said it was a misuse of naval aircraft. The outcome was that Heath was put ashore at Scapa Flow. There was a feeling of sadness about it all, for I could understand both points of view.

We returned to collect RAF Hurricanes and Spitfires from off the Norwegian coast. On the way back the captain told us there would be no flying, which flew in the face of proper practice. I believe he wanted to get the RAF planes back as soon as possible. However, there should have been aircraft up keeping a look out for enemy ships, particularly as it was June and it was daylight practically the whole time. As soon as the captain said this, the personnel of Swordfish Squadron 823 started storing their torpedoes away. A number of aviators objected; but they were told by the chief in charge of the operation that they were getting a lap ahead for leave.

On 8th June we had left the Fleet. It was a lovely summer's day and we were accompanied by two destroyers, HMS *Ardent* and HMS *Acasta*. I wasn't concerned because we had done this journey before. We were sitting in the sunshine when we were stood down for tea. I went below and as I was having my tea I saw through the porthole splash, splash, splash. The messman went up on deck and then came running down to tell us that two German pocket battleships were shelling us.

Our action stations were our aeroplanes. I finished eating my Dundee cake and went up to the hangar. When I arrived there I found a few pilots beginning to congregate. On the bridge our two squadron commanders were talking to the captain. They wanted to take off and attack the bridge of the *Scharnhorst* and *Gneisenau*, knock out some of their sensitive equipment and personnel, and then, if *Glorious* couldn't turn into wind, land on *Ark Royal*. But the captain rejected this idea. He told the squadron commanders it would be like rats about to leave what they thought might be a sinking ship. So we didn't get our Gladiators off.

While we were discussing this a salvo came in and shell splinters were splattering into aeroplanes which began to leak petrol. The damage control people arrived and told us to leave so that they could deal with the mess.

I left and stood by a guard rail with my section leader looking out at the two ships. Then I went to get my Mae West. As I was stepping into the ship's island, a salvo came in, killing three or four sailors who had gone ahead of me. I saw a PO Telegraphist and asked him if he'd got a signal off. He wasn't certain, though he thought something had gone off on low power, and he was hopeful someone would have heard it.

Then down from the bridge came a messenger who told us the captain had been killed and that all communication with the bridge had been severed. I was talking with Sub Lieutenant McLaughlan when we were approached by an Engineer Lieutenant. He had been ordered by the Engineer Commander to go round the ship and inform everyone that *Glorious* had not taken a full supply of oil at Scapa Flow. He stressed that all those who survived should tell the subsequent inquiry. At the time neither McLaughlan or myself appreciated the reason behind making this point. At this point, although the ship was burning, there had been no order to abandon ship. I then went with two lieutenants to the lower flying-off deck to arrange Carley floats ready for launching, and at the same time to muster men on the cable deck below. While we were doing this, four sailors emerged from one of the watches looking very anxious. A young Lieutenant ordered them to return below. This upset the men who explained that their officers had either been killed or severely wounded and that their CPO had ordered them on deck while he closed the water-tight doors behind them. The Lieutenant wanted to send them back, but I was joined by two other lieutenants from 823 Squadron who agreed with my view. The four men's faces showed their relief as they moved off to join the others on the cable deck. We wanted to get all the Carley floats into the water so that when people jumped in they'd be there all together. Unfortunately some character called out 'Every man for himself' and with that they all leapt over the side except for a few non-swimmers. We encouraged them to jump telling them their lifebelts would keep them afloat until they reached a float. One asked a young lieutenant to push him over which he did. 'Thank you,' he said as he was falling into the sea.

After everyone had jumped off I was left there with these two young lieutenants. I offered them each a cigarette and we had a few quiet minutes looking out over the sea. Then they asked me to join them on a Carley float. It was like being invited to tea on the vicar's lawn and having cucumber sandwiches.

I swam to a Carley float some way away. I was absolutely exhausted when I got there and was pulled on. I was bitterly cold. There were no other floats nearby. Twelve hours later, we had drifted to other Carley floats whose occupants decided to swim over to our float because they thought we had food and water, when in fact none of the floats had either food or water aboard. As the ship was sinking we had sent stores ratings below to see if they could locate bully beef and tinned milk, but they had been beaten by smoke and flames.

People were hanging on to the sides. I remember clearly one of them hanging on to one of the ropes. I asked him if he was all right. He looked at me and he said, 'Yes.' And with that he slipped away into a very peaceful death. Another said he was going down below to keep warm. I grabbed him, but he persisted. In the end he took one big dive and swam out ten or fifteen yards and then stopped. He looked as if he was sitting in a little shelter, a little shelter in a field. In the beginning I was asked how long I thought we would be on the float. I reckoned eight hours, possibly sixteen. In the end every one of the fifty-odd people we had slipped away and I was left alone with Marine Hellis.

After three days and two nights we were picked up by a Norwegian trawler which later found Squadron Commander, Bing Cross, and one of his pilots, Pat Jameson.

It was hard to say why I survived. I think it's the way that one is nurtured. In nature, animals, plants and humans are the same: if they are well nurtured from an early age they will stand difficult circumstances far better than if they are poorly nurtured. It was also a state of mind: it was no good being afraid, it is a pointless exercise. Why make yourself, allow yourself to be mentally uncomfortable? I kept thinking that my mother would be unhappy if I didn't make it. The other thing was, is it all worth it? I believed that it was, and that helped greatly.

FROM 1940 TO THE SINKINGS
OF HOOD AND BISMARCK

After the defeat of France in June 1940, the serious question arose over the future of the French Fleet which, now based at Oran in Algeria, might, the British government feared, fall into German or Italian hands.

Stoker 1st Class Vernon Coles, RN

HMS Faulknor was part of 'H' Force. We met our flotilla at sea with the *Hood* and *Ark Royal*, then together sailed south. *Hood* was flying the flag of Vice-Admiral Sir James Somerville. We also had the *Valiant* in company. When we eventually arrived in Gibraltar, we thought, 'God, there's something happening here.' We were even more convinced when we saw that *Resolution* had arrived – another 15-inch battleship. There were also the cruisers *Arethusa* and *Enterprise* and ten other destroyers.

We began sailing on our own, patrolling off Mers-el-Kebir, near Oran. The French told us to shove off. Because we only had five 4.7-inch guns we withdrew and patrolled on the skyline. The following morning, 3rd July, the entire fleet arrived. Captain Holland, who spoke French, went to present terms to the French commander, Admiral Gensoul. The terms were given roughly as follows: put to sea and join forces with the British; or sail to the French West Indies and there de-militarise his ships; or sail with reduced crews to any British port; or scuttle all his ships within six hours of the offer of the British ultimatum. If there was no answer to this signal, we would open fire at 11 o'clock.

We reckoned that Somerville found this pretty distasteful.

However, eleven o'clock came, and we did not hear anything from Admiral Gensoul; but we didn't fire. So the boat went in again with more terms. Admiral Gensoul refused to see the captain. He was told that we would open fire at two o'clock. It didn't happen. Then the terms went in the third time but again they were rejected. Apparently, Churchill was getting a bit hot under the collar about this. So, as there was no reply, five o'clock was given as the deadline and the battle ensigns went up. I was on no. 5 gun so I had a front-line view of the quarterdeck.

At 1755 we opened fire. It was a sad irony. We were not attacking the Germans or Italians, but the Royal Navy's oldest enemy and our twentieth-century ally. The whole fleet was going across and ranging. What a bombardment! I had never seen anything like it. One of our destroyers out on the starboard wing had got so close inshore that she was coming under the range of their 9-inch gun, so the *Hood* just trained her guns to fire at the hill, just below a big fort which was where the firing was coming from. The fort came tumbling down because the blast had undermined its foundations. The French battleship *Dunkerque* was right under a dockyard crane and the *Hood* had to destroy it before she could get at the *Dunkerque*. Her first broadside hit the crane, it was just like a matelot dropping. The second salvo hit the *Dunkerque*. We were firing from a distance of seven or eight miles, which for a 15-inch gun is point-blank range. Our ships sank the *Bretagne*, knocked the stern off *Mogador* and badly damaged *Provence*. Admiral Gensoul then said, 'For God's sake stop firing. You're murdering us.' Over 1100 French sailors had been killed.

The *Strasbourg* got away, along with five large destroyers. We went after her with *Hood*, *Ark Royal* and three F-class destroyers. She had a good start and we missed her. We turned back and joined our fleet. We didn't like firing on the French, but if we hadn't, they might have joined the Germans. Before we got back to Gibraltar the French Air Force came over and dive-bombed us with twin dive-bombers.

Signalman Frederick Humphryes, RN

Mention the Royal Navy in World War Two and people instantly think of the big battleships, cruisers and destroyers. However, at the beginning of the war most of these warships were distributed world-wide, leaving the North Sea and the seas between Scotland and Greenland almost completely unguarded. These waters had to be patrolled for apart from the English Channel, this was the only way out to the Atlantic where the German raiders wanted to attack our convoys. As a result, ocean liners were commandeered by the Royal Navy for this purpose.

The liners were stripped of their luxury fittings and the lower decks and holds packed with empty oil drums in the vain belief it would enable them to remain afloat if holed in an action. These AMCs, or Armed Merchant Cruisers, were then fitted with eight 6-inch guns, many small calibre weapons and, in some cases, depth-charge throwers which made them quite formidable warships, even though most if not all of the 6-inch guns were of pre-World War One vintage, while many were made before 1900. Their main duty was to patrol the area between Scotland, Iceland and the Denmark Straits between Iceland and Greenland (known as the Northern Patrol). Unfortunately they were just as vulnerable to attacks from submarines as any other merchant ship, as they had no sonar or asdic equipment.

I was a signalman on the *Transylvania*, an ex-Anchor Line ship. We, *Rawalpindi* and *Scotstoun* were the first three AMCs to go on patrol, although soon followed by many more. At midnight on 10th August 1940 I was off watch and asleep in my bunk when I was awakened by two very loud explosions, quickly followed by the klaxon for 'Action Stations'. I was up and dressed in a matter of minutes: all the time I could feel the ship heeling over. I raced along the passage to get to the bridge three decks above me and, as I ran, I could see and hear the watertight doors clanging shut, closing off the passages and decks.

When I did reach the bridge the ship was listing well to starboard. Two torpedoes had struck us amidships in the engine-room, a fatal blow as this was the largest void in the ship. The conditions down there must have been appalling; as the ship continued to heel over we could hear the explosive noise of bulkheads and watertight doors giving way under the strain of trying to hold back the sea, and with these noises came a continuous roar, apparently from the engine-room, from ruptured steam pipes and the inrushing sea. The ship was sinking, so the captain mustered his officers on the bridge, thanked them and the ratings on the bridge then gave the order to 'Abandon Ship'. The leading signalman who was in charge of my watch said, 'Go on, boy, off you go and good luck.' I never met up with him again and to this day don't know whether he survived or not.

By now the ship was lying over at an astonishing angle, and the weather conditions were very bad. It was impossible to launch the life-boat port side due to the angle of the ship, and on the starboard side (my boat station) the rough sea and high waves had smashed the boats in the davits. I am a non-swimmer, so it was no use me jumping into the sea. I just clung to a deck hatch. I had no idea what to do, but honestly did not think for one minute about dying as it all seemed so unreal. Eventually, while clinging to the hatch, I heard men shouting to me to jump. Even though it was dark I could just distinguish a small boat, known as a harbour skimming dish, in front of me. I have no idea how I managed to reach the boat – all I remember is that I was in the water with several others clinging to the ropes around the sides of the boat, which was completely full. We soon drifted off away from the ship and in the dark we watched her slowly stand on end and sink beneath the waves, carrying with her very many of the crew. I noticed that, strangely, some lights remained on as the sank. This all happened during the fifteen or twenty minutes from the time we were hit.

I remained clinging to the little boat for the next seven hours. The weather had been so bad that rescue operations had been delayed: by the time they reached the place where the ship had sunk we had drifted quite a few miles away. Eventually we sighted them in the distance and, as I was a signalman, the men in the boat hauled me in and held me upright while I signalled to them with a hand lamp. Fortunately they saw the light and headed towards us. On reaching our position the four destroyers, *Fame*, *Mashona*, *Matabele* and *Ashanti* formed a square in an attempt to create a calmer patch of sea. We drifted toward *Ashanti*, which had lowered her scrambling nets along her side.

As we reached the destroyer's side those hanging on the side of the boat nearest the ship scrambled up the nets first, while we on the other side had to wait until some of the men had left the boat before we could enter it and reach the nets. With the very heavy swell the rise and fall between the boat and the destroyer was considerable; when it came to my turn I mis-timed my jump, missing the net completely. Fortunately the small boat rose on a wave, catching my legs and throwing me up to where a sailor lying flat on the destroyer's deck caught my wrist, hanging on until another sailor helped him pull me inboard.

By this time I was exhausted and numb with cold after all that time in the water. The sailors took me below to a mess where I was stripped of my clothes, given a blanket to wrap around myself and a cup of steaming hot tea, after which I lay down on the lockers for a good sleep. When I awoke I was given my clothes, which by now were dry, and together with the other survivors, a good meal.

We anchored off Greenock and, after thanking the crew members (to whom I am eternally grateful) we were taken ashore. We were met by members of the Salvation Army, who took us to a large hall where we could have a good wash and were given fresh clean civilian clothes plus half-a-crown(2s. 6d.), a bar of toilet soap, a small hand-towel, a packet of cigarettes and a box of matches.

After being debriefed we were sent down to London, where we reported to the RN Transport Office. The chief petty officer said that if we lived within the London area we could have night leave to visit our relations, but only on the strict understanding that we reported back to him by 8am the next day. This we readily agreed to. The following day we were on our way back to Chatham, to HMS *Pembroke*, to await another draft to another ship to continue our part in the war at sea.

Lieutenant Horace Taylor, RNVR

I had volunteered for the Navy at the outbreak of war in September 1939. I was thirty-two and had spent the previous two years doing war service as staff officer to the man in charge of Manchester Central Docks. I was sent a medical form and had to have my ears examined. When I got to the recruitment department they called my name: 'Taylor – Navy rejection.' I felt horrible. So I went home and wrote a letter to the Secretary to the Admiralty. I told them if they didn't do something very quickly, they were going to lose a good chap. My letter went that day and the next my commission came through.

To start with, there were various training jobs to do. I had some funny jobs in my time. At one point I was given a Webley .45 gun and was told to defend the third floor of the Admiralty. I was there until the start of the Battle of Britain. Then I became involved with mine-sweeping, especially magnetic mines. When I first started there were only two of us, but some more chaps came later. We were a very secret society. Nobody knew we existed. We had no Admiralty building of our own, no telephone, no brass plate on the door. The reason for the secrecy was that we were scared stiff that the Germans would find out what we knew about their mines and alter their bombs as a result.

At first the work didn't sound very thrilling to me, but once the Battle of Britain and the Blitz on London began, I realised just how important we were. Magnetic mines were being dropped in their hundreds and London was virtually paralysed. The day I started work, there were 121 unexploded bombs to be dealt with. As the evacuation area for just one bomb was 20,000 people, you can imagine the panic everyone was in. The trouble was, these were the first mines of their kind to be dropped and we had little idea how to handle them. So there were no proper tools. We were working with ladies' hair pins, match sticks, bent nails, a bicycle pump and the bulb of a motor-horn.

My first job was in a big hospital in North London which held 2,000 patients, mostly from Dunkirk. A mine had landed in the front gateway. No one could get in or go out. The mine weighed 2,000 kilos, was two feet two inches in diameter, and nine feet long. Magnetic mines like this one were being dropped by enemy aircraft in the hope of mining the Thames. They had huge reinforced parachutes and when the bomb was released, the aeroplane, now free of the weight, would rise sharply up into the sky. If all went well, the mine would fall into the sea. If it didn't and landed elsewhere, then it wouldn't go off. Or if it did, it would go off when it shouldn't.

These mines had a small fuse, which, if triggered, would go off in seventeen seconds. The mystery of the seventeen seconds was that this was the time the Germans estimated it would take for the mine to sink down into the water. Then the pressure of the water flooding the fuse hole would immobilise the seventeen-second compartment. There was a clock on the other side of the mine which activated it from a magnetic point of view, so that it would stick to a ship's steel hull if one came close enough. Then it would explode two or three hours later. Our job was to take out that little delicate seventeen-second fuse and make the mine safe enough to be moved. Then the army boys would take our mine to somewhere on the south coast where some very splendid scientists would open it up and see how it worked.

It was that little fuse that put the wind up us, because we

knew that if we started it, we'd have seventeen seconds to clear out. So part of our drill was to find somewhere to hide, if we realised it was going to go off. That is not as easy as it sounds. And how far can you run in seventeen seconds? But my first job was so important, I couldn't afford to be scared, with 2,000 wounded soldiers and God knows how many nurses relying on me. The responsibility was shattering.

First of all I got my escape hole dug a hundred yards away from the mine. My assistant, Able Seaman Ross, would stay down there, logging my instructions as to what I was doing with the mine. Then, if something went wrong, at least some information could be passed to the Admiralty.

I told the hospital authorities what I was doing, and told them that if I got the small fuse out, I would blow a whistle, so everyone in the hospital could relax. Because the tension, as you can imagine, was colossal. I was working in full view of the hospital; they were all watching through the windows.

I set to work with the bicycle pump, the motor-horn and a bucket of water. The idea was to put enough pressure into the bulb of the horn to make the mine think it was twelve feet under water, which would immobilise the fuse. That seemed to work all right. Then I started to work on removing the fuse. We always expected there to be booby traps behind the fuses, so when I got the locking ring almost undone, I jammed a bit of stick into the ground to hold the fuse from falling out. Then I tied some rope to the stick and walked off, holding the other end of the rope in my hand, so I could pull away the stick from a safe distance. I was walking away, knowing that everyone was watching, very steady and nonchalant, not scared at all. I was just about to get into my little fox hole when there was one hell of an explosion. It felt as if the whole building was shaking. Well, it wasn't the main charge, it was a big one, because it blew a hole in the concrete path four feet across and blew the mine nine feet away.

I walked back very slowly and carefully. I knew that there

wasn't any danger from the small fuse so I blew a whistle. I hadn't realised what a stupid thing that was to do. Because in no time at all a tidal wave of nurses came out after us. They wanted my tie, they wanted my shirt, they wanted the German parachute. I was nearly pulled apart and the parachute nearly disappeared, such was the relief of the tension. I must confess to having felt some satisfaction after that job, looking at that huge building full of life, knowing that it would be there a bit longer.

My second job was at the Royal Air Force Depot, Uxbridge. For me, this was an easy one. There were no tidal waves of nurses and the fuses all came free smoothly. I thought no more about it, but I was awarded the George Cross.

A much more tricky customer was in a woodland in Oxfordshire. When we found the mine I thought to myself, 'Now where do I go in seventeen seconds with all these trees in the way?' There was an army unit not far away so I went to the colonel and told him I wanted fifty men to carve a way through the forest. He said, 'Who the bloody hell do you think you are?' I was only a Lieutenant and no proper application had been made by the Admiralty. So I said, 'It really is important. May I telephone the Admiralty?' There was a 36-hour delay on the telephones at this time, but the colonel said, 'Have a go.' He didn't know that our squad had a secret telephone code which would get us through to the Admiralty in two minutes. I picked up the telephone and whispered my code and in a couple of minutes I was through. Five minutes later the War Office phoned back and told the colonel to give me everything I wanted.

When I finally got started on the mine, the fuse came out sweetly, thank goodness, but when I started on the magnetic circuit, there was a loud hiss as I got to the 4-inch locking ring. I thought, 'Hell, this has never happened before,' and I jumped back over a stone wall and landed in a bed of nettles. And then I realised what a clot I'd been. The mine had been filled with hot explosives which had shrunk when they'd cooled. I'd just released the vacuum; that was the hiss.

On one occasion, we had a huge bomb in the Southampton basin. It was lying alongside a wall where three big coal barges were moored. The trouble was that two of the barges had been blown up by another mine and had sunk, burying our mine in God knows how much coal. So we moored two barges together and over the space between them, we built a device to support pulley blocks. Then we sent down divers, weighed down with copper suits, to scrape away the coal. The pulley blocks technique failed to shift the mine, so we got an atmospheric balloon. These balloons were four feet in diameter and were supposed to lift about a ton, so we shackled that on to the mine and waited until low tide. The balloon lifted the mine off the sea bed without any problems. Then we secured the mine to our vessel and set sail with a quarter-mile of rope in between us and the mine, just in case it decided to go off.

When we reached the head of a minefield in the Solent, bad weather blew up and the balloon sprung a puncture, so we were dragging our mine through a mine field. Eventually we got another balloon attached and decided to try to beach the mine on the Hamble Spit. We grounded it and when it had dried out, we could see its vital components. Then we left it on the mud bank and went to an establishment called HMS *Cricket*. We explained to the commander what had happened and where our mine was and that we were going to fire it at noon that day. That was agreed on. However, when we fired there was a bit of a thunder clap. We weren't very popular after that. So we thought it was about time we left.

In all the operations we did, I never felt afraid. It was prayer that kept me going. Every morning at breakfast time I'd ask God to hold my hand steady and deal with that treacherous little fuse. Each time my arm was taken in a firm grip and I was in safe-keeping.

But I did get blown up, once. A bomb I was working on went

off and blew me right through two houses. When they found me, I was still conscious. I knew exactly what had gone wrong, and all I wanted to do was to tell my boss what had happened, for the sake of the rest of the crew. But my rescuers wanted to put me into hospital. I was wrapped in bandages. I couldn't see; I thought I was blind, but it was just all the dirt in my eyes. I kept insisting I must go and see the Regional Commissioner but the doctor refused. So I said to him, 'You're obstructing a Naval Officer in the course of his duty.' I suppose he must have thought I was dulally because there was nothing about me to prove I was a naval officer. I didn't have any clothes on because they'd all been blown off.

Eventually they gave in and I was taken to the Regional Commissioner. They let me use the green line telephone and I was able to talk freely to my boss. He was very pleased to know that I was alive and he told me to go to hospital. I ended up in Leamington Spa, in a ladies' ward.

Lieutenant Michael Torrens-Spence, RN

I was appointed to the *Glorious*, the pre-war Mediterranean fleet aircraft-carrier, in September 1937. In July 1939, with the imminent threat of war, the fleet base was moved from Malta to Alexandria. When war with Germany was declared on 3rd September *Glorious* was sent through the Suez Canal to Aden to counter the German surface raider threat in the Indian Ocean. After three months of pretty intensive flying no raiders had appeared. I was then sent home from Aden by P&O. Three new squadrons were required for the new carrier *Illustrious* completing at Barrow, 806 Squadron (Fulmar) fighters and 815 and 819 (Swordfish). In May 1940 the *Illustrious* went to Bermuda to work up with the three squadrons embarked. On 10th June 1940 Italy declared war. This put the Italian Navy and Air Force between Britain and her last army (after Dunkirk) in Egypt. This army had some four divisions facing some fifteen Italian divisions on the Egyptian frontier. The Italian navy at Taranto had two brand new fast 15-inch battleships, with cruisers, destroyers and submarines to match but no aircraft-carriers. The Italian Air Force was deployed in Sardinia, Sicily, the Dodecanese and Libya with numerous fast bomber squadrons (SM 79s) and reconnaissance flying boats. The Mediterranean Fleet had two or three battleships, of late World War One vintage, and one aircraft-carrier, the twenty-five-year-old *Eagle*, with one Swordfish squadron embarked, but she was only good for 20 knots and in need of a refit. In cruisers and destroyers the Mediterranean Fleet was heavily outnumbered. The need to reinforce the Fleet and supply the army in Egypt was critically urgent. The Cape route would have taken far too long. Major reinforcements and supplies, including *Illustrious* and the modernised battleship *Valiant*, were therefore sailed for Alexandria from Gibraltar on 1st September to take on the Italian Air Force and Navy. The operation was a total and unexpected success thanks to *Illustrious*'s Fulmar fighters which shot down the enemy's reconnaissance aircraft. Consequently the Italians were unable to mount any offensive action. The whole force got through completely unscathed.

Admiral Cunningham, the C-in-C, was quick to seize the advantage he now had, amounting to command of the sea, no less. For the next four months the Fleet put to sea every two or three weeks to cover shipping movements between Gibraltar, Malta, and Alexandria. This continued until January 1941 when *Illustrious* ran short of fighters (I will come to this later). The Swordfish attacked the enemy shore bases and airfields by night and provided air anti-submarine patrols whilst the Fulmars dealt with the air threat. By far the most successful and spectacular offensive action by the Swordfish was the attack on Taranto on the night of 11th November 1940. The plan was to torpedo the Italian Fleet at its moorings at a range of 200 miles from the *Illustrious*. We would be up against 21 batteries of AA guns, barrage balloons, searchlights, and underwater torpedo nets, not to mention the guns on the ships we were attacking. Clearly the outcome was going to be anything between a disaster and a famous victory. We would be using torpedoes with magnetic warheads which had just been invented. Up to this point the torpedo had an ordinary contact head which depended on hitting something. This new magnetic head was designed to go off under the ship which would do much greater damage than hitting on the side of the ship. The RAF's Glenn Martin reconnaissance aircraft in Malta had taken some good photographs of where the ships were moored and of the location of barrage balloons and torpedo nets. It was a question of memorising these things and then playing off the cuff when you got there. There was no precedent for judging how it would work. You had to drop the torpedo at a height of 50 feet or less at very close range because of the confined space. Half the aircraft carried torpedoes and the other half bombs and flares. Fifty per cent casualties amongst the torpedo aircraft was probably the general guesstimate. Twenty-one aircraft attacked Taranto. About three weeks earlier we had a fire in the hangar in *Illustrious*. Trying to put in extra fuel tanks, somebody short-circuited a wire and caused a fire which seriously damaged several aircraft so *Illustrious*'s two Swordfish squadrons were short of aircraft. Five were borrowed from the old *Eagle*, she not being fit for the operation.

Lieutenant-Commander Williamson led off the first wave of aircraft at about 2030. My squadron commander, Ginger Hale, led the second wave about half an hour later.

During the attack a hundred thousand rounds were fired at us but only one aircraft was shot down in each wave. I got hit underneath by one half-inch machine-gun bullet. It was the pilot's job to aim the torpedo. Nobody was given a specific target. I dived down in between the moored ships aimed at the nearest big one, which turned out to be the *Littorio*, and released my torpedo. While you're low down over the water and surrounded by enemy ships the comfort is that they can't shoot at you without shooting at each other. I then made for the entrance to the harbour at zero feet and thence back to the *Illustrious*. It's difficult to know whether you have hit the target or not because, once you have dropped the torpedo, you're away. I didn't even see any of the action around me, I was too busy looking for barrage balloons. Once the formation had arrived over the target at about 8,000 feet it was every man for himself. We did not know what damage had been done until the RAF took some photographs afterwards which showed three battleships sitting on the bottom. There was great jubilation aboard *Illustrious* at having had only two aircraft shot down. When we were debriefed they wanted to know if I had hit anything and I could only say that you couldn't miss a big ship at such a short range if the torpedo ran straight. The photographs of that raid appeared in all the newspapers. I was credited with a hit on the *Littorio*. But ships sunk in the harbour can always be refloated. Only one of the three was never repaired. Two were repaired but it took a long time. In March 1941 the Italians still had only one of their battleships in action – the *Vittorio Veneto* – which wasn't hit at Taranto.

The objective of the navy was to try and keep the Mediterranean open for our traffic and to close off the enemy's supply route from Italy to North Africa. In the four months from September to December 1940 there were at least six operations, the whole fleet putting to sea to cover merchant-shipping movements, along with offensive action by the Stringbags. In November and December the Italians succeeded in mounting three or four high-level bombing raids with three-engined SM79s whose Bristol-Jupiter engines were Italian made, the same engines as the Stringbag. They were fast and aimed their bombs at *Illustrious* every time. But we never got hit. On 6th January we were at sea again off Malta to take over a convoy from Gibraltar. We knew that the Germans had sent a Fliegerkorps of Stukas to Sicily, commanded by a Luftwaffe Major-General. Their aim was to sink the *Illustrious*, having

appreciated that she was the key to the control of the Mediterranean, but by now we were down to twelve Fulmars, having
started with eighteen, and of these only five were serviceable.

I landed one at lunchtime after an anti-submarine patrol and
went down to the wardroom for lunch. About ten minutes later
a wave of Stukas arrived and a 1,000-lb. bomb penetrated the
armoured deck and went off in the hangar above the wardroom.
In the consequent smoke black-out, and with red-hot shrapnel
flying about, I made a dive for the wardroom door and got up
on deck. It transpired later that half a dozen people who were
having lunch with me were killed. When the attack developed
we had two Fulmars on patrol, but they had been brought down
to chase some Italian torpedo-bombers, and three Fulmars on
deck, which took off only seconds before the first bomb hit, so
the Stuka attack was virtually unopposed. The Fulmars laid into
the Stukas after they had dropped their bombs, and shot down a
few, but it was nearly a miracle that the ship got back to Malta,
having taken five bombs and having the steering gear jammed. I
spoke to a chap in hospital who had been in the hangar when
the bomb exploded. He said that he had heard a bang overhead
as he was standing in the hangar and he looked up and saw this
bomb 'dropping like a football'. Those were his words. He
woke up in hospital. About 150 men were killed. The Germans
thought they had sunk us, which is partly what saved us. The
Luftwaffe pilots went back and said 'We have sunk her,' so they
stopped sending in more attacks. Funnily enough, when we
were in Greece a few months later, I spoke to a German Stuka
pilot, a prisoner-of-war, who had been bombing us a few
months earlier. Even then he would not believe that the *Illustrious* had not been sunk.

Twelve surviving Swordfish from 815 and 819 Squadrons
landed in Malta and became 815 Squadron. On 23rd January
they flew to Crete with the aid of a following wind. The five
Fulmars also got to Malta and were left there for the defence of
the island. I was then sent to the Western Desert with half of the

squadron, to provide anti-submarine escorts for the coastal traffic to Tobruk, but after three weeks of this the whole squadron was sent on to Eleusis, an airfield near Athens. The object was to attack the two harbours in Albania, Valona and Durazzo, through which the Italians were supplying their army on the Greek frontier. To reach these targets it was necessary to refuel at an improvised forward airfield called Paramythia on the Albanian border, near Corfu, but with no intelligence or daylight reconnaissance and only moonlight to see by it wasn't easy to locate targets.

On the first attack on Valona on 12th March Jackie Jago was shot down, which left me to take over the squadron. Our last attack on Valona was on 15th April, whereupon we were obliged to evacuate by the German invasion of Greece. Altogether we attacked Valona three times and Durazzo and Brindisi once each, but this was only possible when there was sufficient moonlight. Damage assessment was virtually impossible except in the case of the last attack which blew up an ammunition ship.

There was one major diversion in the middle of this Albanian exercise, namely the battle of Cape Matapan. On 28th March, when we were refitting at Eleusis because of no moon, I was ordered to Crete with all available torpedo-armed aircraft, which amounted to just two. We landed at Maleme in Crete at about noon and were given a position, course and speed of the Italian Fleet, which was attempting to attack our troop convoys from Egypt to Greece. We took off at 1700 for a dusk attack.

My young observer, Sub-Lieutenant Peter Winter, did a good job and found the enemy. Before attacking we had to circle for a time until the light conditions were right. While doing so a mixture of eight Swordfish and Albacores led by Lieutenant-Commander Gerald Saunt, arrived from *Formidable*, flying in line ahead at low level. The enemy was in very close formation with all ships making smoke which obliged Saunt's aircraft to drop their torpedoes in succession outside the smoke screen.

At that time we still had no radio communication between aircraft, so that, even if Saunt could have thought out a better tactic, he had no means of ordering it. Being free to act independently I thought it would be a better if I climbed up to about 2,000 feet to get a plan view of the formation in the last trace of twilight. This revealed a bit of sea room clear of smoke on the bow of a major target. I descended into this space and aimed my torpedo at very short range at an easily identifiable cruiser of the Pola class.

The Pola cruiser was virtually stopped. The Italian Admiral Iachino detached two other heavy cruisers, *Zara* and *Fiume*, and two destroyers to escort her, and legged it for home with his main body. This included the new battleship *Vittorio Veneto* which had not been hit at Taranto. Admiral Cunningham was then able to overtake the detached force and sink it by gunfire later in the night off Cape Matapan.

It was subsequently confirmed by Italian prisoners-of-war that the Pola class cruiser was hit by a single aircraft attacking in the manner I described some minutes after the main attack.

After the fall of Crete 815 Squadron was sent to Cyprus with orders to fly a daily reconnaissance to Rhodes to get warning of any seaborne attack on Cyprus from there. The then defences of Cyprus consisted of three Hurricanes and a battalion of Sherwood Foresters, but the threat disappeared when the Germans invaded Russia on 22nd June 1941. By that time the Syrian campaign had begun and 815 Squadron concerned itself with attacking Beirut and stopping the Vichy French running supplies into Syria from the west. The latter was accomplished on 15th June when the Squadron sank the big French destroyer *Chevalier Paul* by moonlight between Cyprus and Syria. The French did not try it again.

This ended my war in the Mediterranean. I was flown home in a Catalina from Cairo to Poole via Malta, Lisbon and Foynes (in the Irish Republic), thirty-two hours' flying time, to relieve Dennis Cambell as Naval Test Pilot at Boscombe Down.

Midshipman Ian McIntosh, RN

When war was declared I was in the cruiser *Sussex* as a midshipman which I'd joined at the start of 1939. We'd had a bit of patrolling off the Spanish coast during the Civil War on the Mediterranean side, then around June the whole fleet moved to Alexandria. We were in fact in Alexandria when war was declared. One of the preparations for war, apart from fusing all the shells, was to sharpen the cutlasses for the boarding party. As this was likely to be led by midshipmen, the idea of sailors behind you with sharp cutlasses wasn't a very cheerful thought!

I had come over to Britain from Australia at the end of 1937 to start my training in Portsmouth with the idea of later transferring to the Royal Australian navy. I always wanted to go into submarines but the Australian Navy at that time had not got any. Firstly, I found submarines fascinating on the technical and engineering side; secondly you all lived very close together and knew each other very well indeed and thirdly, you got responsibility very young: So this was an attractive combination to be in.

Because of the war our training class on HMS *Dolphin* at Gosport was only five or six weeks. I was then sent to go out to Alexandria to be spare fourth hand for one of the submarines out there, but I never arrived because my merchant ship, the Anchor Line *Britannia*, was sunk on the way out. She had around 550 people aboard and was heading for the Cape and then Bombay. After Bombay I was to get further transport on to Alexandria. It was necessary to sail round the Cape because the Mediterranean was somewhat dangerous at the time.

We started off in convoy. But had just left to sail independently. I was in charge of the watch of look-outs up above the bridge, and had just taken over early morning on 25th March 1941. I thought something was wrong, because we appeared to be going in the opposite direction given the north-east trades are pretty regular. When I got up on the bridge I was not surprised to find that we were being chased by an armed merchant cruiser – *Raider E*. The first of some hefty shells started landing fairly accurately either side as a straddle. We replied with our one 4-inch gun, but it was hopelessly out of range and was soon out of action from a direct hit. We were then hit midships, and in twenty minutes the ship was very heavily on fire. We managed to get a Radio Signal off before the captain struck his colours and ordered 'Abandon Ship'.

The raider was good: as soon as he saw the signal he stopped firing. My lifeboat was Number 7 on the starboard side aft. Unfortunately the port side one had been smashed altogether. So there were quite a lot of candidates for my boat. Eventually I got everyone stacked in and we managed to shove off. There were four oars so I got people rowing. Others I got baling because there were a number of shrapnel holes in the wooden boat. I gave one man a baler. He looked at me in blank astonishment and said, 'Oh but sir, we're passengers!' So I used some strong sailors' language and he baled quite quickly after that!

I wasn't officially in charge of the boat: there was a Lieutenant West, RNVR Special Branch, who was a fire-fighting expert, and the third mate who was an excellent man, but he hadn't had any experience in small boats whereas, as a midshipman, I had. So I just took charge of the thing because nobody else seemed to know what to do.

We were about 600 miles west of Freetown, about eight degrees north of the equator. There was a fresh north-east trade blowing and quite a choppy sea. On taking a muster we found we had 82 people altogether. The lifesaving capacity according to the Board of Trade was supposed to be 56 so it was a bit crowded. We had had one or two rafts in tow to start off with: I hauled them in and saved all the rope I could. We tried to keep in company with the remaining lifeboats for the rest of that day. However we were so overladen it was difficult, and we drifted much further downwind. By the next morning all the other boats were out of sight.

We patched the holes with flattened out condensed milk tins which I nailed across the holes with nails extracted from packing cases. I did three of those from the outside hanging upside down with somebody holding onto my legs, the other I had to do from inside because I couldn't reach it. That just about kept the water out. We got the mast and sail up: it was a dipping lug cutter type of sail, just a straightforward sail, very low naturally. You couldn't sail her at all close to the wind. I discussed with the lieutenant and the third mate which route we should take. I thought we should take advantage of the trade winds and sail west for Brazil instead of trying the east. This route was twice the distance, but it would take us less time. Everyone agreed. I had read a book which mentioned the doldrums getting narrower when you got further west: one merchant sailing ship had crossed the doldrums at 33° West. So I said, 'Well, we'll sail due west until we get to 33° west by my estimates and then we'll go southwest and should pick up the southeast trades to make the coast on it.' All this confidence from a book I read!

I reckoned that we ought to ration things for 28 days. Each day a person had an eggcup full of water, one ship's biscuit which was terribly hard to eat, and two tins of condensed milk shared amongst the 82. That helped you to get the biscuit down. After that you could have your water which was marvellous. Throughout the voyage we never managed to catch any fish or birds although one flying fish gave itself up and we tried putting that on a bent pin. Oddly enough after about three days I don't think anyone felt hungry.

After about a week or so some of the crew started dying; the deaths then became really fairly frequent. The odd thing was you could see who was going to die two or three days before they did. You could see when they'd given up hope and, once they had, they died. It didn't matter whether they were lascars, or Goanese or Sikhs or Europeans: it was all the same. It was very peculiar, somehow it was the despairing look about them that gave it away; those who hadn't run their 'three days' picked up all right when we smelt and then sighted the land. They were 38 by then.

We were all suffering from these boils: the cramped conditions, salt water over you the whole time. In the hot periods we poured water over ourselves to help us cool down. When we were in the doldrums we had very heavy rain squalls just before night fall which used to leave us terribly cold. I had read Captain Bligh's account of his time in an open boat when set adrift by the mutineers of the *Bounty*. He wrote that by removing your clothes, rinsing them in the salt water, ringing them out and then putting them on again you were able reduce the chill. I had everyone follow this advice and it worked. Contrary to the views of those days I was a great admirer of Bligh: he was a marvellous seaman.

After about a fortnight when we came to the southwest we had about three days in light shifting winds. We were very short of water and our lips had become thick and caked. We were forced to suck on our buttons, anything we could find. Then to my delight we picked up the south-east trades. During that time we did get the first of a few showers. We desperately gathered all the water we could from the sail. After that and several other heavy showers water ceased to be a problem: we were able to have half a condensed milk tin each twice a day. Then on the 22nd day I smelt land and the water changed colour. This was rather earlier than I was reckoning on, but I knew there was an ocean current drifting us in a favourable direction. However I did not know whether it was good for five or twenty miles a day. I therefore thought it best to ignore it in my estimates. The steering was mostly on the direction of the wind – very regular, and at night you could steer on the stars, which was much the best way. I tended to be on the helm for about twenty hours a day because I found handing it over to some of the others led to the boat being luffed up into the wind. This meant you couldn't get her off the wind; and sailing again without getting an oar out to pull her round was very exhausting.

At about noon we sighted land, a long low sandy shore backed with trees with a few fishing boats. There was a very severe surf running and I wasn't going to try to land in that: we were all fairly weak by this time. So I ran along the coast up to the north-west and then stood out to sea for the night. The next morning we were terribly lucky, it was very calm and we ran into a bay and beached about 200 yards off the shoreline. Everyone made their way ashore. Lieutenant West and I had a general search around the boat and took out anything that was useful. Then we too finally waded ashore. Even though it was only some 200 yards with the water no higher than thigh level, it took us a long time because our legs by then were weak.

We found fresh water which was good, lit a fire using local wood and cattle droppings – a cheerful sign also. We spent that first night lying out and enjoying being able to stretch our legs for a change and drinking the water which we boiled up in a tin. The next morning I divided the boys up a bit: some went to look for shellfish, others to gather firewood, two of the stronger seamen accompanied myself and West to explore inland a bit and see what we could find. We didn't find much in the way of fruit, just a few berries. Making our way back we met two native boys who signed at us. We followed them to a fisherman's village of half a dozen palm-thatched huts housing about thirty people.

We found out we were in northern Brazil, on the north-east coast. We got a message through and arrangements were made to gather us up. We spent about seven hours in canoes travelling up creeks and then a couple of hours in cars and trucks to the state capital, São Luis, where we were looked after very well. Having entered the country illegally without any papers or documents we were first taken to the prison yard where a group photograph was taken of us. Then we were moved off to various hospitals where we were bathed and ailments such as salt water boils were attended to. Within two hours you wouldn't have been able to recognise anyone from the photograph! It wasn't until we were in hospital when they fed us small amounts over short intervals that I did feel hungry. I had lost about three stone in twenty-three days. It was an odd feeling having a shower: one's earlobes were like pieces of paper and of course bones were sticking out everywhere.

They looked after us and fattened us up for six weeks. During that time the fishermen came to see us twice bringing with them presents of fish and mangoes. By then I was able to speak sufficient Portuguese to thank them personally and we gave them some cartons of cigarettes and other things: they were terribly nice people as we found all the Brazilians to be. Theoretically we should have been interned, at least the naval personnel should have been. Basically they consulted Rio, and I think what they roughly said was, 'Well it *was* a British merchant ship, wasn't it?' and we said 'Yes.' They said, 'Well therefore you *must* be distressed British seamen' and we said, 'Yes, we are.' So they said, 'Therefore we *can* repatriate you', and we said, 'Yes, please!'

In the lifeboat I was quite confident, come what may, that I was going to get to the other side: I had very good reasons because I had only just met my wife a little while before: in fact we were sunk the day before her birthday. So I was quite determined that I was going to get back. I was twenty-one at the time.

Able Seaman Thomas Barnham

Before I joined the Navy I was a professional boxer, lightweight. In the Navy I was trained as a gunner and within three months of war breaking out I was on my first ship, the *Voltaire*. She was an Armed Merchant Cruiser, and they'd put eight 6-inch guns on her, but they were 1901, old stuff. We picked the ship up at Portsmouth and went to Malta where they put us on contra-band control. We just toured around the Greek islands for about five months.

Then we got word that we had to go to Canada to escort a convoy. This was 1940. We were the only escort for fifty or sixty ships right over to the Irish coast. Then we had to travel back to Canada on our own for the next convoy. The round trip took nearly three weeks.

We were doing convoys for nearly twelve months. I saw nothing of the war, the only time we saw action was the day we got sunk. In March 1941 we got word that we were going to Freetown. So we set off for Freetown all on our own from Canada. We put in at Trinidad for two or three days and started making our way to Freetown again. Early on 4th April the alarm went off. We could see this ship coming and we kept signalling it, 'who are you, what are you doing in this area?' but it still kept coming and never signalled. All of a sudden up came her guns and they opened up. We all got to our guns but where our shots were falling short, hers were catching us. Within a few minutes we had orders from the officer to split the crew and go down to man a gun in the well deck. When we got down there we found everyone lying dead and when we got up on the gun we couldn't focus it round because it had a direct hit. So we came back up on to our other gun and we just fired away but she kept hitting on us and all of a sudden we went over and the officer said 'Abandon ship.' I didn't abandon ship, I went right through the boat to the stern. I had one or two mates there on other guns. On the way I saw mates of mine lying dead. I went up to the captain who was at the stern, with about twenty other people. He asked me and another kid, a fellow called Ginger McInnes, to go in to the workshop and get some wood to use as floats.

While we were in there a shell came in and Ginger was peppered with everything. I finished up with a nasty cut on the elbow. We came out and all of a sudden the ship just turned over and slung us all into the water. I'm in the water and I see two boys struggling, trying to get on each other's backs. I got in between them. One of them was McInnes and the other a boy called Scott. Neither of them could swim and they were trying to hang onto this piece of wood, so I said, 'Now, cut it out, let me in the middle and we'll just hang on and see what happens.' Then McInnes says, 'Look, Tom', and he held his arm up and his hand was gone. We were in the water about thirty minutes when the boy behind me drowned.

Now all I've got is McInnes, myself and this boy that's drowned behind me. An officer had a life jacket on – you could see his head and shoulders above the water – I shouted to him, 'Pardon me, sir, do you mind coming over here and giving me a hand with McInnes?' He said 'I'm sorry Barnham but I can't swim.' That finished the boy. He kept putting his head on his plank and there was nothing I could do for him. Another lot of lads came by on bits of wood so I went with the other boys and after about two hours the German ship, who'd sunk us, came back.

You could hear t-t-t-t like a machine-gun coming from the ship, and we thought they were shooting at us. We had been given to understand that the Germans were right villains and took no prisoners. One of the best swimmers, a boy from Wembley, just gave up and drowned when he heard the machine-guns. But then the Germans put boats down to pick up the survivors. They brought us back to their boat and bathed us because we were all covered in oil. They had a German officer who spoke English, 'You were given to understand we were firing on you in the water but we weren't, we were keeping the sharks away from you'. Then they took us to the bottom of the boat, gave us a blanket and everybody went off to sleep. Everybody was woken up after a while, given soup and the wounded were attended to while we were there, I think we buried about three or four of our lads. Our officers conducted a burial ceremony but while they were doing that we had all the machine-guns on us.

The Germans worked hard on the wounded and we were well looked after on the ship, in fact Easter came round while we were on board and they sent a bit of chocolate and a bottle of beer to the prisoners. But we were dispirited. I'd lost all my friends on the *Voltaire* and there were quite a number of wounded amongst us.

We were taken to Bremerhaven and then on to a German naval base. We were there roughly three or four months. They supplied us with a shirt, I had a woman's overall and they gave us a handkerchief-like holder for our socks and we had clogs. They had us all working in different parts of the barracks. About nine o'clock in the morning they'd put us in a room all day peeling potatoes. After we'd been there about a fortnight to three weeks they would come in, call one of us out and take us to be interrogated. Once we'd finished with our interrogation they would put us back with the other boys. When I went up for interrogation the German officer offered me a cigarette (if you didn't want a cigarette he'd offer you an orange) and then all of a sudden he started on me – How long had I been in the Navy? Was I a conscript? How many brothers did I have in the services, what were they, naval men, Air Force or Army men. What part of the country did I come from – London? Then all of a sudden he finished up saying, 'Well, tell me who do you think is going to win this war?' Naturally I said, 'We are.' So his reply was, 'Tell me what makes you think you are going to win the war?' and then he goes on and says 'Look, I'll tell you why you can't win the war. We've chased you out of France, we're chasing you through the desert.' Everything he said was correct but nevertheless I still said, 'We're going to win the war.'

After the interrogation two cars would take you to another room where all those who had been interrogated were. They asked you what you'd said and they'd all been through the same procedure as I had. Then after everybody had been interrogated they drove us off to a naval camp, all naval ratings and, on the other side of the camp, the Merchant Seamen's Camp. From there we got into shoes and English army uniform. We were there about five or six months. We used to play football to keep our spirits up and there was always something to do.

Then one morning they had us all out early on parade and a German officer came up and said, 'That lot over there, go back to your barracks and get all your belongings, you're leaving.' There must have been about two hundred of us. They put us in cattle wagons and we finished up in an Army camp, Stalag 344, the biggest camp in Germany.

Lieutenant (E) Louis Le Bailly RN

With the evacuation of Greece ending in late April 1941 and with the need to reinforce Crete, we had to tear into boiler cleaning, change evaporator coils and make good the usual defects. Captain Berthon, my erstwhile chief in *Hood*, gave us particularly useful advice:

Make sure of your steering gear, that everyone knows what should be done if the primary steering system fails; but above all try and ensure it never fails. Bomb dodging is an art your captain and navigator, if they are lucky, will quickly learn. To be successful, instantaneous reaction to speed orders from the bridge and a reliable steering gear are essential.

Everyone assumed that Crete was to be the next big battle. And so we worked hard, preparing for an ordeal which we guessed would try us and *Naiad* to the very limit.

Hardly had *Naiad* come to her buoy in Alexandria early on 12th May than my chief was told we had barely 72 hours to bring all the machinery to immediate readiness. After 19 days of watch-keeping and several severe bombing attacks this struck us as a bit hard: we had not appreciated the Mediterranean pace to which we would have to conform. A run ashore had just been organised when orders came to raise steam for our first operation. By 16th May we were in position north of Crete with two other groups of light forces.

By then the bombing of Maleme and Heraklion airfields had started and we could guess at the soldiers' ordeal as we swept along Crete's northern coast. The German assault seemed to be delayed while the softening up process went on, so we returned to Alexandria to top up with fuel. By 20th May we were back in the Aegean furnace. Our task, the captain explained, with two other groups, was to prevent enemy forces from reaching Crete by sea. To accomplish this would mean spending many daylight hours with little RAF fighter support within range of German airfields in Greece and Rhodes.

History now records that in the first three or four days some 24,000 German troops were to arrive in Crete. Besides 500 troop-carrying aircraft with towed gliders there were more than 800 torpedo and dive-bombers, fighters and reconnaissance aircraft under General von Richthoven, a cousin of the world war one air ace. The airborne attack started early on 20th May. As we fought off dive-bombing attacks we saw Junkers 82s towing gliders and disgorging parachute troops on to the Cretan airfields. That night we swept inshore to assist the army but, though we could see the fighting, we were unable to distinguish German troops from ours so there was no chance of intervening. So close were we that the scent of wild garlic permeated even the boiler rooms. To this day that unmistakable smell recalls those hectic hours.

We engaged six Italian motor torpedo boats and sank or damaged four. As dawn came we withdrew to the southward. High-level bombing attacks pursued us and while on deck I saw *Juno*, one of our destroyer escorts, receive a bomb in her magazine which sank her almost immediately. During the night of May 21/22 Rear-Admiral Glennie with *Dido*, *Orion*, *Ajax* and four destroyers met an Italian escorted convoy. Within two hours the transports were sunk and some 2500 German seaborne reinforcements left to drown or swim ashore. Glennie was lucky. The darkness, during which the Germans had hoped to sneak in reinforcements by sea, was the navy's ally. The Germans quickly realised our night-fighting skills and swopped tactics. They dispatched the next large convoy by day, to become *Naiad*'s target on 22nd May.

Admiral King's force consisted of *Naiad, Calcutta, Carlisle*, the Australian cruiser *Perth* and three destroyers. It should have been joined by Admiral Glennie's force but he had had to return to Alexandria almost out of ammunition. On 21st May the German airforce had concentrated on the land battle. Next day the Mediterranean fleet was their main target. The attack on *Naiad* and the rest of the squadron started at dawn and continued for 15 hours. At 0830 a caique full of German soldiers was sighted and sunk as was another small troopship an hour later. We then sighted a collection of caiques and small merchant vessels escorted by a destroyer and a motor torpedo boat. The destroyer managed to lay a smoke screen and escape but the other escort and several caiques were sunk, while the convoy was forced back to Milos.

By 1100 we had been in action for five-and-a-half hours against high-level, dive- and torpedo-bombers. Our decks had been machine-gunned with phosphorus-tipped bullets inflicting terrible wounds on our short range weapon's crews and setting some of the ready-use ammunition alight. Our high-angle (anti-aircraft) director tower had been hit and a near-miss blew in our starboard side for'd well below the waterline and flooded the small-arms magazine. The inrush of water, for we were at full-speed, burst open the hatch to the messdeck above. The water taken in there brought *Naiad* down for'd and more water started to pour through the splinter holes (400 were later counted) in the ship's side, holes which the damage control parties had not yet had time to plug. A large messdeck was in danger of filling up and I was sent to help the shipwright shore down the hatch through which water continued to gush. So with the survivors of the local damage control party, sometimes up to our necks as the ship heeled under full helm to avoid the next stick of bombs, we wrestled to stem the flooding. Not the least of our difficulties were the mangled bodies of those killed by splinters and the clothing from broken kit lockers which blocked the suction hoses lowering the water level. In the end we had to ask the bridge to slow down for a few moments: no sooner had the squadron's speed eased than *Carlisle* was hit.

By now 'X' turret (aft) had used up its ammunition and 'A' magazine (for'd) still with some left but the turret itself temporarily out of action was flooding up through a damaged bulkhead from the adjacent small-arms magazine, wide open to the sea. So the magazine crew, up to their knees in the rising water and in semi-darkness had to pass ammunition manually from the magazine, along the messdecks and then down into the empty 'X' turret whose guns remained serviceable. Air attacks came from every angle but we were lucky: one air-launched torpedo passed harmlessly under our stern. Another had punched a hole through our stem without exploding.

When the German troop convoy turned back, Admiral King, aware that his squadron's ammunition supply was practically exhausted, retired towards *Fiji* and *Gloucester* who had been sent to support us. Tragedy almost immediately ensued. The destroyer *Greyhound* was sunk by a salvo of bombs. *Kingston* and *Kandahar* went to pick up survivors and Admiral King sent *Fiji* and *Gloucester* to give them cover. In hindsight, this was a mistake. The admiral was unaware that both cruisers were also desperately short of ammunition. The gallant *Gloucester* was hit by a salvo of bombs which sank her. *Fiji*, by now down to firing her practice ammunition, correctly left her and dropped all her Carley floats to help *Gloucester*'s swimmers in the water.

The situation was desperate and a brave and determined Admiral Rawlings, commanding the battle fleet, brought it into the Kithera Channel to support the cruisers, but the cost was heavy and *Warspite* and *Valiant* were both damaged. Next *Fiji* was attacked by a single plane and an unlucky hit blew in her side abreast the engine-room. Then another aircraft scored a further hit and *Fiji* rolled over and sank. Unlike *Gloucester* however, whose survivors were machine-gunned and mostly killed in the water, many of *Fiji*'s ship's company, even without their Carley floats, were picked up after dark by *Kingston* and *Kandahar*.

On 22nd May Admiral Cunningham made the signal: 'Stick it out. Navy must not let Army down. No enemy forces must reach Crete by sea.' But the price of preventing seaborne forces reaching Crete had not yet been fully paid. That night, *Kelly*, with Mountbatten in command, together with *Kashmir* and *Kipling*, was sent to intercept more seaborne troops trying to filter on to northern Crete. After sinking two caiques full of soldiers and bombarding the German-held Maleme airfield on to which troop-carrying aircraft were still landing, the small force turned for Alexandria at full-speed. At about 0830 they were attacked by a posse of 24 dive bombers and *Kashmir* was sunk almost at once. *Kelly*, at 30 knots and under full helm, was hit by another stick of bombs and turned turtle. Her commander (E) and those of the engine-room crew still alive, found themselves in an air-lock, so fast had *Kelly* turned over. Several contrived to swim down through the engine-room hatch and so to the surface. Many of *Kashmir*'s and *Kelly*'s people had been killed in the original bombing; many more were machine-gunned in the oily water. Courageously *Kipling*, despite three hours of intensive attack, rescued a large number of survivors, including Captain Mountbatten.

During a prolonged bombing attack such as we endured, engine and boiler rooms resemble the inside of a giant's kettle against which a sledge-hammer is being beaten with uncertain aim. Sometimes there was an almighty clang; sometimes the giant, in his frustration, seemed to pick up the kettle and shake and even kick it. The officer detailed to broadcast a running commentary suffered a breakdown during the battle so we heard little below, but through the noise and heat of the machinery spaces we came to understand something of what was happening on deck. Suddenly more speed would be called for, then we would hear our 5.25-inch turrets opening fire which told us aircraft were attacking. Next the bridge telegraphs might move to Emergency Full Speed and we would see the rudder indicator go to hard-a-port or starboard at the moment of bomb release. This would be followed by the sound of *Naiad*'s short-range weapons as the bomber pulled out of its dive or the torpedo-bomber dropped its torpedo. We learned to interpret, by the ensuing shake or shudder or clang, the success or otherwise of our navigator's avoiding action. Occasionally the damage control officer would ring me with reports of damage received or casualties suffered; occasionally my valiant chief stoker would report the fuel expenditure and his plans to keep the boilers supplied as our fuel reserves dwindled or seawater contamination from near-misses adjacent to some tanks showed up in his scrupulous testing.

From time to time my chief or I would visit the boiler rooms. Here, for hour after frightening hour, with ears popping from the air pressure, the young stokers knew and heard little of what was going on apart from the obvious near-misses and the scream of the boiler-room fans. On their alertness, as they watched for orders to open or shut off oil sprayers to the furnaces, depended the precise supply of steam available to meet the sudden changes of speed ordered from the bridge, on which *Naiad*'s survival depended. The more imaginative amongst them, no doubt, tried not to think which would be worse, to be boiled by superheated steam, cremated or drowned. Commander Marshall and I, in our respective engine-rooms, spoke often by phone and when not visiting the boiler-rooms one or other would go round the damage control parties and tell the bridge of the situation down below . . .

One irreparable loss was Chief Stoker Whittle, the regulating chief stoker I had selected on my first day as senior engineer. The next six months, in the general air of stability on the stoker's messdecks, confirmed the wisdom of my choice and now he was gone, killed towards the end of the action by a stray splinter as he went about his other task of ensuring the continuity of our fuel supply. He fought for his life for many hours, but when I went aft at night to see him buried with a shell at his feet, the commander broke the near unbelievable news that *Hood* had blown up. That there was another world outside the conflict in which we were engaged was difficult enough to comprehend, that the navy should be fighting two such great sea battles, so many thousand miles apart, was almost beyond understanding; but that the ship in which I had been weaned and I had come to love should have disappeared in seconds was a kick in the stomach.

It was hot and sultry in Alexandria harbour when *Naiad*, well down by the bows, limped in. Overhead was a German reconnaissance aircraft. No doubt the observer could see the masses of shipping in the harbour but he could hardly have distinguished the two large hospital barges which secured on either side of *Naiad*; nor could he have seen the torn bodies lying white-faced on their stretchers or heard the half-stifled groan or tight-lipped jest as they were manoeuvred down the narrow gangway. Nor could he have heard anything from the other barge for, from the dead, lying at last in peace, there could come no sound.

As the last of the wounded were carried down the gangway, we mustered on the quarterdeck. After a service in remembrance of those taken away by the barges and those buried at sea we gave thanks for our own deliverance. Our drawn and rather haggard captain, his arm in a sling, spoke to us of the gun's crews who had fought their guns till they dropped, of the magazine crew who had worked in the dark in a rising flood of water, of the signal boy who had twice swarmed aloft and re-rigged wireless aerials twice shot away and of the Royal Marine who had ditched the burning ammunition from a ready use locker. The captain said: "There was a moment when, due to casualties and damage Stukas dived on us unopposed; no guns were firing. We are here because when I asked for Full Speed, I got more than full speed; and when I caused the wheel to be put over, we turned like a taxicab in a London street. Indeed I would say that, occasionally, during last Thursday, we on the upper deck had moments when we could pause and take stock. But if, for a moment throughout that long action, the engines had faltered or the steering had not functioned, we should now be with those friends we have left lying beneath the sea around Crete."

When our army in Crete could fight no more the Mediterranean fleet, now reduced from four battleships, a carrier, 12 cruisers and 30 destroyers to less than a quarter of that number, had to remove from the rugged southern Cretan shore whatever soldiers were left, in the face of overwhelming air attack.

Just as Cunningham began to believe there were no more evacuation tasks for his battered ships, a personal appeal from New Zealand's prime minister, then in Egypt, triggered one final desperate operation. The fleet's last serviceable squadron, *Phoebe*, *Abdiel*, *Hotspur*, *Jackal* and *Kimberley* was sent to bring off the brave New Zealanders who had fought their way across Crete to Sphakia. Amazingly the squadron suffered no loss, but *Calcutta*, with her brilliant fighting record was bombed and sunk after being sent out from Alexandria to help fight off air attacks against the other ships so heavily laden with soldiers.

Except for those of us who had to remain to keep the coal-fired dock boilers alight to maintain steam to work the pumps (the Arab stokers having sensibly fled) most of *Naiad*'s crew were sent ashore until a parachute mine, lodged under the floating dock in which we lay, had been defused. Thereafter, with the help of the repair ships, we set about welding a great plate over the huge hole for'd and repairing the multitude of splinter holes and other damage. Many of the sailors were helping to restore *Orion* and at the same time remove the remains of the 300 soldiers killed when a bomb penetrated a crowded messdeck during her last trip from Crete. Then, unexpectedly, the French turned on us in Syria and *Naiad* was needed quickly on the Lebanese coast. So, our repairs more or less completed, we undocked, re-ammunitioned, re-fuelled and steamed at full speed to Haifa.

Sub (A) Lieutenant Pat Jackson RN

We did our training at Portsmouth in *Frobisher*. I was a midshipman. Next we went to the *Courageous* as an introduction to aircraft-carriers, after which we went to flying school and I started flying Tiger Moths at Gravesend on 5th May 1939. After tonsillitis I caught up with the course at Peterborough, which was an RAF base. We all had cars and in the evenings we'd meet our girlfriends. Life was fun in those days. War broke out while I was there.

We went down to the south of France for deck landings. First the instructor took us down onto the deck in a Gypsy Moth, just to show us what it looked like. Then we were put in a Swordfish and had to go out and do it alone. People always think deck landings are difficult, but I never found them much of a problem. I drove my car faster than I landed a Swordfish.

Then we came home to torpedo-school at Gosport. I was there until the invasion threat, when everyone was called into active squadrons. I went to join 825 Squadron which had had quite a few casualties, including their Commander. Lieutenant Commander Esmonde, the new commander, arrived shortly before me and almost immediately we went to the Norwegian coast in *Furious* for bombing and anti-shipping strikes. That was in 1940.

In May 1941 the squadron joined the *Victorious* on a convoy out to the Med. We had taken on some new crew, RNVR chaps who had not done any deck landings so we went to sea to give them some experience. On our return to Scapa Flow, we saw the most wonderful sight: the *Prince of Wales* and the *Hood* going at high speed into the sunset. We thought something must be up, they were going so fast and sure enough, as soon as we moored up, the *Victorious* was ordered to follow them out and ploughed across the North Atlantic. We were after the *Bismarck*. She had sunk the *Hood*.

I must admit, there were butterflies in my stomach. The prelude to our Air Strike was horrible, sitting and waiting your turn to get into the ring. You feel, 'God, I'd get out of this if I could,' but once you get into the cockpit and start up and fly in formation, you're just doing what you're trained to do. Just going across the Atlantic at vast speed with little to do except check your aeroplane, through one had butterflies galore floating around. I wouldn't say only in the stomach; almost visible, they were!

Eventually the *Bismarck* was sighted and we were sent off to try to slow her down and do as much damage as possible. It was 24th May, the day before my birthday. We took off at about ten o'clock at night. It was getting dark, the sea was rising and the weather forecast was not good. There were nine of us in the air. We staggered up through the cloud and got an echo on the ASV, so we came whistling down through the cloud and there was the *Prince of Wales*. Fortunately we didn't attack her because we recognised the four guns in the foreward turret. So we pulled away and she sent a signal by light that *Bismarck* was 15 miles from her starboard bow.

We went off, trying to get a bit more height. Then the *Bismarck* saw us and started to let fly, it was chaotic as we went in for the attack. Heavy flak bursts all around and the stench of burning explosives. It was at this moment I felt a tapping on my shoulder from the rear cockpit. I thought someone must have been hurt, so I put my head back and heard Lieutenant 'Dapper' Berrill's calm voice wishing me a very happy birthday. I looked at my watch; it was 0003 on 25th May.

Then we headed back to the carriers. We found them in the dark, purely because Captain Bovelle, bless his heart, used his signalling lamps to make a signal to the flagship. We all landed safely, even though it was dark, with rain and a pitching deck which was good because half the chaps hadn't landed at night before.

The next day, we heard that the German ships had slipped clear of our radar net, so an air search was organised. We lumbered into the air, each on a different bearing from the *Victorious*. The weather was bad, and wherever we looked, all we saw was a small circle of breaking waves immediately below us. Eventually at the end of our search we had to head back as we were running low on fuel. But there was no sign of the *Victorious* where we had expected to find her. We were lost halfway across the North Atlantic and the nearest land, Greenland, was well out of range of our fuel tank, which was nearly empty. All we could do was carry on the search, using the weakest mixture the engine would accept.

I was brought up a Catholic and when I saw the petrol tank register show 'E' for empty, I said three 'Hail Marys' pretty smartish. Then I heard Dapper Berrill shout and saw his glove hand pointing downwards. Below us was the outline of a submerged ship's lifeboat, with waves breaking over it. Someone was looking after us all right.

When someone gives you a lifeboat in the middle of the Atlantic and says, 'Get on with it, chum,' you don't muck around, you get on with it. I decided to ditch immediately, and dropped a smoke float to show which way the wind was blowing. I came down as if I were doing a deck landing and landed in the water about twenty yards upwind of the lifeboat. I stuffed my flying boots full of Verys light pistols and cartridges, and Dapper brought his compass. We had to release the dinghy manually, and it was blowing so hard that it was like trying to control a rather frisky horse. In the struggle with the dinghy, the air gunner, Leading Airman Sparkes, forgot to bring the fresh water bottles.

We got into the dinghy and it took just a few moments to drift downwind to the lifeboat, which was submerged. All we had to bale with was our flying boots, so we set to until there was enough freeboard for us to get on board and get some shelter from the freezing wind. As soon as we were on board, we all felt sick and retched up what was left of our breakfasts. Then we explored the boat, which had come from a Dutch ship, the *SS Elusa*. There was a bundle amidships which we thought at first might be a dead body, but turned out to be a sail bag with a lug-sail and a fore-sail. There were sweeps and a mast lashed to the thwarts. There was also a rusty axe and knife, a suit of clothes and trilby hat, a water-logged tin of 50 cigarettes and a bottle of 1890 Napoleon brandy. There were hard ship's biscuits and a water beaker in the boat's lockers.

We had a tot of brandy to revive our spirits, but it was rather strong on an empty stomach. Then we began to rig the mast using the lashing lines and cut the blade off a sweep to make a gaff, put a splice round it and hauled it up. The boat heeled over and took on steerage, which was a great relief. Now we had to decide what direction to steer. The wind was westerly, force five or six and I thought I remembered from school that the pre-vailing wind over the Atlantic was westerly, so we headed East.

That night we were swamped by heavy seas and had to bail out non-stop. And the wind kept changing all the time; we were in centre of low pressure. I tried to stay calm and sail with the wind, but then you'd find you couldn't make headway. It was like being in a cave. The three of us in a small boat with nobody to push us through. Sometimes I felt the world had given us up.

Dapper was a great comfort. I couldn't have asked for anyone nicer to share discomfort with. He was a Catholic, too, and he kept saying, 'Don't worry, chaps, I'm saying a prayer. You watch it, nine days and we'll be saved.' But Sparkes was a different story. He built himself a little igloo up in the bows using the aircraft dinghy cover and he sat under that saying, 'Why bother? It's only prolonging the agony.'

Since Sparkes had given up and Dapper hadn't much experi-ence undersail, it was up to me to handle the boat. I didn't sleep for the first four or five nights and I started to hallucinate. I thought we were sailing around the moon and the British consul on the moon had called me ashore and said, 'Would you like a hot bath?' and I said, 'Damn right I would,' and I started to walk ashore. Fortunately old Dapper pulled me back into the boat and told me I probably needed some sleep, so I left him to it and slept.

Eventually the strong winds lessened and we concentrated on sailing in a westerly direction, hoping to reach North America. Then we spotted another boat. Everything about it was black. The crew had black rings around their eyes. The officer in the boat shouted across that they were Norwegian, the only survivors from a convoy which had been torpedoed fourteen days before, and there were several dead men on the bottom boards. They were heading for Greenland but had been driven back by gales. He suggested that some of his crew should join us and that we should sail in company to the North. It was a hard decision, considering the state they were in, but I had to refuse. Our boat was lighter and faster than theirs and we would have more chance of survival alone. We gave them the cigarettes and some biscuits and went our separate ways. They were never seen again.

The weather alternated between fresh and gale force winds and during the storms we lost two sea anchors and our rudder. We were all suffering from the cold and the damp. We had to ration the water so we were thirsty all the time. Eating biscuit soaked in cold water gave us terrible toothache and the circulation in our feet and legs slowed right down. Dapper and I kept our flying boots off so we could move more freely and because we needed them for bailing. Although our feet were cold, we kept their circulation going by moving around the boat and whichever one of us was not at the tiller would massage the other's feet.

Sparkes insisted on keeping his wet flying boots on and because he sat in his tent and didn't move around, his feet became much worse than ours. Eventually he crawled aft, saying, 'Christ, I'm in agony.' I looked at his legs and they were going black from the feet up. When I massaged them, they were like bags of ice. He was in serious danger of getting gangrene, so we decided to make for the nearest landfall – Greenland, even though we had little chance of landing near some habitation. We altered course to due North, hoping to spot some mountains before coming too close to the shoreline, and then sail along the coast to an inhabited area. On our eighth day in the boat we spotted some sea birds, then three geese landed on the water near us. We felt sure land couldn't be far away. There was a lot of wreckage in the water and at one point I thought I spotted the periscope of a U-boat and panicked. But it was just a table leg bobbing past.

Then the weather worsened into an Easterly gale, and without a sea anchor and with just a steering oar, all we could do was run before the wind. On our ninth morning in the boat it was sleeting and we were sailing through crashing high waves. Dapper was struggling to steer with the oar and the sails had started to split. It was utterly miserable. I was sitting amidships, thinking, 'Well, I've asked the dear old Holy Mother to look after us and if she's given me this, I can't really ask her again, so I'd better start preparing to meet my maker.' Then, as we were sitting on top of one of these huge breakers, I saw this funny little ship, and thought, 'Oh gosh, I'm hallucinating again.' Like the chap in the desert seeing the palm tree. But the next time we were up on a breaker I saw the ship again. The wind was blowing its smoke in horizontal lines.

I then started panic stations and fired off all the Very lights we'd got. It looked as if the ship would pass without spotting us, but the last smoke puff went off with a louder 'pop' than usual, and they saw us and blasted on their siren. It was music to our ears. They dropped me a line over our bow which I made fast around our mast and this pulled us in under the lea. Some chaps jumped from their deck into the boat to help us. I could stand up but Dapper's hand was frozen to the oar; we had to lever his fingers up. Sparkes was unable to stand at all, so these three husky Icelanders hauled him on board.

Dapper and Sparkes were taken to the sick bay, but I felt fit, I just had tingly feet. Then there was some explaining to do. 'Where are you from? What are you doing?' They thought we were survivors from a German ship. Once I'd convinced the Captain we were not German, he couldn't have been more charming. From then on it was all comfort and good food.

They took us to Reykjavik where a Michael Bratbee came on board to check our identity. Dapper and Sparkes were taken to hospital and Sparkes lost his toes. I went to see the British admiral because I wanted to tell him about the Norwegian boat we saw. He sent a search out, but they didn't find anyone. He also sent a signal to the Admiralty that we'd been found, and some kind civil servant rang up my mother and said, 'You'll probably be glad to know that your son has been found.' She said, 'I never had any doubts about it. I went to a seance the other day and the medium said, "Your son's doing what he likes best: sailing."'

Leading Sick Berth Attendant Sam Wood, RN

The first time I saw the *Prince of Wales* I had come from the Isle of Man, straight from the training ship *St George*. She was the sort of ship you dreamt about as being part of the Royal Navy. It looked awful, frightening – I felt like a little ant. It was greyish blue, and even though it was December, the sun was shining and making everything look even more colossal. The deck was covered in pipes, leaves, portable generators, all sorts. Everything was humming and flashing blue lights. There were lots of people working on it, about 1,300, more frenzied than normally because it was the ship's final days in the dockyard. I was part of the medical personnel in the sick bay, one level down, and the first to arrive. The rest came about a fortnight afterwards, hundreds of them.

One evening we were all sitting down to supper when the tannoy went. The captain was speaking. He told us that two enemy capital ships had been reported leaving Bergen in Norway, and emphasised that one of them was the *Bismarck*. Then he gave us a resumé of what he expected the *Bismarck* was coming out for and said we were going to intercept if possible. He said the *Hood* and the *Prince of Wales* would give a good account of themselves. He then wished us the best of luck.

We had been sailing for a couple of days. The seas were fairly rough. One night it was terrible, awful, high waves, yet nobody was sea-sick. Before that some people had been sick on training exercises. They used to come to the sick bay to try and report sick – we would kick their arses and tell them to get on with it. On this occasion, before we even met *Bismarck*, no one reported sick, probably due to the tension.

When we were organising the battle stations for the medical personnel, I was told to go and pick out a suitable place for myself. I found a position exactly over the 'B' turret, a good twenty feet up in the air from the deck, which was at sea level. The waves were splashing over us. I had a smashing view, better than being at the pictures. It was an armoured wheelhouse with slots in it, some looking to port, some to starboard. The main one was looking forward over the turrets and the bows. All I had to do was move around and look where I wanted, I was the king of my own castle. At the time, with the view, I thought I couldn't have picked a better position. Actually, the way it turned out, I picked the worst place on the whole ship.

My orders were to wait and see what happened, to attend casualties and to get them down to the main clearing stations. There was another leading seaman there with me. We just waited. Every now and again the captain broadcast what was happening and what *Norfolk* and *Suffolk*, who were shadowing the *Bismarck*, were doing, and what signals had been received. Finally, he told us to expect to be in contact at dawn next morning. We remained closed up at Action Stations that night. The steady hum of the ship's engines seemed to calm everyone.

Dawn broke on the 24th May and looking out to the North East I watched the sun's golden orange light rising from the horizon and fusing itself into the dark blue of the night. The first thing I saw of the ships were two smudges on the far horizon. The *Bismarck* fired first. I just saw this orange flash come from her and this cloud of smoke and then the *Prinz Eugen* opened fire. I heard these horrible whistling noises like a train and then, as I looked, a great water spout appeared near me. Even then it didn't dawn on me that it was explosive power, it was as though I was watching a picture. The reality struck when the *Hood* went up.

I was watching the orange flashes coming from the *Bismarck*, so naturally I was on the starboard side. The leading seaman with me said, 'Christ, look how close the firing is getting to the *Hood*.' As I looked out, suddenly the *Hood* exploded. She was just one pall of black smoke. Then she disappeared into a big orange flash and a huge pall of smoke which blacked us out. Time seemed to stand still. I just watched in horror. The bows pointed out of this smoke, just the bows, tilted up and then this whole apparition slid out of sight, all in slow motion, just slid slowly away. I couldn't believe it. The *Hood* had gone.

The armoured wheelhouse we were in had a door which was closed by a big ratchet, nine-inch thick and made of iron. I thought, 'I'm not going to get trapped if this ship is going blow up like the *Hood*.' So I opened the door and headed for the bridge. Just as I was going up to the bridge this shell landed. It came through the front part of the bridge, passed through, and exploded on the compass platform itself. I was sucked up and seemed to float across the bridge and finally came to rest on the deck amidst a shambles of torn steel fixtures and bodies.

That was the first time I had seen casualties to that degree. First-aid parties came up to help me. They were formed of marine bandsmen, writers, and suppliers. There was a multitude of injuries including Lieutenant Esmonde Knight, blood pouring from his face. He was a well-known actor in the pre-war days. While we were looking after them another shell hit the radio direction room, and killed many more people.

When the bridge had been cleared of the wounded, I sat down and reflected. I was covered in dirt and blood and my head was throbbing. In my mind I could see the *Hood* sinking and felt I should have reached and grabbed the bows as they were disappearing. It was crazy thinking, but everything was crazy that morning.

We put a smoke-screen up after we had been hit, but we continued to shadow the *Bismarck* all that day and part of the next. I think we lost her in the evening time. I had just one small glimpse of her afterwards, when she fired at us – that was when she was making arrangements with *Prinz Eugen* to separate, to cause distraction.

I was about three hundred yards from the *Hood*. I will never forget it. I can see it now, even see the paint on the sides of it. We didn't try to go back for survivors, as we had to keep in contact with *Bismarck*. A destroyer went to pick up survivors. There were only three.

Able Seaman Bob Tilburn, RN

I was born in Leeds and when I was ten we went on holiday to Portsmouth to visit relations. It was Navy week and we went round all the ships. From then onwards, it was my one ambition to join the Royal Navy. My father was a policeman and it took me a lot to persuade him to sign the forms, but he did eventually, and I joined when I was sixteen.

After training I was sent to Portsmouth to join the *Iron Duke*, an old battleship used as a sea-going training ship. A few months later there was the Munich panic and I was sent out to Gibraltar to join the *Hood*.

On the *Iron Duke* we were still boys training. But on the *Hood* we were part of a ship's company, doing a job. Our captain, 'Hookey' Walker, had a hook for his left hand. On Sundays he used to change his silver hook to a gold one. In those days you were not necessarily frightened of those officers, you were in awe of them. Because they were so far above you, not only in the mental scale but in the social scale as well. It was still very feudal. Ratings could get as far as a warrant officer but that was it. I once knew a fellow whose father was a Company Sergeant-Major. His father said, 'The men underneath me are more frightened of me than anything else, and that's a good idea because if I told them to do something they'll do it. Rather than being frightened of what they were going to do, they're frightened of me.' With hindsight, I could see the logic of it.

We were involved with the Spanish Civil War, patrolling mostly; joined the Home Fleet for exercises and did one Russian convoy, operating mostly from Scapa. Then we were sent to the Mediterranean for the unfortunate action against the French fleet in Oran. We were all horrified on board. Personally I think that French admiral should have been boiled in oil.

We then came home, went into Liverpool to repair a turbine, and then back up to Scapa Flow. We now did North Atlantic patrolling. The North Atlantic in bad weather is very, very tough. On one occasion there was a very bad storm and we lost all the other ships even though we were using searchlights to try and signal. Four days later, ships were sighted ahead of us. So, general panic stations. In fact it was our tankers, which should have been three miles to the stern of us. The destroyers had disappeared. It was one of the worst storms I've been in. The waves were recorded as being 60 feet high. One wave came over and moved 'A' turret around. 'A' turret weighed 1000 tons.

When I first started off on the *Hood* I was in the shell room of 'A' turret. But later on when I was made a seaman gunner, and when they got rid of the 5.5-inch guns and put the 4-inch dual purpose AA guns, I was on the anti-aircraft guns.

I loved it. I loved watching the water, seeing the waves, seeing the power of the water. I thought it was tremendous. And how the seabirds, the seagulls would fly alongside us against and amongst all these howling gales. And you'd throw a piece of bread up in the air and down they'd swoop and grab it.

I always thought it was tremendous, the sea, but mentally, life at sea was numbing. I started reading navigation handbooks and I got some books about the stars. I would write down how far a star was away, multiplying the speed of light by so many million miles. Just to keep the mind going.

Our food was very, very good, when it was in the fridge. But by the time the chefs had had a go at it, and it was on your plate, it wasn't too good. The *Hood* could carry food for three months for 1,500 people. You weren't living out of a tin of beans or anything like that.

On 22nd May 1941 the *Hood* set sail with the *Prince of Wales* in pursuit of the *Bismarck* and the *Prinz Eugen* which were on their way to attack Atlantic convoys supplying Britain. The *Prince of Wales* had only just come out of the makers' yard and still had some civilian employees on board working on her gun turrets. We went over to Iceland and refuelled there. All the time we were wondering which way the *Bismarck* was going to come. There were three possible ways she could break out: via the Denmark Strait between Iceland and Greenland, or either north or south of the Faroe Islands. The *Norfolk* and *Suffolk*, 8-inch gunned cruisers, were keeping a look out in the Denmark Strait. The next morning, 23rd May, *Suffolk* spotted the *Bismarck* and *Norfolk* and *Suffolk* shadowed her from then on.

The *Bismarck* was approximately 300 miles away. We set off after her and at 2000 went into action stations because we expected to pick her up at midnight. Then the weather deteriorated and at midnight there was a blizzard, so we couldn't see anything. But we still had reports from the *Suffolk* saying in which direction they had last seen her. We switched off our radar in case the *Bismarck* could pick up our transmissions and know there was somebody shadowing her. We were travelling at full speed, about 29.5 knots. Then between 5.00 and 6.00 on the morning of 24th May, we sighted the *Bismarck* in the distance, turned in towards her and opened fire at about 25,000 yards. I was manning one of the 4-inch AA guns on the port side. The *Bismarck* answered immediately with three shells, getting closer and closer and closer.

Then the fourth, fifth and sixth shells hit us. Everyone, even the gun crews, was ordered to go into the shelter deck. There were three of us from our gun who didn't take cover. Then a shell hit the upper deck and started a fire. The ammunition in our ready use locker was on fire and started exploding. The gunner's mate told us to put out the fire, but we said, 'When it stops exploding, we will.' He went back inside to report to the gunnery officer and at that moment a shell flew into the shelter and killed the lot – 200 blokes. We three were still alive, lying flat on our faces on the deck with everything going off around us.

The next shell came aft and the ship shook like mad. I was next to the gun shield, so I was protected from the blast, but one of my mates was killed and the other had his side cut open by a splinter. It opened him up like a butcher and all his innards were coming out. Bits of bodies were falling over the deck and one hit me on the legs. I thought, 'I'm going to be sick,' so I got up and went to the ship's side to throw up. Then I looked up and saw the bows coming out of the water. The *Hood* was turning over. I jumped on to the forecastle which was nearly under water and started to strip off: tin hat, gas mask, duffel coat and all the rest. By then the water had reached me and I was swimming.

I had my sea boots on and a very tight belt. I paddled around in the water and took my knife and cut my belt so I could breathe properly. Then I looked around and saw the ship was rolling over on top of me. It wasn't a shadow, it was a big mast coming over on top of me. It caught me across the back of the legs and the radio aerial wrapped around the back of my legs and started pulling me down. I still had my knife in my hands so I cut my sea boots off and shot to the surface. I looked up to see the *Hood* with her bows stuck in the air. Then she slid under.

It was 6.00 in the morning. It was dark and cloudy but there was good visibility. A heavy swell, about 15 or 20 foot. There wasn't anybody in sight. Further away I could see a lot of clobber in the water, so I swam over. I thought I would get myself one of those little rafts, made of wood and about a metre square. But they were in a fuel oil slick and I didn't want to go in. So I paddled around and I was getting really very cold by then. I spotted two other survivors on rafts, Ted Briggs and Midshipman Dundas. But there was nobody else, nobody else. No bodies, nobody else alive or dead. Just we three.

Eventually, I was getting tired and cold so I got one of these rafts, laid my chest on it and paddled over to Briggs. You know, someone to talk to. He wasn't feeling very well because he had swallowed some of the oil fuel. But Dundas was sitting on his raft, He'd been on the bridge, 40 feet up in the air. Tell me how he did it? He must have flown.

I tried to sit on my raft but every time I pulled it down the other side came up and so I packed it in, because it was falling on my face all the time. We were on three separate little rafts, Dundas, Briggs and me. Where could we go? I mean, the nearest land was one mile straight down. You can't swim, you've just got to hope for the best. An aeroplane came over once but obviously didn't see us.

I'd read one or two of Jack London's books, where in the very cold conditions of Canada you go to sleep and you die. So I thought I might as well go to sleep. So I actually tried to go to sleep on this thing that was tossing up and down. I thought, if I'm going to die, I might as well die in my sleep. And then Dundas shouted, 'What's that?' and I woke up a bit and looked behind me and there was this destroyer coming, the *Electra*.

What a beautiful sight. Then it went straight past us. But I could see the signalman on the bridge who was looking aft and he suddenly sighted us and gave the flash and told the skipper and he turned to pick us up. That was a marvellous sight.

They dropped a scrambling net over the side and two or three of them came down. Waist deep in water, they just grabbed a hold of us. Shot me over the guard rail like a sack of spuds. I was so cold I couldn't move my arms or legs or anything. They took us down below and put us on the mess deck table. They had stacks of blankets. They were expecting to pick up about two or three hundred survivors. We were lying on warm blankets on the mess deck table and the doctor said, 'Right, off with the clothes, blankets on top,' and gave them handfuls of cotton wool to rub us down, to get the oil off and also to get the circulation going. Then one bloke said to the doctor, 'Are we all right to give them a cup of tea?' and the doctor said, 'Oh yes, ideal,' and then went to his locker and brought back some rum and said, 'Drink that.' I was old enough, I was twenty. I was able to swallow it in a cup of tea, half tea and half rum. It was wonderful. I could feel the heat going down inside. I was able to talk, but not very much. I was so cold, numb. I couldn't move my arms and legs. They had to lift my head to give me tea.

Then they put us into the sick bay. Orders came down from the captain: 'We are going into Reykjavik to refuel. Do you want to go ashore into hospital or do you want to stay aboard while we go and sink the *Bismarck*?' He was quite serious, the captain. They were going to go and sink the *Bismarck* when they found her. The *Electra* had half-inch plate and I'd been on the *Hood* with 15-inch plate. 'Oh,' I said, 'I've got to go.' So we went right to the hospital, all three of us.

As I walked into the ward in the army hospital, there was a bloke in bed who said, 'Hey sailor, it's just been on the radio, did you know the *Hood*'s been sunk?' I'm afraid I wasn't very kind to him. Well, I'd been up nearly forty-eight hours. We'd gone into actions stations at 8.00 o'clock at night and we were at action stations all night. We were sunk at 6.00 the following morning. We were in the water for two and a half hours. The water temperature was about 5° centigrade. Just a few degrees above freezing. We went into hospital that evening and the first thing I asked for was a hot bath because I was still covered in oil. Then I went to bed and I was just bang out.

The next day I was very shaky. We were told we must not talk to anybody until we got back to the Admiralty. Don't say anything to anybody at all. I prayed a lot. But there must have been an awful lot of other people who prayed on that ship as well. Ninety per cent at least – why me?

We three were separated, for different reasons. I had been clobbered on my knee when the yard arm hit me, which I didn't realise at the time because I was cold. It wasn't until I actually started to walk on the destroyer that I found I'd been clobbered. Briggs, of course, had oil in his stomach. And Dundas was all right, he got up and walked.

I had been told there were only three of us survivors and more than fourteen hundred had died – but it didn't sink in for a long, long time. That was peculiar. It sunk into me that I was still there, I was alive, I wasn't one of them down there. I think I got, up to a point, happier. Well, it's better being in a hospital than on a ship at sea in the war. The surroundings were better, nicer, warmer, happier.

We were in there about five days and we were sent back to the UK. Our orders were; 'You go on this ferry from Reykjavik to Greenock. You go into your cabin, keep your trap shut, don't talk to anybody. Your food will be brought to your cabin. Don't go out of your cabin. You'll be met at Greenock.' Briggs and I had a cabin together but Dundas, being an officer, had one to himself.

We arrived at Greenock on 29 May and travelled down to London on an overnight train. We were picked up in King's Cross and taken to the Admiralty. After the de-brief, Vice-Admiral Whitworth said, 'Do you want to go to the barracks and get kitted out, or do you want to go on leave until the court of enquiries which will be held very shortly?' So we said, 'Leave,' and went on leave. I was on leave for three months.

After the *Hood* sank my parents got a telegram from the Admiralty, 'Missing, presumed killed.' When I went to hospital in Reykjavik a second lieutenant from the West Yorkshire regiment, came to see me. He said, 'I know who you are, and I know what you are. I'm in the personnel department.' He said, 'I'll send a telegram to your family, give me your name and address.' All I put was, 'Quite safe, I'll write soon. Bob.' They got the telegram saying I was dead and two hours later they got the cable from Reykjavik.

For a long time I was in a state of suspended shock. It took me a long while to get over it. We knew immediately there were no survivors. There was no-one in the water. What I couldn't understand was why there were no bodies. No people drowning or anything, which you'd expect. That is what has puzzled me ever since.

I returned for the board of enquiry. The Rear Admiral in charge of the board of enquiry was 'Hookey' Walker. He asked me something and I said, 'Excuse me, sir, but you'd know more about the *Hood* than I do because you were captain when I first joined it.' They asked me a few difficult questions, the fire for instance. What colour was it? The explosions, what type? Were they like Japanese firecrackers? I said, 'I don't know, I've never heard a Japanese fire cracker.' What colour were the flames? They were trying to establish exactly what was on fire. Which really had no bearing on the actual sinking.

I had no theory at that time. I just told them what I could see. Ted Briggs, he was on the bridge, he could tell them a lot about the bearing, the water temperature, air temperature, signals that were made. I could tell them what had happened on the upper deck. Dundas was also on the bridge.

The *Bismarck* hit us. There was no doubt about that. She hit us at least three times before the final blow. But they were lucky in the fact that they found a weak place. You normally expect the Germans to hit you first, because their range-taking and firing is much better than ours. But once we get a hit we hold it.

In 1943 I went to America to join the HMS *Queen Elizabeth*, which was one of those ships that were clobbered by the Italians in Alexandria and went across to America to get repaired. Then she went home and straight on to the Far East.

The crew didn't treat me as a freak or anything. I'd been lucky, that's all. I kept quiet about it. I thought to myself: my mother, my father, my two sisters, my aunts and uncles, had all thought I was dead. Now, 1418 people were killed, so why should I boast about being alive when each of those 1418 had seven or eight relations who were saying, 'Why you? Why not my son, my brother, my husband?' So I kept quiet about it for a long, long time.

Telegraphist Air Gunner Les Sayer, RN

I joined the Fleet Air Arm as a TAG (Telegraphist Air Gunner). The training was just over a year. You did radio theory, semaphore and Morse Code. Then you did the air gunnery side, shooting, towing and bombing. It was good training but in those days it was run by the RAF not by the Navy, so our pilots were officers and all the ground crew were RAF.

We did our training in Blackburn Sharks and Westland (Wappity). I loved it, my first flight. Another 2s. 6d. a day, and it was a challenge.

My first job was on 811 Squadron. Then I got drafted to 825 Squadron, where Lieutenant-Commander Esmonde was the CO. All the time I knew Esmonde I don't suppose he ever spoke more than twenty words to me, not even in the cockpit. There was just no communication between the ranks. We formed up in the Orkneys. We'd only just got together. There was a nucleus of experienced people, about three pilots and maybe a couple of observers and maybe a couple of TAGS. All the others were brand new and straight out of training.

Normally you would spend at least a couple of months working up, practising torpedo attacks, but no sooner had we got together than we were shunted on to the *Victorious*, because that was when the *Bismarck* came out. She was out to get the convoys. So it was considered absolutely imperative that we got her first. We were the only squadron available and *Victorious* was the only carrier available in that area. *Bismarck* was much too far out of range for land-based aircraft, and most of our squadron were virgins.

The TAGs were not briefed. All we knew was what the ship's company knew, that we were chasing the *Bismarck* and that when we got within her range then the Swordfish would be launched. So we were at the sort of readiness stage, all nine of us TAGs stuffed into a little briefing room. Then we got the call, 'All right, we're away'.

The Swordfish is a three-seat open cockpit design. So the pilot is in the front, the observer is in the middle and the TAG at the back. We could only fire backwards. The weather was terrible. We climbed in a loose formation to about 10,000 feet. We got a blip on our primitive radar and came down to have a look at what it was, thinking it might be the *Bismarck* but unfortunately it was only an American coastguard cutter. However, the *Bismarck* was just beyond that and we had given our position away. So we had to do a low-level attack, and in we went. I was flying with Lieutenant Percy Gick who never spoke to me, but he was a good pilot.

As we went in I was sitting in the back, looking down between my feet. I could see the tail of our torpedo through a hole in the fabric in the bottom of the aircraft. It was like a red fin. I'm sitting there waiting to see that red fin disappear, then I know that the fish is gone and we're away, taking avoiding action. We did a run in and they were letting everything loose from the *Bismarck* and we were fortunate they didn't hit us, mainly because their range finders couldn't get down to speeds that were less than 100mph and our speed was roughly 90 knots.

Gick told us over the speaking tubes that he wasn't lined up and that he was going round again. So we went out to about 25 miles and came back again on our own: all the others were on their way back. So we came in right down at sea level. I'm standing up looking forward at the *Bismarck* and she's getting bigger and bigger and still they didn't see us. I thought to myself, well, they've only got us to aim at, they're bound to hit us, this is your lot anyway, so forget it. But we went in and dropped the fish and turned away and it was only then that they saw us and they let us have everything. Gick was very good. When they started firing their heavy stuff at us we had to count from the time they fired and take avoiding action. Another hazard was the huge waterspouts made by their shells. You could go through the splashes and get pulled down. We did fly through one of these splashes. It came up underneath us and ripped all the underside of the aircraft out so it was a bit draughty! We kept at about ten feet above sea level.

We felt relief when we turned around. I remember saying, 'It's bloody cold back here' because all the fabric had been ripped away, but it was only hazardous from the point of view that we probably didn't have much petrol. I could hear the pilot and observer talking to each other about courses to steer.

We thought we'd hit the *Bismarck*. There was only one known hit and that was amidships, and we thought we'd got it. It jammed the *Bismarck*'s rudders and she was seen to make two big circles. I suppose it was the beginning of the end for her.

When we got back to the *Victorious* it was dark. We had been flying for about four hours and we were right at the end of our endurance. We all got back safely even though, for some of the pilots, it was the first time they had done a deck landing at night.

When we got back we were given bacon and eggs for the first time ever, and also a tot.

She was finally finished by *King George* V, *Rodney*, *Norfolk* and *Dorsetshire* with a loss of 2000 men on 27th May.

CONVOYS, SUBMARINES
AND BATTLESHIPS, 1941–42

Surgeon-Lieutenant Dick Caldwell, RN

We had left suddenly from the west coast of Scotland on 25th October 1941, and headed out westwards and then turned south. There was much conjecture and below-decks gossip as to our destination and plans. We arrived on 5th November at Freetown and, after a short stop there for refuelling, continued southwards and despite the grim war situation we staged the traditional and light-hearted 'crossing the line' ceremony.

It was now fairly obvious that we were heading for Cape Town and it subsequently transpired that President Roosevelt and Stalin had already been informed by Winston Churchill, 'We are sending our latest battleship *Prince of Wales* into the Indian Ocean as a deterrent to the Japanese . . . it can catch and kill any Japanese ship.'

We sailed into Table Bay on 16th November, but our stay in Cape Town, much to our disappointment, was brief, and two days later we set off again with some urgency for Colombo. Secrecy had now broken and the newspaper headlines flared the news 'Britain's newest battleship for Singapore'. Ten days later at Colombo, having called at the tiny wartime base of Addu Atoll in the Maldive Islands, we joined up with *Repulse* and the four escorting destroyers. Incidentally, during our passage out we had heard that the aircraft-carrier *Indomitable* had damaged herself in the West Indies and would not be available as planned to join and support Force 'Z' (as it was to be designated) and no replacement for the aircraft-carrier would be provided. This was a bitter and ominous piece of news.

When we arrived at Singapore on 2nd December the city was brightly lit and certainly, on the surface at any rate, confident that the advent of the two large ships would counteract and lull the now insistent sabre-rattling of the Japanese war-lords. The arrival of *Prince of Wales* in particular, to which the newspapers had already attached the adjective 'unsinkable', was greeted with great enthusiasm and the local press went so far as to state somewhat euphorically, 'the Japanese are caught in a trap of their own making and neither by land nor sea nor in the air do they have a glimmer of a chance of victory . . .' (It subsequently emerged that Japanese minesweepers were already laying massive minefields in the northern route from Singapore and Japanese submarines were already deployed in the same areas.)

The night after our arrival in Singapore a large party was given in our honour. Old friends were met and new friends made and future plans discussed of meetings, of tennis and golf; but these were not to be for early the following day, all leave was stopped – the date was now 6th December.

It was about 3.30am on the fateful Sunday morning of 7th December when I awoke hearing 'Action Stations' shouted and sounded off on the ship's loudspeakers. As I reluctantly got up and dressed I thought it was probably only an exercise, but on arriving at my action station on the bridge I quickly realised from the general atmosphere of tenseness that this was not the case, and on questioning someone I was told that several almost certainly hostile aircraft were reported flying in towards Singapore. The first grey light of dawn was just visible as we stood there – whispering, waiting.

Suddenly someone shouted 'Look!' and pointed. There, far away and very high over Singapore itself, just dots moving in a searchlight beam, were several aircraft. I watched them fascinated. We knew now they were Japs and as I watched them I thought, 'What everyone hoped and prayed would not happen is about to happen now, for just as soon as they drop a bomb, or we fire a gun it's another war to spread misery, death and destruction.' Even as I was thinking this I heard the crump, crump, of bombs answered almost instantaneously by the flaming roar of our guns. So it had happened!

Later, as we gathered round a crackling oscillating wireless set in the wardroom we heard of the fury and treachery of the Japanese strike at Pearl Harbor, and of battered ships and airfields. And I think most of us felt 'Well, the Americans are in! It's round one to the Japs – but now they are for it.'

Gradually we began to get news of the locust-like infiltration of the Japs, and of convoys moving south and of the landing and fighting in the northern tip of Malaya. Late on the afternoon of 8th December we heard the orders we were all expecting and, as *Prince of Wales* followed by *Repulse* led out to sea to whatever was in store for us, we were proud of her – powerful, sombre and sinister. I felt and recognised apprehension – not fear – but tension coupled however with a deepened comradeship with one's shipmates and, hateful though war and its implications undoubtedly are, one experiences a selflessness and this comradeship which is difficult to define. I and many of my friends were aware of this as we stood in groups in the darkness talking, and conjecturing what might be lying ahead of us, and how the Japs would respond to our surprise attack – it was well for our peace of minds that we did not know.

Later there was a sudden silence, then the loud-speaker buzzed into activity. The captain's well-known voice began; there was a large convoy of Japanese ships unloading men and material in a bay in North Malaya. They were escorted by at least two battleships, half a dozen cruisers and many destroyers. We were going to attack them at dawn on 10th December. We had the vital element of surprise. We could do great damage, but we would have to be prepared for quick retaliation and subsequent heavy aerial attack by the enemy.

Well, that was it. Someone said he had heard the names of the enemy battleships and this caused a run on 'Jane's Fighting Ships'. How many guns? What have their cruisers got? We steamed steadily northward, well out to sea in cloudy poor visibility, admirable for our purpose. Then about an hour before the onset of darkness, unfortunately and ominously the clouds lifted, the sky cleared, and shortly afterwards the news flashed round the ship that a Japanese float-plane had been spotted far off on the horizon which was quite obviously shadowing us from a distance and reporting details of our course and disposition. Alas, we had no fighter aircraft available. Our surprise attack was no longer a surprise, and we cursed the fact that sheer chance had revealed us in that short clear period before darkness fell.

We were to be at our action stations all night then, and I wandered down to my cabin, collected a few things I would need, and as I went out took a last look at my cabin with all its personal belongings and wondered vaguely 'What the hell will you look like this time tomorrow?'

My action station was on the signal deck on the bridge. I had first-aid outfits and bamboo stretchers stored there and a telephone communicating with the other below-deck medical stations – there were two of them. I stood there for a long time just leaning over the bridge, looking down at the dark sea with the foam creaming its way aft on our bow wave, not thinking of anything much, and occasionally drifting in and out of the upper conning tower where we could smoke and just distinguish forms to talk to in the eerie blue light. I sat on the deck and leaning against a stretcher, dozed and woke and dozed again. Then somebody shook me and said, 'There is a broadcast just coming through.' It was from Admiral Phillips, the new C-in-C, telling us he had reluctantly decided to cancel our dawn attack. He knew how disappointed we would all be but unpleasant preparation for our reception would now be too great to justify our going in and he intended to alter course and turn south immediately – that was all. I didn't quite know whether I was a bit relieved or disappointed; but I did think that it must have been a hard and also a brave decision to make.

Next morning, as we steamed back south, we received news of suspected Japanese landings further down the Malaysian coast and a destroyer was sent in to have a look. Our reconnaissance aircraft was also catapulted off the ship to explore and report back. However, nothing was found. The morning wore on. Suddenly about 11.20 am we resumed first degree of readiness, and shortly afterwards echoing over all the ships' loudspeakers came that harsh and insistent bugle call, 'Repel Aircraft'. Galvanic in its effects on everyone and dramatic in its results! Every man has his post of duty and gets there by the shortest and quickest route probably plugging cotton wool in his ears and jamming on his tin helmet as he runs.

We were steaming very fast now, *Repulse* and ourselves with our destroyers spread out well ahead of us. Suddenly I saw puffs of smoke coming from one of them. She had opened fire. Looking for the puffs in the sky I saw more and more Jap planes and our own guns started up. A signalman shouted, 'Look at that bastard coming in at us.'

I saw a heavy twin-engined bomber fairly low over the water coming straight in at us, the noise was unbelievable, the roar of all our 5.15-inch armament, the cracking detonation of Oerlikons and Bofors and the chattering ear-splitting rhythm of the multiple pom-poms. They rose through a frenzied crescendo as the bomber approached. I watched him get nearer and nearer, bigger and bigger, I was horribly fascinated and kept thinking, 'We must get him, we must get him.' Then I saw his torpedo fall from the belly of his plane, splash into the sea and then its tell-tale line of bubbles heading for us.

Simultaneously the ship swung round to port to avoid its track and I found myself holding my breath and gripping the rail like a vice as the torpedo passed harmlessly on its way. They were attacking us from high-level too and a stick of bombs came screaming down ahead of us, throwing up huge pillars of water as they exploded in the sea. We avoided another two torpedo attacks on our starboard side and as the second plane banked away there was a cheer from the gun's crews – or rather a roar – as in smoke and like flaming newspaper it dropped lower and lower until it hit the sea and disappeared. A huge oily column of smoke marked its end.

We saw another plume of smoke rising from the sea three or four miles astern. It was certainly nice to know that anything crashing into the sea was Japanese. Then there was a slight lull. So far so good. We sent a signal to *Repulse* asking her if she was all right and her captain replied, 'Yes, we have already avoided 19 torpedoes.'

I had not had time to finish the cigarette I had lit when 'Repel Aircraft' sounded off again and I saw more aircraft heading in our direction from both sides.

The guns roared again and I heard a shout, 'They've hit *Repulse*.' I looked across and saw smoke and flames rising from her amidships. It gives you a nasty jolt to see another ship hit. I went to the intercommunicating telephone to tell the others down below and, as I clicked the receiver back on, there was a dull heavy shuddering explosion.

The 35,000 tons of *Prince of Wales* lifted and then settled with a slight list – a horrid sickening feeling. Verbal comment seemed superfluous. A young marine standing near me said 'W-was that a t-torpedo?' and started, quite automatically I'm sure, blowing up the inflator on his airbelt. Our speed dropped. The whole set-up was changing and I didn't feel awfully happy. I wondered how the medical parties between the decks were getting on. The indescribable din continued. *Repulse* had been torpedoed two or three times now and was travelling very slowly listing badly on fire, but her guns still flashed defiantly. As I watched her there was another heavy sickening jolt – hard to describe – like a sudden earth tremor I imagine. Another torpedo struck us and a huge cascade of water drenched us on the bridge. I went into the upper conning position to use the phone and find out if I was wanted below but it was out of order.

My job was upper deck casualties, so up till now I'd nothing to do but watch it all happening. The commander came scrabbling up a ladder, said 'All right here?' and gave us a grand tough smile.

The ship shook to another explosion. The high-level bombers had hit us with a heavy bomb which crashed through the catapult deck and exploded between decks. My impressions after this were a jumbled medley. I saw the battered *Repulse* hit again and again, list over more and more and slip below water leaving hundreds of bobbing heads, boats, Carley floats and debris.

I saw the track of a torpedo approaching, and realised that in our crippled condition it was going to hit us. It seemed a horrid inevitability waiting for the explosion that followed. I thought if only it was going to get dark soon we might escape but it was only midday. We gave a great lurch again as the torpedo tore into us. We were now practically stationary and listing heavily to port.

I realised that we could not last much longer and had a sudden vivid flash-back of our short-lived but exciting commission in *Prince of Wales* – ten months full of incident, full of highlights, his Majesty the King coming on board; the *Bismarck* action with *Hood* blowing up and sinking just ahead of us; the thrill of taking Winston Churchill across for the Atlantic Charter; his meeting on board with the American President, Franklin D. Roosevelt, and these two great men in our wardroom; grimmer memories of fighting, escorting a convoy to Malta, then the sudden trip out east to Singapore, to this. And inevitably my mind went back to my own previous escape from the *Royal Oak*.

There were casualties on the upper deck now and several had been brought up inside the superstructure. They were attended to and given morphine, and those that were unable to look after themselves were carried and placed inside floats or rafts for it was obvious now that we were going to sink soon. I went up top again for more morphine and, looking aft through the clouds of smoke, saw one of our destroyers manoeuvre alongside us and take off many wounded and as many others as she could manage. She slid clear as our list increased.

There were now hundreds of sailors standing on the sloping deck, they had been driven up from below by the increasing list and the encroaching rising water. We enlisted several of them into first-aid and stretcher parties. With the badly wounded the best we could do was to put them into Carley floats and launch them into the sea on the port side hoping they would float clear or be paddled clear before the ship slowly turned turtle, with its vast superstructure presenting an obvious danger.

On the starboard side men started climbing over the rails and diving and jumping thirty or forty feet into the sea below; but diving off the high side of a sinking ship (although a sound precaution) is a euphemism.

I took off my cap and my shoes and looked carefully round for somewhere to place them (an extraordinary action which I have read and heard of other people doing). I stood for a minute in the orderly crowd waiting their chance and heard a sailor say to his pal, 'Come on, chum, all the explosions will have frightened the bleeding sharks away.'

The ship was heeling over more now and I climbed over the guard rails and slid down to a projection on the ship's side. I stood there and looked down on dozens of heads, arms and legs in the water still far below. Then I said to myself, 'Please God don't let me be drowned,' took a deep breath and jumped out and down into the oily water.

A few minutes later *Prince of Wales* rolled over, her bows rose in the air and she slipped out of sight beneath the waves.

Surgeon-Lieutenant Maurice Brown, RN

It was lovely sunny afternoon in January 1942 when the destroyer *Gurkha* slowly made its way down the swept channel from Alexandria harbour and out to sea. I was on the bridge with the captain and several other officers and it was cold enough to wear a great-coat. In the distance two destroyers could be seen coming towards Alexandria in line ahead. They appeared to be very close together and soon it was evident that the second destroyer was being towed. Our curiosity increased as the distance separating us decreased and shortly afterwards I saw one of the many naval casualties in the Mediterranean at this time. It was obvious that the stern of the second destroyer had been blown off, but the water-tight doors had held and she stayed afloat.

'Must have been an acoustic torpedo,' someone said. 'Follows the bloody ship around till it finds her.'

The two destroyers were now very close and the smoke of a smouldering fire could be seen coming from the exposed stern of the second destroyer. 'Everyone in that part of the ship must have been killed for a certainty,' I thought, trying to picture the incident. These people certainly had had their baptism of fire, and I hoped I would acquit myself well if and when my time came.

My thoughts were interrupted by the captain shouting, 'Let's give them three cheers.'

A line of matelots rapidly formed along the deck and, as the two destroyers drew abreast, three resounding cheers went out from the *Gurkha*, led by the captain from the bridge. I felt that, as each cheer rang out, each and every man on board was expressing the admiration, sympathy and fellow-feeling for those of the wounded destroyer.

After three hours sailing, the captain announced that we were to pick up a convoy and take it to Malta.

There is practically no medical work on board a destroyer for the medical officer which most of them carried. When there is action with numerous casualties several months' work is crowded into a few hours. It was only natural, therefore, that the MO should be asked to do non-medical work like censoring correspondence and decoding messages. The decoding, at sea at any rate, was a not unimportant duty and the messages were usually reports on how many U-boats there were in the vicinity.

That evening after dinner, as was the custom, we spread ourselves round the wardroom either reading or snoozing or just talking. Inevitably two or three officers would start on some topic, anything from philosophy to prostitutes, and before long there would be a free debate in which the whole wardroom took part.

I went to my bunk shortly before midnight. I had one of four cabins, about seven feet square each, which were beside the wardroom. The wardroom occupied the whole width of the ship and, with the pantry, made up a watertight compartment. The four cabins, two of them on the port side and two on the starboard side had a wide passage, or cabin flat, in between which was also a watertight compartment. To get from the wardroom to the cabin flat one climbed a ladder out of the wardroom, through a man-hole on to the main deck, then along the deck a few yards to another man-hole and down a ladder which led to the cabin flat. This arrangement of watertight compartments localised damage to the ship.

I was awakened by the loudest explosion I have ever heard and thrown out of my bunk. I landed on my feet facing the curtain door of the cabin and was very wide awake. The door-way of the cabin was criss-crossed with burning planks. 'This is it,' flashed through my mind and, without stopping to think for a moment, I proceeded to lift the burning planks away in order to get into the cabin flat. My action was purely automatic, actuated by an irresistible urge to escape from the tiny blazing cabin. I never knew the real meaning of 'irresistible urge' before. As I grasped the planks I could feel the heat of the flames in my face and hear the sizzling of the burning flesh on my hands, though I was not conscious of any great pain. The planks were removed surprisingly easily – they had just been stuck to the varnished doorway by the heat – and I was out in the cabin flat.

The flames rapidly died down, and in the ensuing darkness, I could not find the ladder which would take me up through the man-hole on to the weather deck and safety. In the darkness I moved about, groping for the ladder. Several times I crossed the few square yards where the ladder should have been and realised, with a sinking feeling, that it had disappeared. The only means of escape had gone and I was trapped in a watertight compartment. I groped my way round the other three cabins calling their occupants, but nobody answered. Never did I feel so lonely. I could hear the hiss and crackling of a terrific fire, interrupted every now and then by the explosion of the anti-aircraft pom-poms situated high up on the after superstructure.

The wardroom, just on the other side of the bulkhead from the cabin was on fire. Beneath me were the fuel oil tanks, and beneath the wardroom depth-charges and 4-inch shells were stored. Good God! Would the heat of the fire ignite the oil tanks or set off the ammunition and blow the ship to pieces? And I was trapped in a metal box. I could do nothing but wait, and pray that if the ship did not blow up, and the fire was put out, I would be found.

Suddenly I heard a loud clanging noise. It came from beneath my feet. I soon recognised it as the engines trying to turn the propellers, but the propeller shaft was loose in its seating and, after a crescendo of clanging metal, during which I was afraid the whole propeller shaft was going to come hurtling up through the deck, the engines stopped and all was quiet again.

I called for help, but I could hear no voices, and presumed everyone was out of earshot. In any case, no-one could get to the cabin flat because of the fire. Then I heard a voice, the thin piping voice of the midshipman. It came from the wardroom on the other side of that bulkhead which was keeping the fire from me. How could he be alive in that inferno? He was shouting 'Gun lights'. (He wanted the commissioned gunner to get the electric lights working again.) He called three times. In the middle of the third call there was the sound of a heavy object falling and the call was cut short. I felt more lonely than ever. The thought that I might not be rescued hit me. The fear that the ship might blow up at any moment was almost unbearable.

I was aware now that there was a gentle roll of the ship and that, as it moved from side to side, water was swirling around my ankles. I had no idea where this water was coming from but its presence gave me the one thought, 'this ship is sinking'. By now I could vaguely make out the outlines of the cabin flat and presumed it was daylight outside. I had no idea of the passage of time, it all felt so interminably long. Now, when I touched the metal bulkheads, in my half-blind groping in search of the ladder, I got what seemed like a mild electric shock in my fingers. I could not understand this until I felt something hanging from the end of my fingers. I tried to pull this away, too late to realise it was the burnt skin of my own hand which had folded outside like a glove and was anchored at the nail bed. Now I knew that even if I did find that ladder, and could reach the man-hole, I could not undo the strong clasps which held it in place. The water was now up to my knees.

Suddenly the cabin flat was ablaze with light. A sheet of flame spread across the water and set me alight. Automatically I splashed the water I was standing in up over my head, and, as quickly as it came, the flame disappeared. A film of oil on the water had been ignited by the heat of the bulkhead next to the wardroom.

Inexorably the water rose, and my hopes of escape sank. Now I could no longer make out the outlines of the cabin flat. The fire had blinded me! When the water reached my waist and I was still standing helpless and blind I felt a sudden surge of heat and realised that I had again been set on fire. Splashing the water up round myself again soon extinguished the flames.

The water was slowly rising up my body. I calculated I had about fifteen more minutes of life left. When it reached shoulder height I began to have a most irrational, but none the less real, fear that the ship would sink while I was still alive, but trapped inside it. To be drowned in the cabin flat with the ship still afloat seemed a much less horrible alternative. So strong was this feeling that I began devising means of ensuring that I would not be taken down with the ship alive. There was a rack of revolvers in a case on the bulkhead between the two port cabins, but by the time I thought of them as a means of escape, they were already under water. In any case my hands were now incapable of handling a revolver. When the water reached my neck I was swept off my feet with the gentle roll of the ship. This really seemed the end and I yielded again to the lure of self-destruction. The thought of drowning myself occurred to me but even at that moment the instinct of self-preservation proved too strong and the mood passed so that I only got as far as dipping my face in the water once. I was now afloat in the water, which, with the roll of the ship, swished from side to side carrying me with it. I could still see nothing but imagined all the debris of burnt planks, cigarette ends, oil and filth which floated around me. The very fact that there was now no possible escape, no strain of hoping for a miracle to happen, left me wonderfully and illogically calm. I thought of the people who would miss me – the ones who would really grieve for me. I was humbled to discover how very few there were. My mother, my fiancée, my best friend Charles.

How long now? I looked up to see how close my head was to the upper bulkhead. I could not believe it! I could see, and what I saw was a tiny triangle of daylight about ten feet above my head. I immediately swam over to it. When I got there I found a space where solid deck should be. Using my elbows (I could touch nothing with my hands) I climbed through what could only have been the main weather deck of the ship, and found myself in the small-arms ammunition store. A case of ammunition had exploded against the bulkhead and blown a hole in it. I looked at the jagged edge of the metal and shuddered as I thought of touching it with my hands. The hole looked far too small to crawl through. I knew that if I got stuck, or my jersey caught on those jagged edges I could never free myself and would be left half in freedom and half in prison. Squeezing myself into the slimmest possible shape I put my head and shoulders through and found, to my relief, that not only did my jersey not catch, but I was able to lean my elbows on the torpedo tubes out on the open deck, in the clean fresh air and daylight. The contact was unbelievable. Despair was replaced by hope; darkness by light; and the nauseating smell of crude oil, burning clothes, hair and flesh, by the smell of the sweet, pure air. I took in great lungfuls of it as though I had never experienced the sensation before. I was sprawled across the torpedo tubes about four feet above the main deck. Not having the use of my hands, I wriggled down off the torpedo tubes, but as my feet touched the deck I realised my jersey had caught on a projection on the torpedo tube and I hung half suspended and powerless to do anything about it. The main deck (my former ceiling) was awash and the ship was badly down by the stern. I saw sailors up forward and rejoiced that the ship had not been abandoned. My blindness in the cabin flat had obviously been due to the oil in my eyes and not burns.

Then a hand shot out from nowhere and unhooked my jersey. What with the suddenness of the action, my oil-covered feet and a roll of the ship which sent a wave over the deck, I fell and slithered down the sloping deck into the scuppers. Luckily the guard rail prevented me from going overboard.

Willing hands were now helping me, but after walking a few yards my legs gave up and I sank down on the deck. I saw the Sick Berth Attendant passing several times on his duties and each time asked him for morphine. At last he stopped when he heard my voice and said, 'Good God, it's the Doc.' He could not recognise me for I was literally black from head to foot with thick tarry oil. With the aid of a matelot's big strong shoulder under my bottom I climbed the steps to the sick bay. I remember lying in the sick bay and the Sick Berth Attendant trying to clean the burns, but I must have fainted.

My next recollection was of lying outside on the deck, up forward, being strapped into a Neil-Robertson stretcher, a series of bamboo-like slats of wood interlaced and held together with rope. Everything was being done at the double and I realised I was a last-minute job before the ship was abandoned. Owing to the haste, only a simple loop was put round the middle of the stretcher, instead of securing the rope to two tie points, and I was swung out on a davit. As soon as I was swung clear of the ship, my head and shoulders, the heavier half of me, tilted downwards and I was in danger of sliding out of the stretcher on to the whaler waiting to receive me in the sea some twenty feet below. I hung on to the foot of the cone-shaped stretcher with my toes to prevent me sliding out head first. At the same time someone saw the danger and shouted 'lower away'. This matelots did with a will and I went down at high speed and crashed into the whaler coming up with a wave. Immediately I was in the boat the sailors pushed off from the now sinking destroyer. We had only gone about one hundred yards when someone cried, 'There she goes.' I craned my neck up over the gunwale of the whaler to see the ship getting lower and lower by the stern and the bows rising up higher in the air. She seemed to hang, poised like this for some time as though in one last defiant gesture, before sinking slowly, stern first. It was a sight I will never forget.

We were picked up by a Dutch destroyer, crammed with survivors from the *Gurkha*. (Unfortunately, most of the officers were having breakfast when the torpedo struck the wardroom. Only the captain, 'Guns', and a sub-lieutenant who were on duty on the bridge at the time survived.) At last I was lying down, and, glorious relief, an injection of morphine. Never did I revel so luxuriously in the enveloping arms of Morpheus. The thought of the U-boats still crossed my mind but the injection eased my fears as well as my pain and I was soon asleep.

My last memory of that place is of lying on a stretcher near the water's edge in a row with scores of other casualties. There was a clear blue sky and the sun was shining, although the air was cool. Standing off from the shore was a large hospital ship to which the casualties were being taken in relays. I hoped that when my turn came I would be left on one of the upper decks as I was now not a little adverse to dark places below decks. But, alas, immediately we reached the hospital ship I was taken straight into a lift which went down and down until I thought it could go no further. At last, it stopped, but from here I was taken through such a maze of corridors that, even had I been particularly fit and active, I would have had difficulty in finding my way back. Knowing that I was too weak to make any effective escape, I decided that if anything happened to the hospital ship I would not even try. From my position in the bowels of the ship I could hear the anchor being weighed, the slow turning of the propellers and the general familiar noises of a ship getting under way. Soon, to the steady throbbing of the engines, I fell asleep.

Lieutenant John Roxburgh, RN

I left the *Tribune* with my captain, Lieut-Commander Bob Norfolk, who took me with him as his second-in-command, or First Lieutenant (No. 1), to build a submarine called *Thorn* at Birkenhead. After completing its trials we went out to the Mediterranean. I remember being sent for by Norfolk. He was looking rather solemn but there was a twinkle in his eye. He told me a letter of mine had been returned, marked 'Unsuitable'. I read it and it described our farewell party when we left Birkenhead. We had a jolly good thrash and booze-up and afterwards one of our ratings had gone around the control-room swigging all the half-empty glasses. He then got up on deck with a bucket full of gash to hurl over the side, but he was so well tanked up, he forgot to let go and followed the bucket overboard. Fortunately he was rescued. I had described this vividly in my letter to a girlfriend in Canada which had been picked up by the censors as being an 'Unsuitable letter', letting information go to the enemy. The captain laughed and gave it back to me. No action was taken.

We had quite an interesting time out in the Mediterranean in *Thorn* (which unhappily was lost with all hands in August 1942). On 30th January 1942 we were off Dubrovnik where we had surfaced to shell a ship, to save our torpedoes. In the middle of this action the shore batteries opened up on us and we dived quickly near a lighthouse in the middle of a spit of rock offshore. There were shells bursting around us so the captain ordered us to 200 feet. As we were going down we suddenly all fell over without any sound having been made. It was a most uncanny feeling. The captain had ordered 'Starboard 30 (degrees)' but the course ordered to be steered hadn't got through to the helmsman due to the confusion reigning at the time, so we had done a complete circle as we went down and rammed the base of the lighthouse. Thereafter we surfaced and there was the light-house keeper looking down on us pretty excited.

The shore batteries opened up again so we dived and with-drew. When we surfaced that night I went up on deck with the second coxswain to inspect the damage. The whole of one side of our torpedo tubes had been bent round at right angles: the torpedoes were intact but could not be fired due to the blanking off by the bent tubes.

As there was no other damage we continued on our patrol and went up to the port of Pola near the top of the Adriatic, where we encountered a destroyer, an Italian submarine and supporting aircraft on exercises. We watched the destroyer giving the submarine practice attacks. That night, the 30th January, we sank the submarine as it returned to harbour, even though we only had half our torpedoes available. We found out later it was called the *Medusa* with a training class of a number of aspiring submarine COs on board. We had sunk the odd merchant ship before but it was our first warship sinking.

The next day we returned and there was a floating crane over the top of the submarine, trying to raise it, and there were a number of destroyers patrolling in defence. Norfolk wanted to try and sink the crane which I thought was a bit 'dodgy'. It would be very difficult to sink, particularly in face of the strong anti-submarine patrols, and why not let those poor buggers down there survive if they can? But I think most of them perished.

On that patrol we had a group of Yugoslav agents on board whom we were going to land. They were led by a delightful British officer called Major Atherton who had been the Balkans correspondent of the *Morning Post* before the war. They were going to help General Mihailović, as opposed to Tito, and they carried gold sovereigns defaced by a cross from a knife. Unfortunately after we landed them they were picked up by Mihailović partisans who butchered all but one of them, who escaped, for their money.

Leading Airman Donald Bunce, RN

In late March 1941, the German battleships *Scharnhorst* and *Gneisenau* returned to the port of Brest, on the west coast of France, having sunk 22 Allied ships totalling 116,000 tons. They were joined, after the sinking of the *Bismarck*, by *Prinz Eugen*. Their continued presence at Brest was a severe threat to North African and Atlantic supply convoys, and the Admiralty were forced to divert precious capital ships to protect these routes. These three very powerful enemy ships, at large on the High Seas, could have forced us to our knees, so it was imperative that this threat be countered.

A war cabinet meeting, at about this time, concluded that our naval commitments were too widespread, and the task of neutralising these ships should rest with the Royal Air Force. The raids on Brest left the warships damaged, but by no means crippled, and they remained a threat.

During April, high level meetings concluded that it was highly probable that the Brest ships would attempt a dash through the Channel, and this was one month before the German High Command came to the same conclusion. Clause 7 of the Allied Directive which became known as 'Fuller', stated, 'It is unlikely that the enemy would pass through the Straits (of Dover) in daylight'.

Admiral Otto Ciliax was in command of the German fleet, and his planning, with his countryman, the fighter ace Adolf Galland, was meticulous. Weather forecasts and tides indicated the night of 11th February 1942, at 1930, as being the ideal time to sail. A delay of two hours would be acceptable, after that the operation would be postponed.

In brief, the series of events which followed were so bizarre, they beggar belief.

First, the RAF mounted a night raid on Brest at 1930, which, of course, delayed the ships' departure. This, in turn, meant that the submarine *Sea Lion*, on regular nightly patrol off Brest, ran out of time, and, at 2000, retired to recharge her batteries, thus missing the big ships and their destroyer escort, when they sailed at 2130.

The next line of observation was three RAF Hudson reconnaissance patrols, covering the area from Brest to Dieppe. The first Hudson was attacked by a Ju88 night-fighter, switched off its radar and escaped, but then discovered that it could not get the radar to start again, and so the aircraft returned to base. The second Hudson also developed radar trouble, and, likewise, returned to base. When its radar had been repaired, this aircraft got stuck in the mud at the airfield and was not back on station until 2248. Another miss! The third aircraft was working OK, but was recalled to base one hour early because of fog at the airfield. It was now 0630 on 12th February, and the Germans could hardly believe their luck; so, at 0830, the Senior Officer – Escorts – gave their position to German HQ.

It was usual, each morning, for the RAF to fly weather sorties of two Spitfires, but they had strict instructions to maintain radio silence. At 1020 Flight Lieutenant Oxspring took off with Sergeant Beaumont, and at 1030, Group Captain Beamish took off with Wing Commander Boyd, but from different airfields.

Both saw the Armada of ships, which had now swollen to 63, including minesweepers and E-boats, all protected overhead with a constant cover of fighters. Beamish decided not to break radio silence, but Oxspring did, and, amazingly, there is no record by the British that this signal was received; but the Germans logged it and, from then on, expected trouble. It took another hour to convince the British High Command that the danger existed, and, at 1135, Air Vice-Marshal Leigh-Mallory ordered 'Fuller' into action, sixteen-and-a-half hours after the ships had left Brest. At 1155 MTBs (Motor Torpedo Boats) left Dover. At 1210, South Foreland batteries opened up with 9.2-inch guns and fired 33 rounds, and, at 1235, the MTBs attacked, both without doing any damage.

As the British had expected a night passage through the Straits, this meant that everyone had now stood down. This applied to the Swordfish of 825 Squadron at Manston. At 1105, a Wing Commander Roberts, on the Admiral's staff at Dover, began to suspect the worst, and he telephoned Lieutenant-Commander Esmonde, 825's CO, to warn him. He, in turn, brought 825 to readiness. Roberts then attempted to arrange a fighter escort, five squadrons to support 825 and two to attack the German E-boats. At Biggin Hill RAF airfield, the Intelligence Officer was on leave, and had taken the key of the safe with him, so no one knew what 'Fuller' meant. At 1218, No. 72 Spitfire Squadron left for Manston, to escort 825, not aware of the full implications of the action in which they were involved.

As we made our way to the dispersal on that February day, the weather was no different to the previous days, bitterly cold, with snow covering the grass airfield. Blissfully unaware of what was ahead, what dominated our minds was that a planned night attack was now to take place at midday. As usual, TAGs (Telegraphist Air Gunners) were excluded from the briefing sessions and had to rely on the Observer for any 'Gen' (or information). Four TAGs, one former pilot of mine, one Observer, and, of course Esmonde himself, had taken part in the torpedo attack on the *Bismarck*, from HMS *Victorious*, and we were only too aware of the implications of a daylight action. This time it would not be in the middle of the North Atlantic, but in the Straits of Dover, and a warning was ringing in our ears from the RAF types in the mess: a new German fighter, the Focke-Wulf 190 was now operational.

We took off and formed up over the coast, and I exchanged a 'thumbs up' sign with fellow TAG 'Ginger' Johnson, just before seeing Spitfires overhead, and assumed all our escort had arrived. Soon after, we were headed out to sea, in line-ahead formation. I was in the first flight of three, with Esmonde leading, our aircraft bringing up the rear. The second flight was some distance from us, still in 'V' formation. I began to prepare the Vickers Gas-Operated machine-gun, loading a magazine and then sitting down and waiting. The weather was overcast, with low cloud and poor visibility, and the Spitfires were just below the cloud base.

Then it all happened: tracer from a destroyer 'floated' our way, that is, until it came close, when it took on the characteristics of an express train, and in came the FW190s. I don't know how many there were. I was just concentrating on those that were on our tail; it seemed endless. As soon as one peeled off another was in its place, with tracer speeding toward us. After a while they lowered their under-carriage and flaps in an attempt to reduce speed and prolong the attack.

I began swearing away and at the same time fired as much of the feeble .303 tracer in front of the 190s as I could, stoppages permitting; all drill in this respect went overboard, as indeed went any malfunctioning magazine. There simply wasn't time for anything else. From my backward viewpoint, it was developing into a practice shoot for FW190s, and we were the drogue target; they were coming so close, as they peeled off to the port I had a sideways clear view of the pilot. I had a quick visual image of the shells hitting the water, giving them perfect alignment to hit the old Swordfish.

Yet despite everything I had no impending sense of danger or injury to myself. I just considered myself 'fireproof'. Just as suddenly as it had started, the fighters left; presumably our torpedo had been launched, one is usually aware of the drop, but not on this occasion. Now I could look around. I tried to send some kind of distress signal, but the wireless set was dead. However, the IFF worked, and I immediately switched to the distress position, but as this relied on radar contact, at sea level this was a useless exercise.

I turned to the Observer, Mac Samples, to ask if he was OK. He reached down with one hand and brought it up covered in blood; his leg and foot were badly injured. The pilot, Pat Kingsmill, was also wounded in the leg.

Below us I saw some small boats which I thought might be MTBs. As we closed, their true identity was revealed: they were E-Boats and their gunfire immediately began hitting us. But Pat, with great skill, began to crab away, and I, with further oaths, emptied my last magazine in their direction. Then, suddenly, great flashes streaked down the port side; a large square hole in the upper main plane meant that the dinghy had been shot away. We had also lost two cylinders from the engine but we still managed to fly. Not for long. With the tail well down, we ditched perfectly.

On impact, I hit my harness release button and threw it off, then literally, stepped overboard into the Channel, to help Mac. A jerk on my head told me that I had forgotten to unplug the headphones! Thank God a motor launch was alongside. I was grateful, for it was extremely cold! Once aboard, I was bundled down below, to lie between the giant diesel engines, given dry clothes and a cup of 'pussers' rum. Pat was in the wheelhouse, and Mac lay on the after deck, a big matelot attempting to keep him warm, for his injuries were quite severe. The passage to

Ramsgate harbour, at full speed through a choppy sea, must have been a nightmare to the other two. The rum helped me, but the roar of the engines precluded any conversation, leaving me with my own thoughts.

An ambulance was waiting on the quayside and quickly whipped us off to hospital. I wanted news of my mates. At base Edgar Lee (Observer in the second aircraft) told me his pilot had severe back injuries but, to my dismay, his TAG, 'Ginger' Johnson, had been killed early in the action. There was no news of the rest, but there was still hope. Next morning, it became increasingly evident that we who had made it back were to be the only ones!

I was in a daze and it didn't help when, along with the PO Fitter, we were ordered to assemble and pack the kit of the other five TAGs. Stowing photographs and other personal items was very traumatic, but it had to be done, and rather by me than anyone else.

I learnt later what had happened. In the engagement Lieutenant-Commander Esmonde, who was leading the first flight, was jumped on by fighters, as well as being fired on by the enemy ships, and his aircraft was severely damaged, but even with most of his lower port wing lost, he flew on, until he finally crashed into the Channel.

The second aircraft, piloted by Sub-Lieutenant Rose, was attacked in the same manner, Rose was badly wounded and only with the encouragement of his Observer, Sub-Lieutenant Lee, did he manage to keep the damaged aircraft flying, make his attack and, finally, ditch safely. We had managed to get inside the destroyer screen and release our torpedo at about 1,000 yards before ditching.

The second sub-flight of three aircraft was not heard of again, and all nine people were lost.

Even more mishaps were to occur that afternoon. The RAF mistakenly attacked the only destroyer raid we could muster. The only success was that the *Scharnhorst* twice hit a mine and the *Gneisenau* hit another.

Air losses, during this time, were heavy; RAF attacks on Brest had cost them 43 planes. Losses on 12th February were: RAF 37 planes, and the RN six Swordfish.

For the Germans, the whole affair was a major propaganda coup; for the British, after the initial despair, a realisation that one threat to vital Middle East convoys had been removed.

How big a 'fiasco', or 'cock-up', it was can be judged by the fact it was one of only three events during the 1939–45 war that was subject to an 'Official Enquiry'. I would imagine inter-service co-operation improved dramatically when the War Command received the report.

Petty Officer Thomas Gould, RN

On 16 February 1942 we were inshore in shallow water. We could have just about dived, but the Germans were looking for us at sea. We had just sunk a very heavily escorted merchant ship which was escorted by aircraft, MTBs and destroyers off the north coast of Crete, in Suda Bay. *Thrasher* had suffered about three-and-a-half hours of depth-charges, how many I don't know. I don't know if anybody had nerve enough to count them. This wasn't the first time: we had had it before. We were there primarily to map the mines being set by the Germans and then relay the information back.

We surfaced as night-time came and were close inshore on normal duty watch. The skipper, Lieutenant Mackenzie, came down off the bridge and went to his cabin. I went to my Mess but just as I was about to get into my bunk I heard rolling noises outside. I thought, nothing of mine is out there – it sounded to me like the gun-casing, the parapet of the gun. The skipper also heard it because it was just above his head. Anyway I went and reported to the bridge, and he sent the lookout over, Daisy Adams, a gunlayer, who was responsible for the gun, to have a look at what was going on.

Daisy came back to say that there was a large black object on the forecasing in front of the gun platform and a great hole in the super-structure of the platform itself. They told me to come up and have a look for myself, so I did. Lieutenant Roberts was also asked as he was responsible for the outside as well, and was responsible for discipline over and above myself, the coxswain. We took some sacking and heaving lines and when we got through we found it was a bomb.

First Lieutenant Roberts took sketches of the bomb, where it lay on the forecasing while I held it still, as the boat was rolling around. At any moment it was in danger of rolling off the casing on to the saddletank below and exploding. Between us we managed to wrap the bomb in the sacking and tie it with the heaving line. It was too heavy to be thrown clear of the saddle tanks – it weighed about 100 lbs and was about three feet long. We had to manhandle it overboard, really slowly and carefully. I don't think the pilot had enough time to set the fuses. The explosion sounded as if a depth-charge had gone off. If it's very close to the submarine it shrinks the boat and then you hear the steel of the boat coming back to its normal size and shape again: it sounded like sand landing on a tin roof.

To get to where the second bomb was we had to wriggle forward through the outer casing of the submarine. In that confined space there were angle irons to hold the superstructure up, battery ventilations (which are rather large tubes) and drop bollards as well. When we got through I saw that it was another heavy bomb, again 100 lbs, and I picked the bomb up and passed it through to Roberts who came in behind me. I then laid on my back with the bomb on my stomach, and held on to it while he laid on his stomach with his head to my head pulling me by the shoulders. I was being pulled forward with the bomb on my stomach. Every time we moved it made a nasty twanging sound like a broken spring, which it may well have been. Finally we got to the grating.

All this took about an hour. It took us twenty minutes to wriggle in and a bit more to slowly wriggle out holding the bomb. We passed it up to the sub-lieutenant, who was waiting on the forecasing. I certainly think he should have been awarded something more than a mention in dispatches. We passed it up to him, and he laid it down on the forecasing. We wrapped it up with sacking again and put a couple of heaving lines around it. Then he walked forward to the highest point at the foremost part of the boat, and gave a signal to the bridge with a dim light to go astern. As with the first bomb, the boat moved astern as we lowered it gingerly over the bows. When we knew it was on the surface of the water and the boat was moving we let it go, heaving lines as well. Then we ducked and waited for the next explosion, but nothing happened – it obviously couldn't have been primed.

Lieutenant Roberts and myself were awarded the Victoria Cross for what we did. At the investiture at Buckingham Palace King George said, 'How long were you in there?' and I said, 'Oh, about an hour, sir' and he said, 'I bet it was cold.' I said, 'Yes, Your Majesty, but I didn't notice it.' Then he shook my hand and pinned on the Victoria Cross. I wasn't nervous until I saw my wife sitting at the front. We came out of the palace with my wife holding our baby.

Leading Seaman Tom Parsons, RN

I had been on the *Prince of Wales* when she was sunk and was taken back to Singapore. I was then detailed to patrol the Johore Straits in small boats, doing hit-and-run raids. On 12th February 1942 I was sent to HMS *Li Wo*, a converted Yangtze river steamer weighing 1000 tons. Out of a mixed crew from all the services I was the only trained gunlayer on the main armament, an old 4-inch gun made in Japan, which was situated in the bows. The chief bosun's mate, CPO Charlie Rogers, was the captain of the gun and Lieutenant Thomas Wilkinson, RNR, was the ship's captain.

We left harbour on Friday 13th February. Local residents

thought the steamer was being used for evacuation, and there were scenes of panic as we left. We headed for the Straits of Bangka and were attacked many times by lone aircraft, but we came through. On Saturday 14th February we dropped anchor close inshore, hoping that we would not be spotted by enemy aircraft, as the captain intended to go through the eighty miles of the Bangka Straits in darkness. We were spotted by a Japanese seaplane just as we got under way again.

At about 4.30pm we sighted smoke on the horizon off the port bow. It was a convoy, about ten miles away. Lieutenant Wilkinson asked if anyone could recognise Japanese warships and I told him I was familiar with them as I had spent two years on the China station. So I went up to the bridge and he handed me his telescope. I saw one Japanese light cruiser and two destroyers and without looking any more I told the captain the convoy was Japanese, no doubt about it. It later turned out that a heavy cruiser was at the rear of the convoy.

The captain addressed the crew and said, 'There is a Japanese convoy ahead. I am going to attack it and we'll take as many of those Jap bastards as possible with us.' These are words I will never forget. We headed for the convoy and the captain selected a troopship of about 10,000 tons as the target. I had a mixed bag of ammunition in the stand. Six semi-armour-piercing shells, four graze fuse shells, and three A A shells, plus three practice shells.

At about four thousand yards, we opened fire. The first SAP shell was over target, but at least three of our remaining SAP shells were bang on. Fire immediately broke out on the troopship and she was soon blazing furiously and the several thousand Japanese troops aboard were jumping into the sea. Within a few minutes I had used all our ammunition, so Wilkinson selected another target, the transport ship nearest to him, and rammed it at full speed and sank it. I will never forget an RAF sergeant who was manning the Vickers Lewis gun. His deadly accurate fire completely wiped out the four-man gun's crew aboard the Jap transport we rammed. The enemy's gun was about 40 mm and it was this gun which caused our first casualties. I was wounded in the chest. Then as we pulled away, the transport ship sank.

The RAF sergeant opened up on another transport about 200 yards away but the convoy cleared away from us and we came under fire from the Japanese warships. It was a fearful experience as it took them five to ten minutes to find our range, their gunnery was so inaccurate. We heard their shells whistling overhead, always expecting the next one to land inboard, knowing we had to just sit there and take it, helpless and unable to do anything about it. When they eventually found the range, it was all over.

The *Li Wo* listed to starboard and sank stern first. The captain stayed on the bridge but I and many others jumped into the water and started swimming towards the life rafts. The Jap transports closed in, picking up their own survivors, as we expected they would then come and pick us up too. But we were in for a shock. They came right at us and deliberately rammed our rafts. We realised just before they hit us what they were doing and quickly dived into the sea. Then I watched that transport go among a group of survivors and manoeuvre amongst them with their churning screws, killing at least a dozen. They machine-gunned us as we tried to get away from the sinking ships. Then they threw grenades and even lumps of coal and wood at us in the water. Out of a crew of over one hundred, only ten of us got ashore alive. Seven lived to celebrate VJ day.

Bandsman George Lloyd, RM

I was one of fourteen Royal Marine bandsmen who worked in the Transmitting Station (TS) of HMS *Trinidad*, a wonderful, incredibly fast cruiser. We'd been trained to operate the computer which controlled our main armament. The TS was right down near the bottom of the ship below an armour-plated deck. On one side were the ship's oil fuel tanks, and, on the other, the magazine.

On 29th March 1942 we were escorting a convoy on its way to Murmansk. We were crossing the Barents Sea when we picked up three unidentified ships on our radar screens. It was 6.30am. In those days no-one could trust radar 100% and we didn't want to attack one of our own convoys or Russian destroyers that were in the vicinity. Visibility was poor, so we had to wait until we were close enough to identify the suspect ships. When we were less than two miles away, visibility cleared and the three ships were identified as German destroyers. Immediately the captain gave the order to open fire and we hit the leading ship with our first salvoes.

Everything seemed to be going well until, suddenly, there was a huge explosion on our port side and our lights went out. We had been hit not by the German destroyers but by one of our own torpedoes. Something had gone wrong with it, and it came round full circle and exploded into our port side.

There were twenty-one men in the Transmitting Station when the explosion happened. I was working the switchboard close to the ladder which was the only way of getting in or out. Straightaway our band corporal vanished up the ladder and out of the hatch. He just did a bunk.

Then the emergency light came on and we found that the explosion had broken communications between our computer tables and the turrets, so Warrant Officer Gould, who was in charge, shouted to me to try to telephone the bridge. But the lines were dead. Gould then ordered a signal sailor to go up to the bridge and report that all the lights were out and our lines were completely dead.

By this time oil from the oil fuel tanks started pouring down through the open hatch. I moved a few yards to the other side of the room to get away from it. Then the oil became a strong cascade and Gould shouted, 'Shut the hatch!' But no-one moved. Everyone seemed to be completely paralysed with fear and stayed glued to his position. Just like so many hypnotised rabbits, standing waiting to be drowned. No panic, no movement.

Again, Gould shouted, 'Shut the hatch, shut the hatch!' The oil was now up to our groins. Thomas Barber ('Lou') went to the ladder and tried to climb it but he was knocked back by the force of the oil. I went over to help him and suddenly I became really angry. I said to myself, 'God, you can't do this to me, I have work to do, music to write.' It was that anger which saved me. When Lou tried again to get up the ladder, I went after him and pushed. He couldn't move so I shouted, 'Shove, Lou, go on, shove!' and then he moved a little bit. I thought of my wife, Nancy, and started to climb the ladder.

I have no memory of what happened after this until I crawled out of the hatch two decks up. They later found that another sailor had tried to get out after me, but the hatch had come down and broken his back. So I was the last person to get out of the TS. All the rest were drowned in that cold black oil.

My next memory is of trying to haul myself out of the hatch leading on to the mess deck. Lou had disappeared. I lay on the deck totally exhausted and unable to move. Then I crawled across the mess deck and up some iron stairs to an upper deck where I again lay down. I felt like a burnt-out cinder. On the deck below there were first aid fellows and security people. One was standing above the ladders going down to the lower decks and shouting, 'Anybody there? Anybody below?' I wanted to shout that help was needed in the TS but I couldn't speak. I had no strength.

I was just lying on the deck, saturated with oil, when a sailor came along and said, 'Get yourself to the bake house, Bandy,' so I crawled to the bakehouse where somebody gave me a blanket. That's when fear overcame me. Quite frankly, I was scared out of my mind. Just lying there in a state of shock, no reserves left, I couldn't stop shivering.

Somehow, the damage control parties managed to save the ship and we crawled to Murmansk. Everyone around me was terrified that we would be a sitting target for the U-boats which ambushed convoys coming into Murmansk. But the destroyers, *Oribi* and *Fury*, maintained an anti-submarine screen around us and the armed minesweeper *Harrier* went ahead of us all through the night. When we arrived in Murmansk the next day, people seemed to come to life again with the sheer relief of arriving safely. But I couldn't keep still, and shivered all the time.

They could do nothing for me. In those days, they didn't understand shock. I managed to walk off the ship but by the time I reached naval hospital in Scotland six weeks later I had reached total collapse. Almost comatose. My wife came to see me and the doctors told her I was a hopeless case. I would have to spend the rest of my life in hospital. So she said, 'If you can't do anything with him, you'd better let me have a try.' For years, she didn't get a wink of sleep, I was always screaming. But eventually I recovered. She saved my life. And I did write music.

But I am still haunted by the picture of those silent men standing motionless, the tiny emergency light bulb giving its dim light, the cold black oil engulfing their bodies. It is a picture that will always live with me.

Lieutenant-Commander Roger Hill, RN

On 24th June 1942 we got a cypher from the Admiralty ordering us to sail that night for Hvalfjord in Iceland. We were to join the Russian convoy PQ17. I was then in command of *Ledbury*, a Hunt class destroyer. After a wild two hours' oiling, storing, getting spare gear and reliefs and topping up with extra ammunition, we were under way. The feeling on board seemed to be one of cheerful excitement, as well as some trepidation.

We arrived in Hvalfjord on 26th June and the next morning I went ashore to the convoy conference. The large room was filled with all those taking part. Admiral Hamilton who commanded the four cruisers was there, small, quiet and courteous. I knew him from Combined Operations days and reckoned nothing would ruffle him and he would never give up fighting.

Then there was Jackie Broome, the close escort leader from the *Keppel*. From the fleet destroyers there was Alistair Ewing in the *Offa*, whom I much admired, Jock Campbell in *Fury*, and Adrian Northey in our sister ship *Wilton*.

The masters of the 35 merchant ships sat in rows with bundles of books and charts on their laps. There were a large number of American merchant ships and at least one Russian, the tanker *Azerbaijan*. These ships all carried war material and this convoy would have supplied a complete army and airforce of, say, a small Balkan country. There were some 500 aircraft crated and on deck, as well as tanks, guns and ammunition of all sorts.

The Western Approach destroyers included the ex-American four-stacker *Leamington* and there were three corvettes, three minesweepers and four old trawlers. Two anti-aircraft ships, the *Palomares* and *Pozarica*, a 'Ranger' tanker, three rescue ships and two submarines made up this fleet.

The conference was well run, the explanations were clear and the emphasis was on the defence the escort would give against air and submarine attack. I had a brief chat with Douglas Fairbanks, Junior, who had a liaison job on one of the American cruisers. He was a most unlikely person to meet in Iceland enroute for Russia.

I returned to my ship full of confidence in our leaders, and, as we steamed down the fjord, I briefed the officers and ship's company. I told them we would have some really good shooting at high-level and torpedo-bombers with quite a chance of a go at some U-boats. I tried to pass on the confidence I felt in Admiral Hamilton and Jackie Broome. I told them we would be in three watches in order to give them as much rest as possible, since, when anything happened, we would go to action stations.

On the afternoon of 30th June we sighted the great mass of

shipping in their orderly nine columns. I was on the starboard quarter of the convoy, with *Offa* in the next square to me and *Leamington* next to her. The evening and night passed peacefully. Daylight lasted all through the night and from now on there was no darkness.

At 0900 we were well inside the Arctic Circle. It was still a flat calm, with scattered patches of fog, and the big merchant ships hardly seemed to be moving on the cold, glassy sea. The little escorts were zigging and weaving about, sniffing at suspect echoes like gun dogs. I swept the horizon with my binoculars and saw a U-boat on the surface about six miles away. We turned towards her, signalling *Offa* and *Leamington* to join the chase. I planned to open fire at ten thousand yards, but *Offa* fired too soon and the U-boat crash-dived. We did a square search for an hour, but got no contact, and at 1045 *Offa* ordered us back to the convoy.

I was bitterly disappointed; it was the first U-boat I had sighted on the surface during the whole course of the war.

At 1130 on 2nd July we sighted the returning QP13 convoy. It was obvious the Germans were saving all their fire power for us, the loaded convoy. At 1300 a Blohm and Voss shadowing seaplane joined us and flew round the convoy in a big circle, just out of range. Sometimes he would fly ahead and land on the sea, to save on diesel, and lumber off as the leading ships approached. It was a nasty feeling to know that our exact position was always known to the enemy. We fired an occasional single round at him if he got a bit careless. We wanted to perfect our very low-angle fire to be ready for the torpedo-planes.

At 1630 we sighted a flight of Heinkel 115 seaplanes manoeuvring astern of the convoy and trying to get in with torpedoes. Six attacked on the port quarter but did not press home their attack. Surprisingly, there were no more attacks that afternoon or during the 'night'. The feeling in the ship was that we had beaten off the air attacks without loss, and everyone was very cheerful. I was puzzled; previous convoys had been attacked about every six hours when at their closest to enemy airfields in Norway.

At 1300 on 3rd July when we were steering east to pass between Bear Island and Spitzbergen, *Leamington* sighted a U-boat and asked me to join her. We spent the afternoon playing hide-and-seek with U-boats until 1700. By then we were thirty miles astern of the convoy, so we headed back.

Suddenly, coming clear of the fog, there was a U-boat going at full speed after the convoy about seven miles ahead of me. He was making 17 knots and as I turned to bring all my guns to bear when he was five miles away, he crash-dived. We searched for him without success; I think there was a layer of colder water that they dived below and the asdic did not get through.

The convoy was attracting U-boats like a magnet, and if only there had been hunter groups to spare, what a killing we would have had. But this was 1942, and there was no ship or plane to spare anywhere. The U-boats had never been so bold; I had seen seven on the surface in the last two days. By midnight we had rejoined the convoy, topped up with 88 tons of oil and were zigging in our square, wondering what in hell was going to happen next. The night hours were peaceful, except for the usual asdic contacts and depth-charging. We were now past the nearest point to the enemy air bases and were nearly 300 miles from the North Cape. I felt, if we got through 4th July without serious loss, we were almost home to Archangel.

At 1600 on 4th July we started to get aircraft on the radar screen and soon sighted some Heinkel 115s flying around the stern. A torpedo from one of them hit and sank the *Christopher Newport*. Then a few Junkers 88 appeared and did some high-level attacks; no ships were hit, but this proved to be merely a diversion. At 1819 we sighted six or seven aircraft low on the horizon. I closed the convoy, thinking this would be a bombing attack, when suddenly the whole horizon on our side was alive with planes. We counted up to 26 but there was no time to count more. I saw they were Heinkel 111K which carry two torpedoes each, and we opened out to meet them.

They came at us like a cavalry charge, so hard and fast that they could not turn away, but after dropping their torpedoes, continued through the fire of the fifty ships and away the other side. We started firing at a group going from left to right, and then saw a single plane coming right at us. Our shots were bursting all around him and I think he crashed, but just then two torpedoes were coming straight at me and I went hard-a-port to dodge them. Then a plane came over from the other side of the convoy and I put the oerlikon onto him. I could see the shots going into his wing and the fire starting. The plane swerved to port and *Offa* blew him to bits. Now a great mass of smoke and flame went high in the air as torpedoes hit the tanker *Azerbaijan* and two other ships.

The whole sky around the convoy was a mass of bursting shells. Tracers were going in all directions and the sea was boiling with the falling shrapnel. The noise of the gunfire was continuous, and in the centre a great pall of black smoke was slowly rising where a ship loaded with arms and ammunition had been hit. Suddenly the firing stopped. The planes had gone. The damaged ships were falling back, with the rescue ships and escorts standing by. For the size of the attack, the losses were small. We reckoned we had won this battle, and the enemy had really taken a beating, but in fact only three aircraft were brought down against three ships hit. The R/T was full of instructions from Jackie Broome in *Keppel* to the ships astern. *Azerbaijan* was rejoining, having put the fire out. The tone of the talk was cheerful and it was felt that the enemy had done his worst.

At 2025 the Commodore hoisted a string of flags. The yeoman knelt down and, using his big telescope, called out the letters for someone to write down. Then he looked them up in his code book and said to me, 'The Commodore's Chief Yeoman has made a proper balls-up this time; that signal means,

'Convoy is to scatter.' 'Put the answering pendant at the dip,' I replied (which means, 'Your signal not understood', and makes the originator check it). I saw that the destroyers near me had also got the answering pendant at the dip. The Commodore's ship lowered the flags and then hoisted the same ones again, and at the same time Jackie Broome in *Keppel* came up on the R/T, 'To all destroyers "Strike", repeat "Strike".' 'Christ,' I thought, 'here we go, surface attack by the *Tirpitz*,' and I searched the horizon with my glasses. I called for the first lieutenant and steered for the head of the convoy.

In fact three signals had arrived in close succession from the Admiralty. The first ordered the cruiser force to withdraw to westward at high speed, the second ordered the convoy to disperse due to threat from surface forces, and the third, 'Most immediate' signal said, 'Convoy is to scatter'. Because these messages had come from the Admiralty we never doubted that the *Tirpitz, Hipper* and some large destroyers were just below the horizon, and about to open fire on the convoy.

As we steamed through the convoy to join *Keppel* the crews of the merchant ships cheered us and we waved back. A paragraph from some naval action orders kept going through my mind, idiotically, 'The ship's company should change into clean underwear before going into action so that wounds are not contaminated.'

From way over on the edge of the ice, the four cruisers came streaking across the bows of the convoy. *Wilton* and *Ledbury* were stationed astern since we could only do 25 knots, which was the speed of the fleet. Adrian Northey made some rude signals to me, and I insulted him back, feeling comforted that he was with me in this hopeless battle. For our cruisers had only eight-inch guns and virtually no armour, and would be blown out of the water before their guns were inside the range of the 15-inch guns of the *Tirpitz*.

My plan was to join the torpedo-carrying destroyers and give fire support as they went into the attack. We would turn as if firing torpedoes, and throw some big armour-piercing shells over the side. Privately, I decided that, if we got that far, we would go on and try to ram the *Tirpitz*. I piped the port watch to supper and tried to eat a sandwich, but it stuck in my throat. I think my stomach was three decks below.

The puzzling thing to us all on the bridge was that no-one, Admiralty, Admiral Hamilton or Jackie Broome, had given an enemy position. We searched the horizon with the big director telescopes and all the bridge binoculars, but it remained a hazy, empty line. We never doubted for one moment that we were going to attack a bigger force to save the convoy, but, eventually, hours later, we realised that no surface action was going to take place after all and that we were running away. We were leaving the convoy, scattered and defenceless, to be slaughtered by the U-boats and aircraft.

At about midnight the most terrible and harrowing signals started coming up to the bridge from the radio office. They were coming through on the Merchant Navy wavelength. 'Am being bombed by large number of planes.' 'On fire in the ice.' 'Abandoning ship,' and, 'Six U-boats approaching on the surface.'

I discussed with the pilot whether we should quietly slow down, turn round and go back to look for the survivors of the convoy. I thought for months afterwards this was what I should have done. But discipline is strong, our orders were clear, we were miles away by then, and, the ever-governing factor, almost out of fuel. So, bitter, bewildered, tired and utterly miserable, we stayed with the admiral and the cruisers. Underneath the bitterness was the sneaking relief of having survived, of which I also felt ashamed.

I have always felt that, as the merchant ships were going to almost certain destruction, then we should have gone back and taken the same chance and we would have got some of them to Archangel. Even though we would probably have lost the destroyers as well once the oiler was sunk – still we would have tried. As it was 23 of the 34 merchant men were sunk by U-boats or aircraft. Never will I forget how they cheered us as we moved at full speed to the attack; and it has haunted me ever since that we left them to be destroyed.

OPERATION PEDESTAL

By the summer of 1942, the Germans and their allies were in control of most of Europe. Malta was the unconquered British bastion of the inner Mediterranean and the whole Allied cause depended on its successful defence. But by August 1942 Malta was on the verge of surrender. Only five merchant ships had reached the island that year, three of which had been sunk in the harbour at Valletta before they were discharged.

Operation Pedestal, the despatch of fourteen merchant ships to Malta in August 1942, marked the turning-point in the siege of Malta and of the war in the Mediterranean. The story of the operation is told by six survivors.

Lieutenant-Commander Roger Hill, RN
(Hunt class destroyer *Ledbury*)

Operation Pedestal was the last all-out attempt to get a convoy of merchant ships through to Malta. Their food was running out and they had no aviation fuel, no submarine diesel and nothing for the dockyard. Malta had virtually stopped.

If the convoy failed, Malta would have to surrender. The Governor of Malta, Lord Gort, said to me, 'You can make the garrison eat their belts, but the three hundred thousand civilians have to be fed or evacuated.'

The convoy of over fifty ships left Gibraltar on 9th August 1942. Thirteen merchant ships and the 10,000-ton Texaco tanker, *Ohio*, steamed in four columns. They were all big, fast ships and the speed of the convoy was 15 knots. Around them was a screen of 26 destroyers. Close round the convoy were the anti-aircraft destroyers, like my *Ledbury*, and the battleships

Nelson and *Rodney* each of which had nine 16-inch guns, steamed astern of the two outside columns. The anti-aircraft ship *Cairo* had a roving commission near the convoy and *Jaunty*, an ocean tug, followed along behind.

Three aircraft carriers, *Victorious*, *Indomitable* and *Eagle* followed the convoy inside the destroyer screen. They carried a total of 72 fighters and were constantly altering course into the wind to fly off and land on the patrols. The cruisers *Sirius*, *Phoebe* and *Charybdis* careered about keeping an anti-aircraft guard on the carriers. Finally, there was the old aircraft-carrier *Furious* with her own destroyer screen, whose job it was to fly off 38 Spitfires when we were about 500 miles from Malta, as reinforcements for Malta's depleted squadrons.

As we approached down the Mediterranean we were entering a cauldron of attack. Crete and Greece were in German hands and would be used for air attack, then of course the long toe of Italy, Sardinia, and Sicily was all aerodromes. About 20 submarines and 40 E-boats were also waiting for us. It was just like another Charge of the Light Brigade.

Officer Cadet Frederick Treves, RN
(Merchant vessel *Waimarama*)

We were at action stations as soon as we got into the Med on the evening of 9 August so I would have been up in the fo'c'sle with Bowdrey. He was the oldest man in the ship and I the youngest. He was looking after me. He even held my hand when we were being bombed.

The sea was very calm and the convoy was going very slowly. It was a moonless night and we were in total blackout when I saw all these twinkling lights strung across the sea like jewels. I asked Bowdrey, 'What are those?' and he said, 'I think they're Spanish fishing vessels. They're probably telling the Germans we're just coming into the Med.'

The first action I saw was late on 10th August. Some spotter planes went over and the fleet put up a terrific anti-aircraft barrage, especially the 16-inch guns on the *Nelson* and *Rodney*. I think no 16-inch gun had ever been fired at that angle before and the whole sky was puckered with little puffs of smoke cloud. It was an enormous umbrella of fire, absolutely terrifying. The feeling of terror it evoked is impossible to describe.

As well as this huge barrage of anti-aircraft fire we could hear the scream of the destroyers, that extraordinary wailing scream destroyers made when tearing around trying to find the submarines which had been detected somewhere. The next day, 11th August, I saw the *Eagle* go down. I heard two or three huge explosions so I rushed out of the fo'c'sle on to the forward well deck and saw the *Eagle* on its side. It had been torpedoed by a submarine.

There were little tiny dots like ants all over the side of this vast belly coming out of the sea. It was all the crew trying to get into the water from the side of the ship. In the distance all the destroyers were rushing around in circles trying to find the submarine, their sirens blaring. Even above this noise you could hear the people on the *Eagle* screaming as the ship sank.

It was an enormous blow, but 800 people were saved from the *Eagle* and they were taken back to Gibraltar by the tug, *Jaunty*, which was having trouble keeping up with the convoy.

After the *Eagle* sank things began to liven up much more. They started to bomb the convoy constantly and I don't know how many ships went up in the next forty-eight hours. The noise was just indescribable, bombing day and night, torpedoing, and the firing of guns in retaliation. The Stuka dive-bombers would dive on the ship and the siren on the plane's bodywork would make this banshee noise which increased and increased and increased as they did a kamikaze-type dive on the target and then released the 500-lb bomb. We suffered that for days.

Lieutenant-Commander Roger Hill, RN
(*Ledbury*)

The *Ledbury* was fitted with a loudspeaker system and on 10th August the telegraphist tuned this to the carrier fighter control officer. We listened to the calm voice of the control officer talking to the fighter leaders. This served as a useful early warning of air attack, as the carrier's radar had a greater range than ours, but we also became very interested and involved with the fighter pilots. Our favourite was a Red Leader who was a real comedian and sometimes put on a Yankee drawl.

On the evening of 11th August we heard the fighter control vectoring the fighters on to approaching enemy bombers, and heard the excited voices of the pilots as they attacked: 'From Red Leader, large number of bandits below me to port – attacking, I say again, attacking.'

The first attack was from high-level bombers. We had a nice steady shoot at them and as the shellbursts increased around them, they dropped their bombs well away from us and turned away, chased by our fighters. At 2000 about forty Junkers 88s attacked in shallow dives, but no-one was hit in either attack.

The fighters were staying up until the last minute and we could hear them saying, 'I've got no petrol, I've got no petrol!' and they were landing on the aircraft carriers with their tanks empty. One or two crashed on to the carrier and burst into flames. As the planes crashed they were just thrown over the side to keep the carriers clear.

Before dawn the next day (12th August) we could hear our fighter planes warming up and the first patrols took off at first light. At 0915 there was an attack by about thirty Ju 88s. They pressed on right through our gunfire and dropped their bombs all amongst the convoy. This was the first time I had ever seen bombs in the air dropping close to the ship. One was close enough to wet a gun's crew as it landed in the sea. Rather frightening.

All that day we were bombed. At 1300 the merchant ship *Deucalion* was damaged and later sunk. That afternoon we were listening to our old friend Red Leader going for some 'bandits'. Then control called him, 'Red Leader, Red Leader?' but there was no reply. Then 'Red Two' came up, 'Red Leader has just been shot down.' We were heartbroken.

Then I saw a parachute coming down and I thought, 'Blimey, that might be Red Leader,' so I rushed over to pick him up. I hung over the side and said to my first lieutenant, 'What is he, Jimmy?' and he said, 'A fucking Hun, sir. Three more parachutes coming down to starboard.' 'Let them go to hell,' I replied.

That evening our troubles really started. A flight of dive-bombers came in, supported by fast German fighters and our Fleet Air Arm chaps were completely out-gunned and out-speeded. The dive-bombers were targeting our carriers like a disturbed wasp's nest, screaming down almost vertically, one after the other. And our fighters were following them right into their own ship's fire, trying to shoot down the dive-bombers. It was the most spectacular sight I'd ever seen.

Captain 'Eddie' Baines, RN
(Hunt class destroyer *Bramham*)

On 12th August the bombing started in a big way and at around 1300 the *Deucalion*, one of the merchant ships, got hit by one bomb and had a near-miss with two others. She was not vitally damaged but she came to a halt because she was making water and they wanted to see what was wrong with her. *Bramham* was a 'rescue' ship so we came up alongside her.

We were greeted by the sight of the *Deucalion's* boats being lowered in great panic and people tumbling into them and rowing over to us. The officers and particularly the captain standing on her bridge were absolutely apoplectic with rage and saying, 'Send the boats back!' which I would have done, anyway.

So when the boats came alongside our scrambling nets, we jumped on the men's knuckles as they came up over the edge. They called us a few choice names but we invited them to choose: either they could get back into their boats and stay there or go back to the *Deucalion*. So they thought better of it, recovered their nerve and returned on board.

Deucalion now could only make 13.5 knots so we were ordered to escort her to Malta by what was known as the inshore route, along the coast of North Africa. It was just as unpleasant on the inshore route as anywhere else and we got bombed on the way. Then at dusk a couple of torpedo-bombers came out of the murk and popped a torpedo into *Deucalion* and blew a bloody great hole in her stern. She was burning down below and there was obviously no hope for her, so the captain gave the order to abandon ship.

Then we had to sink her by going up close and dropping depth-charges. We didn't want her to get picked up by the enemy as a propaganda prize. The scare was that she would blow up as we went alongside, as all the merchant ships were carrying high octane aero spirit and huge amounts of ammunition. She seemed to be settling by the stern so I left her, and when we'd been steaming at 23 knots for about an hour I saw an explosion astern and it was the *Deucalion* blowing up.

Junior Radio Operator John Jackson, MN
(Merchant Vessel *Waimarama*)

During 12th August we had a number of alarms but our fighter protection saved us from direct attacks. But that evening at about 1835 I saw a flight of Stukas coming out of the sun, flying very low, peeling off one after the other and diving straight on to the carrier *Indomitable*. There was no other target they were going for. They were going for the *Indomitable* and they were going to have her.

Nelson opened up with her 16-inch guns and we all fired our guns. The ship rattled with the vibration. But nothing seemed to stop these planes and they continued to attack. A lot of bombs missed, but about the fourth or fifth plane coming down scored a direct hit and did a lot of damage. We saw terrific clouds of smoke and spray and *Indomitable* vanished from view in the smoke.

We were getting close to the Pantelleria Straits which were too narrow for the heavy warships to manoeuvre in. At about 1900 the aircraft-carriers, the battleships *Rodney* and *Nelson*, and several cruisers turned around and we were left with a fairly small cover: the cruisers *Manchester*, *Kenya*, *Nigeria*, the light cruiser *Cairo* and a number of escort vessels including the *Ledbury*, *Bramham*, *Speedy*, *Penn* and five or six others. So we continued, a bit deflated. But at that time everything was intact, apart from losing *Deucalion*. If all went well, we'd be under the cover of the Spitfires from Malta by the next morning.

As we reached the Pantelleria Straits it was getting dark. The convoy started to form into two columns to pass through the narrow channel swept for mines by the destroyers. Then, without any warning, we heard a loud explosion and saw that the Admiral's ship *Nigeria*, in column ahead of us, had been hit amidships by a torpedo from a U-boat. She heeled over to starboard in a cloud of smoke. A few seconds later, *Cairo* was torpedoed and hit in her stern and she swung round to port, seemed to settle in the water and stop. A second later the tanker *Ohio* was hit amidships and caught fire. This was bad news. The *Ohio* was the most important ship in the convoy because what Malta needed most was oil.

The whole convoy immediately took evasive action and carried on at full speed. From then onwards, right through into the night it was just like Dante's Inferno. It was unbelievable. Half an hour after the U-boat attack there was a big low-level bombing raid. We were alongside the *Clan Ferguson* at the time. She was carrying the same cargo as us: aviation spirit in five-litre cans on the foredeck and lots of ammunition and petrol for

Malta. Then she got hit by a Ju88 and it was just like someone holding a piece of rag soaked in petrol and putting a match to it. A terrific sheet of flame shot up into the air about half-a-mile high. She went down very quickly and how anybody survived I don't know, but they did. About sixty people were rescued.

So we knew what we were facing. But, funnily, we didn't really think about it at the time. We thought, 'Poor old people on the *Clan Ferguson*, but it's not going to happen to us, we're not going to get hit.' If you didn't think like this you could never go on.

Captain Dudley Mason, MN
(Texaco oil tanker *Ohio*)

Minutes after *Nigeria* and *Cairo* were hit by torpedoes, there was a bright flash and a column of water was thrown up to mast-head height. A second later, flames shot up into the air. We had been hit amidships on the port side, halfway between bow and stern. There was a hole in the port side 24 feet by 27 feet, reaching from the main deck to well below the waterline. The deck on the port side was torn up and laid right back inboard almost to the centre-line and was buckled beam to beam. The flying bridge was damaged and the pump-room was a shambles.

I immediately rang 'Finish with engines', as the pump-room had caught on fire and flames were bursting out of the kerosene tanks, whose lids had blown off. I had previously told the chief engineer that he was not to stop the engines whatever happened unless I gave him the order to do so. I gave the order now because the pump-room was on fire and the men were in danger.

The gunners were still firing, ignoring the flames and the bombs which were falling all around the ship. Some men were running for the boats but I told them, 'Come on, let's get that fire out.' They grabbed fire extinguishers and set to work.

It was then a case of fighting the pump-room fire. At first I thought it was a forlorn hope, but we went to work with foam fire extinguishers and managed to put out the flames much more easily than I had expected. We also put out the flames in the kerosene tanks and replaced the tank lids, although these could not be screwed down as they were badly buckled.

While we were fighting the fires the air attack was still going on. The planes were diving to mast-head height to drop their bombs, and we had several near misses.

I sent for the chief engineer to ask him how long it would take to raise steam, as the steam had dropped back while we were stopped. Fortunately, since we had a diesel generator, we were able to raise steam again within ten minutes, instead of the usual three or four hours.

I had been forced to stop not only to fight the fire, but because our steering was out of order and we were turning in circles, making us a danger to the *Nigeria* and *Cairo* which were lying stopped near us. We tested the main engines and found they were all right, but stopped until we rigged up the emergency steering gear aft.

I had a signal from Admiral Burrough, who had been taken off the *Nigeria*, asking how we were getting on. I told him we should soon be able to get under way again, but since our gyro was wrecked, I requested a destroyer to lead us once we were under way. The *Ledbury* came to lead us on with a blue light astern and we got under way at about 2130 and followed her throughout the night.

Steering was rather difficult. The chief officer took the wheel aft and was directed from the forward bridge by me using a telephone line which, fortunately, was still intact.

A merchant ship ahead of us was burning to the water's edge and I was afraid of catching fire from her so I requested the *Ledbury* to steer further away from her as our kerosene tanks were open to the sea. The chief engineer reported all well in the engine-room and we were now averaging 15 to 16 knots, following the *Ledbury* round the minefield past Cape Bon. I had been concerned that the speed might break the ship's back, but the hull was showing no undue strain.

Lieutenant-Commander Roger Hill, RN
(Ledbury)

After being damaged by a U-boat torpedo at 2000 on 12th August, the *Nigeria* turned round and went back to Gibraltar with far too many destroyers escorting her. As far as I was concerned it didn't matter a tuppenny cuss how many cruisers we lost; our job was to stay by the merchant ships. I was horrified when I saw how few destroyers we had left.

After the U-boat attack there was a very clever attack from high-level bombers combined with a low-level torpedo attack. The *Clan Ferguson* on my starboard side was hit and blew up and another, the *Empire Hope*, was set on fire. After these attacks the convoy was in disarray, with several ships on fire and many others going in the wrong direction. I went alongside them with a loud hailer to get them going on the right course again. Then I came across an American ship, the *Almeria Lykes*. The captain was a bit stroppy and said he was going back to Gibraltar, he didn't see there was any point in going on. So I told him he wouldn't have a hope in hell without an escort and if he joined up with the others he would be in Malta tomorrow. He came round like a lamb and joined up with the convoy. But he was sunk later on.

As I went to rejoin the fleet, I came across the *Ohio* lying stopped in the dark so I went alongside and called out to Captain Mason. He seemed very cheerful and in control. He said they'd put out a fire and had set up emergency steering gear, but they had no means of navigation. So I said, 'Well, I'll put a dim light on my stern and I'll lead you.' So they joined in astern of me and I led them right into the coast because I reckoned that was the safest place to go. Soon we were belting along at 16 knots, which was great.

We had hot soup, stew and cocoa served up all over the ship and apart from people manning the telephones, the whole crew slept on deck at their stations. As we rounded Cape Bon and steered south there was a spectacular sight ahead of us. Tracers tearing through the dark, star shells bursting and heavy gunfire. Italian E-boats from Pantelleria were attacking the convoy. We were lucky we were missing it all. Four merchant ships, *Wairangi*, *Santa Elisa*, *Glenorchy* and *Almeria Lykes* were sunk that night and we received a signal from the cruiser *Manchester* saying that her engine-room was flooded and she was on fire.

Early the next morning we led *Ohio* back into line with what was left of the convoy.

Officer Cadet Frederick Treves, RN
(*Waimarama*)

The night of 12th August was horrendous. Bombings, emergency turns to starboard and port, flames, ships going up, huge explosions. I saw our sister ship, the *Wairangi*, go up in a sheet of flame. Like us, she was loaded up with high octane aero spirit, 500lb bombs, oerlikon shells, pom-pom shells and a bit of food for Malta.

There was a slight lull on the morning of 13th August. I went to the saloon and found that some of the chaps had been getting at the liquor locker. The chief steward was way beyond recall. Then the sirens went and I rushed to my quarters on the fo'c'sle, right across the well deck. As I got to the door at the side of the fo'c'sle, a bomb fell and I was blown through the door onto some bags of lime and my old friend Bowdrey fell on top of me to protect me. I thought I was going to die and I started to get very numb. But Bowdrey moved off me and I managed to get up and went out onto the well deck. It hadn't quite dawned on me that the ship had been hit.

There was black smoke everywhere, flames were burning aft of the bridge and the deck was slanting to starboard, so I thought, 'Well, I'm being a terrible coward, but I think I'd better go.' I made a very quick decision and darted to the port side of the ship, forgetting the rule that you should always leave the ship on the side nearest the water. I tore up the tilting deck, grabbed the side rail and dived into the water. I had a helmet on, which was lucky, because the water was full of debris, and a kapok life-saving suit. The wind had been blowing to starboard, but as I dived it changed direction and fanned the flames away from me and towards the rest of the crew. The flames were 600 feet high.

I bobbed up to the surface like a cork. There was debris and people screaming all around me, 'I can't swim, I'm drowning!' I was quite a good swimmer and I felt terribly calm and tried to organise everybody, telling them to stop wasting their breath by screaming for help. And I kept blowing my whistle in morse code, trying to give them instructions. This pathetic little whistle playing, 'de de de de'. Stupid thing to do; they couldn't hear me. I saw the wireless officer, Jackson. He couldn't swim and I pulled him out because the ship was sucking him up back into the flames.

Then I saw my friend and mentor, Bowdrey. He was standing on a raft, his arms were outstretched and he was screaming for help, he couldn't swim. It was a picture I'll never be able to forget. He was drifting back into the flames on this raft. I started out towards him, but I realised he was very near the flames and the raft would be too heavy to stop. So I turned over and swam away. That has haunted me all my life. I was a coward. He'd done everything for me and I didn't do anything for him. That affected me greatly.

The *Ledbury* came into the circle of flames to pick up survivors. They were still being attacked and we were being machine-gunned in the water by German and Italian planes. Captain Hill talked to us all the time through his loudhailer. Eventually they lowered a wooden boat and dragged me on board.

Junior Radio Operator John Jackson, MN (*Waimarama*)

On the morning of the 13th I was talking to the liaison officer in the chart room. He said, 'Jacko, I reckon we'll be in Malta in four or five hours. We'll be all right.' And then we heard aircraft approaching and headed for the port side of the bridge where both our action stations were. As the liaison officer stepped out ahead of me there was the most enormous explosion and a wall of flame came between the two of us. An absolutely solid curtain of flame. That was the last I saw of the liaison officer.

The captain's steward had just brought his breakfast up on a tray and stood there in the middle of the chart room. He was only a lad, sixteen or seventeen. I shouted to him, 'Come on, let's get down the companionway to the next deck,' so we jumped down the companionway and got out on to the port side. It was a sight you can hardly describe, thick black smoke, flames and the ammunition exploding. The ship had started listing over to starboard and I could see about twenty men already swimming around in the water. The ship was enveloped in flame except for the small patch where these men were swimming around, so I shouted to the captain's steward to follow me and I jumped feet first over the side. I don't like water and I couldn't swim – it had to be pretty hot to get me to do that.

As I came up I saw the ship's bows sinking and I struggled away as best I could. The water was full of wood and debris and the fire was very very close and it was getting very hot. As I was floundering a young cadet, Freddy Treves, came up to me in the water and said, 'Jacko, lie on your back and don't move; I'm going to tow you away.'

Now the one thing I'd always heard was that drowning people always struggle, so I told myself, 'Don't struggle, Jackson, this guy's going to tow you away.' And so he did. He got me by the arms and pulled me, very slowly, away from the flames, which were increasing all the time. Then a whacking great spar of wood came along side and he said, 'Can you grab that spar?' and I did and I heaved myself on to it. And he said, 'Right, are you OK now?' and I said, 'Freddy, I'm fine, you carry on, off you go.' There was no question, he was a very brave lad.

So I found myself paddling away from the flames. I was quite confident. All around me people were shouting and screaming. A lot of people perished in the flames. Then I saw the *Ledbury*, a little destroyer, approaching. They put a whaler into the water and played a hose on it as it went in and picked the people out of the flames. And then Captain Hill put the bows of his ship into the flames, picking people out of the water, it was unbelievable. The captain was a brave man, but my golly, so were the people in the whaler.

I was in the water with the cook and another person nearby. Then the *Ledbury* picked the whaler up and started to move away and the cook said, 'They're going to leave us, they haven't seen us'. I remembered my whistle, and I blew it and they spotted us and swung the ship around and the three of us got up the net and scrambled aboard. Then they doped us with morphine to take the shock away.

Lieutenant-Commander Roger Hill, RN (*Ledbury*)

At 0730 on 13th August about a dozen torpedo-planes came in low from the port beam and a flight of Junkers 88 came out of the sun. A stick of bombs hit the *Waimarama* and she blew up with the biggest explosion I have ever seen. The flames were about six times the height of my mast. The *Melbourne Star* was 600 yards astern of the *Waimarama* and she couldn't avoid going right through the flames. The people who were aft in the *Melbourne Star* all jumped over the side because they thought their own ship had been hit, which gives you an idea of the intensity of the flames. The Admiral made to me, 'Survivors, but don't go into the flames.' Now, you've got to realise that I had been on PQ17, a convoy to Russia which had been ordered by the Admiralty to scatter because they thought the *Tirpitz* was about to attack. I was a close escort of that convoy but the Admiral signalled to us and told us to take up station to protect him against submarines. We all queried this and flashed at him, 'Could we go back to the convoy?' but he said, 'No, take up your station.' So we left the merchant ships at high speed and it was simply terrible. Something I have never ever got over in my life, not even now. That the navy should leave the merchant navy. The merchant ships were nearly all sunk. And it was in the Arctic and if a man was twenty seconds in the water he was dead.

My crew had felt just as badly about this as I did. So when we were going with this convoy to Malta I said, 'As long as there's a merchant ship afloat we'll stay alongside it and to hell with any signal we get from anybody.' And I got all sorts of signals telling me to go back to Gibraltar and to do all sorts of things, but I just threw them over the side. I was determined to stay with the merchant ships. When the *Waimarama* blew up and I went into these flames I felt I was redeeming myself for the disgrace of leaving the ships on the Russian convoy.

So we went towards the flames. I did not think anyone could have survived but as we approached there were heads bobbing about in the water, black with oil. I put down a whaler and she stayed outside the flames and picked up all the people she could find. I spoke to those we passed through a loudhailer, saying, 'I must get the ones near the fire first,' and they shouted back, 'That's all right.'

I took the ship into the flames. The fire was spreading outward over the sea, even to windward, and it was a grim race to pick up the men in the water before the flames reached them. When we got into the flames you couldn't see very much in all the fire and smoke and the heat was tremendous. Even on the bridge I had my hand over my beard because I thought it would catch on fire. I wondered how long my ship could stay there without blowing up. There was the odd survivor in the water and my sailors put a strap round their waists and jumped over the side and pulled these chaps into the landing nets. Terribly burnt, some of them. Then they were rushed along to the sick bay where the doctor looked after them.

We got everybody we could see and I thought, 'Well, thank God, I can't see any more, I'm going out astern.' So I started to go astern but the coxswain called up the voice pipe, 'There's another man over there, sir.' And I said, 'Coxswain, all I can see is flames and smoke.' He said, 'No, I saw him raise his arm, he's over there, sir.' So I had to go in again which I didn't want to do at all. We picked up this chap, Jackson, a wireless operator.

When we finally got out of the flames we found we had picked up a total of 45 survivors, only 19 from the *Waimarama* and the rest from the *Melbourne Star*.

At 1115 we came up to the *Ohio*. She was lying stopped, with *Penn* dropping depth-charges around her. About half-a-mile away, the big merchant ship *Dorset* was also lying stopped with *Bramham* standing by. The convoy was about ten miles away being bombed.

I suggested to *Penn* that I should take the *Ohio* in tow, but just then I received a signal from the Admiral at Malta telling me to go in search of the cruiser *Manchester*. I decided to obey the order, even though it meant leaving the *Ohio*. I think what decided me do this was my shortage of fuel; I thought the *Manchester* would be able to give me some fuel during the night.

We set off and relaxed into two watches to give the hands a chance to bath, eat and sleep. I felt I must get some sleep, but after just about an hour there was a cry of, 'Captain sir, enemy aircraft, enemy aircraft!' I ran on to the bridge and there were these two planes coming towards us. At first I thought they were Beaufighters from Malta, but they were Italian torpedo-bombers.

I spoke over the loud hailer to my eager pom-pom crews, 'Now you're going to get these. Wait, wait, let them come in.

They think they've surprised us. Let them come in. Right, open fire on the left one.' And they opened fire and you saw all these little bursts of flame on the front wing of the left plane and he went straight down. I said, 'Shift target right-hand,' and they fired at him and he went right down. Everybody was cheering and shouting and singing.

Then there was a great cry; the second plane had dropped a torpedo and it was coming straight for us. I went hard to port and it missed the stern by what seemed a few inches. Then I thought, this is a terrific boost to morale. So I said, 'Splice the mainbrace, stand fast the Hun.'

We failed to find any sign of the *Manchester* so we turned towards where we thought the *Ohio* might be.

Captain Dudley Mason, MN
(Ohio)

At 0700 on 13th August we caught up with the convoy after being led through the night by the *Ledbury*. The convoy was now in two columns, our position being at the end of the line, owing to our defective steering. At 0800 the heavy bombing attacks started again. We sustained many near-misses, but there seemed to be no damage to the ship. Then the *Waimarama* had a direct bomb hit and blew up. The *Melbourne Star*, following her, could not avoid the flames and steamed straight through them. The *Ohio* just managed to clear the edge of the flames by going hard to port.

During these attacks we were constantly receiving orders by wireless to make 45-degree emergency turns. It was quite impossible to execute these in the time given. These orders were also transmitted over the radio telephone, and the wireless orders were always several seconds behind, thus causing misunderstanding and confusion.

At about 0900 a Junkers 88 crashed into the sea close to our bow and bounced on to our foredeck, making a terrific crash and throwing masses of debris into the air. A little later the chief officer telephoned me from aft in great excitement to say that a Stuka had landed on the poop. Apparently this plane had also fallen into the sea and bounced on to our ship. I was rather tired, having been on the bridge all night and I'm afraid I answered him rather curtly, saying, 'Oh, that's nothing. We've had a Junkers 88 on the foredeck for nearly half an hour.'

At about the same time a near-miss right under our fore-foot opened up the port and starboard bow tanks, buckled the plating and flooded the forepeak tank. The *Ohio* vibrated violently forward to aft, amidst a deluge of water.

Despite these problems, we were making good headway. The weather was fine with good visibility, smooth sea and light airs, and we were steaming at 13 knots, steering approximately east. At 1000, when we were 100 miles west of Malta, a large plane flew right over us at about 2,000 feet, banked slightly and dropped a salvo of six bombs, three falling close to the port side and three close to the starboard side. The *Ohio* was lifted right out of the water and shook violently from stem to stern. The *Dorset* was hit by bombs at almost the same time.

At 1030 the main engines stopped as the two electric fuel pumps were out of commission. The steam pump remained intact, but it was practically impossible to keep the vacuum with this one pump. We managed to get the main engines going again, as there was only a little water in the engine-room, but we could only do about three to four knots. Then one of the boilers blew out and extinguished the fires. Enemy planes continued to bomb, but our gunners and crew kept up a deadly and accurate barrage, and no further damage was done.

Ledbury offered to take us in tow, and we reckoned that with our own power we would be able to make 12 knots. But at 1045 the second boiler blew out, extinguishing the remaining fires, and the vessel stopped. The *Ledbury* then signalled that she had to leave us to go to the assistance of the cruiser *Manchester*. Bombing was still going on.

At 1130 the *Penn* came alongside and we gave her a 10-inch manilla tow rope from forward, but the attempt to tow from ahead was hopeless as the ship just turned in circles, finally parting the tow rope. I signalled to the *Penn* that the only hope of towing the *Ohio* was from alongside, or with one ahead and one astern to steady the ship. We were still being bombed while stopped, so I asked the *Penn* to take off my crew until more assistance was available, to which he agreed, and at 1400 the *Penn* came alongside and took off the whole crew.

At 1800 two motor launches and a minesweeper, *Rye*, came out from Malta to assist us. I called for a small number of volunteers to return to the *Ohio* to make the tow ropes fast, but the whole crew voluntarily returned. The tow ropes were made fast to *Penn* and *Rye*, both towing ahead. The bombing attacks were still going on and at approximately 1830 a plane dropped a bomb directly on the fore part of the boat deck, which passed right through the accommodation into the engine-room, exploding on the boiler taps. It made a shambles of the after-accommodation and the boiler-room, and the crew were blinded and choked by the powder from the asbestos lagging. The engine-room ventilator and falling debris fell on Gunner Brown, causing numerous internal and external injuries.

I did not see any use in remaining on board the stopped *Ohio* with the consequent risk to life from continuous air attack. As the attempt at towing was proving unsuccessful with the assistance available, I ordered the crew to the boats, from which they were divided between the motor-launches and destroyers, and I lost track of them.

During the night the destroyers tried to get the *Ohio* in tow again, with the assistance of the destroyer *Bramham*, which came alongside in the night. But they were not successful. During the night some of the crew of the destroyers went aboard the *Ohio* and manned the guns through that night and the next day. Also during that night the 400 survivors in the destroyers took advantage of the stores and clothing on the *Ohio* and had also took away most of the wreckage of the two planes on the foredeck and the poop as souvenirs.

In the early hours of 14th Gunner Brown died and we buried him from the stern of the *Penn*. At about 0800 enemy air activity recommenced and continued. The *Ledbury* returned after a fruitless search for the *Manchester* and offered assistance. I was now in one of the motor launches about three cables astern of the *Ohio*.

At 0900 a near-miss fell just astern of the vessel, carrying away the rudder and holing the vessel aft, putting huge strain on the main deck which had already been weakened by the torpedo hit in the pump-room. The *Ohio* began to settle by the stern as the engine-room flooded. I watched the ship settling aft and sent a message to the *Penn* for my chief engineer and chief officer to assist as much as possible with the air compressor gear. I assumed these people were on board the *Penn*. The reply was, 'Come aboard.'

It was then about 1030. The *Penn* was towing alongside the *Ohio* on the starboard side and the *Bramham* was alongside on the port side and the ship was making headway. When I got on board the *Penn* I found that thirty of my crew, mostly officers and engineers, had been taken to Malta by a motor launch when it had developed engine trouble. I was left with only two firemen, two greasers and two other seamen belonging to the *Ohio*. So I boarded the *Ohio* and made a complete examination of the vessel with the assistance of these men.

We sounded all the empty spaces and tested the air compressor gear. The empty tanks were still intact and dry, but the kerosene was overflowing from the port tanks and the water was flowing in through the hole in the ship's side, forcing the kerosene up with it, as all the lids were buckled and nothing could be done with the compressed air. *Penn* was endeavouring to keep the engine-room pumped dry but the water was gaining six inches per hour. The mean free-board of the *Ohio* was now 2 foot 6 inches and the stern half of the vessel was expected to fall off at any time as the ship was now buckling more in way of the pump-room. She was drawing 40 feet aft instead of 29 feet.

From this examination I came to the conclusion that the ship could still be saved and would last at least another twelve hours, provided she did not break in half at the main deck where she was buckling, in which case the stern half would probably have fallen off, leaving the forward section still afloat and salvable. I passed this advice to the senior naval officer and also told him that if the after-end did part, towing operations would be easier and we should still get 75% of the cargo to its destination. This conclusion I continued to impress on all those interested, insisting that it could and must be done.

Captain 'Eddie' Baines, RN
(Bramham)

I was standing by the damaged *Dorset* when, about three or four miles away, I saw the problems that people were having with the poor old *Ohio*. The *Penn* and the *Rye*, a minesweeper that had come out from Malta, were trying to get the *Ohio* moving and I could see without even using my binoculars that they had got it all arse about face and really were not achieving much. Then the *Dorset* was sunk and after picking up the survivors I made my way over to the *Ohio*.

I went up to the *Penn* and said to him over the loud hailer, 'Wouldn't it be a much better idea to tow with one destroyer on either side rather one ahead and one on the stern?' He agreed and decided that, come dusk, we would do that.

At about one o'clock in the morning I went to the starboard side of the tanker and *Penn* went on the port side. Unfortunately on the port side of the ship there were some big flanges sticking out which had been blown out by a torpedo. The *Penn* was bigger than my *Bramham* and his stern overlapped this flange.

He was very frightened that he would damage his own ship by bashing it against this flange, so he said he was going to cast off. I said, 'Look, can't we stay put and get on with it? The sooner we get to Malta the better.' But he said he didn't want to get to Malta with a ship with just one screw. I saw his point so we both cast off.

At first light *Ledbury* arrived back from her search for *Manchester* and offered her assistance. I went alongside the port side and positioned myself so the flange was clear of my stern. *Penn* went to the starboard side and so we secured and made tracks for Malta.

Through trial and error we discovered that if the *Ohio* took a swing to starboard the *Penn* should increase speed by a third of a knot which would very slowly check that swing and would bring her back again. And the swing would go past the right course and come towards my way so then I would increase speed slightly. So in fact the actual course was a zig-zag, but it worked extraordinarily well.

At 0900 a bomb holed the tanker aft and she started sinking. By this time the remaining merchant ships in the convoy, the *Port Chalmers*, *Rochester Castle*, and *Melbourne Star* had safely reached Malta with their escorts. Leaving us poor sods with this old crock, tied together with cobwebs, sinking slowly in the middle of the sea.

Lieutenant-Commander Roger Hill, RN (*Ledbury*)

On the morning of 14th August we headed towards where we thought the *Ohio* would be but she was much further behind the rest of the convoy than I had expected. We found her in the company of *Rye*, a minesweeper which had come out from Malta, *Penn* and *Bramham*. *Ohio*'s boilers had blown up and there was no hope of getting her engines going. So we had three destroyers and a minesweeper circling around the damaged tanker, whose cargo was intact and Malta less than a hundred miles away.

It was absolutely vital to get the tanker to Malta but the difficulties were immense. She was slowly sinking and she had this great big plate sticking out and, as you tried to tow her, she turned to port all the time. I put a wire onto her quarter and when they tried to tow her I pulled on this wire to try and keep her straight, but I put too much power on and the wire broke. So then I went and took her in tow with a big manilla rope. *Rye* took a line from my fo'c'sle to keep my bows up. *Penn* lashed herself to the *Ohio's* side to keep her straight. This was fine and we were off, making about two knots.

Then a crowd of nine dive-bombers came screaming down at us. It was horrible to be held by tow ropes at each end, moving at two knots and quite unable to dodge. We all lay down on the bridge as a 500-lb. bomb whistled over the top of the bridge and splashed alongside the fo'c'sle. Luckily for us, it did not explode; it was an oil bomb, designed to set the tanker on fire. *Ohio* had a near-hit in the raid and started to settle by the stern.

Just as the bombers were flying away, we spotted some Spitfires from Malta chasing the Stukas over the sea. We had radioed Malta to report the dive-bombing attack, but the Spitfires had only arrived in time to chase the Stukas away. Unfortunately, none of us had any radio with which we could talk to them directly.

When the attack was over, we were in confusion. The *Ohio* and *Penn* were pointing towards Malta and *Ledbury* and *Rye* were pointing in the opposite direction. The chaos of wires, ropes and cables hanging down into the sea had to be seen to be believed.

We finally got ourselves disentangled and then *Bramham* lashed herself on the port side of *Ohio* and by shouting to each other she and the *Penn* got the *Ohio* moving and kept her on the right course. The destroyers alongside were about half the length of the tanker and she was very unwieldy. When she swung badly I put my bows against her and pushed her round.

The afternoon dragged by slowly and we longed for darkness when there would be no more threat of attack from the air. I felt if we had any more bombs around I would lie down on the deck and burst into tears. That evening at dusk we spotted the cliffs on the south side of Malta. All the sailors and survivors on deck cheered at the sight. Now we only had our own minefields to get through and perhaps an E-boat attack to face in the night. We stayed at action stations all night with permission for everyone to sleep except the man on the phone.

In the night there was quite a circus act. A tug came out from Malta with masses of people on her bridge all shouting at once. Then she rammed *Penn*, made a hole in her wardroom and disappeared into the night.

During the night *Ohio* made several attempts to blow herself up on our minefields as she swung off course, but each time the destroyers alongside pulled her up and I gave her a push in the right direction. As we were pushing her round the last point for the run to Valletta, the coastal defence opened fire. They thought they had spotted E-boats. We made signals to try and stop them firing but they kept on. So eventually I got a big light flashing and I said, 'For Christ's sake, stop firing at us!' and they stopped.

In the early morning as we approached Malta I walked round the ship and looked at the sleeping members of my crew. They were lying in duffle coats, one head on another chap's tummy, faces all sunburnt and lined with the strain of the last few days. I felt proud of them, and grateful we had got through it all without a single casualty. The pom-pom's crew were closed up and ready, training their guns. I climbed up and said, 'Good morning, aren't you going to get any sleep?' and they said, 'Oh no, please sir, just one more attack, can't we have one more attack?' I said, 'Christ almighty, haven't you had enough attacks?' They were great people.

At daylight we came round the corner to the entrance to the Grand Harbour. I pushed the *Ohio* round with my bows and followed her in. It was the most wonderful moment of my life. The battlements of Malta were black with thousands of people, all cheering and shouting and there were bands playing everywhere. It was the most amazing sight to see all these people who had suffered so much, cheering us.

The *Ohio* was pushed by tugs to the wharf to discharge her oil. Her stern was so low now that water was washing over her after deck. Within five minutes they were pumping her out in case she was sunk by enemy bombing.

We berthed the *Ledbury* in the French creek. I went quickly around the ship, looked in on the wounded, then got some dope from Doc, took off my clothes and then, oh boy, did I sleep.

Junior Radio Operator John Jackson, MN (*Waimarama*)

After the hell of the past three days it was unbelievable joy to see the entrance to Malta's Grand Harbour. I went ashore with the survivors of the *Waimarama* and the *Melbourne Star*. The fourth officer of the *Melbourne Star* was sitting opposite me in the stern of the whaler as we went into the harbour. I saw his face as he caught sight of the *Melbourne Star*, and he burst into tears. He was tough, he wasn't a baby. It was as if he had seen a ghost. I'll never forget his face.

Then I saw the other surviving merchant ships, the *Brisbane Star* with a great gaping hole in its bows, the *Rochester Castle* and the *Port Chalmers* lying almost discharged of their cargoes. A band was playing and crowds were lining the quayside, cheering. It was real *Boy's Own* stuff. You actually felt you had done something.

Captain Dudley Mason, MN
(Ohio)

At 0600 on 15th August, when we were in the Malta Channel, two tugs made fast fore and aft, but the destroyers remained alongside. At 0800, by magnificent seamanship on the part of the two destroyers, the ship entered Malta Harbour and discharged its cargo safely.

DIEPPE TO ITALY, 1942–44

Ordinary Signalman Les Seldon, RN Command

I joined the navy on 5th December 1941 and trained at HMS *Collingwood* which was about two miles away from my mother's house in Gosport. I wanted to be a signalman and it was a six-month course. You take four exams before you pass out as an ordinary signalman, which is the lowest of the low.

My first draft was at HMS *Dundonald*, the combined Operations HQ. I joined on 10th July 1942. There were fifty from Portsmouth, fifty from Chatham and fifty from Devonport. We were put through a ten-day course of dealing with wireless sets and radio telegraphy. I was a visual signalman so I had been taught Morse, mechanical semaphore and flag signals. We had to learn the meaning of ninety-seven flags. Some of those were the same flag with a different meaning depending on whether we were in port or at sea. We were taught codes on top of that and we did the basics in code-breaking.

After a fortnight, they got us on the parade ground and read out a list of thirty names, including mine. They said, 'You gentlemen have volunteered for the Naval Commando.' As it turned out, only one of us had actually volunteered. We were kitted out with uniforms and clobber and were told we were going for specialist training near Oban. However somebody grabbed hold of me and said, 'A signalman has gone sick, so you're wanted in B6 section.'

I joined my new section, rather bewildered. We left the camp and marched about two miles up the road, some of the lads pushing a wireless barrow (a double-ended, tubular-framed pram, with a Type 22 Set built in) to Brassie railway station and caught the next train to Glasgow. We were then put into a lorry, driven for several hours, and dumped way out in the Scottish countryside. We were supposed to practise various signalling methods and survive on our own, sleeping rough with one army blanket each. Luckily, it was early August and the weather kept fair. We were in contact with Dundonald via the 22 set and after a couple of days we were called back, only to find that we were leaving the next day for the south of England.

We travelled to London by train, then in the back of a lorry to a village called Crondall, not far from Aldershot. Sub-Lieutenant Evans, who was running the show, told us we were to wear our naval uniforms whenever we were in the village because the information had been put around that we were all survivors of sunken ships and had been brought to the countryside for recuperation. I don't know who they thought they were kidding.

The next day we were all in battle dress. The more experienced men told 'little lambs' like me that we were preparing for the Dieppe raid. I didn't have a clue what they meant or where Dieppe was. I learnt later on that the aim was to take Dieppe, hold it for a few hours and destroy anything of military value.

Every day that week we fell in with the wireless sets and signalling equipment, drew a packed lunch each, jumped into lorries and drove out into the open country. I had no equipment and nothing to do and one hot sunny day I was so bored I fell asleep. The next thing I knew was a kick in the ribs and a voice saying, 'What the hell do you think you're doing?' It was Sub-Lieutenant Evans who was on a motorbike, checking up on each station. I asked him what I was supposed to do, with no signal gear and nobody in sight. He mumbled, 'Well, bloody well stay awake,' and drove off.

The following Monday we were told we were going down to Salisbury Plain to put on a big exercise for Mr Churchill. All the lads said, 'Don't be so bloody daft. We know we're going to Dieppe.' My friend, Keith, showed me the Smith Wesson Colt

45 and bullets he had been issued with and told me he was leaving the next morning to join a tank landing-craft. We left the next morning by lorry and at six o'clock that evening we arrived at Newhaven. We'd had nothing but water all day so that night they gave us a delicious hot stew. Blokes were joking and calling it 'the condemned man's last meal'. How right they were.

We left for Dieppe at 10pm that same night on a naval motor-launch which was acting as an escort for four or five R-boats (motor minesweeper). I was on the bridge with a telegraphist. Commander McClintock was in charge of the landing-craft throughout the raid and we were sent on board as his communication. It was a beautiful moonlit night. As we came out of Newhaven we could see all the landing-craft heading out to sea. There were dozens and dozens of them.

Halfway across the Channel, one of our R-boats broke down and all the commandos on board were yelling at us. We took them in tow until they got their engine going and then carried on. The commander explained to me that the moon would soon go down and we would be in darkness, which was ideal. It took about six hours to get across. As we were approaching Dieppe, an array of lights suddenly went up in the sky. The commander said, 'What the hell's that?' I thought it must surely be the Air Force bombardment and the ack-ack going in. But he said, 'No. The bombardment has been cancelled; were not getting one.'

We were looking at the lights which were on our port bow. It looked just like pretty fireworks going up in the sky. I was using my binoculars and suddenly I saw a boat coming up to us flat out. It was a German armed trawler and it passed our bow by about thirty feet. It could easily have carved us right in half. She was so close that I could actually see the chap at the wheel. As she passed us we started bucking and dipping in her wake and I thought we were going to turn over. We had five little landing-craft behind us. How the hell they survived it, I'll never know.

Then the commander said to me, 'Oh good. They've left the lights on on the harbour mole.' There was a point just along the coast which also had a light on it. So he had an exact fix of where he wanted to be. We had to drop our commandos in a gully in the cliff. We went right on to the beach and grounded our bow while the five landing-craft and No. 4 Commando emptied out.

It was absolutely dead quiet. The men wanted to go up the gully but their radio operator told mine that it was full of barbed wire. They were just wondering what to do when another message came through to say that somebody had found that by using the fixings at the end of the barbed wire as ladder steps they could get around the wire and in. So the lads went in to take on the guns that Lord Lovat and his commandos were attacking. We were on Orange Two beach and Lovat was just around the point on Orange One beach, trying to go around the other side of the gun emplacement.

We left them and went back along the coast past Pourville, where they'd made another landing. Commander McClintock had to get back down to White beach at Dieppe itself to see about the others, because once the commandos had done their job, they'd be off.

At White beach, where the casino was, all hell was let loose. I saw plenty during the war, but never anything like I saw there. There were bodies lying on the beach, massed up, and bodies floating right in by the shore. They were mainly Canadians. Their bodies were dragged down by their helmets and boots, but the big pack kept them floating on top. Those that were still alive were huddled up by the sea wall. A bit later on in the day, the edge of the water was absolutely red with blood.

Many of the lads who should have got ashore never made it. It was impossible. There were machine-guns all along the front, coming from the hotels. There were hundreds of windows in the casino, each seemed to have a machine-gun. Then there were rifle men up on the cliffs throwing stick grenades over. The front of Dieppe itself is quite flat. I went back there for the first time in 1986 and saw the distance between the hotels and the first road and the bloody beach; it's something like two hundred yards with a lot of shingle. That's the ground they would have to have covered. I stood there and thought, 'That was murder.'

All this time I was attempting to send signals to the lads of the Naval Commando ashore, but they were all dead by then. Then I was sending light signals back to the First Destroyer Flotilla, some way out to sea. *Calpe* was the headquarters ship and *Fernie* was the deputy-headquarters ship. So I was signalling back to them. The commander was trying to tell them it was impossible to get ashore because the gunfire was so heavy and all the communications were knocked out. We were requesting what to do. They were still sending landing-craft ashore. There were some German landing-craft in the inner dock in Dieppe. The Royal Marine Commandos' job – once the town had been taken – was to go in, get those landing-craft and bring them back to the UK. So the Marines were laid off ten miles offshore, in some French Chaucer boats (which were like little gunboats), awaiting their opportunity. At around 11.00 am some silly bugger sent the signal – I actually saw it – to send the Marines in. It would just have been murder. They had a big smoke screen down and Colonel Phillips, RM stood on the stern of the landing-craft as it was going in and realised that he was getting pounded to hell. He signalled to the others to get back and not attempt it. I think two landing-craft got in and got hit and Colonel Phillips was killed. I saw the Marine boats going into the smoke, but you couldn't really see anything because the mortar fire was like hailstones.

On the beach people were just cut to ribbons. My own best mate, Keith, I was told later was bending over attending to a wounded person and he got hit and fell on a big boulder. Then another mortar bomb hit him and he was so smashed up he couldn't be recognised.

Our craft was attacked. The commander and I were were on the bridge along with a New Zealand sub-lieutenant, when a German plane came down. Everyone was banging away at everything by this time. We all ducked down and right alongside of me was a spare oil drum full of oil. I heard this 'thwuck' right by my ear. I didn't take any notice. I stood up and oil was running out of the drum. One of the crew took the oil drum down and found this bloody cannon shell in there. If it hadn't gone into oil, I would have been blasted to kingdom come.

From eleven o'clock onwards the commander was sending landing-craft in to try and get men and the wounded off. They would load up with wounded and get away from the beach and then get shot to pieces in the sea. A hell of a lot of them went that way. A couple of destroyers went in to try and re-lay smoke but they had to turn away before they met each other which left a big gateway in the middle. All the German guns were firing out through that gateway and all the British guns were firing in through it. Two RAF aircraft came from opposite ends of the beach right down to sea-level and laid smoke from their exhaust pipes to fill that gap. I have always thought those two pilots should have been given VCs that day because, although they were getting gunfire from both sides, they still flew through it.

A Spitfire was shot down and a parachute came down a little way out to sea. We went out to get him and, as we went to pick him up, the parachute got wrapped around one of the propellers. We got that pilot on to the *Calpe* before she sailed. She was absolutely loaded with wounded all over the decks. We started to leave too, but a mile or so away from the beach, the commander said to me, 'Do you think this boat could tow a landing-craft on one engine?' I stupidly said yes. So we turned back 180 degrees and went back to the beach. I wondered why I hadn't kept my mouth shut. We got back to the smoke and came across a MLC (motor landing-craft), which was for carrying lorries, loaded with troops. Its engine had broken down and they were waiting, stranded. There was speculative firing going on around the smoke screen. We got a tow-rope and started to tow her. We had to turn to port to go along the beach a bit to swing back out to sea. Lo and behold we came across another

MLC loaded with troops so we got another tow-rope and tied them on. Then we put straight out to sea. I thought, 'Thank God. Let's get home.'

It was one or two o'clock in the afternoon. I'd had no sleep, nothing to eat and nothing to drink. I hadn't even had a pee since six o'clock the evening before. We saw that the *Berkeley* – a destroyer – was sinking. She'd been hit with bombs. I flashed the signal and the *Albrighton* – another destroyer – replied that it was okay, they'd got the survivors off and they were going to sink her because there was no way they could tow her.

There was absolutely nothing else in sight, just an open sea. We felt isolated. It was a boiling hot day. The sun was beating down and I thought I was imagining things, because I looked out to sea and said to the commander, 'I don't know if the sun is baking me brain, but I can see a fire in the water.' He turned slightly to port and headed towards it and it was a little landing-craft. Its engines had caught fire. There were about five blokes on it who wouldn't have stood a chance. We went alongside of them and let them climb into the MLCs. Just after we left it, the burning craft went 'gurgle, gurgle' and sank. So I thought to myself, at least I'd had a mission, saving some of the lads' lives.

There must have been at least fifty or sixty lads on the landing-craft we were towing. We got back to Newhaven and the commander asked me to make the signal requesting them to open the gates. The reply came back: 'Port closed. No more entries.' I reported that to the commander who was standing alongside me and he said, 'Make to him, "Open the gates or I open fire".' So they opened the gates and let us in. The port was absolutely massed with tank landing-craft and there were ambulances and wounded all over the jetties.

As we got into the port, my telegraphist was talking to the ship's telegraphist and I was standing by the bulkhead when my legs started giving way. He said, 'What's up, Ginge?' I said, 'I'm going to sleep. I'm bloody knackered.' The telegraphist asked me if I'd had anything to eat. I said, 'No.' Two seamen got hold of me and gave me what I thought was a banquet. It was sausage, egg, bacon, mash, tinned tomatoes and a lovely hot, sweet cup of tea. When I'd finished that my head was nodding on to the mess table, they slung me on to one of their bunks and I went straight off to sleep. I slept all night and they woke me up the next morning. I went up on to the jetty with the telegraphist and one of our officers was there. He said, 'Where the bloody hell have you been?' We'd been reported missing because we were asleep and hadn't reported in.

We went back to Crondall and got our leave passes straightaway. The next day we were on leave. In the pubs at Crondall that night, they put some of those old white enamel pails on the bar, full of booze. All the lads had to do was help themselves. Quite a few drowned their sorrows.

I had ten days leave so I went home to see my mother, father, and married sister. When I got in my mother said, 'Oh hello, boy. What're you doing home?' I told her I'd been to Dieppe and she said, 'Oh have you, son? That's nice.' She didn't have a clue what it meant. When I got back to Newhaven, some old lady gave me a pre-war photograph of the casino at Dieppe. I carried that in my wallet all through the rest of the war.

Wren Dorree Spencer (née Roelich)

After reporting to the training base I was told that I was to become a cook. 'Ha ha,' I said, 'pull the other one. I want to be a driver or boat's crew, or something like that, and in any case I loathe cooking and even my soft boiled eggs are hard.' It wasn't a joke though. The navy had decreed in its wisdom that I was to be a cook, so that was that; and after the first shock, I thought, it might not be so bad. I could learn to cook delicious dishes, and surprise my family when I went on leave.

The second shock came when reporting to Portsmouth Barracks, eyeing with delight all those delicious sailors who, for some reason, seemed to be running. Perhaps it was the cold?

Suddenly my companion and I were hailed in a loud voice by a man in a different uniform, who turned out to be a Warrant Officer. 'Well,' we thought, 'this is great. We are rising in the world already.' But when he reached us, as we kept sauntering on, we saw to our amazement that he appeared to be very angry and red-faced.

'Why aren't you wearing your raincoats?' he shouted. 'Well, it isn't raining,' we replied in surprise, thinking he was a bit touched. He went on, 'It's the rig of the day. If you had bothered to look at the notice board, you would have known.' Feeling a bit deflated by now, especially as the sailors all appeared to be smirking, even though they were still running, we apologised, thinking to humour him, but he still seemed to be angry and demanded to know why we were actually walking on the quarterdeck. To us it looked like ordinary paving stone, and we said so. The poor man seemed to be having some sort of fit, but after a few minutes of silence, when he seemed to be trying to swallow, he said quietly, 'Everyone runs on the quarterdeck, it's a tradition.' Well I ask you, to be running in a thick coat when it wasn't raining seemed absolutely potty, but rather than upset him again we set off at a run.

The third shock came when we were told to report to the galley at six o'clock. Thinking that was all right by us, we were absolutely horrified to be enlightened that it was 6 am and not 6 pm. 'You're joking,' we wailed, 'we aren't awake by then!' 'Don't worry,' we were told, 'you'll be awake all right.' And so we were, to shouts of 'Wakey, wakey, rise and shine, the morning's fine!' How the heck they reckoned we could rise and shine at that hour in the morning was beyond us, but we made it, reporting to a freezing galley, to be confronted with piles and piles of carrots and potatoes to be peeled.

Talk about penal servitude. We felt like convicts, especially as there didn't appear to be any cups of tea arriving, and we had had no breakfast. Feeling cold and a bit let down, we set to without a will, with stomachs rumbling, to peel those horrible spuds, which seemed to be leering at us with their beady eyes. Suddenly there was a commotion. One of the rookies had fainted. The officer in charge rushed to get her a cup of tea, whereupon the crafty so-and-so opened one eye and winked at us. We begrudged her every sip of the tea she didn't deserve and, with mouths drooling, all decided to do a faint the next day. Needless to say, we couldn't find the courage.

Our first training fortnight soon passed, not as bad as we first had imagined, and with lots of laughs, and we toughened up very quickly. It was quite sad when we were all drafted to different bases and had to part company.

My first base was Stamshaw camp which was composed of Nissen huts. Our hut was bitterly cold, warmed only by a small coke stove in the centre. We used to draw lots to see who would sit in front of it; the poor girls right at the back were really cold and had to wear their outdoor clothing, while the front ones could almost sit in pants and vests.

I was absolutely horrified on my first duty morning shift to have to report to the galley at 4 a.m., walk through a deserted camp, with frost thick on the ground and wrestle with an old-fashioned stove which had to be raked out and lit with wood and paper. A bit different nowadays, I think. Have you ever tried washing up huge greasy pans with cold water and fingers too cold to feel anything? They bred them tough in those days!

Warmth though did arrive, when the sailors poured in for breakfast queuing up for the bacon and eggs, which we poor mugs had been slaving at for hours, only getting grumbles for our work. I remember the Indian sailors I served with for a year were the most courteous. Always very polite, they gave us perfume which they stuck in their own ears on cotton wool, providing us with lots of giggles.

We used to stand outside in the moonlight, and watch our bombers going over, knowing that many would never return, 'Silver wings in the moonlight' was the tune of the time. Then at Christmas 1940, about six months after I'd joined the WRNS, my first fiancé, Elvin, was killed over Hamburg – he was an air-gunner. He was my childhood sweetheart and we were going to be married in April on my twenty first birthday. After he was killed, I had a bit of a breakdown, and they decided to send me up to train at Westfield College in London as a switchboard operator. I hated that job, being inside all the time. My first appointment was at the Admiralty – it was all underground. I got into trouble there straightaway – they said, 'You do this, and you do that,' which I did, and this voice said, 'Can you put me through to so and so?' So I said, 'Who shall I say?' 'Just say Ike,' and I said, 'And I'm Minnie Mouse.' Actually it was General Eisenhower. He was very sweet over it, he said don't make anything of it, but I got really pulled over the coals.

I decided that job wasn't for me, so I put in for another category, as a driver. I hadn't driven before. Halfway through my driving course they decided that I was to be drafted. I said, 'But I can't, because I don't know how to drive! I'm only half-way through the course.' 'You can do it, you can do it, you're a driver.' And they sent me to this place at East Meon in Hampshire. I was petrified, I knew I couldn't drive.

I went up to one of the Canadians there and said, 'Look, I keep telling them that I haven't passed the driving test, but they want me to take a bus-load a sailors into Portsmouth tomorrow! I can't drive!' And he says, 'Get into my lorry, we'll see.' Of course I got into the lorry, we went round and round the camp and the poor blokes in the back were jumping backwards and forwards because I was stalling and starting so much. When we came out he said, 'No, you're quite right, you can't drive.' I was sent back to Portsmouth to my intense relief, and continued my driving course – passing first time.

Of course, I knew a lot of the Canadians who took part in the Dieppe raid. August 1942, it was. I served for a while at a combined operations depot where they trained at East Meon. It was a sort of a hush-hush place, you weren't allowed to talk about anything that was happening there. So many of them were killed. They were lovely chaps, they seemed to be all big and tough and lots of laughter – it was a tragedy.

During Dieppe, when our soldiers were stranded on the beaches there, I was at HMS *Mercury* at Portsdown Hill; it was a signal school. I was a captain's driver; I had to drive him down to Southampton. I can remember standing out there at dawn. It was quite a thick mist, very eerie because it was so silent. I saw all these little boats going out to rescue the stranded soldiers.

I was engaged then to a chap named David and he was killed at sea that day. He was on one of the bigger boats which couldn't get close into the shore. The rowing boats and small boats were ferrying the chaps from the shore out to the bigger boats, and his boat got a direct hit, with a line of soldiers waiting to get on board.

I remember being drafted to HMS *Lizard* late at night. It was a shore base in Hove, opposite HMS *King Alfred* where the officers were trained. I was met by a 'Wren', Ruth Brown, dressed in a duffel coat, hat and pyjama trousers. You're not supposed to change into pyjamas on night duty. She'd forgotten to put on her bell-bottoms, just rolled out of the bunk!

I have many happy memories of HMS *Lizard*. Being an MT (Motor Transport) driver by then I used to serve at night in the MT rooms, so of course there was no bathroom, and we weren't supposed to bath or get undressed. But the mother of one of the drivers had found this hip bath, and sent it to us – it was really luxurious, filled with hot water, in front the open coal fire. One night, however, the duty officer was doing her rounds early, accompanied by two male ratings. We rushed to the poor girl in the hip bath, trying to hold towels in front of her. We didn't manage to cover her before they got there. I think the sailors really thought it was their birthday! I could see their eyes bulging. We all had a dressing-down the next day, and weren't allowed to use the hip bath again.

In spite of everything we had such fun. Perhaps we were

aware that it might be a short life, and we were determined to make the most of each day. There was such an air of comradeship everywhere, we were all pulling together, helping those who had been bereaved, so many in such a short time.

I met my future husband, Jack, at HMS *Lizard*, because he had been put on shore-based duty having contracted asthma while returning on a ship from Singapore. He could have chosen to be invalided out, but he loved the Navy so much he spent a year driving lorries instead. He died in 1977, aged fifty-eight, I have never found anyone else. You have to put a brave face on, the war taught me that.

When the war was over I went to live in London and work at Harrods. It was like stepping into another world. When we were in the navy we didn't have to worry about fashion books, clothing coupons, so in that respect we were spoiled; and we always had plenty to eat. I remember making cocoa in a saucepan at night and it was so thick the spoon almost stood upright in it! I'm not saying we didn't work hard, because we did. But returning to civilian life, missing all the companionship and laughter, took a lot of getting used to. In spite of everything, I wouldn't have missed it for the world.

Ordinary Seaman Dick Wilder, RN

I joined *Impulsive* in Southampton after that it had had a major refit. *Impulsive* was the last of the many I-class two-funnelled destroyers built between the wars. The ship had four 4.7-inch guns, a high-angled gun, four torpedo tubes and multiple 0.5s on the searchlight between the two funnels. The speed was about 35 knots. Radar had just been fitted and we had asdics, or sonar as it is now known.

After a brief work up in Scapa Flow we set off for Valfjord, near Reykjavik, in Iceland and acted as part of the escort for the capital ships there. After two months we set off for Seydhisförd to join the escort for the Russian convoy PQ18.

The main section of PQ18, comprising 32 merchant ships, had assembled in Loch Ewe and sailed with a small escort to rendezvous off Iceland with a joiner section of eight ships. The Convoy Commodore was Rear-Admiral Bodham-Whetham in the freighter *Temple Arch* whose master, Captain Sam Lamont, had already completed two return runs to North Russia. The close escort was under the command of Commander Russell, in *Malcolm*, and he had with him two 'A'-Class destroyers, three ocean minesweepers and four anti-submarine trawlers.

For only the second time in the war, a light Escort Carrier was to accompany the convoy – this was the *Avenger*, under the command of Commander Colthurst. Three Swordfish aircraft were embarked for anti-submarine patrols and, for air defence, there were twelve Hawker Hurricanes. The carrier had its own escort of two 'Hunt' class destroyers.

To protect the convoy from attack by heavy surface units, there was a fighting escort of 16 Fleet destroyers, of which *Impulsive* was one. Also as a protection against surface units there were two submarines, P614 and P615. If the enemy units were detected, the submarines would leave the convoy, submerge and attack. Also in the escort were minesweepers and corvettes.

To boost the air defence capability, two anti-aircraft ships were stationed with the convoy. The *Alynbank* and *Ulster Queen* were former merchant ships armed with eight 4-inch AA-guns.

The convoy was made up of forty ships, mostly British and American. In addition there were two oilers for refuelling the escorts and one rescue ship, the *Copeland*, a former passenger-carrying coaster owned by the Clyde Shipping Co. Also, in tow of three escorting trawlers, were three MMs, 105-foot craft armed with close range weapons and with a rescue capability.

In command of these forces was Rear-Admiral Bob Burnett in the cruiser *Scylla*. This was a brand new vessel designed to carry eight to ten 5.25-inch Dual Purpose guns but, due to wartime production problems, she had been completed with eight 4.5-inch AA-guns and had been nicknamed 'Toothless Tiger'. However, she provided a useful addition to the convoy's AA capability and was an excellent command ship being fitted with the very latest radar equipment and good communications.

Long-range protection against surface forces was provided by heavy units of the Home Fleet patrolling in the Iceland-Spitzbergen area in such positions as to be able to steam towards and hopefully intercept any enemy ships approaching the convoy from the Norwegian coast. These forces were commanded by Admiral Bruce Fraser, Second in Command, Home Fleet, in Anson.

To support all forces afloat were two oilers anchored in Bell Sound, Spitzbergen, which supplied bunkers for the fighting escorts. A force of destroyers was detailed to protect them.

Along the Norwegian coast were six of our submarines (five British and one French) lying in wait to catch any German unit leaving the safety of the fjords to harass the convoy. Air cover was provided by long-range Catalina flying-boats based on Sullom Voe in the Shetlands, and a squadron based in Northern Russia. They carried out long-range reconnaissance and anti-submarine patrols. The entire operation was under the command of Admiral Tovey in King George V at Scapa Flow.

These units totalled 65 warships and, with the convoy and auxiliaries, there were 110 ships participating in the operation. They were formed up in a conventional formation of a broad front of ten columns, with 4 or 5 ships in each column, with the AA ships, oilers and the rescue ship being allocated convoy positions. The convoy stretched across the ocean for miles. Its speed was 8–10 knots. The convoy left Iceland for Archangel on 2 September 1942. The route was designed to keep us 330 miles from the Norwegian coast but this didn't stop the Luftwaffe making concentrated attacks.

During the whole passage we remained at defence stations, four hours on, four off. My place of duty was on the 4-inch high-angle gun just astern of the after funnel. This meant that when we came off the bridge having done half an hour's stint as lookout we had some shelter to thaw out a bit and doze off for a while, because lack of sleep was probably the hardest thing to bear. Even though it was only September there was ice forming on the guns and upper decks and to counter-act the cold I wore three jerseys, long johns, no.3 trousers and my overalls, topped with a duffle coat, cossack hat, scarf and gloves.

The cold was only one of our hardships. In *Impulsive* we were luckier than some because we were able to sling our hammocks and get spasmodic sleep. Fortunately too, the mess decks were reasonably dry and the only leak we had was cured with the Chief Stoker's chewing gum.

On 8 September, PQ 18 was sighted by a Focke-Wulf long-range bomber on patrol and from then on we were constantly shadowed, mainly by BV138 flying-boats. First blood was drawn on 12 September when *Faulknor* successfully attacked and sank U-88. This U-boat had penetrated the screen, was detected by the destroyer's asdic and sunk by the first five depth-charge pattern set at 150–250 feet.

The next day, 13th September, Hurricanes from *Avenger* attempted to drive off a BV138 shadowing the convoy and were appalled to see their .303 bullets ricochetting off the plane as it dodged into the clouds.

A Swordfish spotted a U-boat on the surface twenty miles astern of the convoy at 0815 but it dived before an attack could be made. However, U-408 and U-589 had worked themselves into an attacking position and successfully torpedoed *Stalingrad* and *Oliver Ellsworth*, the third and fifth ships in the starboard column. This was at 0900. I heard the 'crunch' of the explosions and saw for the first time ships being sunk. The feeling of fear this aroused in me I have never forgotten.

Meanwhile, air activity was building up. At 1100 a Swordfish observed a BV138 dropping an object into the sea fifteen miles ahead of the convoy. This was reported as a possible mine and the commodore then ordered an emergency turn to 45° to port. The same Swordfish sighted a U-boat surfaced ten miles ahead of the convoy but the attempted attack was thwarted by a BV138. Another U-boat was sighted twelve miles on the port side at 1400.

At 1435 radar detected a large group of aircraft and for the next hour it was apparent that aircraft were massing for attack. Hurricanes constantly drove off small groups of Ju88s expending much ammunition without apparent success and had to return to *Avenger* to refuel and rearm.

The main attack developed shortly after 1530 when a force of 28 Heinkel 111 torpedo-bombers and 17 Ju 88 torpedo-bombers came in from the starboard quarter followed by 20 Ju 88 dive-bombers. The torpedo-carrying aircraft appeared in waves over the rim of the earth like a swarm of locusts, flying just above the waves. The commodore ordered an emergency turn of 45° to port. Then all hell was let loose as the merchant ships and escorts opened fire with every gun which could be brought to bear. We fired as many rounds as we could under maximum elevation. It was hard pushing rounds up the spout like this but when the devil needs, you do your utmost. While we were firing I did not have time to be afraid, but looking over the side during a lull and seeing torpedoes speeding by was frightening to say the least. Our firing, although erratic, caused the aircraft to drop their torpedoes badly, some appeared to nose-dive, others either bounced off the waves or hit tail first, but some ran true. With more than forty aircraft, each carrying two torpedoes, inevitably some torpedoes found their target. One of the first ships to be hit was the *Empire Stevenson*. The torpedo detonated her cargo of munitions and she went up in a tremendous explosion, a yellow flash, then a great red cloud ascended to a height of more than 3,000 feet. The next astern, the *Wacosta*, bore the brunt of the blast which devastated her upper works, then, as she steamed on, the burning remains of the *Empire Stevenson* descended, much of it falling on *Wacosta*.

Whether she could have withstood this onslaught will never be known because she was then struck by a torpedo. Other ships fatally hit were *Afrikander* in column 9 and *Oregonian*, *Macbeth* and *Sukhona* in column 10, also *John Penn* in column 7 and the lead ship in column 4, *Empire Beaumont*.

Having dropped their torpedoes, the enemy aircraft swept over the convoy or to be more accurate, through the convoy weaving between these ships making it difficult to fire at them without hitting our own ships. They came so low and close that the aircrew could be seen. Passing one destroyer the airmen waved and this was returned by the seamen in the form of two fingered gestures and advice. Then, down through the clouds, the Ju88 dive bombers made their attacks. To see an aircraft aimed directly at you and knowing that it is the pilot's intention to blast your ship to pieces is somewhat disconcerting. It was, therefore, the aim of every gun's crew to dispatch as many projectiles as possible into the aircraft to reverse the position. The attack ended in stalemate. No ships were hit yet some suffered superficial damage. No aircraft were shot down but many were hit. The aircraft flew away pursued by *Avenger*'s Hurricanes which had been caught replenishing when the Luftwaffe commenced their attack. The convoy steamed on, licking its wounds and astern was a scene of desolation: four sinking freighters, the sea dotted with lifeboats and life-rafts and the surface covered with wreckage and, slowly moving around searching for survivors, were the three ML-MMs who had slipped their tows and were doing sterling rescue work.

The respite was short – only a hour. Nine Heinkel 115 float planes attacked but were repelled by the Hurricanes. Sadly, one Hurricane with its pilot was lost. Then the last attack was made at 2030 by twelve Heinkel 115s. The guns of the escorts repelled the attack and two aircraft were shot down.

And so ended at last the first day of major assault on the convoy. The big attack was the most devastating torpedo attack of the whole war, eight ships being sunk or destroyed in less than eight minutes. The gunners in the escorts and convoy had fought hard and several aircraft had been destroyed and more damaged.

The next day, 14th September, U-boats were active in the early hours. U-587 was detected but eluded attack by *Impulsive* and torpedoed the tanker *Atheltemplar*. Later a Swordfish sighted and vectored *Onslow* to a U-boat which was then attacked and breaking up noises were reported. Aircraft made several attacks and appeared to be concentrating on *Avenger*, but all were beaten off. Twenty-two HE 111s and eighteen Ju 88s attacked at 1400 with torpedoes. *Mary Luchenbach* was hit and blew up in a similar fashion to the *Empire Stevenson*, her only survivor was picked up half-a-mile away. Seventeen torpedoes were fired at *Avenger*. Her Hurricanes destroyed 5 bombers and damaged 17.

Similar attacks continued throughout 15th September but no ships were hit and no successes were reported by our forces. Forty-five aircraft took part in the heaviest attack. Several submarine contacts were attacked but there was no evidence to support a kill.

However, early next day, 16th September, soon after the convoy had altered course to the southeast, *Impulsive* picked up a firm contact, which was U-457. John Whittle was officer of the watch at the time. When he got an urgent message from the asdics he rang the alarm bells, reduced speed and fired the depth-charges. On the previous day I had been deafened by the gunfire and could literally hear nothing. At the time I was the port after-lookout on the bridge and heard nothing of the excitement going on around the bridge, not even the alarm bells. I had no idea anything was happening until I saw the depth-charges being hurled into the sea and then the terrific volume of water erupting from just beyond our stern! Then oil and wreckage came up to the surface; we had destroyed the submarine.

PQ 18 was now almost out of range of the Luftwaffe so at

1600 Admiral Burnett left the convoy with part of the fighting escort of destroyers to rendezvous with QP 14, a convoy of 'returned empties', many of which were survivors of PQ 17. Later *Avenger* and *Alynbank* joined QP14 leaving one AA-ship, *Ulster Prince* to continue to provide support for the remainder of the convoy's journey to Russia.

On 17 September the weather became foggy and the ships were once again within range of land-based aircraft and they were shadowed by Ju 88s from Norway and supported by a Catalina from Russia. U-boats continued their harassing tactics and once more the bombers attacked. The *Kentucky* was hit by a bomb and disabled and the minesweeper *Sharpshooter* took her in tow but she was again attacked, set on fire and then blew up. The remainder of the convoy, now reduced to 27 merchant ships with their escorts, continued towards the North Russian ports in deteriorating weather and experienced problems due to inferior pilotage, groundings and further air attacks before reaching harbour on 19th September.

Telegraphist Air Gunner Les Sayer

I did PQ18 in the *Avenger*. There must have been about forty merchant ships and forty escorting ships. It was a hell of a big fleet. PQ18 was one of the most horrific experiences of the war for me. It was all right until we got within range of the Luftwaffe in Norway and then we were under constant attack by high-level bombers, torpedo-bombers, dive-bombers and submarines. I don't know how many ships they sank. It was something like eleven on the first few attacks.

We were flying Swordfish on anti-sub patrols so you could be airborne while these attacks were on or you could be on the carrier which was under attack anyway. On the *Avenger* there were three operational Swordfish at any one time and a half a dozen Hurricanes. The Hurricanes did a great job but they had difficulty in dealing with 42 torpedo bombers coming in one attack. We spotted subs almost every day and some were sunk, caught by depth-charges. We carried a couple of depth-charges so we could have a go as well. We would sight them and report them, but if you got within range of the Blohm and Voss seaplanes you would be pretty anxious because their cannon could get you at ninety knots without too much of a problem. The Blohm and Voss was a big type of seaplane which they used for shadowing duties.

The German pilots had bags of courage, looking at it from a purely airmanship point of view. Each of those 42 aircraft had two torpedoes, not one. Some of them carried the torpedoes that went round in ever-decreasing circles so if they miss you the first time they might get you the second time.

We lost a couple of destroyers but on that convoy it was the merchant ships that went down. The Liberty ship, an ammunition ship, was hit and went up just like a mini atom-bomb. We just had to keep going, we couldn't have stopped. It's terrible when you see debris floating around, upturned dinghies or lifeboats with no-one in them. It's very cold out there; you don't last very long in the water.

One thing which stands out in my mind is standing on the flight deck of the *Avenger*. An enemy plane had been shot down, I suppose at the head of the convoy, and the German crew were sitting in their dinghy and were floating down in between the lines of the ships. They came right along side the *Avenger* and they were shouting, 'Comrade!', and the guy next to me said, 'Die you bastards, die.' And I thought 'No, that could have been me.'

It was obvious that PQ18 wasn't going very well but the previous convoy PQ17 had been an even bigger disaster. They didn't have sufficient ships, they scattered. But PQ18 stayed together, and did much better than PQ17.

We didn't go all the way to Murmansk. We turned around because the captain of the *Avenger* said the Swordfish crews were so fatigued that he wasn't going to guarantee their safety.

You did three hours in the air, three hours on standby and three hours off. You did that for about three days and fed on Benzedrine tablets to keep you going. You didn't notice the tiredness until afterwards when the whole thing was over.

When I got back I was emotionally drained and found it very difficult to relax. PQ18 was the one experience which rammed home to me the futility of war. All those people, all those innocent people, and all those ships, lost. It's the utter waste.

Chief Engine-Room Artificer Trevor Lewis RN

On Sunday 13th September 1942, we slipped out of Haifa in company with our sister ship, *Zulu*, carrying three hundred and fifty Royal Marine Commandos and soldiers, bound for an unknown destination but obviously prepared for a landing on some stretch of enemy held coastline. Both *Sikh* and *Zulu* were painted Italian grey with red and white recognition stripes on the foc's'le, presumably to hoodwink enemy aircraft. To us simple sailors, known to be superstitious, this was another bad omen and gloomy forecasts were flying around on the lower deck as to what could happen going into action under Italian colours. Still no-one on the lower deck knew our destination, although we were informed that the ships would enter the outer harbour of Alexandria, for last minute topping up with fuel, under cover of darkness.

It was dark when we entered harbour in Alex, and fuel lighters were soon alongside – it was then we learnt our destination. The Arab crewmen on the lighters were shouting up at us 'You go Tobruk eh?' – another bad omen of things to come. After fuelling to the limit we sailed immediately for what we now knew to be a Combined Operations raid on Tobruk, described later by Admiral Harwood as 'a forlorn hope'. The plan was for *Sikh* and *Zulu*, known as Force 'A', to break the boom at Tobruk, enter the harbour and destroy all shipping, landing the Marines and soldiers who would capture the town.

Our guns were also to silence the German batteries at the mouth of the harbour. The Long Range Desert Group would then come in from the landward side to attack the garrison, who would be caught between two fires. So much for the plan, which turned out to be a disaster; the Germans had been forewarned of our arrival through the criminal lack of security in Egypt; as every Arab seemed to know the whole plan.

We arrived off Tobruk around 3am, stopped two miles offshore and began lowering our assault craft with the Royal Marine Commandos. They set off for the beach and were soon involved in heavy fighting. The second wave of assault craft turned back, much to the annoyance of Captain Micklethwaite who slated the CO on the upper deck, before ordering him and all his detatchment for'd on the messdecks. We had moved a mile inshore when at around 5am a searchlight picked us out, wavered for a moment, and then held us as all hell broke loose. The German 88mm guns in the batteries concentrated their fire on what was I suppose a sitting target.

As *Sikh* began to circle to seaward, shells from the German batteries found the range and with a terrific explosion a salvo of 88mm shells exploded in the gear room. In the engine-room we saw the oil pressure fall to zero, and immediately closed the throttles to stop engines. Another salvo of shells landed aft and wrecked the steering gear, and 'A' gun for'd blew up with all its ready ammunition after a shell scored a direct hit: the Royal Marines who had been sent for'd to the messdeck suffered a dreadful fate and were burnt to death. Attempts to flood 'A' and 'B' magazines to put the fire out were hopeless.

I reported to the bridge, 'Lubricating oil pressure failed, Sir, Main engines stopped,' and Captain Micklethwaite himself came to the voice pipe. In a calm, authoritative voice he said, 'CERA, we must try and get out of range of the shore batteries – half ahead both engines.' We both knew what the result would be – seizure of the main engines, which would be the end of us all. Another violent explosion rocked the ship, and I went aft to the gear room, up the hatch and along the upper deck to see if anything could be done to restore lubricating oil pressure. Dropping down the gear room hatch, it became obvious that nothing could be done: the port and starboard fuel pumps had been smashed by the force of the explosion, the compartment was four to five feet deep in oil and water, and both the Leading Stoker and Stoker who had been on watch appeared to be dead. Clawing my way through the oil and water and clambering over twisted metal I reached both bodies and saw they had been killed outright: I had to confirm this before returning to the engine-room.

On the upper deck it was a shambles; twisted torpedo tubes and jagged pieces of metal littered the deck. Some of the Royal Marines had escaped from the for'd messdeck but had been caught in the blast of the explosions. They were screaming from terrible burns, with their skin from neck to fingernails trailing behind them. Some leapt over the side in their agony.

Miraculously when I dropped down the engine-room hatch again we had still not received a major hit in the engine-room. The Chief Gunner's Mate Harry Seymour was still firing back at the shore from 'X' gun in the after turret, but this was the only bark *Sikh* had left, all the other guns having been put out of action. The main engine throttles had been opened to Half Ahead and the ship began to move: with my senior ERA, we tried desperately to bring a small auxiliary oil pump into play to supply oil to the main engine bearings.

We soon found that the ship was going round in a circle, as the salvo of shells landing near the Tiller flat had destroyed the tiller mechanism. The Engineer Officer went down with a small party to try to connect the hand-steering gear but it was impossible. After a few minutes of watching the engine-room tachometer turning ahead, there was a loud rumbling noise, tremendous vibration throughout the ship and then a violent booming. At first we thought we had been hit in the engine-room, but then realised the port and starboard main turbines had seized up solid from lack of lubrication.

After reporting the situation to the bridge we got the Captain's reply, 'Thank you CERA, stand by for further orders.' He was an inspiration to us all with his cool, calm way of giving orders in times of crisis, and this was reflected in the behaviour of my engine-room staff. With two ERA's, a Leading Stoker and two Stokers they all carried out orders without question right to the end: both boilers were still keeping up a head of steam and the generators in the engine room were still providing light. The worst thing for us was the failure of the forced draught fans when the temperature on the engine-room plates rapidly rose to well over 120°F; with hot metal and escaping steam all round us, breathing became difficult.

Sikh was now helpless, stopped and unable to move again under her own power, when the message came down from the bridge that *Zulu* would come alongside and tow us clear of the shore batteries and out of range of the guns. *Zulu* closed and a line was passed; all the time shells were still whistling around us, some exploding in the water, some causing more damage both forward and aft. *Zulu* was hit but not disabled, and after frantic efforts on both ships the line was secured and *Zulu* began to take the strain and pull us clear. I remember thinking my chum Charlie Manship would be down in the engine room of *Zulu*, and silently urged him on; sadly it was not to be. An 88 mm shell hit *Zulu* on the quarterdeck, carrying away the bollard and towing wire, whereupon Captain Micklethwaite ordered *Zulu* away. She laid a smoke-screen between us and the shore and headed off for Alexandria at about 0700.

'X' turret continued to fire back at the enemy, but it was obvious we were finished as we could not get out of range of the guns on shore. Enemy aircraft appeared and dropped a few bombs, but it seemed they were more interested in *Zulu* than in us. It was not until much later that we learned that *Zulu* had been sunk, after being hit in the engine-room by a stick of bombs, and Charlie Manship killed. Ironically, *Sikh*, having been blasted both fore and aft, suffered not one major explosion in the engine-room.

Soon after 0730 Captain Micklethwaite himself rang the engine-room with the order, 'Abandon Ship, CERA.' We left the engine-room together after a last look round and shook hands all round at the top of the engine-room hatch. By this time the ship was settling in the water, and as the shelling seemed to have stopped for the moment Alec Sutton and I decided to see if we could salvage anything from our mess before going over the side. A shell had exploded on the bridge immediately above our mess and the blast had ripped through the Mess Flat, bursting open lockers, cupboards and doors. I found my old reefer jacket with snapshots of my wife and children in the inside pocket. These were to be a source of great comfort in the next few months. Strange though it may seem, a small bottle of rum was still intact. We drank a couple of tots of neat rum each, after which I think we could have taken on Rommel and the whole of the Afrika Korps single handed.

It was time to go, so clambering down to the break of the foc's'le on the starboard side we jumped into the water and swam away from the ship: most of the survivors were already in the water. When we were two or three hundred yards from the ship we saw our captain haul down our Battle Ensign from the foremast, then walk down the starboard side to repeat the process at the aftermast, before jumping into the sea. He was the last man to leave the ship.

It was not long before the end came for *Sikh* as she heeled over to starboard and finally sank. We were left feeling alone in the world, shocked, afraid, yet still struggling to survive. It is a solemn, heartbreaking experience to see the ship you have loved going to the bottom.

The survivors now gathered together in small groups, some clinging to mess tables or benches they had managed to throw over the side, others, hanging on to the Carley floats. The badly wounded and those who had been burned, we managed to put into the Carley floats whilst those of us who were uninjured trod water and hung on to the side ropes. Fortunately the sea was fairly calm and we tried to cheer each other up, though men behave very differently in such circumstances: some cry – usually the result of shock, not weakness; some curse with a long tirade of abuse against everyone else; some laugh and try to crack jokes – 'Where's that bloody taxi I ordered?', or the most standard Naval joke, 'If only Mother could see me now she'd buy me out.' And some just give way to despair and slide away into the depths. It's difficult to stop them when you are clinging to your own life, as it seems at the time, literally by a thread. After an hour or so the cold starts to creep in, even in the Med, and with the cold a kind of despair as you begin to resign yourself to the inevitable.

The bombing and shelling had stopped and all was quiet and peaceful, but with no friendly ship in sight all hope of rescue seemed to have gone. You just wonder how long it will be before the end comes. The laughter, the cursing, the joking, gradually die away as men struggle to keep afloat: many a silent prayer is offered.

Suddenly someone shouted 'A ship!', and we saw a large landing-craft type vessel bearing down on us, together with a high speed launch, both flying the German Swastika. Fear of another kind came to us: these were Germans, our enemies.

They came alongside each group of survivors and hauled us out of the water. The wounded were handled carefully and with compassion, and two or three dead bodies were taken up with a degree of reverence. Those of us who were uninjured were hauled inboard and laid out on deck like so many stranded fish, then they came around to each man with a tot of brandy, stuck a cigarette in our mouths and offered us a light. The wounded were taken below for treatment.

These were the men of Rommel's Africa Korps, and when we were taken inshore to Tobruk it seemed as though the whole of the Africa Korps were there to see us being brought in. We heard afterwards that Field Marshal Rommel himself was there to greet our captain who, thank God, had also been rescued and brought ashore with four or five other officers. We were taken first of all to Navy House for interrogation, after a brief word from Captain Micklethwaite to survivors of the ship's company. The officers and men were separated. We were very much prisoners-of-war.

Our interrogations were conducted by the Italians, watched over by the Germans, and it soon became obvious that they treated us prisoners with more respect than they did the Italians, their own allies. The Italian officer interrogating me took my snapshots of the family and was about to throw them away when I protested. The German officer holding a watching brief barked at him, looked at my snaps and handed them back to me with a click of his heels.

Lieutenant John Roxburgh, RN

In December 1942, while serving as the spare Submarine Commanding Officer in the Tenth Flotilla at Malta, I was summoned to take over command of P.44. later named *United*, when her Commanding Officer went sick. I was all of twenty-three at the time and the youngest CO in the flotilla.

I sailed in *United* on my first patrol in command and had a bit of luck. Ships were pouring across the Narrows between Sicily and North Africa with supplies for Rommel. It was a very hot area which we dubbed 'the Cauldron'. From Malta one had to go along the south coast of Sicily to Cape Bon and the Tunis area. Normally the first patrol of a submarine CO was a quiet number in a quiet area. However at this stage of the North African battle ashore it was essential that every submarine available was sent there to intercept Rommel's supplies, and we had a pretty lively time. We didn't sink anything but we were troubled with depth-charges.

I well remember my first attack in earnest. It was on a heavily escorted convoy of three or four supply ships. I had manoeuvred *United* into a firing position on one of the convoys when I found myself in the direct path of an oncoming escort. I went deep to duck under the destroyer as I ordered 'Fire'. Just then the escort dropped a pattern of depth-charges as it passed over the top of us. In the ensuing 'kerfuffle' the order to fire was late in reaching the torpedo compartment. We missed!

Depth-charges didn't bother me too much. You assumed you were going to escape them, and if you didn't, it would happen very quickly. I would be much more frightened as an infantry-man in a battle with bullets flying around than being depth-charged.

We encountered 29 destroyers and 15 other targets on that patrol. Apparently the crew were all horrified at how young I looked. The other thing they wanted to know was: was I married? Because my predecessor wasn't married and was obviously after a VC, they reckoned that, because I was married, I might want to live: this gave them confidence!

On the way to that patrol we'd been down off Bizerta and we were moved up to Trapani in the north-west of Sicily (the principal base of the Italians' anti-submarine patrols). We were to join Commander 'Tubby' Linton, VC, on that patrol line with two other submarines. We were moving up at night on the surface and it was glassy calm, dark with mist on the horizon. You couldn't see much and there were E-boats patrolling in the area. Silent passage in such conditions was imperative; at the same time I had to charge my batteries and run the engines which, of course, was noisy. We compromised by proceeding slowly charging the batteries as quickly as possible whilst listening for the E-boats. This delayed us reaching our ap-pointed position. Because I failed to reach that patrol line, a ship got through. When I saw 'Tubby' Linton afterwards he ticked me off for not making my position in time. I told him there was a lot of phosphoresence in the water. When it was flat calm, porpoises darting around like torpedoes can be pretty frightening. There we were going along quietly when suddenly two enormous great white tracks, phosphorescent as hell, came hurtling towards us. These were genuine torpedoes. I thought, 'This bloody torpedo is getting pretty close; I had better clear the bridge and get below.' Then I thought, 'It will pass in a second, and if it hits, well, at least I have slightly more chance than if I am down below.' So I stayed on the bridge for an extra second. I often wonder if I wasn't being a bit of a coward but I stayed there just to watch the result of the torpedo. The track actually went under the submarine which meant that the torpedo had passed ahead. The second track went astern which meant the torpedo had probably passed under us. Then I got the hell out of it. The next day I had an encounter with a merchant ship. It was an eventful first patrol in the 'Cauldron'.

In those days in the Med, we had no air-purification system in submarines. With 33 crew and a very small hull, at the end of a normal 15-hour-day's dive you were not gasping for breath but you were breathing deep. At the end of 18 hours it was uncomfortable. On 17th January 1943, on my second patrol, we were again in the 'Cauldron' and off the island of Marettimo, where we attacked and sank an Italian destroyer *Bombardiere*, which got in the way of a salvo of torpedoes I aimed at a supply ship in another heavily escorted convoy. We were subsequently depth-charged quite severely and then hunted all through the night; there was no way we could surface and draw in fresh air, so come the dawn we had been dived for over 24 hours, and I could see us facing another 18 hours submerged next day. We went deep and I ordered all activities to cease: no cooking, no reloading of torpedoes, everyone was to turn in, no activity, nothing. Which we did. We heard a convoy pass overhead and by the end of that time it was bloody uncomfortable. We were gasping for breath. Some of us had to do some work, but most of the chaps were straight out. While most were sleeping the navigator worked out the time when it was OK to surface – obviously as soon as it was dark. We came to periscope level at about seven o'clock. The setting sun was still glowing on the horizon. There was a huge groan when I announced we would have to stay down at least another half-hour.

Because we had fired torpedoes the air pressure in the submarine was high which makes breathing carbon dioxide more lethal. As soon as I was confident it was dark we surfaced and opened the conning tower hatch to relieve the air pressure in the submarine; this was after $36\frac{1}{2}$ hours submerged. When I came to open the hatch I ordered the signalman who was following me to hang on to my legs so that I was not blown over the side with all the air escaping from the submarine. I realised as I climbed up on to the bridge that if the enemy were present we would have no alternative but to scuttle the submarine and surrender. I just couldn't see how we could fight. I had not told anyone this, it was just in my mind. As soon as I was on the bridge I had the most agonising splitting headache. I felt as if my head was going to burst. I threw up. I was as sick as a dog, totally useless, as everyone else was down below.

However, we soon recovered ourselves with the engines running, sucking precious fresh air into the submarine and starting to charge our flat batteries, when after half-an-hour an aircraft flew overhead and we dived in a hurry. This half-hour on the surface undoubtedly saved our lives.

When we returned to Malta twenty-four hours late we had been given up as overdue and lost. One of my first steps was to go into the wardroom and order my ration of one can of beer per month from the Maltese steward. To this he replied, 'Oh Senor, Lieutenant Stevens thought he would drown his sorrows and considered your beer would be better for him on earth than for you in heaven, so he drank your beer.' Steve and I were just friends at this stage; subsequently he became godfather to my daughter and after the war I was best man at his wedding and godfather to his daughter. But just then I could have strangled him – alas, he had already sailed on patrol!

The medics worked out the dosage we would have been under for CO_2 poisoning and it was very high. We had a young Commando officer on board, because we were going to blow up trains and sabotage tunnels. We didn't in fact do it on that patrol but it was one of our plans. He was physically fitter than we were. I put in my patrol report that he was the least affected on board by the CO_2 poisoning. Most people were very quiet and sleepy most of the time. No-one did anything silly. No after-effects.

On another occasion I was patrolling off the toe of Italy at the entrance to the Straits of Messina. It was flat calm. One used to go deep, then come up for a periscope look, and then go deep again. One could not stay at periscope depth in the clear waters of the Mediterranean because aircraft could see you. The first lieutenant was on watch whilst I slept. He stayed deep a little too long and when he came up there was a U-boat coming straight at us on the surface. He called me and I rushed to the periscope and turned to get off the U-boat's course on to a firing track. The U-boat was pretty close and by the time I had got on to the track it was too broad, too fine an angle and too long a range to fire. The bastard was going past when I had a clear view of about six chaps on the bridge, stripped to the waist and wonderfully sunburnt, the German swastika ensign flying in the breeze only 500 yards away. She was a sitting duck if only I could have got on to her track.

I was beastly to the first lieutenant after that and subjected him to a routine, for the next hour-and-a-half, of going down to 125 feet and returning to periscope depth at regular intervals just to make sure he didn't stay deep too long whilst on watch. He became a novelist after the war and put this incident in his book!

On another occasion off the toe of Italy we sighted a ship about 7,000 or 8,000 yards away, very broad on the bow. I roared in at it for three-quarters of an hour flat out, got very close, fired four torpedoes and sank her. She was escorted by a destroyer and an aircraft and they both clobbered us with bombs and depth-charges.

When I returned to Malta and made my report, the RAF sent me a series of photographs recording the whole attack. It was quite extraordinary. A RAF pilot in a Spitfire flying at 25,000 feet returning to Malta from a photo reconnaissance over Taranto had witnessed and photographed everything. Below him he could see the picture unfold. He had photographs of the torpedoes roaring across the ocean towards the ship; two torpedoes hitting, two more going on into the blue; the aircraft coming in to bomb me and the destroyer turning round and roaring back to depth-charge me. The whole picture. He was even able to confirm the range I had fired at accurately!

Lieutenant Bill Jewell, RN

I joined the submarine HMS *Seraph* while she was being built at Vickers in Barrow. I was there for about six weeks during which time we made one or two changes. We carried out the necessary trials, did a three-week work-up and on to Holy Loch to prepare for war. At the end of 1942 we sailed to the Mediterranean to patrol the North African coast during the November landings. General Mark Clark and a team of Americans joined us for a short trip – it was his first time in a submarine. We put them ashore on a bay near Oran for a conference to arrange the landings in North Africa.

Having got back I was sent to collect General Giraud from the south of France; Captain Jerauld Wright, USN, came aboard as nominal captain. We had to wait for at least a couple of days before we could go in to Miramar. Giraud had great difficulty in getting down to the coast because he was always being followed by the Germans. He eventually came off in a fishing boat from the shore. They came alongside and we put a plank across for him which he promptly fell off! Our wireless broke down as we turned back to Gibraltar but fortunately a seaplane was sent out, picked them up, and took them to Gibraltar. We followed in slow time, arriving four days later.

On one patrol we were sent to Cape Bon to look at Galita island, the only lighthouse in the area which the American Texas Rangers were planning to take. We went around the island with the colonel and two of his staff officers for some time, looking at everything. We must have been seen because they kept the periscope up for too long. Night was falling when we started off back and shortly afterwards an Italian submarine came up close by us. We both fired torpedoes and we both missed, but we rammed them at about 200 feet and surfaced immediately afterwards. The bow was seriously damaged so we had to head off back to Blyth for repairs.

Halfway through these, I was sent down to the Admiralty, to meet Lieutenant-Commander Ewen Montagu in the Intelligence Department. Briefly, they were trying to think up ruses to disperse the enemy. After the North African landings the next obvious target was Sicily, indeed it was so obvious that, as Churchill said, 'Anybody but a damn fool would know it is Sicily.' Operation 'Mincemeat' was devised to hoodwink the German High Command that Sicily was only a cover target, the real objectives being Sardinia in the west and Greece in the east. Montagu dreamed up the idea of putting a body into the water so it would be picked up. 'Major Martin' was supposed to be a Royal Marine officer on Mountbatten's staff. The corpse could carry what purported to be vital secret documents to ensure that the other side was misled in predicting where we were going. Among them was a personal letter to General Alexander from General Archibald Nye, which was actually written by him.

I just looked at it as another job to get on with, I really had no feelings about it either way. I'd done some fairly clandestine operations already so it seemed only logical that they should consider me the right man for the job. I enjoyed going down to London to see my parents because until then I'd only seen them for about two weeks throughout the war. Montagu asked me how long the boat was going to take to repair, and I had really no idea but I put it at about a month. He seemed to think the whole operation would go well and we decided that he would arrange everything until we'd got to Holy Loch after our repairs and a brief work-out.

In Spring 1943 Montagu and an Air Force officer came up to the depot ship at Holy Loch to deliver 'Major Martin'. They came alongside with a refrigerated canister about six foot long and about the width of a man's shoulders. It looked like a small torpedo. We lowered it into the fore-ends and hung it on the torpedo rails. Nobody except myself knew what was going on and there was quite a lot of speculation about what this thing could be. There were rumours that it was a secret weapon. We sailed within an hour of taking delivery and set off for the Mediterranean. We had no real problems apart from being bombed twice, which was par for the course anyway.

On 30th April, 1943 we arrived south of Huelva where Spain and Portugal meet. Intelligence hoped that the canister would drift inshore from this position where it would surely come to the attention of the Spanish authorities. By this time the crew had decided that the canister was some form of meteorological device for predicting the weather. I explained that they were on no account to talk to anyone about the matter, either then or in the future.

When it was really dark, we got as near as we could to the estuary. The first problem we encountered was an enormous fishing fleet which came out, passed over us and beyond. We closed into the coast and lifted the canister on deck on to the fore-casing. We shut everyone else down below and put the hatch down. All the other officers and I went down on to the casing, unscrewed the lid of the canister and took the body out. Both my father and brother were doctors so I didn't have a problem handling the corpse. The poor devil had died in a lunatic asylum in London and was about thirty-eight. That was the macabre aspect of the whole scenario. I was supposed to check that he had all his private impedimenta about him. He was dressed in a Royal Marine uniform and all his letters and documents were in a case attached to a chain which led to the pocket of his great coat. They'd been able to find someone who looked very like him in the Admiralty, so they were able to take a photograph to produce his official pass.

Intelligence had taken every precaution to ensure the authenticity of their decoy. As well as the false plans, he was provided with passes, theatre ticket stubs, keys, money and personal letters, including two from his fictional fiancée, Pam. These rather imaginative love letters had been written by some of the girls at the Admiralty who probably had plenty of experience in writing to absent loved ones. Poor Pam had been so naive:

Your letter came this morning just as I was dashing out – madly late as usual! You do write such heavenly ones. But what are these horrible dark hints you're throwing out about being sent off somewhere – of course I won't say a word to anyone – I never do when you tell me such things, but it's not abroad is it?

Previously I'd had a look through the prayer book and got some idea of how the burial service should be. You never do burials from a submarine and I'd never done a burial at sea before. So we read this out over him and pushed him quietly over the side. We ran the propellers full out astern to move his body towards the shore and sent him on his way having no idea whether he would get there or not. We then set off to Gibraltar. Absolutely everything had gone according to plan. The greatest difficulty we had was getting rid of the canister because it was designed to be refrigerated and had tiny compartments all around it. We started off by putting a charge inside the thing, but nothing happened. The charge went off but the canister didn't sink. Then we tried firing machine-guns through it but it took about 400 rounds and still didn't sink. So we had to blow it to small pieces with another charge and eventually it went down.

As we tied up in Gibraltar, somebody came on board and handed me a folded piece of paper. I opened it and read it. It said that the body had arrived successfully. Really that was the last I had to do with it. The enemy must have swallowed 'Mincemeat' whole because they mobilised a lot of troops to Sardinia. Believing the Allied forces were coming up through Greece, the German High Command moved all the armoured divisions from Sicily to Greece. When the time came, there were very few troops in Sicily and the loss of life from the invasion was minimal. 'The Man That Never Was' (as he came to be known) really changed the tide in that area.

From Gibraltar, I was sent straight to see General Patton in Oran. I was to be a marker submarine for the landings in Sicily. I found Patton very arrogant. He seemed to think that nobody but an American was good for anything at all, but after the troops were ashore in Sicily, he did get into a boat and come and see me to thank me for everything we had done.

Acting Leading Seaman Eynon Hawkins, RN

I was a senior gunner in charge of the army and naval gunners aboard the tanker *British Dominion*. It was nearly 10,000 tons. We had a 4-inch gun, a twelve-pounder, two Oerlikon-guns and two machine-guns. There were four naval gunners and five from the army. We went on a convoy across to New York. From there we went down to the West Indies and Trinidad. We formed a convoy there of seven ships, all tankers, bound for Gibraltar. Two more tankers joined us two days after and then there were nine tankers altogether. Of course we were sitting targets. Only two actually got through to Gibraltar. Seven of us were sunk by submarines.

This was the first time I came under attack from torpedoes and submarines. We were under attack for ten days. They always attacked in the night, we couldn't do anything really. We had two corvettes as escorts and they really had their work cut out. We saw the fires on the ships in front of us, we could hear the men screaming in the water asking for help but we couldn't stop. I was on the 4-inch gun when the Oerlikon guns opened fire to draw the escort's attention because they had seen a periscope. The corvettes charged them to draw them away but they kept coming back. We had to just keep ploughing on through.

We were the last to be torpedoed. I was very lucky to be on watch on the 4-inch gun right on the poop deck. The first bang was amidships where we were hit by three torpedoes. We were carrying benzene and it went up just like striking a match. Luckily most of the people were sleeping on deck.

I swam away from the burning ship but then I heard someone crying for help. It was a man we used to call Maltese Joe. He was in a terrible state, and so was his lifebelt. I pulled him away from the ship and got my face and hands burnt in the process, luckily not too badly. I was trying to swap my lifebelt with Joe's to keep him afloat when I heard someone else crying out. So I left him and swam back over and pulled another man over. When I got back, Joe was dead. I don't know whether it was from shock or burns.

There were seven or eight men in the water near me and they were all in a panic and swimming like hell. I took charge and told them to keep together so we'd have a better chance of getting picked up by the corvette when he came back for us. They listened to me because I was a senior gunner. I think they realised that we had a better chance if we stuck together. I kept telling them the corvette would come back when she'd chased the submarines away. I'd seen the corvettes go back when other ships had got sunk before us. They were still dropping depth-charges and that is what I was most frightened of. I could hear them coming near and I could feel the explosions in the water. The ship was still blazing.

We were an hour and a half in the water. The water wasn't too cold; the sea was calm, not choppy. We all had these lights and I asked for volunteers with me to put their lights out to make sure the batteries would last longer. Then this corvette came back picking up the survivors. They saw our lights. As the ship came alongside we were shouting, 'Help, help!' and they were telling us to keep quiet because submarines could pick up our noise.

I was very tired when I got on to the ship. They wrapped us in blankets, we had a drop of rum and then we had to go and be interviewed by the corvette captain. That was the first time I had seen our captain, Captain Miller. He had a bandage round his head and a cut on his neck. He was very pleased to see me. He had lost thirty-six out of the fifty-three crew.

I was glad to be on board that corvette. Then it sunk in about the loss of my shipmates. We were all like pals aboard on one ship. They must have had a terrible death; we could hear them screaming. The people asleep in the cabins didn't have time to get out. Even some of the crew asleep on the deck didn't make or, because it happened so quick. It was a quick decision I made to jump. I didn't know whether I would be picked up, but if I hadn't jumped I would have been burnt to death. I didn't have time to think which is the better, to drown or be burnt? They dropped me off at Gibraltar. A week in hospital, a little time in barracks being kitted, and then they sent us back to England on the *Renown*. I came back to Devonport, got rekitted and was given a month's survivor's leave. I got the Albert Medal, which in 1971 became the George Cross.

Sometime later I was up in Hull, doing a gunnery course. I had to go in front of this officer and he snapped at me and said, 'What's that ribbon you've got on there?' I said, 'The Albert Medal, Sir,' and he said, 'You've got it on the wrong side.' 'Well,' I said, 'that's where he put it.' 'Who put it there?' he asked. I said, 'The King,' and he said, 'Oh, we had better leave it there then.' I left the navy in 1946.

Able Seaman Ken Oakley, RN

On the night of 19th December 1941 Italian two-man submarines got into Alexandria harbour unseen by following a ship in, and managed to plant explosives under *Queen Elizabeth* and *Valiant*. Very daring and well executed too. This meant that the Mediterranean Fleet was now deprived of all of its major battleships. Morale in the Fleet was devastated.

Back in England after this disaster, I was sent to barracks in Devonport. Then I received a draft chit, 'You lot from here to left, Scotland, number 1 . . .' At Glasgow we find a lorry waiting outside the station, which takes us to a little place called Baigh and there, under canvas again, we were told that Lord Louis Mountbatten had issued a signal on taking over Combined Operations.

He wanted naval men to be on the beach with the first wave of assaulting troops, naval men who would speak naval language to people who were coming in to commit the ultimate 'crime' of beaching their craft. They were to be trained in all commando techniques, etc. This meant we forsook our blue suits and wore khaki and army boots, but we wore sailor's hats with the khaki. At first it was Combined Operations, then it became Royal Navy Commando. We trained very hard up there, working with the army. Eventually we moved in with the Yankee army, at Inveraray and ended up with them in Algiers.

In Algiers one of our chaps went on a little sortie with one or two friends, found a bar, had a few drinks and they were coming back when they were challenged. They didn't know the password so the next minute a hail of fire was descending on them. So my friend, John, pulls out his .45 and returns fire, at which stage someone shouted in English, we are American soldiers, that of course ended that. When the smoke cleared one of the Americans was lying wounded. He wasn't dead but the bullet had grazed his head. So my friend goes along and puts on a dressing and, while he was doing this, all the others slipped silently into the night and disappeared. The next thing he knows he has been arrested and thrown into jail for shooting this American soldier.

He stays in jail overnight and then our Senior Naval Officer, Commander Ranson, visited the jail to find out what it was all about, and on being told he said, 'Well you must release the prisoner to my jurisdiction. He will be dealt with on board.' The Americans let him go and, on getting him back on board, the commander gave him a kick in the pants and said, 'Behave yourself, make sure this never happens again. Get on with your duties.' John was very lucky to get away with that.

After further training back in Scotland, we set off in January 1943 in a troopship to the Middle East for the invasion on Sicily. We went round the Cape then up the coast and landed at Port Taufiq at the end of the Suez Canal on the Red Sea. We now had to do exercises with the assault group we were going to land with in the bay.

After one such sortie we had a medical inspection. When the medical officer got to me, he asked, 'Mm, what's that? Can't you pull the skin back any farther?' I said, 'No Sir.' 'Mm, I don't like that at all,' he said. 'I think you'll have to have something done about that. If you put that back on the beach and it grows over any more you would be in serious trouble. I think we had better send you ashore to be circumcised.'

So I went ashore to an army camp and the medical officer came in, stripped me to the waist and told me to sit down in the chair. I was sitting down, with a local anaesthetic. He said, 'Now let's have a look'. The scalpel out at the ready, he added, 'I'm going to show you something you've always had and never seen. It is easy making the first cut with the scalpel, just like skinning a banana.' Second cut, third cut and as he is speaking so he is doing it until he gradually cut it all off, and there I am, exposed. 'Put the dressing on, now you better go and have a rest.' I was looking at it while he was doing it; I was just sitting in the chair. What an experience. I stayed in hospital there under canvas in the desert for about three days. Oh, it was painful. Then they sent me back to the ship and of course all the lads were ready then, all raring to go. I told them what had happened. They all wanted to see.

Over the past few months the great assault ships had been loaded with men and materials. We had crept up the Suez Canal one at a time and assembled at Port Said. Early in July 1943 we were ready to sail for Sicily.

We were spotted by enemy aircraft four days before 'the day' but they didn't attack us; in fact it was a lovely cruise. At midnight on 9 July we were at anchor eight miles from Avola on the south-east coast of Sicily, our immediate objective. After a good meal we put on our equipment and manned the assault boats. I was sitting right in the stern of the boat. At last the order came 'lower boats', and we were away. The sea was so rough that our boat was thrown against the ship. Away went the 2-inch mortar, swept over the side. One soldier said, 'It's time they supplied us with umbrellas,' as another great sea swept over us.

Then came that very difficult time between ship and shore when you wonder if you will survive what's up ahead. The boats were tossed all over the place and the soldiers were seasick, but they had cardboard boxes to vomit into and this helped them a lot. Suddenly a flare burst over us – we'd lost the element of surprise, but we still had about a mile to go. Our formations split up and made for their own landing places, with fire from enemy machine-guns directed at us. There was also anti-aircraft fire and light machine-gun fire and the occasional shell.

Our Bren guns engaged the enemy machine-guns and we began to get our bearings. We had landed in almost exactly the right place so it didn't take us long to set up lights and signs to call in the second flight. We waded out along the length of the beach, finding the best landing places. We could not find the beachmaster. I was detailed to find him and make a report, so off I went towards the Marina D'Avola. I joined up with four more 'B' Commandos but still couldn't find him.

We were approaching the marina tower when a sniper opened fire at us. We took cover and shot back. Our cover was a ledge towards the top of a small cliff and in order to get back to the beach, we had to cross a lot of open ground. We had decided to make a dash for it when the sniper opened up again at a man coming from our beach. He appeared to be hit – he rolled in the water and floated away. Later on we found out that it was the assistant beachmaster who was playing 'possum'.

A little later we made a run for it and got back to the beach safely. No other 'B' Commandos had landed and the beach-master had not appeared so we did our best to get the craft in and direct the avalanche of men ashore.

About this time, nearly an hour after 'H' hour, a battery in the hills began to shell us. A landing-craft carrying about 250 men was the target. It was beached and the men were pouring off down two ladders, but near-misses and one hit were making things hot. I waded out and told the men to jump for it as the water was not very deep. A few jumped and I steadied them as they fell. My gunnery training said straightaway that the next one was going to be on target. Then it came. A terrific explosion and I felt myself fading away into oblivion.

I came to under the water. I felt numb and shocked: had I been wounded? Or maybe some limbs were missing? I couldn't tell, but then felt someone clutch my legs and drag me down again. I lost all reason and kicked like mad until I was free and shot to the surface. A body floated by, its limbs still kicking, it must have been the man who clutched me. There was skin where people had been blown out of their skin – if you ever had tripe that is what it was like, arms, legs.

I staggered through all this to the shore and collapsed there for a few moments, then looked around, completely dazed. My comrades were fleeing for cover and in the water men were crying for help. I went back into the water again to help a man whose arm was hanging on by a few bits of cloth and flesh. He said, 'My arm! Look, it's hit me.' I didn't say anything but managed to get him to the beach and lie him down. I collapsed then, exhausted, those shells still coming down far too close for comfort.

Then I heard a voice crying, 'Help me, oh God, help! Help!' I looked up and on the gangplank was an army captain I had been speaking to earlier. I ran to him up the ladder and saw both his legs had shattered and were dragging in the water. Goodness knows how I got him to the beach. He was a dead weight. I shall never forget the way he thanked me as I lay there almost sobbing at all these terrible sights; so this was war!

I pulled myself together, and saw that the landing-craft had been hit almost directly above where I was standing. How did I get away with it? A man or the remains of him was splattered all over the side.

A few more 'B' Commandos landed but the beachmaster still hadn't turned up and only one assistant beachmaster was there to take charge. Craft were coming in all the time.

Then the beachmaster turned up. I went out to take a line to another landing-craft that had beached on a false bar – a hill of sand made by water movement – a little way out of the beach, the men were coming into deep water in full kit. I took a rope out to give them some assistance. One man clung onto me and I said, 'Ditch your helmet, ditch your bag.' 'No I mustn't,' he said. 'I must hold on.' So he is holding on, he is holding on to me and pulling me under. Anyway I kicked clear of him, I was exhausted at this stage. I was quite a way out and Commander Ranson came up in a boat with one of our chaps. I was in dire straits. I hailed him with what little breath I had left and they threw me a line, but I missed. So I was left until they had picked up two soldiers and then they threw me a life-belt and towed me to the beach, where I collapsed again.

I came to and swilled my mouth out with fresh water; it felt as if I had swallowed half of the Med. In the meantime along came an LCA, a Landing craft (assault), and I am getting the people off there and one of the chaps, his nerves gone completely, clung to floorboards, 'No, no I can't, I cannot do it.' I said, 'OK,' to the crew. 'Take him back.' They had to take him back on board the parent ship. He was an army chap, in really bad shock.

There were plenty of guns and ammunition lying about on the beach. So I set up a Bren gun on a tripod as an anti-aircraft weapon and when a Messerschmitt 109 came over to strafe the beach I opened up on him with it. I don't know whether I hit him but I certainly put up some opposition. He was having too much of his own way. In the end all visible signs of enemy resistance disappeared and our troops and equipment started pouring ashore.

At dusk the enemy bombers returned; this became their practice for the next few days. After four and a half days of night and day work on the beach amongst all that carnage, we boarded a Landing-Craft (tank) and sailed to Syracuse, then to Malta, and on to the dear 'Old Country'.

All the way back, I couldn't get those terrible sights out of my head, they would keep coming back.

Corporal Joe Humphrey, RM

I was a member of 40 Commando. We were sent up to Ayrshire. The idea was to train across the sand-dunes of the seashore at Troon. Over the weeks we learned to move very fast, taking our equipment with us to the edge of the water, over the sand-dunes, and on to the main road. Really hard work, but we gradually got used to it. And we wondered why.

Very soon we were told. We got on the trains, we were down to Gairloch, where we boarded the troopships – I was in the *Derbyshire*. In there too was 1st Canadian Division – we had taken the 2nd Canadians into Dieppe. Our Chief of Combined Operations, Lord Louis Mountbatten, spoke to 40 and 41 Commandos, on the shores at Gairloch. He told us we were going on the greatest amphibious operation of all time, and as soon as we struck anchor sailing down the Clyde we would be told, and we were: it was the invasion of Sicily.

We got going immediately: looking up plans, maps and illustrations. We all had books with some Italian language in, while the NCOs had to study the beaches and their approach. They took us all the way down to the Bay of Biscay, straight to Gibraltar and along the Mediterranean, and finally, on 10th July 1943, we were there.

We had a very long run in; they reckoned it was seven miles. As we approached the beaches the sea got very very rough indeed and our boats were scattered. Every Marine Commando was feeling so sick, I don't think we could have cared if the whole German army was waiting for us on the beaches. However, I was on the boat carrying No. 1 Platoon, and I was No. 1 Section, so I was going to be first out of the boat. On board with us was our troop commander, Captain Michael Ephraums. We had got to like him so much that we would follow him to hell and back – which we did, more than once.

When we hit the beach, we hit this shallow bit. We had to go up on top of that and then back into deep water, up to our necks, away and up the beach. There we were, on Lake Dia; this was an unopposed landing.

Our first objective was an Italian barracks. We surrounded that, caught them absolutely unawares, got them outside and took them prisoner. Then we began to run into a bit of trouble, but not too bad – there wasn't too much fight in the Italians, and we began to round them up.

One or two sad things: the countryside was so rough there that they couldn't use motor vehicles, and their guns and mortars were towed by horses. Well, unfortunately, to stop them we had to shoot the horses, and it was a terrible thing that couple of days, because this hot sun was beating down on these dead horses and dead men. The Italians would sooner not fight at all, they gave themselves up in hundreds, but we also learnt a hard lesson there. When they would move a white flag – or white handkerchief or whatever – we would go across the fields to bring them in. We very soon stopped that because those that had some courage were acting as snipers, and picking our fellows off. We very quickly learnt to wave them in, make them come across the fields to us.

We tore across the country, and this is where I had perhaps my biggest thrill of the war. We were advancing in arrowhead formation; I was the man right in front, with my Bren gunner and the rest of my section right beside me. But my goodness, I never was more alive than then: I was watching every window, every doorway, every bush, the brow of every hill, wondering all the time if the enemy was there.

However, we got down into Syracuse and gradually we had the whole thing under control. At first the Italians, obviously enough I suppose, were very shy of us; they not only shut all their doors, they pulled down all their blinds, nobody appeared on the street, and we went through these deserted streets. Finally we got to the main square of Syracuse, and we started cooking up – meat and vegetable stuff out of tins.

Our next big target was a port called Augusta, which at that time was behind the enemy lines. Our ship was the *Ulster Monarch*, and 40 Commando was now led by Colonel Manners, who had been a lieutenant in Dieppe. Our orders were to take the port of Augusta, the harbour installations, the signal stations, and berths. 'A' troop, the troop I was with, were ordered to take the railway tunnel before the Germans or the Italians could blow it up. It was away up the mountainside, so we had orders to be on our toes and first ashore. We had to run, not double, but run, double file, right through the docks, right through the town of Augusta, and up this awful hill: it was stony, shingle, potholes, scrub, bramble, weeds, nettles, you name it. We had to save this railway tunnel at all costs.

When we eventually got up there, we stopped. We could hear voices in the tunnel. So we surrounded it with our Bren guns and rifles at the ready I called out (in English because I didn't know anything else), 'Come out or we'll open fire!' Eventually two men and a woman came out, holding a white handkerchief. It's as well we didn't open fire, because in that tunnel was practically the whole population of Augusta. They knew that the 8th Army was approaching, they could hear the guns in the distance and the bombers had been over, and they had all gone to the tunnel for safety.

We left some men in charge of them, and went up over the top of the tunnel, up over the hill. I must say, it was there I nearly met my end, because a German rifleman opened fire and I swear I felt the bullet go past my head. We started shouting and roaring, then a young German officer and six Germans appeared. I think to this day it was a complete mistake on their part. They spoke English, and called out, 'Comrades!' I shouted out, 'Put down your guns and come forward!' and they did. When they came forward and saw that there was only five of us, he was furious. But that was it – his guns were behind him, and we had six prisoners.

We held on at Augusta until 8th Army came up. Augusta, as a port, was secured without any damage. We didn't have much more action in Sicily after that. We then went up into the hinterland south of Messina which was full of trees but behind the enemy lines – we'd come in from the sea and tucked our boats into the shore – we hid among the long grass. Out on the road we could see Italian and German soldiers passing up and down, but we weren't ordered to do anything, just to lie low and stay put.

The next thing we knew was that Sicily had been taken. The Americans had gone round the other side, and they had taken Palermo and eventually reached Messina. That was it; all over. I must say we were all smiles, because the sand-dunes on the shore where we landed weren't anything like those at Troon, they were far less hazardous. After I hit the beach and then the road, I gave a great yell of delight, I was so surprised. It was a great feeling.

Lieutenant John Bridge, RNVR

Up until June 1940 I taught physics at Sheffield Grammar School. When war broke out I felt that I could take no active part in killing another man. So, when the navy wrote to me in May 1940 asking me if I would like to volunteer for bomb disposal I immediately said 'yes', because you needed an honours degree in physics for the job and it didn't involve taking another person's life. In fact the whole idea was to save lives, so it fitted in with my philosophy.

I was interviewed on 6th June 1940, was commissioned on 13th June and joined the first group to be trained in naval bomb and mine disposal. There were eight of us; six were physics teachers, one was the son of an admiral and the other was an explosives expert with ICI. I didn't get to know them very well as the training courses were so short. The first course with the RAF lasted five days, and the second course in mines lasted just three.

We were lucky with our RAF lecturers. The one who taught us about bombs was a civilian called Harrison who had solved the problem of how the electrically operated German fuses worked. The other lecturer was good on shells, which were easier to handle than bombs as they didn't subject you to the same threat. By the end, I felt they had taught us all they knew and was fairly confident about handling electric fuses. However, all of us learned far more later, on the job, than we did on those training courses.

After training I was stationed in Plymouth and was responsible for defusing bombs in the south-west. My responsibility was naval, meaning bombs or mines in dockyards or naval establishments, as well as any found below high-water-mark on the beach. However, there was an understanding between the RAF, army and navy and the vast majority of bombs which I rendered safe were not actually naval responsibility.

I tackled my first bomb on 6th July, just seven days after being stationed in Plymouth. It was 50 kilos in weight, about six foot six inches long and 8 inches in diameter and was lying on the surface in a back street. As it was my first bomb I was a bit cautious. The first thing to do was find the fuse and get at it without disturbing the bomb. If you shook the bomb, you were in trouble because it could be fully armed.

If you could see the fuse, you'd look for the number, which would tell you the sort of fuse you were dealing with. In this case it was ELAZ 19, an electric impact fuse. For these fuses we used a discharger to drain away the current, after which the fuse was safe and you'd unlock the locking screw and remove the fuse. After that the bomb was relatively safe; it only contained high explosive. Luckily, my first bomb was no trouble and I rendered it safe in a few minutes.

Over the next thirteen months I disarmed about 110 bombs, not to mention incendiaries. The most dangerous I faced was in the Plymouth blitz of March 1941, when we had to deal with fifteen bombs in three days. One had fallen in Devonport dockyard and, when I arrived, I found its delayed action fuse was ticking. It was the first time I'd met a bomb with a ticking fuse. Normally I'd have applied a magnetic clock-stopper while removing the fuse, but this was a big bomb, 250 kg, so it had two fuse pockets, one at the back with the ticking clock, and a second, booby-trapped fuse at the front. I had to immobilise the booby trap fuse before I dealt with the clock, because if I put the clock stopper on the clock, the magnetic field might have affected the spring in the booby trap and she would have blown up.

This was a nerve-wracking business. I knew the bomb could blow up at any time, yet I had to immobilise the front fuse – which took at least five or ten minutes – before I could stop the clock.

I immobilised the front fuse without any trouble and then turned to the second fuse, put on the clock stopper and pressed the button. But the clock carried on ticking merrily. So I reversed the current but the clock just would not stop. There was only one thing to do: to go up from the bottom and take the whole thing out. I don't mind telling you, it was frightening. There I was, sitting on this bomb with my spanners, taking the fuse out and thinking, 'I hope this doesn't go off while I'm sitting on it.' All that took about an hour, the worst hour of my life. I was looking death in the face the whole time. Only recently I had seen my first corpses, a husband and wife who'd been beheaded by an unexploded bomb that went through their air raid shelter. It really made you think.

Another tricky customer was in May, two months later. A bomb had dropped into a valve chamber which controlled the flooding of a dry dock in Falmouth. We arrived at low tide and found the bomb lying in six feet of water at the bottom of this chamber, which was 35 feet deep and 6 feet square. I stripped off some of my clothes, climbed down the girders to have a look at the bomb and tried to get my thoughts together. I had no idea how I was going to tackle it.

The bomb had been in the water for two days, so the chances were that the salt water had drained its electrical charge and made it relatively safe. So I prodded the bomb with a boat hook and found that it had been damaged; there was a hole in its side. That gave me a clue. If I lashed a good rope to the boat hook, I could get the hook in the hole and we might be able to lift the bomb to the surface. This would save me diving in and attaching a rope to it underwater. Luckily, it worked and the men hauled the 250 kg bomb to the surface. I watched to make sure it didn't snag on the girders. When we got it to the top, it was a simple matter to defuse it. For that I was awarded a Bar to the George Medal.

After Plymouth I spent six weeks in Portland, and then went to Scapa Flow for the winter. It was bleak and cheerless there. There were no bombs and only a few mines to deal with. I spent most of my time going around the ships, teaching them how to deal with unexploded bombs. During the six months I was there

I visited over a hundred ships. Even so, the navy thought I didn't have enough to do so they sent me to lecture to ships' companies on how to behave if taken prisoner-of-war. The amount they knew at that time could be written on the back of a postage stamp. I found it less than satisfying, because I hadn't got a real message to put across.

So it was a God-send for me when they sent me to Simonstown in South Africa. It was a gorgeous life; the Cape Peninsula is one of the finest spots in the world and there was no rationing and no blackout. I lived in a hotel and had plenty of spare time, so I read some confidential documents about the development of underwater weapons. I realised that there was no-one in Simonstown who could tackle such weapons, so I thought I'd better get trained to be a diver, just in case. I put the idea to the admiral in Simonstown and he said, 'Yes, good idea, arrange it forthwith.' So I started training immediately.

On my first dive I only went down 12 feet and my left ear started to bleed. I went to see the doctor and he told me to lay off diving for three weeks and to go down slowly next time. I did, and it was fine. Diving was a novel experience and I enjoyed it. The water was clear and warm and the diving suit was very substantial, which gave me confidence. You had a big helmet with a pipe going up to the air pump, a safety rope around your middle, and a thin line which was the only system of communication in those days. Every fifteen minutes they'd give the line a tug on the surface, and you'd tug back, to show you were all right. Eventually I became a fully qualified diver, and it turned out to be quite fortunate that I was.

In 1943 I was sent to the Mediterranean as the Allies were due to make an assault on the Italian mainland. Many of the nearby ports had been mined and were unusable. News came that a bomb disposal party had been sent to do a recce at Messina harbour in the northeast of Sicily. They had spotted some underwater charges and, unfortunately, five out of the seven men in the party were killed when they tried to tackle the charges. My captain turned to me and said, 'I want you to go to Messina, find out how this accident occurred, what the present situation is and how you are going to tackle it.' Just like that. Clear cut. He was a man after my own heart.

So off I went to Messina, which was still being shelled from across the Straits, but was otherwise fairly safe. I went to see the two survivors who were still in hospital. They said they had located bunches of charges lashed together about forty feet down in the water. They had tried to pull the charges up the surface using a thin line with a hook at the end, with a derrick and a lorry to do the pulling. But while the lorry was moving, the charges had snagged on something, there was an almighty flash, and the consequence was five men dead, two injured.

So that was how the accident occurred. What was the present situation? Fortunately there was a small rowing-boat available and I got one of the ratings to row me around carefully about five yards from the quay so I could look over the stern and down at the bottom. I could see at least two more groups of charges and other things I couldn't identify. So that was the present situation. How was I going to tackle it? The answer was: get me a diving suit; I'm not going to do it the way they tried.

The diving suit arrived on a Sunday and the Allies were due to invade Italy on the following Thursday. In my squad were two qualified divers. One of them was Warrant Officer Stone. He had been trained in the navy and the navy does things by rote: you do this, then you do that, and then you're allowed five minutes for a cigarette. Petty Officer Woods did one dive, but to me the whole thing seemed too slow. So when he came up and took his helmet off, I said, 'From now on I'll do the diving.' I knew it wouldn't go down very well because officers don't usually dive and these trained divers had to be my attendants, which went against the grain. I was well aware of this and ignored it. When Stone didn't call me 'Sir', I didn't bother him. I just told him what to do. And from that point I did all the diving.

I planned the whole of the operation while lying in bed, which is where I did most of my planning. I'd found that the under-water charges were in two parts: three charges and a new mechanism, lashed together with wire. The biggest challenge was to lift them out of the water safely. So I asked W/O Stone and the ratings to make me a special four-legged 'tripod' to support a pulley block. I put four wires around the pulley, one for each part of the underwater charge, and positioned the 'tripod' at the water's edge.

The next challenge was to separate the four parts of the charge. I could have cut through the steel wire with a hacksaw, or I could use a one-ounce charge instead. The method was of considerable importance, so I explained the pros and cons of both to the naval officer in charge, Captain Campbell, who immediately decided I had to do it with the explosive charge (the other method would have been very risky for me). I was heartened to hear his decision. So I went down and put on an inch of plastic explosive, came up and blew it from a safe distance. It worked beautifully; the wire was cut and the charges and the mechanism were all splayed out on the sea bed. So we pulled the mechanism to the top. It consisted of two cylinders with a cable between them. The top mechanism was for firing and the bottom mechanism was a charge, and my hunch was that, if you could just separate the cable, the danger would be over. I called for a volunteer to do the cutting and told him (A/B Peters) to cut the cable strand by strand. It worked. We pulled the three depth-charges to the surface with a lorry and then moved on and retrieved the other set of charges safely, using the same technique and on the same day.

Over the next few days we dealt with 207 depth-charges and unidentified objects. By this time Warrant Officer Stone was calling me 'Sir'. I'd done over twenty dives by the Wednesday morning and the harbour was almost clear. All that remained were some unidentified objects. Captain Campbell came up to me and said, 'You've done enough. You should rest now.' I knew that, with luck, I could finish the job so I disobeyed him and dived again on Wednesday morning. By noon on Wednesday I was able to go to the captain and tell him the harbour was clear.

As a result of that they were able to use the harbour for the Allied landings in the toe of Italy and the invasion went off far faster than planned. At one point they were three days ahead of their schedule. That gave me great satisfaction. For that operation I was awarded the George Cross, PO Woods and A/B Peters were awarded George Medals, and W/O Stone a King's Commendation.

It was an amazing war altogether. And all eight members of my original training group survived it. Absolutely incredible.

Engine-Room Artificer Vernon Coles, RN

I left HMS *Faulknor* and went back to Portsmouth to do my trade test for engine-room artificer (ERA). I passed, became an ERA and went over to Victory Barracks which I didn't like very much because, after all the action we'd seen, life was dead. I had a couple of drinks one Sunday and foolishly volunteered for submarines.

I got over to HMS *Dolphin*. I performed the joining routine and medical on the Monday, the Davis Escape in the tank on the Tuesday and, on the Wednesday, I was on the train up to Scotland and Holy Loch. I arrived on board the *Forth* – the submarine parent-ship. The engineer commander said, 'Now you people think you're going to be sat in a classroom, learning all about submarines. Well, you're the first class to arrive and the training for ERAs has changed because we've lost so many. You'll have to do your training at sea, in the boats.'

It was frightening the first time I heard the water rushing up around us in the quick diving tank. After about four or five months they asked for volunteers for Special Underwater Services. Again it was on a Sunday, just after tot time, so I volunteered. That night I was on the train back to *Dolphin* in Gosport. They gathered us on the Tuesday morning. About nine of us had volunteered and we all had to be ERA submariners. So far we'd done a few trips and sunk a couple. That wasn't much, just coastal stuff; nothing to write home about.

We had to go to a selection committee with Lieutenant Hezlet. He was a man's man. We did five days in the tank getting used to being underwater. We used to play ludo on the bottom of the tank on a big steel board and the dice were about four or five inches square. We used to toss them in a bucket and then go swimming after them to see what score we had. On the last day's diving they put wooden blanks in our goggles so we couldn't see anything. We were sent down for two or three hours just to give us confidence in the units.

We used to wear Sladen diving suits. They are very loose and you get in through the apron in the stomach. Then you bring the top down like a jumper and seal the hole with a jubilee clip. The helmet was a soft-top built into the suit. There were eye-pieces like those in a gas-mask. The oxygen supply came through a mouthpiece which was strapped onto a harness on the back.

We were taken over to Portsmouth dockyard but, at this stage, we still didn't have any idea what we'd let ourselves in for. One morning we got into a boat with Lieutenant Hezlet and were given a strict escort to a room in a shed while they phoned for permission to open the inner door. We went into a building and saw our first midget submarine. X3 was the first X-craft but she was already in use for training in Loch Striven, Strathclyde; the one we saw was X4 and she was lying all opened up, her total length when finished was 51 feet. They used to build them in three sections. The bow section was built in Hull, the control room in Portsmouth and the tail in Devonport. We had a good look at her before she was bolted together. It was a little frightening.

We went up to Scotland to Port Bannatyne, on the Island of Bute. We took over a hydropathic hotel there, and a shooting lodge at the top of Loch Striven called Ardtarig, which had belonged to Lord Geddes. The beauty of this was that in 1922, at the time of the 'Geddes Axe', Commander Varley and Commander Bell were among the officers who were kicked out of the Royal Navy, so they had started building their own boat. They were the ones who started the midget submarines. So they had the greatest delight in kicking out Lord Geddes in order to take over his shooting lodge for the midget submarine base.

The ERAs started intense training. We had to carry on diving in cold water. We used to dive in our helmet suits off the old sloop *Tedworth*. We overcame our fear within days. When we went out in X4 for the first time, it was just like sitting in an aeroplane. There were scuttles you could look out from. We soon got our confidence in them.

We had to chop down trees for winter fuel at the loch. They were all owned by Bryant and May so they were not very happy at the end of the war to find the trees gone. We spent half the day training in a midget submarine and the other half chopping down trees.

We all lived in the shooting lodge together. There were lots of officers there, and they took all the rooms except for one. That was for the ERAs to eat and sleep in. It was our mess. They had a delightful bar down below but we didn't have one. Commander Bell did give us the privilege of having a bucket of beer a night. We used to take a cup to our room and quaff it.

We had an advanced training base right up on the north-west coast of Scotland at Loch Cairnbaan. That was known as HHZ, and was where the final training took place. Meanwhile the X-Operational class had been designed and built down in Barrow. When they came along, we could see they'd been thrown together, they were so noisy. They looked delightful though. We had three in a crew; two officers and an ERA.

I wasn't chosen on the first operation, but I was chosen for the passage crew on the X10. That went very well. These new boats were a vast improvement on X3 and X4 but they weren't good enough to go when the time came. We all had to go on to a floating dock. Meanwhile, one chap chucked his hand in, and I got a job with an operational crew. Everybody was entitled to throw their hand in right up to the last minute. Three of them did that, so a few of us had to jump in immediately and take over. This was poor management. When we heard the list of ERAs who had been chosen to go, we knew damn well in our mess that some of them wouldn't make it. If you spoke with an Oxford accent or your father was an officer you were in, never mind whether you could use a spanner or not. It was seamanship officers who were making the decision. They even chose a Frenchman to go – that was foolish because if he'd been taken prisoner he'd have been executed. He decided not to go at the last minute.

Our mission was to attack the German Fleet. They were in Trondheim at that stage but then they moved to Altenfjord. When the German ships came in from the sea, it was noted that they always moored tied up fore and aft, so they were always on the same compass bearing which made the attack easier. The object was to lay two-ton charges, one under the bow and one under the stern to break her back. There were two tons of explosive in each charge. If she didn't sink it was just too bad; she would still be no good as a fighting unit. We were going for the *Lützow*, the *Scharnhorst* and the *Tirpitz*. The explosives were carried in two charges secured to the side of the boats, but they had their own ballast tanks so that when you released them, it didn't make any difference to the trim.

We knew very well that three men couldn't manage. It meant that, if the diver had to go out to cut himself through nets, it left only two men in the boat who could neither carry out the attack successfully nor get the boat back home again. The boat had two control positions. The forward one was the steering position where the ERA sat. He opened the main vents and kingstons to dive and surface the boat. He also had the HP airline and the chart table to his left. In practice, the captain did all that himself. The after control position was where the first lieutenant sat. He had a set of hydroplanes and could steer from that position. He was responsible for the trim, and he controlled the trim and compensating pumps. He also had the engine and tail clutches and the engine and air compressor controls. The captain was at the periscope. If the ERA went out, it just couldn't be done.

Just before the attack the staff decided to put in a fourth member. He was a diver from the Chariots. That improved the situation but also reduced the diving time because the extra man would burn off twenty-five per cent of the oxygen. We couldn't generate oxygen at all.

Then somebody on the staff took the ERA out of the passage crew. When we went on passage, we were due to surface every six hours to run the engine, dry the boat out and put a charge in. It meant that with three in the boat, they were four hours on watch and two hours off. The tow to the *Tirpitz* attack was ten days. That was hell. I've no idea why they did it because the oxygen supply wasn't an issue.

During exercises we used manilla tow-ropes, which had been breaking wholesale. So we tried out nylon tow-ropes and had no trouble whatsoever. When the day came for the big attack, three boats had nylon ropes and three had manilla. The three with nylon ropes were all 'wavy-navy' (RNVR) and the three with manilla were Royal Navy. I don't know why there was such a discrepancy. Don Cameron, VC, was with the Royal Navy Reserve. He was a sea-going man but he was still considered 'wavy-navy'. He wouldn't go unless he had a nylon rope. He knew what he was doing.

The great day came and we sailed. The first boat was X6 under tow to the *Truculent*. We followed half-an hour after behind the *Syrtis* under Lieutenant Jupp. We were sailing at half-hour intervals. Four days out, the first tow-rope broke. That was X8 and she was lost for about thirty-six hours. They got her to the surface and Captain Jack Smart decided to press on on the same compass bearing. He bumped into one of the other towing submarines who then reported back to the Admiralty that he'd got this other boat alongside. Captain Lt. J. P. H. Oakley turned the towing-boat back and they renewed contact. In so doing, X8 bumped against her as they tried to pass the second tow-rope across. It sent one of the charges ticking so they jettisoned it very quickly and tried to make a quick get-away. It was set at 'safe' but it exploded and caused so much damage it set the other charge ticking. They had to drop that one quickly and get away. They scuttled X8, so that was the first boat lost.

X5, X6 and X7 were to attack the *Tirpitz*, X8 and X9 the *Scharnhorst* and X10 the *Lutzow*. X9 was due to surface at eight o'clock in the morning for fresh air so the *Syrtis* slowed down. Our telecommunication with the passage crew X9 had broken down after the third day out, so we had to throw three hand-grenades over the side to tell her to come up. We did that and she didn't surface. All we had was the broken part of a tow-rope to pull in. Our boat hasn't been seen since – she must have gone straight down. Paddy Kieron was the captain, 'Darkie' Heart the able seaman and 'Ginger' Holitt the stoker. They were three damn good people. That was a shocker for us. We reckoned it happened at about six o'clock in the morning because we checked the engine-room register. The ERA on the throttles didn't report the sudden increase in revolutions. That meant that the *Scharnhorst* was out of the attack.

On the sixth day out Godfrey Place's tow-rope broke. He and one other survived but First Lieutenant Bill Whitham and the ERA Bill Whitley went down. X6 and X7 got the *Tirpitz* but no other boats were taken. X6 was taken with Don Cameron, John Lorimer, Dick Kendall, and the ERA, Eddie Goddard. X5 had nylon tow-ropes and was under Henty Creer, but she was lost. He got into the fjord all right but one can only conjecture about what happened to them. So one-and-a-half crews were killed, one-and-a-half were taken prisoner and three got back.

We'd have got them all if we'd had nylon tow-ropes. It was a good attack, but it could have been fantastic. It could have changed the course of the war. We were very depressed because, after all that training we'd been through, we found that everything had gone up in smoke. The whole flotilla was wiped out. We only had six boats and they'd all gone down. There were six more being built.

Later on we picked up X24, which is now outside the museum at Portsmouth.

We were later sent to Scapa Flow to test the defences. There were so many people there to observe us being caught on asdics, or whatever, but we just sailed in with no trouble at all and surfaced in the Flow. They were staggered when they realised they had no defence at all against the enemy, despite the earlier loss of the *Royal Oak*.

After testing the Scapa defences we went into Bergen to attack a floating dock but through sheer bad luck and a multitude of small boats traversing Bergen harbour, Max Shean the captain, had very little opportunity to use the periscope so we got under a large merchant vessel, the *Barenfels*, and sank her instead. The date was 14th April 1944.

Lieutenant Godfrey Place, RN

While *Unbeaten*, in which I was serving as first lieutenant, was refitting in November 1942 – the captain of the 12th Submarine Flotilla asked me, 'How would you like to join us and sink the *Tirpitz*?' I said that sounded a good idea and the next thing I knew I was preparing for Operation 'Source'.

The 12th Flotilla consisted of midget submarines known as X-class. They were designed by a man called Farley, a submarine captain of the First World War. The boats were just over fifty feet long, weighed 35 tons, and could dive to 300 feet. Each craft carried two huge mines on the outside of the pressure hull, each of which contained two tons of explosive. The method of attack was that you would drop these huge great charges underneath a ship and hope to get away in time before the clockwork timers detonated the mines.

We spent the summer of 1943 training in Scotland. The original plan was for three of the six X-craft in the fleet to attack the *Tirpitz*, two the *Scharnhorst* and one the *Lützow*. All three ships were lying in inlets off Altenfjord, an area of Norway which wasn't terribly well known. We had good pictures taken by reconnaissance planes, but we didn't appreciate what type of anti-torpedo nets they would have to protect the harbours. We assumed they would be similar to the English nets which went down only to about 40 feet and, always with a gap underneath them. On the last practice run all six of us 'escaped' undetected. We really thought it shouldn't be too difficult.

The plan was for the submarine fleet, manned by passage crews, to be towed across to Norway by orthodox submarines and slipped when in reach of Altenfjord. All the X-craft were to go by different routes, so that we couldn't be found together. The attack crew for my craft – the X7 – was to be myself, First Lieutenant Bill Whitham, Lieutenant Bob Aitken and the ERA, Whitley. The X7 left on 12th September, just three weeks after I had married my wife, Althea.

The first two boats to leave had five-inch tow wires, but there were only four-inch wires available for the rest of us, and they all parted at some point during the tow. One boat, X9, was lost on passage. The X8 broke away, unknown to its parent sub-marine, and paddled around in rough weather until being picked up, but it had taken such a buffeting that it had to be scuttled. So that left just four X-craft: ourselves in X7; my best man, Henty-Creer, in X5; Cameron in X6; and Hudspeth in X10. As we'd lost a third of the fleet on the tow we were ordered to forget the *Scharnhorst* and the *Lützow* and attack just the *Tirpitz*.

I decided we should take over from X7's passage crew on 18th September, although the weather was bad. Just as our parent submarine, the *Stubborn*, got under way again the tow wire parted, so Bill Whitham and I spent three exhausting hours struggling to set up our only remaining spare, a 2.5-inch wire.

The next day we spent mostly sleeping, until the evening when the weather cleared and we came up to the surface to charge our batteries. During supper we heard an alarming noise from up forward. I went up on deck and saw a green and black German mine caught in our tow wire and bumping against the bow. One of the mine's horns had already broken so I quickly pushed it off with my foot while I freed its mooring wire from our tow. I breathed a sigh of relief as I watched the mine floating astern and when I got below we toasted Minerva – the mine with the crumpled horn.

We slipped on the following evening, 20th September, just after dark. I wasn't particularly aware of the other three X-craft, but I assumed they would be somewhere nearby. The going was easy and all the warnings we'd had about tides and the difficulty of finding where you were didn't seem to apply at all.

At dawn the next day X7's internal exhaust pipe split and the fumes had to be extracted with the air compressor. When we entered Altenfjord I could see the *Scharnhorst* at anchor out in the middle of the fjord. It was a tempting sight, but I had to ignore it and carry on to attack the *Tirpitz*.

That evening we cleaned up the boat while Whitley made rough repairs to the exhaust and charged the batteries. Then at 0100 we dived and made our way to the entrance of Kaafjord, where the *Tirpitz* was lying. We found a gap in the anti-submarine nets at the entrance and entered at a depth of forty feet. Just as we were coming up to periscope depth to check our position, I caught sight of a motor-boat and we were forced to dive again, still uncertain where we were. After a reasonable pause I brought X7 up again, but we hit a torpedo net at 30 feet and stopped dead. The water was so clear I could see the mesh of the net through the periscope. It was a double thickness of six-inch square mesh, nothing like the nets we used in England. We tried going slow speed astern but with no success. It took an hour of struggling backwards and forwards to break through the net. Then we sat on the bottom for a while to let the giro steady itself before we pressed on. We were already well behind schedule.

At 6.40am we sighted the *Tirpitz* at a range of about a mile. My plan for the attack was to dive down deep about 500 yards from the target, pass under the torpedo nets at 70 feet and lay the charges, then escape under the nets. At 0705 I took X7 down to 70 feet for the attack but we hit a net and had to disentangle ourselves. We tried again at 90 feet, but got even more firmly stuck this time. When we finally came clear and rose up to the surface I saw that, somehow, we had got under the net and were now about thirty yards from the *Tirpitz*'s port beam. We actually broke surface at that point but no-one spotted us, even when we gave the target's side a glancing blow. So we slid underneath and dropped one charge forward and one aft. As we dropped the second charge at 0720 we heard the first sounds of counter-attack from the enemy. It was not directed at us, as it turned out, but at X6 which had been spotted after dropping its charges.

Our charges had a time delay of about an hour but the timers had proved unreliable so it was imperative we escape through the nets as quickly as possible. The charges dropped by the other X-craft might go up at any time after 0800. For the next three-quarters of an hour we nosed around just feet from the sea floor, looking for a gap in the nets and rapidly losing all sense of our exact position. We tried most places along the bottom of the nets, and even broke water sometimes, but couldn't find a way out anywhere. The HP air was getting dangerously low and eventually the situation was so desperate that I decided to try going over the top of a curtain net between two buoys. We surfaced, gave a strong thrust and flopped over the net. Then we dived down to the bottom and tried to get as far away from the

Tirpitz as we could before the charges went up. But at sixty feet we hit yet another net and while we were struggling to get free the explosion went up, a continuous roar that seemed to last whole minutes.

The explosion shook us free of the net but also damaged X7, so I took her down to the bottom to assess the damage. The situation was not promising. Water was coming in through the hull glands, but none of the pumps worked and our HP bottles were empty. When we surfaced to check our position our night periscope was hit by enemy fire, and at this point I decided to abandon ship. As the Germans were dropping depth-charges we decided to try a surface surrender. With some trepidation I opened the fore hatch just enough to allow me to wave a white sweater. The firing stopped immediately so I climbed out on to the casing, still waving the sweater. We had surfaced close to a battle practice target so I thought, 'That's fine. I'll hold on to the practice target and bring the crew out.' Just then, the X7 bumped into the target and the curved side of the target forced our bows down, letting water into the hatch before I had time to close it. Unfortunately the boat hadn't got enough buoyancy to stay on the surface and she went down, leaving me standing on the practice target. I felt fairly confident that the others would get out all right but, as it turned out, the only one to escape alive was Aitken, who was a trained diver, and he was picked up in a comatose condition. Whitham and Whitley had run out of oxygen before they could escape.

So there I was, standing on the battle target, wearing just my underclothes, sea boot stockings and army boots. I felt ridiculous as I was taken on to the quarter-deck. The *Tirpitz* was in chaos. One chap kept running up to me and saying, 'How many boats?' and 'You will be shot.' I had a sudden vision of Gabby, the town crier in a cartoon film of *Gulliver's Travels*, saying, 'You can't do this to me, you can't do this to me – I've a wife and kids, millions of kids.' What I actually said was, 'I'm an English naval officer and I expect to be treated with due courtesy.' But I wish I had known at the time that the likelihood of my being shot on a crowded deck was very small.

Also aboard the *Tirpitz* were Cameron and the crew of X6 who had scuttled their craft and surrendered after laying their charges.

I spent the rest of the war as a POW in Germany. Initially I was taken to the Naval Interrogation camp. This was a complete waste of time because the only secret about the operation was the fact that small submarines were able to breach their defences at all.

I reached the POW camp nine days before Christmas 1943. There I was, at the ripe old age of twenty-two, thinking, 'I'm going to get out as soon as I can.' So a group of us attempted a wire-cutting escape in about the second week of January. When it failed we were all given a month in solitary confinement which was very pleasant because you could have a bath in front of the stove, on your own. When I got back to the main camp everyone was saying, 'Silly young fool, he's only been here five minutes'.

By that time it was clear that Germany was going to lose the war, so I decided to sit it out. We had a radio and could listen to the news from everywhere. I heard about my VC in February 1944 when it was announced on the news. There was a little bit of a celebration, but I was too busy feeling hungry and thirsty to care very much about the award.

It was only when I flew home at the end of the war that I heard what had happened to the rest of the X-craft. X-10 had got lost in a fjord and was picked up by one of the parent craft, and X-5 was lost with all hands, no-one knows when or where.

Eventually I went to receive my award from the King and the Queen. This was the first investiture she had attended so we were given a special briefing. The chap said, 'The Queen will probably ask where you got your award and all you have to tell her is in which regiment or squadron and give the theatre of war.' The Queen actually asked, 'What are you doing now?' I was then working on future X-craft designs which was supposed to be super-secret, so I couldn't think of anything to say. Then I remembered that the King had been to see us a little time before, so all I said was, 'His Majesty knows!'

Lieutenant Henry Leach

By early 1943 the real contribution to the war of continuing to run convoys to Russia had decreased markedly. On the other hand the enemy threat in those Northern waters had been maintained at much the same level. For although the U-boat threat had been reduced the surface element (now the battleship *Tirpitz*, the battlecruiser *Scharnhorst* and the pocket battleship *Lützow* together with destroyers) was stronger. Thus the military case for further Russian convoys now turned mainly on their value as 'bait' to tempt the German surface forces into action. The convoys ceased.

But there were also political considerations and by the autumn it was decided to re-start the convoys later that year. Paradoxically the conditions for the reception of the ships at the Russian terminal were hopelessly inadequate. It appeared that the Russians, far from being grateful for vital war stocks run through at considerable risk and at the cost of many brave lives, went out of their way to be difficult and obstructive.

The merchant ships berthed at Murmansk, one of the gloomiest towns in the northern hemisphere. Repeatedly bombed by the Germans from airfields just across the Norwegian frontier, it had been reduced to a state of rubble and dejection. In winter the uncaring inhabitants shuffled about like ghosts. In summer the whole town stank with a stench so vile as to be hardly bearable. The disorganisation, muddle and inefficiency on the part of the shore authorities were incredible and the effect on the morale of the seamen was deep.

Conditions were no better for the escorting warships. They

were allocated an open anchorage at Vaenga, to seaward of Murmansk in the same Kola Inlet.

Being in Kola was like being in a trap with the knowledge that it might be sprung at any moment. The amount of rest and relaxation obtained was commensurate and nearly everyone was glad to put to sea again where they felt that at least they were 'in with a chance'.

Admiral Sir Bruce Fraser, Commander-in-Chief Home Fleet, knew all this from his Commanding Officers. Now, with the restarting of the convoys, he determined to visit Kola to see things for himself and to try to sharpen the Russian Commanders into doing better. Flying his flag in the battleship *Duke of York*, he sailed from Scapa Flow with the cruiser *Jamaica* and four destroyers to provide distant cover to Convoy JW 55A which had left Loch Ewe on the West coast of Scotland on 12th December.

At that time I was a young Lieutenant of twenty in *Duke of York*. My action station was Officer of the Quarters of 'A' Turret – four 14-inch guns each firing a shell of over 3/4 ton to a range of 18 miles and each manned by fifty men.

A few days before departure our own captain (Brian Schofield) after only three weeks in command, had hurried south to stand by his wife who was desperately ill. Twenty-four hours before we sailed Guy Russell transferred to us from *Nelson*, an unusual occurrence which led the discerning to suspect that something out of the ordinary was impending. Guy Russell was a big man in every sense of the word – physically, in leadership, in charm and in his understanding of human nature. He had a well-developed and unique method of registering commendation or reproof to his subordinates, based on his intimate knowledge of London. For the former he would grin and drawl 'Bond Street', while a coldly growled 'that was pretty Whitechapel' had the opposite effect.

The visit to Russia, though the first of its kind by a British battleship, was unremarkable. We entered in a howling snowstorm and left a few days later in another one. *Duke of York*, *Jamaica* and their escorts returned south to Akureyri in Iceland to refuel. On the night of 23rd December they put to sea again in distant support for the next convoy which had sailed from Loch Ewe three days earlier. It was this latter convoy, JW 55B, leaving as the slower earlier JW 55A arrived at Kola, that it was hoped would provide irresistible bait to the German surface forces lurking ready to pounce in the North Norwegian fjords. Further bait was provided by a third convoy, RA 55A, sailing south from Kola on 22 December with a heavy destroyer escort. To the north additional distant cover came from the cruisers *Belfast*, *Norfolk* and *Sheffield*. This British trap was now set; would the Germans spring it?

The weather had deteriorated and even a great ship like *Duke of York* was bucketing about in a manner which precluded anyone lying on a camp bed for long. Few slept much. Over all hung an air of expectancy and uncertainty. What was the enemy up to? When would we meet him? Would we meet him at all? Doubts on the latter generated the greatest anxiety.

We did not meet him that night. But soon after the black dawn of a long, dark, storm-ridden Boxing Day, cold and fatigue were ameliorated by definite news of our impending target and for the first time the real prospect of action that day. *Scharnhorst* had attacked the convoys but had been successfully intercepted and had withdrawn, later to attack again from a different quarter and again be driven off. This was a much-needed tonic.

Scharnhorst turned south, pursued by our cruisers. This presented the Commander-in-Chief with a dilemma: would she attempt to break out into the Atlantic to carry out further raiding operations like the *Bismarck*? Or would she return to her Norwegian base? Instinct inclined the C-in-C to the latter view and he adjusted course to intercept accordingly. Events were to prove him right.

Bruce Fraser's tactical plan was clear. Unless the enemy

opened fire first, *Duke of York* would not engage until the range had closed to 12,000 yards; *Jamaica* would illuminate the target with starshell and was disposed accordingly.

Then came the long-awaited order:

'All positions stand-to.'

In an instant tiredness, cold and seasickness were shed and all hands became poised for their individual tasks.

'Follow Director,' and the huge turrets swung round in line with the Director Control Tower.

'All guns with armour-piercing and full charge load, load, load.' The clatter of the hoists as they brought up the shells and cordite charges from the magazines. The rattle of the rammers as they drove them into the chambers of the guns. The slam of the breeches as they closed. These were music to all.

Then a great stillness for seemingly endless minutes, disturbed only by the squelch of the hydraulics as Layers and Trainer followed the pointers in their receivers from the Director.

'Broadsides' and the interceptors completing the firing circuits right up to the Director Layer's trigger were closed.

A glance at the Range Receiver whose counters were steadily inexorably ticking down until . . . 12,000 yards . . . the fire gong rang 'ting ting' and . . . CRASH, all guns fired and the Battle of North Cape had started.

It is an indifferent view through a turret periscope, especially in rough weather, but two things of significance stick in my mind. The first was that when *Jamaica*'s starshell illuminated the target, *Scharnhorst*'s turrets were clearly seen to be still trained fore and aft. Astonishingly, after being trailed by our northerly cruisers for the whole of that day, she was caught completely by surprise by *Duke of York* and *Jamaica*. I heard later that the captain and admiral on *Scharnhorst* were obsessed by the risk of RDF transmissions being intercepted by Direction Finding equipment with which the British were known to be equipped. Although they had considerable faith in the effectiveness of their RDF, they preferred not to use it for this reason.

The second incident was that at an early stage in the action my no. 3 gun misfired, so reducing my turret's output by 25%. The rules for this were unequivocal: wait 30 minutes, open the breech, remove the cordite cartridges and drop them overboard. Entirely prudent for peacetime but arguably too rigid for a war situation in which time and output were crucial to success. I compromised – waited five minutes and ordered the gun to be unloaded and the charges ditched. The God of Battles was with me.

Scharnhorst turned east and, despite the best endeavours of *Duke of York*'s Engine Room Department, it became clear that she had the legs of us in those conditions. Steadily, gallingly, the range counters clicked up as the enemy drew away. I cannot adequately describe the growing frustration of those few who were in a position to realise what was happening: to have achieved surprise, got so close, apparently done so well, and all for nothing as the enemy outpaced us into the night. To conserve ammunition fire was checked when the range ceased to be effective on an ahead bearing where the ship's movement generated the greatest fire control errors. The resultant despondency was profound.

Suddenly the range steadied, then started to close. Had we done it after all? We gained rapidly; our own secondary armament of 5.25-inch illuminated with starshell and fire was re-opened with the 14-inch. We closed right in to point blank range. *Scharnhorst* was ablaze from end to end. Men could be seen leaping over the side into the icy sea, and death within minutes, to escape the inferno. It was a terrible sight. Thirty-six survivors, including one Petty Officer but no officers, were picked up by the destroyers and later transferred to *Duke of York*. It was over.

One's feelings? Almost a blankness of shock at what had been done. Some relief that it had gone the way it had. Little exultation – the closing scenes were too grim for that and the remoteness of actions at sea precludes hate between sailors.

Pride in achievement. And a great weariness. It had been a long day's night.

Corporal Joe Humphrey, RM

With all the reinforcements coming in, we moved over to the other, western, side of Italy, and started training on the hills around Naples. These were very steep hills with orange and lemon groves. We would climb these steep hills and then run down them at full speed. The coming-down business meant you took two or three steps and jumped! Land and run again, jump! And run again. It sounds dangerous, but it was good fun.

This was January 1944. Eventually on about 14th or 15th January we moved up to the front line in front of Monte Cassino. Monte Cassino was the strong point of the Gustav line, and it was manned by German paratroops who were well entrenched behind barbed wire fences and minefields. In front of that was the Garigliano river. We were to open up the big assault on Monte Cassino.

We had to go across the Garigliano in rubber dinghies. The river was in full flood; by the time we got to the other side we were slightly downstream to where we should have been, but we eventually got on to a sunken road and then all hell was let loose. This time, instead of being in the front, my section was at the back. In all the other raids we had led them in. In this one we were at the back, and we began to take casualties. The first one to go was a good friend of mine, Tom Ockwell. He stepped on a mine which killed him, and Sergeant Shea, coming behind as platoon sergeant, was blinded. And the fellow in front was torn up the back.

We did what we could for them, but there wasn't much we could do, because we had to go on, but we left them a couple of extra field dressings in case they were needed. Then another good friend of mine, Lance-Corporal Taffy Hastings, also stepped on a mine, and was killed. That night lots of our friends were killed either by mines, hand-grenade or bullets. And eventually I was hit in the shoulder myself, by shrapnel from a hand-grenade. I fell, and Jimmy Steedman, got over to me. 'All right?' he asked. I said, 'No. I can't see.' I just couldn't believe it. He said, 'You must . . .' I said, 'I can't see!!' Little did I know, but that was me on the way back to England.

It was explained to me later on in hospital at Naples that the shrapnel had hit my shoulder, but that the suction of the grenade had taken my eyes. I was told that if a bomb was up against a window, it'll blow it in; if it's a certain distance from it, it'll suck it out. Well, it had sucked my right eye out, and squashed my left one. So, I was on my way back, thinking I was a prisoner, because I was being carried by Germans. Eventually I was put down and this English fellow spoke to me, asked me how I was. I asked him, 'Are you a prisoner too?' He said, 'You're not a prisoner!' I said, 'Those Germans are carrying me.' He said, 'No no no. They brought you in, you're their passport. We're going to get you back across to Garigliano now.' They took me across the river, and I was lying in this house called a casualty clearing station, where this German was screaming something I couldn't understand. I said, 'Oh, for Christ's sake, shut your big mouth.' I'd seen our fellows killed, and wounded, I knew all hell was being knocked out of them up there. Then a RAMC bloke came over to me and he says, 'Look, you have to, er, leave him alone. He's a German soldier, he's just lost a leg right up to the hip.'

We went back to Naples, to hospital there, and the casualties were so vast that every bed was full; there were stretchers up the middle aisle. Two days after I was in, the Matron came stumping up the ward. 'Corporal! Is that yours?' She put a condom in my hand. 'That's disgusting,' she said. I said, 'Wait a minute'; she didn't, she went away, so I said to the ward sister later, 'Would you ask the matron to come and see me?' I had to explain to her that when we were doing the commando land-ings, we put our paper money in one of these things and tied it in a half hitch. I was forgiven after that. But, a few days later, she came to me and said, 'Do you know a Sergeant Shea?'; I said, 'I do, he's my platoon sergeant.' She said, 'Well, he's in a side ward, and he's not too well. There's another bed in there – would you mind sharing it with him, because we think that if there's somebody there he knows, it will help.' The funny thing was, when I did join Bill Shea in the side ward, he went quiet. He'd been shouting, 'Share that among you!' and all this sort of thing, trying to throw hand-grenades all over the place. He'd been heavily hit, and he was delirious.

Eighteen of us flew out on a plane from Naples to Tunis, all eye cases. The RAF bloke in charge of the plane told us that a German fighter had come up. Our plane was marked with a Red Cross and this German fighter circled right round us and then let us go. We finished up in military hospital in Tunis, for about a week, and then we went up by hospital train to Algiers.

Sharing the eye ward there were quite a few blokes who later became St Dunstaners. On the way home the physiotherapists were working on my shoulder, which had been pretty badly damaged, and I began to hear of how a blind person could work as a physiotherapist. And that is what I became.

Lieutenant Bill Johnson, RN

I first met Captain Walker when I was on the secretarial staff of Captain 'D', Liverpool. It was a shore base with a lovely big house; from there we used to administer all the convoys going in and out of Liverpool across the Atlantic and to Freetown. I was the CB officer, in charge of the distribution of confidential books and ciphers to all the ships on the convoys. We used to get reports of proceedings in from all the senior officers of the escorts. The reports from HMS *Stork*, the 36 Escort Group commanded by Commander Walker soon came in to prominence. At one point while under attack by U-boats, Commander Walker found he had to make a vital decision: whether to leave the convoy only partially protected while he (and possibly another ship) went off to hunt the U-boat, or to stay with the convoy in order to give it full protection. He decided that the only way to stop the U-boat sinking any further ships was to put it out of action, so he went over and sunk it. We always looked forward to reading his reports of proceedings – they were written in his own inimitable style, lots of touches of humour.

Eventually, after doing this trip, the powers that be thought he needed a rest. So they promoted him to Captain and made him Captain 'D' Liverpool, a shore-based job, so then I was actually on his staff. He lived quite close to me and we got to know him socially. While he was captain there, we also formed a concert party which we took to hospitals and service establishments. We called it the 'Shakers' and he was one of our fans, always coming to our shows. During that time he managed to get the ear of the Commander-in-Chief, Sir Max Horton, and was able to put some of his somewhat revolutionary ideas to him. Eventually he got his way, and support groups for the Atlantic convoys were formed. The problem was that the convoys had to go across the Atlantic with escorts, and there was a black gap in the middle where there was no aircraft cover. The U-boats knew this and they used to indulge in wolf-pack tactics, forming-up in order to attack the ships going across this unprotected area. The function of the support group was to protect the convoys and their escorts going across that two hundred miles gap. If a U-boat popped up we could detect it up to a hundred miles away by HFD (high frequency direction finding), and go off and hunt it as a group, still leaving the convoy fully protected. Captain Walker was made Senior Officer of the new founded second escort, or support group, in *Starling*, an AA-sloop, now called a frigate. The others were *Wren*, *Wild Goose*, *Cygnet*, *Kite* and *Woodpecker*, all sloops.

In the first four months in the *Starling* they sank five U-boats. At this point I had spent about two and a half years on Captain

'D's staff at Liverpool and I was asked if I had any ideas about moving on. I said, 'Well there's only one job I'd like and I don't suppose that I've got a hell of a chance of getting it, and that is secretary to Captain Walker.' Before I knew where I was I was at sea in HMS *Wren* in order to get my sea legs, which I thoroughly enjoyed. We had one of the waiters from the Savoy as our wardroom steward, so everything was done very well, silver service and everything. We were to go down as guinea-pigs to try and find a defence against a new weapon – the first guided missile, called a 'Chase-me-Charlie'. These were mounted on small gliders and released from the parent plane which directed it by radio towards the target. We had a lot of scientists on board to try and work out a defence – they hoped that we'd be attacked by it. The only defence they had dis-covered was an electric razor – it messed up the radio-control! So we all brought up a lot of electric razors so that, if one of these planes appeared we could switch them on in the hope that the baby 'plane' would turn around and blow its parent plane up.

At that time the U-boats had also developed acoustic tor-pedoes which were attracted by the noise of the screws (or propellers) attacking the ship. They would home on to those screws. One way to stop them was to reduce speed to seven knots. However, the *Starling* had also got a new secret defensive weapon called the Foxer. The idea of this Foxer was to make lots of noise well behind the screws by towing lots of rusty old iron behind the ship. The *Starling* tried it on but they got caught up with the wires, so they let it go and Captain Walker refused to use a Foxer again.

The Foxer put the *Starling* slightly out of action, so he sent a signal across to *Wren* saying that he was changing commanding officers over and coming across so he could carry on the operation from *Wren*. He came aboard with his staff. He had another secretary with him at the time who came over as well. I was more or less a passenger at that point; it wasn't until we got back to Liverpool for the next trip that I officially took over duties as his secretary.

The night before I took up the job, I'd arranged to have a farewell party ashore. It wasn't until that evening that I discovered I was supposed to be on board right then. So I transferred the party from ashore to the ward room of the *Starling*. Everybody turned up and whilst we were having drinks before dinner there was a knock on the ward door, and there was Captain Walker. 'I'm sorry to interrupt your party but my steward is ashore; may I have dinner in the wardroom?' Needless to say, we were only too delighted. We put him at the head of the table, we thought naturally he would sit there, but he said he wouldn't hear of it. He said, 'This is your party, I'm only a gate-crasher.' He went down to the end of the table with some of the Wrens and we had a hilarious evening – that's when I saw him do his party trick of standing on his head and drinking a glass of beer. He would then invite people to do the same thing and when they were upside down he would pour a pint of beer down their trouser leg.

On the first action I was involved in, we went to sea in October 1943. We were in the *Starling*. We had some very rough weather, we were hove to for about four days. I was thrown out of my bunk into about twelve inches of water in my cabin. After that I slept in a hammock, immediately outside the captain's cabin and below the bridge. Not only was that more comfortable on the rough sea, but it meant that if any signals came in for the captain I could take them in to him. That is how I knew, particularly on the sixth trip, that he never had more than four hours consecutive sleep, because I was the chap who had to wake him up with the signals.

Walker was in charge on the bridge. He was a very strong disciplinarian, but a very caring man. He always took requests for compassionate leave very sympathetically. He liked to be on the bridge as much as possible, because he liked to be seen by the ship's company in order to give them confidence. He was also a shy man, he didn't show his feelings except occasionally when people didn't do as he hoped, then he would throw his cap on the ground and jump on it.

On that first trip, on 6th November, we attacked a U-boat with a 'creeping' attack. The *Kite* had picked up a radar echo and the lookout spotted the U-boat as it came out of a patch of fog about five hundred yards ahead. It was in such a good position to have a shot at the *Tracker*, which was a small aircraft carrier, and made a good target. *Kite* fired some charges immediately. The U-boat did fire a torpedo, but with the dropping of the depth-charge and *Tracker* turning away, it missed. *Starling*, *Kite* and *Woodcock* were stalking the U-boat; we were in asdic contact. We got reports from the cabin on the bridge. I was on the other side of the bridge making notes of what was going on. The timing was particular, if we increased speed too much we would have become targets of one of these 'gnats', these acoustic torpedoes. However, we had to increase speed so as to drop depth-charges without blowing ourselves up.

On this occasion it was pitch black, but they had a steady asdic contact of the ship. We followed the U-boat and then at dawn, *Woodcock* was instructed by Walker by loudhailer to switch off his asdic. He then directed *Woodcock* to a position over the U-boat. The U-boat knew when they were being pinged; they could hear the attacking ship as the pings on its hull got more rapid, and take evasive action. It was busy concentrating on the steady pinging of the *Starling*, which was some distance away. So then the *Woodcock* increased speed, and it wasn't until the depth-charges dropped that they knew she was there: they never knew what hit them. It was so simple. That was the 'creeping' attack which we did very successfully.

You could hear the underwater explosions and very often you could smell the diesel oil. Bodies eventually came to the surface. There were no survivors. The only thing there was the headless and tailless torpedo which came to the surface. We had to pick up bits of wreckage, as evidence, and we had to find human remains in order to claim a kill. At first the doctor had to pickle these human remains, but when they arrived at the Admiralty it was opened by a Wren who passed out on the spot, so they didn't think that was quite such a good idea. However, we had to take some evidence back.

The *Kite* said it had been a large U-boat, a 'Milch cow', used to supply the other ones. We spliced the mainbrace and I put on a show over the radio to celebrate.

That was the first U-boat, sunk at 7.30. At 1.00 we got a HF/DF bearing on another U-boat, about twenty miles away. Now it was their turn, the *Woodcock* and *Kite*, to look after and shield the aircraft carriers. The *Starling* went in with the *Wild Goose*. *Wild Goose* had a good contact but *Starling's* giro compass was thrown out of action by a shallow depth-charge explosion. When this had been repaired, Captain Walker directed *Wild Goose* into another creeping attack, to fire twenty-six charges. Something went wrong and she only fired ten. Walker was in a fury at his own mistake, because his most trusted ship had let him down and because, in the middle of the attack, he was told that his giro compass was not two degrees out of line but nine. He threw his cap on the deck and jumped on it. *Wild Goose* only said, 'This is most unusual.' He started to send a rude signal to them when he was interrupted by a loud underwater explosion and the asdic operators reported unmistakable breaking-up noises. Diesel oil came to the surface and, believe it or not, up popped another headless and tailless torpedo. So, instead of sending this stinker to the *Wild Goose*, he sent a message to splice the mainbrace. In his report of proceedings he said, 'I would have staked my last penny that the attack was bum, and I should have lost my money.'

The sixth trip of the second support group was in January 1944. This time we were with two aircraft-carriers, the *Nairana* and *Activity*. The *Starling* had with her the *Wild Goose*, *Kite*,

Wren, *Woodpecker* and *Magpie*. The captain would issue very brief orders to all the commanding officers, as he didn't want people signalling to ask him for instructions. They were to do as they thought best, but tell him what they were doing. They knew exactly what they had to do anyway because we had the plan of campaign; as soon as we got the U-boats, the black flags went up and we were off. We also knew exactly what the other people were doing. We worked very much as a team.

Captain Walker didn't like working with the carriers. However, we were instructed to take our own aircraft with us as we couldn't get aircraft support across the middle of the Atlantic, which in theory was absolutely splendid, but the mid-Atlantic can be a rough sea. It is extremely difficult to get planes off a heavy deck and almost impossible to get them back on again. But they did make jolly good targets for the U-boats and acted as a bait.

This was to prove itself when on 1 February, the *Wild Goose* suddenly got a shout from the bridge that there was a submarine echo to starboard. It looked as if the U-boat was trying to get a shot at the *Nairana*. Commander Wemyss from the *Wild Goose* immediately ordered, 'Hard to starboard, full speed, hoist the attacking flag, tell leader on radio that I am attacking.' The *Wild Goose* attacked; *Magpie* went to go in with her. *Wild Goose* told the *Nairana* to get out of the way, then dropped a ten-charge pattern to scare the U-boat off before it could target the aircraft-carriers.

Captain Walker then told the *Kite*, *Wren* and *Woodpecker* to screen the *Nairana*, while he went in to join the *Wild Goose* and *Magpie*. *Magpie* tried an attack but without success, so she went off to assist in screening the carrier. The *Wild Goose* and the *Starling* carried on hunting. Walker said, 'When the *Magpie* left to join the remainder of our force, *Wild Goose* handed me an asdic contact with the Boche on a plate.'

They were in contact with the U-boat by asdic when they carried out an operation 'plaster'. This involved attacking abreast: they went in at five knots, dropping in all some sixty depth-charges set to explode between 500 and 700 feet at five-second intervals. You can imagine the explosions. They were terrific, throwing from the stern and away from the stern.

After dropping the depth-charges all sorts of things came up: oil, clothing, planks of wood, pulped life jackets, books and the mangled remains of bodies. That was U-502. Again we sent out our boats for the remains and spliced the mainbrace.

Five days after the attack on the *Nairana*, we joined forces with the west-bound convoy, SL147. We were told that, by virtue of seniority, Captain Walker was not only senior officer of our group, but also of the escort. He was in charge of all the ships in the convoy. It was a terrific responsibility – there were eighty-one ships and two aircraft-carriers. Joining a convoy at sea is quite an experience. You go for days and days seeing nothing else but the five or six ships that you're in company with, and then suddenly on the horizon you see the silhouettes. As you get nearer, it's rather like coming into a town: it looks like civilisation. This particular convoy seemed pleased to see us. We had signals that there were at least fifteen U-boats converging on them. Actually there were twenty-six, although we didn't know that at the time.

Wild Goose was six miles ahead of the convoy in the port quarter when her port bridge lookout sounded an alarm which rang through silence, to be repeated in dozens of ships spread across miles of the Atlantic. Their lookout had sighted a U-boat on the surface with only the conning tower showing, about a mile and a half away. Walker ordered the convoy to alter course. The U-boat was preparing to ram, but realising he had been sighted he crash-dived. But instead of diving deep and taking avoiding action, he stayed at periscope depth to keep track of *Wild Goose*'s movements. Again, the same Able Seaman who spotted him drew attention to this, but they couldn't get the depth-charges to bear on it. All they could do was fire with the machine-guns. This eventually persuaded it to down periscope and dive away.

Wild Goose then got an asdic contact and directed the *Woodpecker* into a 'creeping attack'. When the last depth-charge had exploded the *Starling* came up. Walker took one look at the surging water left by the depth charges and sent a signal across to the *Woodpecker*: 'Look what a mess you've made.' They did a cross-check and Walker then directed the *Woodpecker* into a creeping attack. She dropped twenty-six sets of depth-charges to explode at maximum depth, probably about 700 feet, although they could have gone much deeper. (As the depth-charges were improved over time they were able to go deeper and deeper.) There was a tremendous explosion – we had got it!

We fired snow-flake rockets so we could see the wreckage. We picked up a German coat and some other things. From Naval Intelligence later on we were able to recognise it as the U-762, a big one. Sometimes the wreckage gave us clues as to what it was. We spliced the mainbrace that day.

The next U-boat was ten miles ahead of the convoy. It was found through HF/DF signalling by wireless on the surface at 6.00am the next day. Walker sent *Magpie* and *Kite* to investigate. *Magpie* was still some distance astern of *Kite*, who was racing to catch up. However, she sighted a U-boat as it came out of a patch of mist, steaming fast toward the convoy and only 800 yards away. Fortunately the commanding officer realised the danger of being attacked by a 'gnat', or acoustic torpedo, so as the U-boat crash-dived he did the usual drill, reducing speed to seven knots and firing a single depth-charge in the hope of counter-mining a gnat before it could strike home. A second or two later a violent explosion threw a column of water twenty yards on *Kite*'s port beam. The depth-charge had actually counter-mined the 'gnat' warheads, causing a double explosion.

Kite then increased to full speed and ran over the diving position to fire a full pattern of ten depth-charges. She got no result, so set off to hunt the U-boat. At the moment when *Kite* and the U-boat sighted each other, *Wild Goose* obtained a radar contact with another U-boat which was little more than a mile away on the convoy's port bow. Also fearing a gnat torpedo, she reduced speed to seven knots and fired off a starshell. The first shower revealed the U-boat about to dive. Then there was an explosion – the gnat, having failed to pick up on the propellers, had exploded at the end of its run.

We couldn't see what was happening. We didn't know at that time what they were doing. It wasn't until we joined *Wild Goose* at about 8.30 in the morning that Captain Walker was again handed the asdic contact 'on a plate' by *Wild Goose*. He directed *Wild Goose* on two creeping attacks. These gnats were all about, and another went off at the end of its run.

After we'd fired the depth-charges on the second creeping attack, oil came to the surface, although there was no other sign of damage. The carriers which had been diverted steamed near the *Starling*, and the senior officer there signalled Walker, 'Good Luck. Hope to see you again.' Walker replied, 'We seem to have nabbed a couple of particularly tough babies, will be rejoining soon.'

Just as the convoy was moving away, a shallow-running torpedo was suddenly spotted racing towards the ship. There was no time to pick up speed or take avoiding action. Walker immediately ordered, 'Hard to Port, stand by depth-charges, shallow setting, fire!' The U-boat had come up to the surface, fired this torpedo and then gone down again. We all fully expected to be hit – many sailors were flat on the deck but, incredibly, the depth-charge counter-mined the torpedo, which exploded only five or ten yards from the quarter deck.

The ship seemed to leap in the air. A huge wave rolled over her. The compass went out of action, electrical switches were thrown open, but the greatest tragedy was that every bottle in the wardroom was shattered into fragments.

There wasn't time to be frightened. This situation illustrated the discipline that the captain was able to exhort. If they'd paused to think, if they hadn't been so disciplined, they would have said that the captain must be crazy firing a depth-charge at this slow speed. But thanks to the training and discipline they immediately did exactly what they were told and saved our lives.

Almost without a pause more depth-charges were thrown out away from the ship while we went hard to port. Then *Starling* went with *Wild Goose* for more briefings and attacks. We followed up with another 'operation plaster' at about 10.00 in the morning, which finally produced human remains and wreckage. Captain Walker then went on to see what was happening to the *Kite* and the *Magpie*, which were ten miles ahead. They hadn't had any joy in attacking, although again on one occasion a gnat had been fired in self-defence as the *Kite* had stepped in to begin her depth-charge barrage. Again the depth-charges immediately counter-mined the gnat torpedo. From the *Starling* we could see this terrific crash, and through all the water that was in the air it looked as though *Kite* had been hit. Then when the splash died down we could see that she was still there. So, the attack was continuing. It was close enough for us to see.

Next, the *Magpie* went in with a creeping attack but got no results, until Walker suddenly remembered that the *Magpie* was equipped with a hedgehog – a multi-barrelled mortar bomb thrower that could destroy only if one or more bombs scored direct hits. He directed the *Magpie* into a hedgehog attack, which was from the head of the ship instead of the stern. It actually scored a direct hit. According to his report of proceedings, 'I was highly tickled by this hedgehoggery. Complicated instruments are normally deemed essential to score an occasional hit with this weapon. But under my order over the RT, *Magpie* steamed into attack and fired off her bombs when told, as if firing depth-charges for a creeping attack. To score two bullseyes, like that first shot, with somebody else's 'hedgehog' a thousand yards away was, of course, a ghastly fluke, but amusing considering no instruments at all were used, for his gyro compass had been put out of action from that other attack. That was the fourth attack of the day and Walker had been in command for thirty-six hours without a break. There were 81 merchant ships depending on him, two aircraft carriers, a close escort of six and our own sloops. And we did it without any loss of ships.

By this time we had been in action quite a long time, but we were getting sandwiches and cocoa. He snatched his first two hours' sleep for nearly three days after the fourth attack when we'd run out of depth-charges. We had a Norwegian tanker come alongside us so the lieutenant could take over the bridge while the captain was resting. We went along in line abreast with this tanker and they transferred all these depth-charges at sea. The ships were both rolling heavily but had to be twenty-five yards apart, and we had to keep them at that distance while the charges were hauled over singly by hand. This was a very dangerous operation, as each roll of the tanker threatened to capsize the sloop. Sometimes the depth-charges sank below the surface or were carried away to bump dangerously across the ship's side. With the very last depth-charge they sent along a bottle of brandy, which we were glad to see.

While we were loading the depth-charges, *Wild Goose*, *Woodpecker* and *Magpie* had gone to protect another convoy, HX278. On the next day, 12th February, they came across a U-boat creeping up on the convoy from the stern. *Wild Goose* as usual made contact and then went in with the *Magpie*. After an hour's attack, during which some fifty-odd depth-charges were dropped, *Wild Goose* made firm contact at last and the commander, Captain Wemyss, tired of what he called this 'groping around and dot-and-carry-on business', went in for a full blooded plaster attack. They duly heard breaking-up noises, so we were sure that was a kill. We were still some way away. At first there was some doubt as the doctor was not sure the remains were human – sometimes the Germans sent up animal carcases to fool the attacking ships. But we all went back to inspect the site, and it was clear another U-boat had been sunk – U-424.

After a couple of days without much action Captain Walker decided to sweep astern of the next convoy we joined, ON224. The Admiralty, however, told him to rejoin the convoy. At that moment the *Woodpecker* put up her black flag indicating she'd found something. So Captain Walker did what another sailor had done, saying that he didn't see the signal. He went off to attack this U-boat with the *Woodpecker*. From what I can remember we spent all day attacking this boat with no luck. Eventually the captain said, 'It's got to surface to charge its batteries so we'll just wait.' About 5.30 in the evening the lookout in the crow's nest couldn't get the words out quickly enough. He pointed and we saw the U-boat on the surface. We opened fire and got several hits: soon they were all abandoning ship. The U-boat engineering officer went back down with the scuttling charges and it was blown up.

All the survivors came aboard, although we wouldn't let them on until they gave us the number of the U-boat and the name of the captain. What I used to do with those chaps was to take off all their diaries and personal effects. As soon as they were all dried off I would lay them out on the table, having extracted any stuff which might be useful for the director of Naval Intelligence, and I got them to come in one by one and claim their belongings.

In the report of proceedings Walker said he signalled the group to splice the mainbrace and he wrote, 'The enemy threw in the towel after receiving a big wallop in the belly from *Starling*'s last creeping attack.' This was on 19th February at 5.00pm. That was the sixth sinking.

Then *Woodpecker* reported having her stern blown off by a gnat. It hit her, and the depth-charges went up by her sinking stern as we formed a screen around her. The *Starling* went alongside and threw a tow-line over to take her in tow.

On the way back one of the officers on *Woodpecker* woke up

and found the sky over his head instead of the bulkhead. We took off all the ship's company, and eventually a tug arrived to take her in tow to Liverpool. Then unfortunately a storm sprang up when she was practically in the sight of Land's End, and *Woodpecker* sank.

Finally we arrived at Liverpool. It was 9.00 on a very dull morning. Before we got into harbour we got a signal from the Admiralty saying the Prime Minister and the War Cabinet wish to convey their congratulations. Then the First Lord of the Admiralty, A.V. Alexander, went by in the *Philante* and passed by us signalling a personal congratulation, then we came into Gladstone dock. We were cheered into the harbour. There were hundreds of people there. There were 2,000 officers, sailors and Wrens lining each side of the dock. Military bands were playing, 'A-Hunting We Will Go'. Captain Walker's wife was at the side, and his son and my wife were there as well. The First Lord made a speech which compared the trip that we'd done with the battle of the Atlantic, considering the effect upon the enemy. He compared it to the Battle of Trafalgar. Captain Walker was awarded his third DSO and two years' extra seniority as Captain. And if he'd lived he'd have been in the running for Flag Rank.

When he formed the Second Support Group, Captain Walker wrote: 'Our job is to *kill*, and all officers must fully develop the spirit of vicious offensive. No matter how many convoys we may shepherd through in safety, we shall have failed unless we can slaughter U-boats. All energies must be bent to this end.' No-one doubted that by the time he died – on 9th July 1944 of cerebral thrombosis, brought on by overstrain, overwork and war weariness.

First Officer Diana Barnato Walker, ATA

When the war started I joined the Red Cross, but some friends in the Air Transport Auxiliary (ATA) said I should join them –

they needed pilots. I had learnt to fly in a Tiger Moth but hadn't done any flying for years.

The ATA trained in their own way. They categorised aircraft into six classes and you learnt one in each class, then you could fly anything in that class. We flew dual control, then solo, had classroom lessons and were even taught a little engineering. Once you had trained on twins you were sometimes a taxi pilot and sometimes a delivery pilot. Taxi pilots fetched and carried everybody to and from the beginnings or end of link-ups of their jobs. Delivery pilots ferried aircraft to where they were needed. I delivered many types of aircraft but flew more Spitfires than any other type – by the time I was twenty-two I had flown 260 Spitfires as well as many other different types of aircraft.

On 6th May 1944 I married Wing Commander Derek Walker. Marriage didn't stop me, or him, flying. After our honeymoon Derek returned to duty with the 2nd Tactical Air Force while I went to my ferry pool. On that historic date – 6th June 1944 – I delivered an AOP Auster from Hamble to Tangmere to replace theirs which had been blown over by gales. Later that evening I flew a Fleet Air Arm Albacore from Hamble to Eastleigh. Whilst I was tootling along the coast, I saw tanks moving on the roads, on their way to being loaded on to ships in the ports. Bailey bridge sections were also ready to be towed with the ships.

On 27th June, three weeks after the Normandy invasion, my CO at Hamble called me to Operations. 'Diana, your return job! I want you to be very careful and if you don't like it, don't take it. Go around it very carefully, run it up, test everything, then leave it if there is anything suspicious.'

She added that after my flight up to Hawarden in a Vultee Vengeance IV (an American single-engined two-seat dive-bomber used by the RAF and Fleet Air Arm), the ferry pool there would fly me to Royal Naval Air Station, Burscough, north of Liverpool, where the RAF were sending in a special ground crew for an aircraft which two naval pilots had disliked. The first pilot had done a precautionary landing there while the second had aborted his take-off because, he said, something was wrong.

I couldn't wait to get to Burscough. When I did, I found the aircraft in question was a gull-winged naval thing with elbow-bent wings, standing forlornly by a blister hangar with its ground crew, plus transport, in waiting. I looked around it as I spoke to the senior airman. He said they couldn't find anything wrong with it at all. They, and the other ATA pilot who had flown me over, were all waiting on my whims. Will she, won't she? – I could almost hear them thinking.

At first I thought it was a Corsair, but reading my delivery chit I saw that it was a Grumman Avenger I, an American torpedo-bomber used by both the American Navy and our Fleet Air Arm. It was a big aeroplane, weighing nearly 11,000 lb. empty, 2,000 lb. more than the Corsair.

With great relief to everyone, I agreed to take it. I opened up very slowly, taking off while watching the speeds and temperatures closely. When I reached 5,000 feet I throttled back to cruising revs and boost, and flicked the switch over to check the supercharger, whereupon the revs and boost disappeared downwards. So, nearly, did the Avenger and I.

Something, as the FAA pilots had reported earlier, definitely wasn't right. What was wrong was now obvious – to me. The supercharger was linked up the wrong way round. Knowing this, I was able to fly all the way to Worthy Down in Wiltshire with the switch in its wrong position, but we didn't blow up.

Margot Gore, my CO, called me to her office the next day, telling me the 'authorities' had rung through to ask her to commend the pilot on finding the fault on their Avenger that had mystified the male sex. I grew at least an inch in stature after that interview, thinking to myself, 'There you are, the ATA training must be better than the Navy's!'

I got hold of another Navy plane a few days later. I was at Speke, near Liverpool, having to fly a Blackburn Skua to Eastleigh. The Skua had been used by the Fleet Air Arm since before the war, but by 1944 it had been relegated to training or target-tugs.

I didn't even take the trouble to read all the makers' handling notes. After take-off the undercarriage came up and the red lights showed it was locked up but the undercarriage warning horn still blew! I was condemned to fly the one-and-a-half-hour trip with the horn trying to deafen me.

When I landed the mechanic in charge told me if I pushed a test button for the horn once or twice the horn might have unjammed. 'It was in the notes, Miss!' If I had taken the trouble to read them all I wouldn't have gone to bed with a raging headache and ringing in my ears. It was an unpleasant flight. I didn't like the Skua at all.

Large flying-boats were the only type of aircraft women pilots were not allowed to fly. We could fly the Air-Sea Rescue single-engined amphibious Walrus and Sea Otters off land, but not off water. Margot Gore said the high-ups at ATA thought that if women pilots got stuck out for days with large flying-boats in some far northern place with Navy or RAF crews all sorts of antics might ensue.

I flew my first Walrus on 3 July 1944, a Walrus II belonging to 277 Squadron at Shoreham, flying it to Wroughton. It was my least favourite aircraft. It was difficult to get into; either a climb and hoist up the outside of the cockpit or a crawl along the inside of the hull, past anchors and cables. They were awash with paraphernalia that was murder for elbows, knees and finger-nails. After opening for take-off nothing much seemed to happen at all, it just rolled along with everything clanking in the back. It didn't get airborne before the control column had biffed you in the bosom several times over the bumps. When you hauled back, nothing much happened either, until it felt like getting itself airborne. Then it wallowed and flew much more like a boat than an aircraft.

It took a lot of elbow-grease to wind up the undercarriage. This made only two knots difference in its dreary cruising speed of 83–88 knots, so we usually left it down. It climbed at 75 knots, approached to land at 65 knots, and clanked on to the ground at 53 knots. Not much scope, with its speeds in no way critical to the pilot – provided the engine worked.

ATA handling notes said the rudder and elevator were very sensitive during take-off. As far as I was concerned, nothing was sensitive about that clattering lump of flying machine.

The Hamble girls cleared the factory at Cowes, Isle of Wight, and flew – if you can call it that – the Walruses to one of the various Fleet Air Arm stations or maintenance units. My friend Anne Walker didn't like the Walrus either – who did? Except, of course, the people who were saved or collected from the sea by virtue of its amphibious characteristics.

Anne took off one day in a cross-wind, a hazardous perform-ance with all that double-wing. She swung, finishing up at the end of the take-off run in a haystack. She was knocked out and the whole caboosh, aircraft and haystack, went up in flames. Fortunately, a baker's delivery boy was cycling along the lane beside the aerodrome boundary. He pulled her out of the conflagration, then rescued his bike plus a lot of burnt loaves of bread. Bread was rationed but he offloaded some of the singed stuff. Anne brought it back to the cottage we shared for tea. We said that when we had guests to stay, she should do it again.

Philippa Bennett was a first-class pilot with a four-engined rating: very reliable, and really good. On a rare occasion, for her, she was given a Walrus, and meticulously pumped up the wheels en route. However, she forgot to pump them down again. She made a really beautiful, gentle landing, as she always did, with everything, but on the two underwing floats.

The ground crew jacked up the Walrus and pumped down the wheels. The landing onto the smooth grass of Eastleigh aero-drome had been so good (unlike most of mine) that the floats were not even dented.

A male pilot from another ferry pool was in a Walrus flying

north towards the Wrekin in Shropshire. He was over the Severn River where it winds through a deep-sided culvert with forests on either side, when he had a complete engine failure. He didn't have much choice, but, rather than crash into the tops of the trees, he pointed into the narrow cleft and landed on the water. He threw out the anchor and waded ashore. The pilot was highly commended for saving his aircraft, but the Walrus proved to be slightly damaged when the tide receded.

At Hamble, on the misty afternoon of 29 October 1944 Alison King, the Ops Officer, peered round the mess door and said, 'Oh, Diana, if you're not doing anything, there's a Vengeance here for Gosport. Would you like to pop it over? We'll send a van to collect you.' Although it was a request, one never refused.

Gosport, a Fleet Air Arm station, was only around the corner from Hamble so although the weather was foggy, it wasn't far to fly. Signals told me that there was some work going on at Gosport, so I had to be careful of any runway obstructions.

I had flown over there a few days earlier and had spotted a lot of road-work signs with red danger lanterns, so I was going to have a good look before landing anyway.

I was just about to start up when Alison came rushing towards me. 'Diana!' she shouted, 'do you know it's only 400 yards?' 'Mmm, yes!' I replied casually, nodding, then started up. Alison, looking a bit nonplussed, shrugged her shoulders slightly before turning back towards the ATA hut. I wondered why she had worried to tell me. After all, surely she knew that an old hand like me wouldn't ever go off, even for ten minutes without first checking with Signals for anything un-usual, which is why they had told me about the works and the runway length. I knew you could land very short with a Vengeance, so I'd have more than enough room.

When in the air, I found it really was very poor visibility indeed. It was also already starting to get dark. I was able to fly very low along the coast, then into the circuit at Gosport. There, to my amazement, through the ever-increasing fog and darkness, I could just make out that there was absolutely nothing at all blocking any part of the runway. It was completely clear.

When I got back to Hamble, I gave my delivery chit to Alison, saying, 'You know, it wasn't only 400 yards, but the entire length of the runway was clear. What were you going on about?'

She said: 'The latest Met. report came in after you'd left the mess, showing that the weather was deteriorating, and it was already down to 400 yards in the fog there, and decreasing fast. I just wanted to warn you to stop you going. You wouldn't take any notice of what I said. It was the visibility, you goose, not the runway length!'

Derek survived a terrible war only to die in an air crash in the circuit of RAF Hendon. He was buried eighteen months after we married.

I continued to fly after the war and by 1969 I had more than doubled the flying hours I had done when the war ended. I have flown over 120 different types and mark of aeroplane. I wouldn't have missed a single type, a single hour or any one of those flights. Not even the Walruses!

Lieutenant-Commander Ian McIntosh, RN

Early in May 1944 I was in command of *Sceptre* and sent down to the Bay of Biscay with a list of six ships to sink: they were running iron ore from Bilbao to the French Atlantic ports. They had been unmolested for a long time. I studied weekly intelligence reports for the previous two years or so from which I gained a clear idea of their turnaround time, the state of the tide they would sail as well as knowing the ships themselves. None was terribly big: the largest was a 7,000-tonner. I was given all sorts of restrictions: I wasn't to offend the Spaniards, hurt them or damage Spanish property or ports. However I could go into territorial waters, as long as I wasn't caught.

Just to the east of Bilbao, heading towards the French coast, I got my first ship in a night attack as she had just sailed after loading: it was about the third or fourth biggest. She was in territorial waters but I was outside, so that was all right. It was, I must admit, rather a lucky shot.

This action rather stirred the Germans up. They had anti-submarine patrols sweeping along the coast trying to look for me. I followed the second largest as it came out of Bilbao and went along the coast a little way to the west to Castro Urdiales where there was a loading gantry. He certainly was in territorial waters, but he was under way when I started my attack on him. I didn't regard that place as being a Spanish harbour, not within the full terms of the reference. He had just got a picking-up rope on the buoy when my first torpedo hit him; I then put another one in to him to make sure he settled firmly on the bottom. That really did stir things up.

The biggest chap of the lot was in Bilbao and was due to come out. I was longing to get at him but obviously they had delayed his sailing a bit. Escorts kept sailing up the coast: I counted about a dozen. Although I was keen to get this bloke, I was anticipating a lot of trouble from the escorts because the water conditions were on their side. I might have got him but I was sure to be hammered. However at that stage I was hauled out. I went down to Gibraltar with the idea of doing another patrol in the Bay on the way back, but by then the second front of D-Day had happened, so I was taken back up north well clear of all that brouhaha.

When I finally got back to England I was sent for by Admiral Cunningham, the First Sea Lord who said, 'Well, McIntosh, you've got something to explain, haven't you? Tell me about it.' So I told him and I said that I had perhaps stretched the rules a bit during the last attack, but I thought it was near enough all right. He listened and finally said, 'Well, the bloody ships are sunk. Well done!' Two months later when I was down in Submarine Headquarters the Chief of Staff said, 'By the way, McIntosh, we told the Foreign Office that we'd severely reprimanded you. Have another gin!'

FROM D-DAY TO VE-DAY

Lieutenant-Commander Roger Hill, RN

At 1900 on 5th June we were in position convoying Group G9, which carried the assault troops for Gold Beach – the 50th Division. It was a great moment – at last we were under way and off for France to finish the war. Even if ships were sunk all round us, we were going on to the beaches with anything that stayed afloat. I felt a sense of relief that our object was crystal-clear and there were no difficult decisions to make when casualties started.

All through the night we overhauled the line of shipping which was now an endless stream. 'We have built a bridge of ships from England to France,' Admiral Cunningham had said and we passed it all keyed up for explosions and losses, ships on fire and everything that goes bump in the night, but nothing happened.

The mine-sweepers had done their job and the coastal batteries and the mined beaches had been plastered by Bomber Command during the night. At daylight 900 Flying Fortresses came over high and dropped their bombs in the same area. As the roar of their engines and noise of the exploding bombs died away, there was a sudden pause and quiet.

We had all studied aerial photos and knew that our target was an 88-millimetre gun and a concrete pill box which enfiladed our beach. At 0625, when we were just over four miles from the beach. We were working on the right-hand English beach – Gold – to our right the cliffs rose to Port en Bessin. I turned into the tide, to bring our six 4.7-inch guns to

468

bear, and opened fire. At this moment *Jervis* was truly at the sharp end of the war.

Since we were the first to fire we were able to spot the explosions of our own shells and to move on to the target: we continued to plaster it, but I felt sure we had knocked out the gun. It was necessary to make absolutely certain, lest they lay low and then opened fire on our people as they went up the beach. So we kept firing for thirty-five minutes. We wore earpads on the bridge, since the noise of the guns was really painful, and all orders had to be shouted in the few seconds between salvoes. The cruisers joined in from further out to sea and all the destroyers on either side were blazing away. Each ship was flying a big battle white ensign. It was a thrilling moment.

At about 0715 the rocket landing craft appeared and lay off our Green Beach. Suddenly she fired, and we could see the six hundred rockets fly through the air. Each of these was the equivalent to a six-inch shell. No-one could be alive in that beach and most of the beach mines must have been exploded. We all increased to rapid fire for ten minutes and watched in awe as the shore and low hills around the beach leaped and rocked in the hailstorm of shells. The big gun seemed to have stopped firing at us, but the 88-millimetre persisted and kept landing right alongside the bridge, but we could not see the flash of the gun. At 0730 the tanks were going over the edge of their landing craft and swimming ashore.

Suddenly we could see them on the beach, like little models – moving forward, stopping, firing, and moving forward again. Coming in from the big ships were the flotillas of the landing craft, and as we watched (the guns still blazing away), they formed in line abreast and were rushing for the surf line of the beach. I found myself banging the bridge with my clenched first, 'By God, we're ashore in France, we're back in France again.'

Now the craft approaching and landing on the beach were continuous, mostly landing tanks.

They went in at an angle to the beach because of their slow speed and the strong tide. I saw *Saumarez* lead four other destroyers right into the shore and they all plastered some strong point in a village. Suddenly, as I watched through binoculars, I saw flashes of explosions from below a church as shells hit the craft on the beach and one was soon on fire.

We opened fire with two forward turrets; the first salvo was over, the second short. The guns were then brought 'Up two hundred'. We turned to starboard to bring the after turret to bear. The six guns were firing beautifully, the right guns loading with armour piercing, and the left with direct-action high-explosive. We could see the concrete emplacement and the shells were bursting on it and all around. It was a wonderful sight and I let the guns go on for fifteen minutes. Then we lay, loaded and ready, to see if they fired again, but there was no sign of life or of gunfire.

Marine Stan Blacker

606 Flotilla (Landing Craft (Mechanised), or LCM, Mk111), E Squadron, Royal Marines, was formed without craft at HMS *Westcliff*, a Royal Navy Shore Establishment at Westcliff-on-Sea in December 1943. In January they moved to HMS *Cricket* on the banks of the River Hamble to await the arrival of its craft and to join 'E' Squadron.

Our training for landing craft had been very rushed over a short period of time and, as a Flotilla, we had only ever done one beach landing in practice with training landing craft and Dutch troops when we had carried out an early-morning land-ing on a small island in the Blackwater River.

Each flotilla consisted of 16 craft with six flotillas to each squadron. Each craft had a crew of four, a coxswain, two deck-hands and a mechanic. Every fourth craft had a signalman. Our flotilla had three officers. In February the 16 LCMs duly arrived up the River Hamble. Seeing them filled us with dismay and left us wondering if we would ever reach the beaches of France! These LCMs had been brought back from the landings in North Africa and Sicily and were in a terrible condition. Each craft had cracked welding and engine trouble. Out of all the 4,200 landing craft that took part in D-Day, the LCMs were the smallest craft to make their own way across. Each was powered by two 9hp marine diesels giving each craft a maximum speed of 9 knots. The well-decks were open to the sky and provided no protection whatever against weather. The maximum load was one tank or 30 troops with kit. With the naval maintenance party working flat out and all ranks of the Flotilla's own efforts for some six weeks before D-Day our LCMs were as good as we could possibly get them.

On 3rd June we were ordered to parade and Captain Gooding, RM, our CO, informed us that the hour of action was drawing near and to remember that we were Royal Marines and that our Country depended on us. He then told us that all identity must be removed. I can remember amongst my belongings dropping in a picture of my mother and sister taken in the garden at home and wondering if I would ever see the picture, or them, again. Our only identity was now the two identity discs on a piece of string around our necks.

About 3pm on 5th June we were ordered to stand to. The Padre appeared and asked us to take off our helmets and kneel in three ranks. He then said, 'The Hour of Battle draws near and the thoughts and hopes of the Free World are upon you. Please God give you all the courage to face and beat the enemy.' We all said the Lord's Prayer and then marched through the camp to the Landing Craft. The men of the Royal Artillery on the AA guns all wished us good luck.

And so we sailed in a drizzle and under heavy clouds to the rendezvous point off the south coast of the Isle of Wight, St Catherine's Point. Because of the bad weather, all the LCM flotillas began to lose formation and the signalman in every fourth craft received orders for us to make our way independently across, and to follow the bigger landing craft and merchant ships to our destination!

Before we sailed we had been issued with chewing gum to prevent seasickness, but with the rough seas and our craft being flat bottomed, the continuous buffeting made a lot of the troops, and some of the crews on board, seasick.

As dawn appeared our flotillas had again become badly scattered, but the first rays of light enabled us to see a small merchant craft which told us of a minefield ahead and that the path through it would be marked with green flags on small buoys, which we soon saw too. Had it not been for that very small merchant ship, our flotillas would have sailed quite happily into the minefield. Shortly after clearing that minefield one of our LCMs signalled that they had broken down. We replied that we would turn back to take them off on to our craft. However they said that they would stay with their craft and try to get the engines going again. This proved a bad decision as they could not get going again and they drifted into Le Havre, where they were taken prisoners-of-war.

We could now see the mass of shipping ahead of us. Our flotilla had now become so scattered that, out of the 14 craft left, only two were in contact with one another. As we approached the beach we saw that the whole coast was ablaze and I thought 'My God, we will never get in there alive.' With all thought gone of being the third wave in, with our scattered formation and late arrival owing to the terrible crossing, we headed, together with some other craft, for the Red section of Gold Beach. As we approached, the beachmaster waved us back. We circled for some time until the beach was clear, then we were called in to hit the beach with ramp down and off went the lorry. As we hit the beach we saw two dead soldiers being washed by the sea: poor buggers.

By 11am all 14 of the flotilla had arrived and unloaded. We continued all day ferrying troops and ammunition, our LCM taking load after load of 25-pounder shells in cases of two.

When arriving at the beach, these had to be unloaded by hand, back-breaking work after the tiring journey across.

Each time we landed at the beach, we could see the long white strips of tape marking the tracks through the mined beach which had been laid by the Royal Engineers. When the tide receded we saw how lucky we were that the tide was high enough to carry us in, as the obstacles on the beach were everywhere – row upon row of wooden poles, each with an explosive charge attached. The pole was anchored by a chain to the seabed to allow the pole to float up and down with the tide and, should you hit one, the charge was sufficient to blow at least the bottom out of any small landing craft and sink it.

That first day was a very long one.

Acting Lieutenant-Commander Edward Gueritz RN

My Army opposite number, the Beach Group Commander, Lieutenant-Colonel D.H.V. Board, and I took passage in LCH185 which was the 'flagship' of Commander E.N.V. Currey, Deputy Senior Officer of the Assault Group and leader of Group S3 under Captain Eric Bush (who had carried out his first assault landing at Gallipoli when he was fifteen). During the training period in Scotland they had been responsible for working up the Assault Group, and not least the skills of the units which were to provide the close-in support for the assault troops.

Royal Naval Commandos wore khaki battledress and the same load of equipment and weapons as other units in the Beach Group. We had distinguishing marks on our helmets for easy identification; as a Principal Beachmaster my helmet was painted blue. My own contribution was a red scarf and a walking stick.

The scene on a beach in the early stages of an assault landing is seldom encouraging. The situation on Red Beach, Queen Sector of Sword Area, was therefore much as expected, not least the fire from enemy guns, mortars and some small arms. Of two tank landing craft beached to give fire support on the eastern edge of Red Beach, one was on fire, and some wounded were crawling up the beach.

A number of armoured vehicles were standing halfway up the beach, some firing; flail tanks were operating to explode beach mines; beach exits were jammed with vehicles impeded by soft sand and mine explosions. The sharpest impression, as always, was created by the sight of bodies scattered on the beach from the water's edge. One of these turned out to be my immediate superior, Commander Rowley Nicholl, who was Deputy Naval-Officer-in-Charge of the Sword Assault Area, not dead but severely wounded, having insisted upon accompanying the leading beach parties. We had been right to expect casualties among the early landings of the naval beach parties, and each of the first reconnaissance parties suffered losses. A little later a beachmaster was killed when a mine exploded. As I stopped to talk to Commander Nicholl, Colonel Board went on. We did not see him again until we found his body in the evening only a short distance along the beach lying beside his dead escort.

The task of No. 5 Beach Group and its associated Royal Naval parties, including Commando Fox RN was to bring order out of chaos, or at least to organise the chaos as far as possible. As soon as we landed we had to reconnoitre the beaches and set up signs to mark the beach limits, approach channels, and navigational hazards. Landing Craft Obstruction Clearance Units (LCOCU) cooperated with Royal Engineers to clear beach obstacles, explode mines and booby traps, and mark potholes and quicksands. Landing Craft Recovering Units (LCRU) with waterproofed or amphibious vehicles brought help to damaged or stranded craft.

While this was going on the Beach Group, with its many specialised units, began marking the beach exits, carrying out mine clearance, laying beach roadway across soft sand, recovering drowned or damaged vehicles, ministering to the wounded and directing the ever-increasing flow of traffic. We had to keep everybody moving: momentum had to be maintained. It was sometimes necessary to speak sharply to keep groups of men moving to clear the beach, even in one case some military policemen.

On Queen Sector circumstances conspired to create very considerable congestion on the beach and just inland. Traffic congestion impeded the forward movement of the Intermediate Brigade, 185 Infantry Brigade, which came ashore hot on the heels of the assault brigade at about 9.30am. This Brigade had intended to press forward with the tanks of the Staffordshire Yeomanry to attack Caen. Also 41 Royal Marine Commando had landed on Queen Green Beach to swing right towards the Canadian Sector, while 4 Commando of 1 Special Service Brigade, led by Lord Lovat, moved briskly over Red Beach to swing left and join 6 Airborne Division over the River Orne. Commandos were easily distinguished by their berets, whereas everyone else wore a steel helmet. It had not been possible to clear many of the obstacles from the approaches to the beaches before the tide, accelerated by the wind, had swept over them. When the Naval Officer-in-Charge, Sword Area, Captain W.R. Leggatt came ashore, it was decided to hold off incoming flights of landing craft to enable the beaches to be cleared. The Reserve Brigade, 9 Infantry Brigade, did not land until mid-afternoon.

As the day went on there was sporadic shelling and mortar fire on the beaches; the first air raid, by a lone Focke-Wulf, came at 5pm. Barrage balloons were flown by many ships, but later they lost their popularity among those on the beach when it was realised that German gunners were using them for ranging on beach targets. Some further enemy air action occurred later causing confusion as the airborne reinforcement and re-supply flights for 6 Airborne Division flew in towards the River Orne. These flights necessarily passed close to the ships lying off the Beach and there was a good deal of trigger-happy firing.

During the afternoon 6 Beach Group, accompanied by RN

Commando, arrived ashore and we were able to reallocate responsibilities within the Sword Area. The commander of 6 Beach Group took command of both Beach Groups until he was wounded during the night, as was his second-in-command who relieved him.

By the end of the day it was reported that 130,000 Allied troops had landed by sea, including 50,000 Americans and 75,000 British and Canadians. The Sword beaches contributed 29,000 men, second only to Omaha, together with about 2,000 vehicles and 1,300 tons of stores. Nearly 8,000 British troops were landed by air. Total casualties among the British forces were reported to be 4,300.

The work of landing men, vehicles and supplies continued on Sword Beach for the next three weeks of the Build-Up phase, interrupted by a violent storm which lasted for four days and caused havoc in the whole Allied landing area. In spite of powerful fire support from battleships and cruisers offshore, German mobile guns continued to inflict damage and casualties in ships and craft and among those working in the Beach area. I was wounded in the head during the evening shelling on 'D-plus-19' (25th/26th June).

Ordinary Signalman Jack (Buster) Bown, RN

Having joined the Royal Navy as a 'Boy, second class' under the direct entry scheme, in 1944 I found myself as a very young ordinary signalman on HMS *Kellett*, a fleet minesweeper. Our flotilla was sweeping in Lyme and Swanage bays, when our captain received the signal ordering the flotilla to 'in sweeps' and to proceed to where there had been some action, to do what we could to help.

As it transpired, we were being sent to the catastrophe off Slapton Sands, where German E-boats had attacked a fleet of US Landing Craft who had been rehearsing for the D-Day landings. I remember the dozens of corpses covered in fuel oil floating in the sea, and our ship's boats being lowered to recover them. We had about seventy brought aboard, but only one was still alive and he died shortly afterwards. The flotilla returned to our base at Portland where the dockyard abounded with ambulances, but there was not much that could be done for the poor blokes. There were 638 killed.

Shortly afterwards, in May, German planes came over and dropped mines right inside Portland Harbour. Most shipping had to 'stay put' until the small sweepers cleared them up. On 5th June we sailed for an unknown destination but, owing to bad weather, we were forced to return. On the following day we sailed again, and this time it was the real thing. The flotilla was placed under the command of the US Admiral on board USS *Ancon*, who ordered us to sweep as far into the beaches of 'Utah' and 'Omaha' as possible. Suddenly, during the early dark morning of 6th June, there was the most almighty crashing and banging: our sweep cable had fouled another one. We were no more than a few hundred yards from the occupied coast. Our captain asked on the intercom what the racket was all about. When told he made a swift decision: 'Tell the silly bastard to cut the fucking thing adrift!'

As daylight appeared I saw what was, to me, the most fantastic sight I have ever seen. The sea was completely covered in ships of all shapes and sizes, the sky full of planes towing gliders with the now white-striped identifying marks. Shortly before 6am every ship that had guns opened up with a barrage of fire, so the whole of the French coast as far as the eye could see appeared to be bathed in one long, continuous concussion wave.

The landing having been successful on our part we sailed back to the south coast where we promptly ran aground on the rocks and stove a great hole in the bow. The poor *Kellett* was finally helped into Portsmouth. As we came in belching black smoke (she was a coal-burner), and with a huge list to port, HMS *Arethusa* passed us in the opposite direction taking King

George VI across to France. *Arethusa* made a 'well done!' signal to us to which our first lieutenant replied, 'They're round and they bounce'!

Petty Officer James Hinton, RN

I was an electrical artificer on HMS *Scourge*, a fleet destroyer. We arrived in Portsmouth on 27th May 1944, my twenty-first birthday. All those in the PO's mess gave me their tot of rum and I got a bit sauced. For the last few days of May we were allowed restricted leave ashore but then leave was abruptly cancelled. We began to stock up on ammunition and waited for orders. On the afternoon of 4th June we set sail, but the sea was too choppy and the invasion was postponed for twenty-four hours.

After lunch the next day our captain told us that we were going to be in the vanguard, leaving that afternoon. We would be escorting the minesweepers through the British and German minefields and taking part in the initial bombardment of the French coast. There was some apprehension and a lot of excitement at this news. The captain would always hold a little service before we left to go on a convoy or other action. He had his own version of the Breton prayer and he would say, 'Dear God be with us. Our ship is so small and the sea is so great.' He was Lieutenant-Commander Balfour, a magnificent captain, very approachable yet very stern, and respected by the crew.

We set to work preparing the ship for sea. As an electrical artificer I had a lot to do. Warships are heavily dependent upon their electricity supply and checks needed to be made on the condition of the generators, switchboards, emergency power supplies and gun-firing circuits, amongst other routines.

At 1535 we hauled in the anchor and set out for France. The crew was very alert, tensed up, proud and excited. We were a young crew with an average age of nineteen. At twenty-one I was the youngest petty officer aboard. As we set out for France many of us looked back at the English coast with mixed feelings;

what were we heading for and would we see England again? How would we cope with a mass attack from the air and how well would we be able to defend the British land forces and armour in our care? Would the E-boats and U-boats come out to engage us from their lairs on the French coast? We thought of our loved ones and friends. I had just heard from my wife, Mary, that we were expecting our first baby in December.

As we crossed the Channel, we were in constant fear of attack by enemy bombers. We saw a plane circling in the far distance, and prayed it was not the enemy to give warning of what was taking place. At last dusk fell and the chance of being attacked diminished. But there was soon another hazard to face: the minefield ahead. At 10.15pm we closed with the minesweepers and reduced speed to about three knots. The captain ordered all not working below decks to muster on the upper deck. We could see quite well around us for it was a moonlit night and the sea was very bright. We watched loose mines bobbing threateningly close to the ship's side. Two or three rubbed the ship's side and one fellow put his fingers in his ears. It needed only one of those horns to knock against us for the ship to be obliterated.

A welcome distraction from mine-spotting was hearing a heavy continuous drone overhead and watching our airborne troops fly over in gliders towed by their tug planes. Quite a few silent prayers were said for them.

After we got through the minefields we separated from the minesweepers and headed for the French coast. We were the first warship to arrive off the Sword sector, two miles off Ouistreham on the extreme left flank of the British invasion area. Then we helped to guide through some of the bigger warships, the *Warspite* and others, to their bombarding positions. At around 0430 we saw one of our sister destroyers, *Svenner*, torpedoed. She had a Norwegian crew. As she went down her bow and stern stuck up like a defiant V for victory. We were not allowed to pick up survivors, but one of our sister ships, HMS *Swift*, was nearer to *Svenner* and the captain could not bear to see the crew struggling so he let his engines idle, drifted towards them and picked up a hundred people.

As dawn broke we could see the enormous size of the armada that had made its way across the English Channel. Literally, the sea was full of ships, like huge stepping stones, going seemingly all the way back to our home ports. We could also see some enemy movement ashore, but I don't think they had seen us. We all felt very impatient for action. Eventually *Warspite* opened up and the bombardment began. We had a major who went ashore and directed our firing and we knocked out our first target, a German gun position, quite quickly, although shrapnel from its return fire came too close for comfort. Then we lost contact with the major, so from that time on our Gunnery Officer was solely responsible.

I had a free warrant on the ship and went around checking gun circuits, searchlight and signalling lamps and, if there was a problem, I was there to fix it. I watched the bombardment. The most impressive were the multi rocket-firing ships. They were firing their rockets over the heads of the troops going in, we were firing over the top of those and the *Warspite* was firing over the top of us. So there was terrific fire-power. It was exhilarating.

By now the sea between us and the shore was filled with craft carrying tanks and men, all passing our starboard beam and heading for the beaches. We were instructed to go in and lay down a smoke-screen and give covering fire for these small craft. We went in to about a mile from shore which was too close because we were being out-gunned. The Germans had 6-inch guns and ours were 4.7-inch. We saw some landing craft which failed to get there and we saw some of the tanks going down. The noise was terrific, and all the flashes; it was like make-believe. You really couldn't believe it was happening.

Then we went back to our fire position. We watched the action on the beaches through our binoculars and rangefinder. Our troops had very good support from the special tanks which set off the mines with great flailing chains and others which threw flames into the German gun-posts. These tanks gave our forces a good start. The wounded, and survivors from sinking craft, were being picked up by the landing ships and craft which had managed to get their weapons and people ashore. The wounded were taken back to hospitals which had been set up all over the south coast.

We kept up our fire for two-and-a-half hours and then we were ordered to break off and go along the eastern flank to protect *Warspite* and *Ramillies* from attack by E-boats and U-boats. Although we were still at action stations the crew was a little more relaxed and hot drinks were taken around to everyone. We protected the warships for two hours and then resumed our bombardment of enemy gun positions. One post after another. There was a lot of debris and shrapnel flying around, but we were lucky and there were no casualties.

At 2200 we were sent out to patrol the sea lanes and were twice attacked by Junkers dropping high explosives. The first two just missed our stern and, about half an hour later, a string of six high-explosives straddled our beam, three on each side, but missed us. The explosion sent vibrations right through the destroyer's structure and drenched the bridge.

When D-day was over at midnight, we thought, 'Well, thank God, we had a lucky day.'

Able Seaman Ken Oakley, RN

On the evening prior to the landing we were given a briefing by the senior arms officer and I will always remember his final words: 'Don't worry if all the first wave of you are killed,' he said. 'We shall simply pass over your bodies with more and more men. This landing must be a success, whatever it costs.' What a confident thought to go to bed on! I was in the first wave. Of course the Padre, Bishop Maurice Wood, said a few words.

We were called very early the next morning, around three o'clock, to stand by our boarding stations. We were in position for the launch and boarded the Landing Craft (Assault) which was tossing about very badly because the weather was still blowy. We had a gangway down to ours. It was awkward to get into because the LCA was pitching and tossing. Finally we were all loaded. About thirty of our unit were in this craft. We were all split up so that, if there were any losses, we didn't lose the whole unit.

The landing craft made for the shoreline some five miles distant, which is quite a long trip. It was still dark at this time and I remember, after we had proceeded some way, that I could see the star formations in the sky. However we could hear the bombardment passing over us, huge shells from the battleships hurtling ashore, the screams of the different types of shell and, as daylight broke, I saw a rocket ship discharge its full load of rockets towards the Merville battery area. It was fantastic; the whole scene was a sheet of flame. Incredible.

All around the sea was one mass of craft, landing craft of all kinds, shapes and sizes. A lot in our immediate area were LCAs because we were going for the initial assault. There was a good feeling as we went forward except that most of the army were seasick. I wasn't very happy myself. However when we got within sight of the shore we were getting spattered with light gunfire, nothing very heavy at this moment. Finally we got within sight of the stakes, the dreaded stakes, with the shells and mines on, which protected the beaches. Our coxswain did a marvellous job. We were headed straight for this stake and I could see the 56lb. shell lashed to it. In just the last second, he missed it. He got it just right. He steered us in between the stakes and got us ashore without touching one of those shells.

At the order 'Down Ramp' we were all surging ashore. We were in a few inches of water. All around were craft beaching and chaos and more gunfire was pouring down on us. We ran, under fire, up to the top of the beach where we went to ground, about a hundred yards from high-water. People were going down and screaming and crying all around us. As we hit the sand at the top of the beach we took stock of our bearings and realised we had landed almost exactly in our correct positions. We landed on Queen Red One, Sword Sector, Colleville sur Orne.

To our left the patterning of mortar fire seemed very intense but we seemed to be just under the arch of fire so that we were relatively safe. The main part of the mortar fire seemed to be to our left, further down, which suited us fine but for the people that were in it, it was awful. A commando was screaming, 'Help me, help me,' and I looked at the beachmaster as if to say, 'Should we go to help him?' but we couldn't. My duty was to stay with the beachmaster; he was my prime responsibility. The commando had a huge pack on his back anyway which would protect him from various splinters and shrapnel. It didn't look good at all, but he wasn't the only person who was in dire straits all around us. The mortar fire was very intense. Some people were filtering through, only some, not many. Then behind us came the roar of a tank. A Duplex Drive tank had managed to get ashore. He pulled up behind us, opened his hatch and fired, and that was the end of the mortar fire. One shot, honest, no more than that one shot screamed over our heads, whoosh, and it must have gone straight down into the bunkers. Fantastic, I thought, a great job.

We were then able to proceed. There was still some odd light machinegun and rifle fire coming down. The tank was off and gone, he was in the business of getting through and knocking the next one out. It was great, because the DD tanks were able to float the last few hundred yards, they had the propeller hood all around and they could switch from the track to a propeller in the tank itself. So they were launched off the LCTs – Landing Craft (Tank) – some two hundred yards or so from the beach and floated in under the drive of their propeller. As soon as they hit the beach they switched back to their tracks, cast off the flotation skirt, and they were in business. And there you are, one of these chaps comes in with this damn great tank and makes the mortar look like a pea shooter.

We were now left with the business of organising the beach, getting everything moved off the beach and getting the signs laid. The beachmaster's responsibility was to get that beach cleared, get it organised, and he was the senior officer on the beach, irrespective of rank – whether the army guy was a general or whatever, he was the man in charge of the beach. He sent his various teams to do the clearing, get the stakes out, get the roads laid down for the heavy vehicles. After some time one of our chaps came up to me and said, 'Oh, Ken, can you help me? Sid is down there, very badly wounded.' Sid was an old friend and we had gone on leave together. He had been the assistant beachmaster's bodyguard and his duty was to put the left-hand extremity sign for our section on the beach at the beachmaster's order. This sign was a huge great pole with a flag on it. So I went along to Sid who was lying some two hundred yards away. He was severely wounded. The assistant beach-master said to me, 'He caught it across the back. His kidneys were hanging out. I've pushed them back in and shoved on this dressing. Can you get him to the first aid post?' I said, 'Yes. Will do.' We had to half carry him, half drag him. The fire was not too bad; the mortar fire had subsided but we got the occasional rattle of machine-gun fire. We got Sid to the first aid post and left him there under a bit of canvas. He was going to get some attention and be looked after. Then I had to go back to my duties at the shore line. More and more craft were coming in continuously and I was directing them. The trouble was, when the soldiers came ashore their first reaction was, 'Let's group up and have a little check and then we'll have a cup of tea.' We had learned on exercises that you must not allow this to happen, you must keep the beaches clear and the momentum going. If the beach is clogged up the whole impetus is lost. You have to keep it moving. There is no other way. This is what we were doing, chasing them, telling them to get off the beach, that is your exit, that is *your* exit, over there, over *there*.

The beachmaster, Lieutenant Commander Gueritz, had a complete list of everything that was coming in and the designated signs to be put up. So all that was well in hand. The troops were a bit bewildered and a bit sea sick and one of our assistant beachmasters had been wounded in the shoulder, so he had used his white waistcoat to serve as a sling for his arm. The army had decided that if the assistant beachmaster wore a white waistcoat they would be easily recognisable, forgetting that the white waistcoat would also make him a prime target for the Germans.

Suddenly the air was split by a piercing sound of bagpipes. Along the beach, some hundred yards away, a piper was marching up and down. There was Piper Bill Millin filling his bag up and getting his wind. Lord Lovat had asked him to play a few tunes. Lord Lovat came up behind Bill, formed up his troops and they marched off in parade ground style, straight up into the village of Colleville. It was amazing. How could he have the pipes on the beach amidst all this battle noise? Shells screaming and fire all around. And silently, as the sound of the pipes died away into the hinterland of the beach, we got back to work bringing the landing craft in. That was a real high point in the whole landing.

In the early afternoon the beachmaster came to me and said, 'Ken, I've arranged for Sid Compston to be taken to Arromanches for medical attention. We can get him on to a hospital ship from there quite easily. He'll be better looked after than staying here in the first aid. Would you go with him to look after him?' Sid was pretty ill by now with an infection, but we had penicillin powder to put on his wounds which killed off the infection. Sid survived and recovered; he was later best man at our wedding.

We were still getting shelled at various times from the area of the Merville battery and their mobile guns which they were firing at intervals to disrupt our work.

On the third day the beachmaster said, 'Ken, I want you to go as the representative of our unit to a funeral this afternoon of all those that were killed on the beach. They are being buried today.' The Pioneer Corps had been designated to clear the beaches of dead bodies and put them in canvas bags. The burial took place in an apple orchard. The bulldozers had scraped out three huge trenches between the trees to a depth of about three feet. The bodies were laid side by side. The smell was appalling. We stood with bowed heads and the padre of each denomination read the prayers. I will never forget that funeral. A lot of good men were killed and buried there. It seems an ironic place to bury the dead, in an apple orchard, but it is still there today.

So back we went to the beach and we were still getting craft in. The beachmaster's responsibility was to get material in which the army particularly wanted. If they wanted armour-piercing shells of a certain size they had to come in in preference to food supplies or anything else. The beachmaster had immediate contact with the ships offshore through beach signals. We had a beach signals chap with us all the time with a radio to pass messages.

Telegraphist Alan Higgins, RN

The day before we sailed for the D-Day landings we, and a few more Landing Craft ship's companies were mustered in a large boatshed in Newhaven. A Royal Navy captain gave us a pep talk which went something like this: 'You men have done a great job at Pantellaria, Sicily, Salerno and Anzio and have earned the reputation of being "the cream of landing craft". As such, the Admiralty had seen fit to reward you.' This caused great speculation amongst the assembled crews: medals, leave, promotion? However, all such speculation was crushed as he continued, 'You have been given the honour of landing on the extreme east flank of the landings at Sword beach, which is expected to be the most hotly contested, and I know that you will conduct yourselves commensurate to the occasion.' Well, with that bit of information under our belts, we realised that we were in for a hot time.

For the invasion we were flotilla leader and carried a Lieutenant-Commander, RNVR, in addition to our two-ringed skipper, Harry Collinge, and a sub-lieutenant, RNVR, who was the no. 1. After loading the troops, we anchored in Shoreham Bay, whilst the powers-that-be decided whether or not the invasion was on or off. The accommodation for the troops, however, could at best be described as primitive, consisting of rows of wooden, ribbed seats, just like park benches. It doesn't stretch the imagination to envisage what conditions were like after a few hours of being packed like sardines, with all the equipment, weapons and webbing required for landing and storming the beaches. The stench of vomit alone was terrible, most of the troops being seasick. However we duly sailed that evening.

As dawn broke, the sheer size of the operation became apparent. There were battleships, cruisers, destroyers and dozens of other types of craft all going south; hundreds of all types of ships with one purpose – to land and support an army in Normandy.

Through the ring of bombarding vessels we sailed and, as the beach grew nearer, one could see splashes as shells and mortars homed in on and near the landing area. As we reached the beach and began unloading the first casualties were sustained. Orders were for all wounded to be landed on the beach. There was one soldier being helped by two others, his left foot and boot as one, in a mingle of flesh and leather. I shall never forget the almost apologetic look he gave me as he passed by.

A Landing Craft (Tank) shot alongside us and on to the beach with its cargo of tanks ablaze and ammunition exploding. AB Harry Gee, a Yorkshireman, was on our foc's'le blazing away with his Oerlikon 20 mm-cannon – a brave effort, bearing in mind that the air was alive with bullets and shrapnel.

As I ducked back into the wireless offices, we sustained a direct hit. The usual smell of cordite and the cries of wounded men came from the packed no.3 troop space, where a shell had entered and exploded, leaving wounded and dying men as the shrapnel made its exit from the port to the starboard side. Our skipper shouted down the voicepipe for me to see if no. 3 troop space was cleared. This I did with great alacrity, as I knew from past experience that as soon as we had disembarked all our troops, we could kedge off the beach, and reach the relative quiet among the offshore fleet. However, as I was halfway down the ladder, a soldier who was sitting on the bench with his back to me, turned and said, 'Come and help my mate, Jack.' I replied, 'You better get off quick, mate, all the rest have landed.' He replied, 'I can't – my leg has had it – help my mate.' The water was pouring in and although not deep as such, it became a hazard to wounded troops, who were in danger of drowning, as well as making their injuries worse when the ship was rolling.

As I came to the soldier who had called out, I saw that his leg was hanging off below the knee, so I opened the tin of morphia ampoules and jabbed one into his thigh with the attached needle. Turning to his mate, who was semi-conscious, I undid his webbing and tried to set him on the seat next to his wounded mate. He was a big chap, and his gas mask kept catching under the seat. I said, 'Try and help yourself, mate,' but all I got was a vague, incoherent mumbling. I finally got him seated and saw that both his legs were shattered below the knees, so I jabbed a needle of morphine into each of his thighs. These tins of morphine were flat, contained six to eight ampoules, each having a needle attached which could be used by removing the cap from the needle and then squeezing the drug into the casualty.

By now, some other crew members had arrived in the troop space, and the task of getting the dead and wounded up to the deck above began. One soldier looked all right at first, but a closer look revealed a hole of about one inch in diameter behind his ear. He just sat dribbling in a semi-haze. The total extent of his injury wasn't known, and he and the rest of the casualties were put aboard a destroyer, which carried a medical officer. We had only one wire stretcher, so most of the wounded were carried up the ladder, one man supporting the shoulders with his hands under the arms and one man supporting the legs. Not the most satisfactory way of handling wounded men, as the one supporting the shoulders would be kicking the wounded man in the back as he struggled up the ladder.

One of the men I was helping must have had internal injuries, for his face was a leaden colour and he just sighed and gave up the ghost as we reached the top of the ladder. The skipper had told us to try to comfort the wounded as best we could, but just what can one say or do under those circumstances? It was a mercy that we found a destroyer with medical facilities aboard in very short time. The dead and wounded were placed all along a narrow passage on the port side, and the wounded were kept as comfortable as was humanly possible.

After passing all the dead and wounded to the destroyer, we sailed directly back to Newhaven where, when the tide went out, we were left high and dry on what was called a 'gridiron', a wooden platform on the bed of the harbour. Some workmen from the Southern Railway pumped us out and welded dozens of patches of shell damage in a very short time. That night we were loaded again, and thus began what was to be a daily shuttle to the beachhead, the only 'respite' being riding out of the five-day storm, which caused severe damage to all the unloading facilities.

I must record my admiration for the courage and fortitude of the British 'Tommy'. At Anzio, I had expressed these feelings to one particularly brave soldier. He turned to me and said, 'Jack, let me tell you something: I couldn't get off that tin box ship of yours quick enough.' Horses for courses?

Ordinary Seaman Ronald Martin, RN

On *Warspite* we started preparing for D-Day with a practice in Scotland, then we sailed down the west coast to England. D-Day was postponed for twenty-four hours so, having got to the English Channel, we spent another half-day steaming up and down the Bristol Channel until ordered to go back. Eventually on 5th June we were off. We stopped at Plymouth to embark a Russian admiral, a Russian general, a whole pile of war correspondents and photographers and a fat Chinese naval officer. Why he appeared on the scene I'm not quite sure, but he was appointed to my director.

As twilight approached there were 6,000 or 7,000 ships off the south of the Isle of Wight, which was a magnificent sight. The soldiers, poor devils, were so sea-sick, they were leaning over the sides of the landing-craft. Led by a fleet of minesweepers we crept very slowly towards Gold Beach at the eastern end of the beach-head. We arrived just as dawn was breaking and at 0530, or just before, we sighted what we thought were torpedo E-boats coming out from Le Havre to attack us. I opened fire with the port armament. Almost at the same time the 15-inch guns opened up against our first shore battery. So the *Warspite* lays claim to firing the first shots of the invasion. We sank one of the E-boats and the rest retired to Le Havre and didn't come out again. During the next five or six days, we continued bombarding all our targets. There were a few sporadic air attacks but we had air supremacy so there was nothing to worry about from that side. We were helped by both shore spotters and Fleet Air Arm spotters; they were very accurate. We demolished all our targets successfully.

On D-Day itself no-one was having any meals. Instead we had action rations, a big paper bag containing a Cornish pasty – or 'tiddy oggy' as we called them – a couple of apples, a bar of chocolate and that was it. They passed seven packages up to my director and the Chinese officer whom we'd taken on board presumed that they were all for him, so he ate the lot. As a result we had nothing to eat on D-Day. The paymaster commander brought the captain's parcels up on to the bridge personally. The captain took one bite from his tiddy oggy, and said, 'I must say this is very wholesome,' then threw it straight over the side.

One unique situation arose when a German tank commander, hiding with a whole fleet of Panzer tanks in a wood, covered in bushes and twigs, made the mistake of lighting a cigarette while sitting on top of his tank. He was spotted by aircraft. We pin-pointed the target and gave an order unique in naval gunnery history of '15-inch, fifty rounds, rapid fire. Commence.' That was almost impossible because of the time it took to load the one-ton shells, follow their pointers and so on. However, there was a method in that madness because the first broadside fell slap in the middle of the wood and then as the succeeding ones started, because of the human error and the time lag, the shells were chasing the Germans as they started to run away. We got reports back from the aircraft that it was very successful. We could knock a chap off a bicycle at twenty miles.

We then ran out of 15-inch ammunition after nearly four hundred rounds. So we went back to Portsmouth where we loaded ammunition all night. Halfway through the night we got a signal saying that the Americans had got themselves into all sorts of bother down on Omaha beach. Their bombarding wasn't going very well and they had specifically asked for *Warspite* to go down and sort them out. We went straight there to bomb the German troop emplacements with the aid of aircraft and spotters. They would communicate by radio to give the map coordinates. Then we went back to our original bombarding positions and carried on bombarding.

We were told that we had to go up to Rosyth because the 15-inch guns had worn out. We set sail on our own, through the Straits of Dover and up the east coast. Just off Harwich we hit a radio-controlled mine on the port side and that stopped the ship in her tracks. It shifted the port propellers forward by about six feet and put them all out of gear. We limped up to Rosyth and the engineers in the dockyard did a magnificent job. The old crate could still do fourteen knots if pushed. We were sent back to Portsmouth.

Brest had been occupied by the Germans, but they had fallen back into several forts for a last-ditch stand. In August the *Warspite* was asked to go and help shift them. So we went down to Brest and bombarded the shore forts and the British Armoured Corps with their Churchill flame-throwing tanks were also doing the job ashore. Between us we got the Germans so annoyed that they finally gave up and Brest was liberated. We suffered very few casualties at that time. Most of them were only wounded by splinters. There was nothing serious. We were under artillery fire from the shore occasionally, but not for long because we put all their batteries out of action.

We were then asked to go along to Le Havre to help the British army take over the town, so we bombarded their shore batteries. Finally, the dear old lady's last sortie was to Walcheren in the Schelde estuary in Belgium where the commandos and the rocket landing-craft were going to attack the Germans. By then the poor old ship, after two world wars, had really had it. We finally limped back to Portsmouth where she was put into reserve.

Acting Lieutenant-Commander John Roxburgh, RN

At the beginning of 1945 I was given command of a brand new submarine *Tapir*, fresh out of Vickers at Barrow-in-Furness. On 12th April we were on anti-U-boat patrols off Norway. I was trying to sleep after a night on the surface charging our batteries when Donald Duckers, who had been with me in the Meditearranean and was my tried and tested anti-submarine sonar operator, reported yet another diesel engine noise. I had been called by him before that morning and it was usually a small fishing boat, so I got pretty rude. Finally he called me over the intercom, 'Captain in the control-room, Captain in the control-room, U-boat surfacing.' I rushed in and there was a U-boat (U-486) surfacing at 3,000 yards. I fired eight torpedoes and sank him. No survivors from that one.

A week before I had heard a submarine surfacing in my patrol area. I followed it to the surface and identified it as a U-boat moving away. I gave chase and was closing the range on an apparently unsuspecting target on a straight course. Just as I was getting into a firing position I was astounded when my quarry suddenly flashed a bright aldis signalling lamp at me with the message, 'Don't shoot, Steve here.' This was the Lieutenant Stevens (now in command of *Turpin*) who had pinched my solitary ration of beer over three years before in Malta when he thought I had had it. He had inadvertently, in thick foggy weather, been patrolling in my area off Bergen and had discovered his mistake from star sights that evening. He was naturally trying to get the hell out of it as fast as he could and was pretty certain it was *Tapir* which was after him. He was lucky.

I then went out to the Far East sailing from the Clyde just before VE Day. I wanted to get my hat-trick. I had sunk a German and an Italian submarine and I was now keen to get a Jap. I got out there but within a fortnight the war was over. Whilst I may have been glad when the war started, I was even more glad when it was over.

Marine Noel Barker

At our POW camp at Landsdorf the Germans were in charge. Our officers didn't have command over us, as command goes: when you are POWs you are all the same. I don't know what happened to the officers, whether they got taken in transport or not. I never saw them after we were all captured at Calais in June 1940.

I only saw my own mates. We were sleeping in fields and in

barns. What food we had was inedible half the time. One time there was a barrel standing in the gateway of the field, full of this meat which was green and crawling with maggots. We ate it because there was nothing else to eat, just wiped the maggots off and ate the meat. People were getting ill, but no-one died that I know of, although it is possible that I didn't hear. Several were shot trying to escape and roughed up as well. You got the butt of a rifle round your head if you said anything out of turn. I wasn't one of those, I managed to escape that.

Then I got sent to the coal mines with a couple of my mates. I had never been down a coal mine before, so I hadn't the faintest idea what it would be like. I remember the first day: we went down in the cage. It was a bit scary to start with. It was a long way from the pit shaft. We went in on trucks: actually one of our blokes got killed on that. It was run by overhead electricity and because it was bare, they warned you to be careful when you got out.

The coal seams weren't level; they were on a slope. There was this chute that the coal used to come down and a bunker controlled the flow of the coal into a truck underneath. They put me on clearing up the coal; a lot of it fell off the chute and, if you didn't keep it clear, it would all choke up. Quite often I would just sit there and let it choke up. I would put my light out and make out it had blown out. It quite often did get blown out when they fired.

I got on a good job going round oiling all the machinery, and that's where I really got my own back. All this stuff that was shunting backwards and forwards had to be kept oiled but, before pouring in the oil, I put a handful of coaldust in first. That wore the bearings out. They were always changing parts. The whole damn lot had to come out. They never did twig on, so I had them there. One of my friends got taken away after throwing a cup of hot coffee in the face of a guard one day, I never saw him again.

We weren't that far from the pit head, but they always

counted us a dozen times on the way over. Coming back we used to have a shower. We had working clothes but the footwear wasn't very good; we had wooden clogs which were damned uncomfortable. The only thing they were good for was killing the rats in the hut: they used to come over your bed and run all over you.

There wasn't much hope of escape, we just didn't have the facilities. There were stories about having passports made and God knows what else. I don't know how they did that but I certainly couldn't do it where I was. We used to play a game called Ukkers (Ludo) in the evenings. Also we played chess and bridge: they were the two games which I learnt while I was there. And we had a bloke who actually carved a set of chess men.

We also set up our own theatre. I was keen on electrics before I joined the Marines so I did all the electrics. We had several good actors dressed up for all the parts. They even managed to get dresses somehow for the women's parts. The Germans didn't watch these shows: they knew we had the stage, but we were OK until the Gestapo came round, and smashed everything.

The actual guards weren't too bad. The chap in charge of us when we first went there was an old chap. He was very good, he turned a blind eye to lots of things. I don't think he had a lot of time for the Nazis. But he hadn't been there all that long and there were so many escapes that they took him away and pulled a new bloke in. He was a really hard bastard: when he looked at you his eyes went right through you. He said, 'The next man that escapes from here I will bring back and shoot.' That night two blokes went over the wall. They were away for about a week and when they did catch them, this bugger was out there on the pit head waiting. He pulled his pistol out and shot one. The other managed to get away, but the other guards knocked him down. Then the bloke shot him. They weren't satisfied with that, so they pulled the two bodies back into the compound, laid them out and left them there for a week or more. The Geneva

Convention made no difference to him. There weren't any more escapes after that.

We worked seven days a week – no weekends. We were allowed out in the compound after we got back from work. I didn't do much in the way of outdoor activities, though we would walk around the compound for a bit of exercise.

We didn't have any news coming through. The Germans used to supply us with a monthly magazine about all the British planes they had shot down and all the ships they had sunk, which we ignored. It wasn't until just before D-Day landings that I managed to scrape together enough bits and pieces to make myself a wireless set. I made it with cats' whisker and a bit of crystal. The crystal was easy to get because it was in the carbide lamps. It was the other bits and pieces that were more difficult. I managed to get a couple of ear phones from the telephones down in the pit, I pulled them off the wall. But I needed a plug. I thought, well I'll have that bugger off the wall – it looks a bit loose. So I yanked it away. All of a sudden my body started going in and out, then I was flung off right between a load of trucks which fortunately weren't moving. When I got up I felt bloody marvellous. I don't know if I have felt so bloody good in all my life. Anyway I got my plug and a bit extra: I was lucky really. I got my wireless working so I was able to hear of the advance of our troops through Europe. Someone had drawn a map, so we were able to see how the advance was going. I used to lie in bed at night listening to it: one night I fell asleep with the damn thing on and it was only the guards, making such a bloody noise which warned me in time to grab the lot and put it under the bed.

I had two operations while I was there. I had my appendix taken out. In hospital you couldn't have been treated better, they were marvellous. Later on in the war I had something wrong with my inner ear. They didn't have any general anaesthetic, so they did it with a local anaesthetic. They had to cut the bone out of the back of the ear using a hammer and chisel. I remember every second of that. By Christ it was like a sledge-hammer banging into my head. Those doctors were fantastic.

We lost a Jewish lad, not from the British army. He had a tumour on the brain. You wouldn't have expected they had much time for him, but they did everything for him. He could speak several languages: when I sat up with him when he was in a coma and dying, he went through the whole lot of them, ending up speaking Yiddish. The doctor came to verify his death. He covered him over, stood at the end of the bed and, making the sign of the cross, said a prayer. I wouldn't have believed that of a German to a Jew, but he did it. I am not a religious man myself, but that was very moving. He must have known about the concentration camps. Everyone knew.

We were moved out of the camp because the Russians were closing in on us. We only knew when they told us to pack up all our stuff and get out in the middle of the night. It was dead of winter and bloody cold out there. We were marched all together covering 1,200 kilometres south into Germany and all the way down to Vienna. We were on the move for four months.

We passed Auschwitz when the Jewish prisoners were being moved out: they were literally like skeletons and were so bloody hungry they were asking us for food. They were literally skin and bone. It was terrible.

Many died on the march from frost-bite and one thing and another. I never thought I would get through it. The worst I got was a fungal infection, Chinese foot. My heels were like rhinoceros hide. We had the same pair of clogs all the way through. I didn't have socks, only a piece of rag to wrap around my feet. It was cold. We couldn't bury anyone that died, we didn't see what happened to them, we just kept marching – they wouldn't let us stop.

When I was first captured a French priest came round asking for our names and addresses, saying he'd write down and let 'them' know where we were. I gave him my address. In the meantime the navy had put out my name as 'lost, presumed dead', at Calais in 1940. Which my family read. They didn't know until about twelve months later that I was actually alive and in a prison camp. Then they had another four more years to wait. I was able to write to them and I got letters back.

We eventually met up with the Americans – General Patton's Third Army. We saw them coming in the distance, a whole column of tanks. He was sitting up there in the front tank. When they came up to us in the village they disarmed the few guards who were left and the first thing the Yanks said was 'Do you want a gun to shoot these bastards?' If they had been the guards that had been there originally, I would gladly have shot the buggers but they changed them over before we got there. These ones were as good as gold. How could you shoot them?

General Patton sat up in his tank and said 'Go and knock on any door and make yourself at home for the night.' It was a little village somewhere in Germany or Austria. Me and my mate went and knocked on this door and asked if we could stay and they said 'Yes, come in.' They were nice and kind. They couldn't speak any English but we could talk German. In five years we had learnt it. It was only a bed we wanted really. We didn't have a bath. They only had the one bed and they insisted that we both had this bed with a duvet: I had never seen a duvet nor even heard of one. You can imagine what happened when we got under: what with the heat and the lights there were fleas all over the bed by the morning. I felt terrible because I didn't want to take their bed but they insisted. I mean, even though they were Germans, I still didn't like to. They gave us breakfast and we were then moved off.

We were marched to an aerodrome. This was the first time I had been in an aeroplane. It was a Yankee plane, a troop carrier with seats down the sides – a Dakota. We went up in this thing and suddenly—oomph! We came down about three hundred foot. Then it went up and down again; what a blooming trip that was. They took us to France where we got into one of our own Lancaster bombers. It could carry quite a few in the body. I managed to climb up in the centre gunner's cockpit and I had that all to myself. All was fine until we came over England and were about to land. Then one of the bloody engines cut out. I thought 'Oh no, not all this bloody way just to be killed just before we land.' Anyway, we did land all right.

That was it. They sent us back to Chatham. I was eighteen when I was captured so I was twenty-three by this time. We were only there long enough to be checked out and put in new uniforms, then we were sent home on eighty-three days leave after five years.

My Dad was at Chesham station to meet me. Mum was at home because it was late at night. It was the first time my Dad ever kissed me. When I wrote to him, he had replied, 'It might seem a long time now, but once it's over it won't seem too bad'. We walked back from the station and met my younger sister and Mum at the front door – she was over the moon. I was pretty thin, around nine or ten stone, having been about twelve stone when I went away.

Able Seaman Thomas Barnham, RN

When we arrived at Stalag 344, in 1942, it was full of army personnel except for one compound which had a few Air Force lads. Those that weren't NCOs had to go out to work, working on farms, all different jobs. Some were billeted out permanently, some of them worked in coal mines or brick works. At this camp we had a boy who was an Imperial Amateur champion boxer. Another camp asked for him to go and box at their camp, which the Germans agreed to. But he wouldn't have it, he said, 'I'm a regular in the Services and if I get beat I've got to live with it.' So one morning we got up early, I had a couple of mates with me, an English officer and three Germans. We set off and we travelled half the day and I boxed at this camp and won.

The Germans had the front seats. After that I had it made. We had roll-call at seven in the morning, but when they came and said 'Aufstanden,' which means 'Get up everybody,' they said

'Boxer, bleiben, you can lie in, stay,' so I never used to go on roll-call. Only a silly little thing but I appreciated it, and that's what happened every morning after a boxing match. They'd never cry 'Well done,' but they'd always give me a lie-in, which was real luxury. And I never lost a match.

We were treated reasonably well. First thing in the morning you'd either have black coffee or mint tea. At 11.00am you'd get four or five jacket potatoes and a black loaf between seven with a bit of butter and a bit of meat; then about 12.30 you'd get a pea soup or Sauerkraut. That was your lunch and at about half past two or quarter to three you'd either get your coffee or your tea again, that was your meal. That was all you got, but fortunately we used to get one Red Cross parcel a week each from England. But if we ran out of them we could go probably two months before they'd come in again. I was very fortunate because of my boxing. An English army officer said to me, 'What food do you get, my friend?' I said, 'I get the same as you, sir' although I knew he was living a lot better than I was. So he says, 'You've no extras at all?' and I said, 'No, I get Red Cross parcels the same as the rest of them,' and 'Oh,' he said, 'Something's got to be done about this,' so he gave me a chit so that I could get an extra Red Cross parcel a week. But there were a lot of hungry lads, so whatever I got went in the middle and was shared out, so it hardly meant much.

Towards the end of the war the Germans brought thousands of Russian prisoners in and put them in the camp next to us. There was only barbed wire in between. We watched these people walking and they looked at us as though the wind was blowing through them. They were starving. Typhus broke out and a lot of them died. There was a Russian kid there who was about sixteen and any time we ever threw any bread over to him, which we often did, before he could get it all the other Russians had it. So I said, 'I want to get that kid and bring him into our camp'. One day I cut the wire, brought the kid in and put him in English uniform. He stayed with us two months in our camp. Couldn't speak a word of English, but we used to sit him on our bunk and say, 'What's your name?' and we'd teach him to say, 'Monty Banks' in English; 'Where have you come from?' 'London.' 'Where were you caught?' 'Arnhem.' Four or five little questions which he knew the answer to. An English officer came to me one day and he said, 'We'll toss him back, because if typhoid breaks out in this camp I'm going to hold you responsible and put you on a court martial.' But if you've been a prisoner for four-and-a-half years you don't care, so you can guess what I told him to do.

I must have been at that camp about two and a half years and then they shifted us to a camp in Obersilesien and while we were there the Russians came in.

The Germans put the whole camp on a march, bar those that were sick. I suppose there were a few thousand on the march and there was thick snow. I pretended to be sick so I didn't have to go. About three weeks later they sent off everyone who remained on cattle wagons and we travelled for about five or six days and finished up near Munich.

The Yanks were coming towards us so then everybody had to march, sick or not. We marched all night and slept during the day. Our guards were all old men, seventy or more and they kept falling asleep on the march and we had to wake them so they could take us on. After the first night I'd had enough – I had huge blisters on my feet. So I planned to escape with seven mates of mine, including Monty. An officer came to me and said, 'I hear you're going to bugger off tonight,' and I said, 'Yeah, I'm not having any more of this.' He said, 'You're taking the Russian, with you?' and I said, 'He wants to come,' and so he said, 'Well look, do yourself a favour and the boy a favour, don't let him come because ninety-nine percent, you'll get caught and he's got no chance. You being English, you'll get away with it, but if they know he's a Russian they'll shoot him.' So I left Monty behind with a mate of mine. He later told me Monty was taken off by some Yanks, but I don't know what happened to him after that.

The rest of us got away and finished up in a barn. Some German farmers looked after us for a while, but we were getting a bit restless, so we went out and nicked two cars, a BMW and a Mercedes-Benz, and half of us went in one car and the other half in the other. We drove right through Germany and into France. Whenever we got low on petrol, English or American lorries would give us cans of petrol. We finished at a place called Nancy and when we got there the Yanks pulled us in and put us on a plane home.

When we landed they put us on a train and we finished up at the naval base at Havant in Hampshire. They supplied us with a naval uniform, and gave us our back pay, which was about £200 or £300. Enough to buy a house with in those days.

Corporal Bernard Slack, RM

Six months after leaving Normandy we went into the Commando base to be reformed, as part of the 116 and 117 Brigades. I was in 33rd Battalion of 117 Brigade. At the time no-one knew that there was only five months to go before Germany capitulated and the war ended. First 116 Brigade went. Then we were getting ready, when out of the blue they picked out 33rd Battalion. We'd done all this training, we'd unstitched all identification, green-painted every bit of brass, so they put us all on one side, saying hang on a bit, we'll tell you what's happening later on.

They sent the 33rd Battalion back into France, under a commando brigadier of Czechoslovakian descent. In France we were doing infantry training, keeping it up, and all of a sudden, one night along comes a transport and we are taken to an airfield in Belgium. Nobody knew what was happening. I always remember the brigadier. He gave us an hour's 'Any Questions?' It turned out that, although under the armistice agreement the German Army had surrendered, the German Fleet had not, but the general public didn't know this.

The German Fleet was ordered off the high seas and, depending on their tonnage, their ships were told which port to make for. The big battle wagons were told to make for Kiel where I was, with the Royal Marines detachment there.

A boom had been thrown across the main harbour. We were outside the boom on landing craft, and our job was to board them; the Royal Navy was inside the boom. There were nine or ten of us on the boarding party – we were lucky, we'd got a German-speaking officer with us. We had to board them cold – mind you, it was handy that we each had a Thompson sub-machine-gun under our arm. The German ships had been told to have either the steps or the rope-ladders down ready, and no hanky-panky.

The very first thing we always did was to take the skipper off for interrogation ashore. They always say that the Germans are OK when they're being led. We always used to make sure the crew could see him being taken ashore. Imagine you've been a gunner in the German navy. You've looked after your gun, you've polished it, there's not a speck of dust gets on that gun, then along come a load of boot-necks and blow the ruddy thing up! So what's your re-action? Not surprisingly we lost some men.

Our CO would go aboard the ship, relay the skipper ashore, leaving about six of us on board, and then he'd come back for us. We had to go down the line of crew and take everything off them which had got the eagle and swastika on it. And then we blew the breeches on the guns fore and aft to make sure they couldn't fire. We left a skeleton crew on and the rest were taken off by Royal Navy patrol boats, and then, and only then, was it passed through the boom into the inner harbour for the Royal Navy to put about a hundred men on and go through it with a tooth comb. We weren't the real demolition party – our job was to see that there was no mucking about. Their weapons were supposed to be all piled up, but when we went over the side we had no idea if they'd obeyed us! We were hoping to God they had done.

We tried to make the crews keep standing to attention while we were on there, but some of our men had to fire into the deck of the ship at their feet, to get them to keep still, or fire into the air to let them know we were there. We didn't bother what was done: the Marines teach you to use your own discretion.

The U-boat base at Kiel had got a town actually underneath it. The biggest problem wasn't the German navy, which we were taking into internment, it was the DPs, the displaced persons. There was a big torpedo shed, with all the torpedoes on cradles waiting for the British experts to check. The torpedo fuel was wood alcohol, which was 98% proof. These DPs had got keys to the shed, and they were draining the fuel into cups and drinking it! We had to deal with all this; we used to mount patrols through this underground place and shoot. We just used to fire down halls and let the bullets ricochet; they'd soon stop, but you could still hear them moving about.

Kiel was terrible. There was shipping, railway, warehouses, big cranes, all rolled into one. It was totally demolished. Going through Hamburg was just as bad – people were living in tin shelters on the street.

Back in France we were all issued with a little handbook by the Intelligence Corps. Inside it said, 'You have the honour of being the advance guard of the army of occupation. Your future conduct will most likely influence the round-table conference, you're ambassadors for Britain.' Yet there we were in Hamburg dodging the bricks. You didn't look round for something bigger to sling back at them, you just bit your lip and kept your composure. Hamburg was like looking out from the top of a hill, and all you could see was bricks. There were trolley-poles sticking out of the rubble, bus roofs showing – it was shattered.

The Royal Marines were ordered to keep a riot squad on 24-hour call. To be a member you had to be over five foot eleven inches tall. I was six-foot-one. We got called out to these camps outside Kiel where the DPs were. Once one of the DPs killed a deer, out in the forest. They brought it back and there was a fight going on, the guns were out, the knives were out, we had to go out there and deal with it all.

They shot one of our officers and dumped him in the canal. He was twenty-two years old. I was in the funeral party. They did find out the farmer who did it. I believe the main thing he killed him for was his shoes. That's what we were up against.

Another time, we were trying to clear a river, which was full of boats upside down with their propellers showing, and lots of other rubbish. On this river were these brothel barges for the German soldiers. There was a hell of a 'do' going on there, murders and gunfights. The girls were out of work, and were only too happy to accommodate any man. I had to go there and clear them out, shut them down.

They were big barges with beds in – sea-borne brothels. We got propositioned ourselves, but we had more damn sense than that.

Eric Williams
Official Naval Reporter

As an official Navy reporter, I was the only journalist permitted to witness the official end of the U-boat war. It took place on Thursday, 10 May 1945, at Loch Eriboll, a narrow inlet in the north coast of Scotland. At seven o'clock that morning I stood on the crowded bridge of a frigate with Captain M. J. Evans who was in command of the operation, and scanned the sea for signs of approaching U-boats. The frigate's crew were closed up at action stations, in case there was any trouble.

At last we spotted a blob and mast and a faint smoke haze on the horizon and the black hull of U-1109 slid towards us. Our guns ranged on her and the U-boat's crew came into focus. I noticed their grey-green uniforms, unkempt beards, pallid skins and the peaked caps of the officers. This was the face of the enemy I had never seen in four years at sea.

I had met a U-boat before in the mid-Atlantic. It had sunk the ship I was on which was carrying old women and children. Since then I'd had a personal interest in U-boats.

We looked for the swastika, but it was not flying. Instead, a ragged green flag of surrender flapped at the mast. Our armed guard leapt aboard and mounted the bridge. The U-boat's commanding officer offered a lame Nazi salute and a few seconds later the Royal Navy's white ensign stood proudly on the conning tower.

Another U-boat had been sighted and, as it approached, we went alongside in a launch and I boarded her. Our guns were trained on her bridge. I asked the sullen CO what had made him join the U-boat service. He drew himself up and said, 'All Germans want to go to the front. I wanted to do it; it was doing more for my country.' He sounded as if he was repeating a vow.

More U-boats came in to surrender and, as I talked to their crews, I built up a fascinating impression of these brave, clever and determined men. Discipline was the backbone of their character – implicit and unquestioning obedience. They preferred to be known as soldiers, not sailors, and they obeyed automatically. When I asked one officer whether he would obey an order he knew to be wrong, he smiled and said, 'But that would not happen. We do not get wrong orders.'

After surrender the U-boats were inspected and then sailed in escorted convoy over to Lisahally in Northern Ireland, where the official surrender was to take place. I sailed over in U-293 in the care of its commandant, Leonhard Klingspor, and a small armed guard. Klingspor was 27, dark, virile and energetic, and he spoke very good English. I stood with him on the tiny bridge on the first evening and talked.

He claimed to have sunk ten ships since 1942. He was very pleased about that. He said he thought it would have been much better for Britain to have allied with Hitler against Russia. When I told him about the concentration camps he smiled and said, 'Propaganda – all propaganda!'

It was a pleasant evening and I felt relaxed and happy. Klingspor gave a quick cheerful command down the conning tower hatch and a few seconds later the sound of Mozart came floating up. Later it was Wagner.

I turned in at about midnight, but was woken a few hours later by the roll of the boat and the crash of water down the conning tower. I put on oilskins and struggled up to the bridge to find a gale blowing and seas breaking over the boat. Klingspor was on the bridge. 'When I say, "Watch out" get under the bridge,' he said. I realised I was now dependent on the seamanship of a U-boat captain. Klingspor gave me a belt which I clipped onto the bridge. He was in his element. He said, 'I like this weather. It is good for attack. The escorts can do nothing.'

He described how he would chain himself to the bridge and ride a following sea, letting the waves break under him, riding in to the attack. I could only admire his courage, but I felt sick and went below.

Later, Klingspor told me about his family, his wife and two children whom he had not seen for fifteen months. He launched into a diatribe about Germany's persecution by the rest of Europe and finished up by saying, 'See, we shall make you a good Nazi yet!' His self-assurance was baffling.

As we approached Culmore Point we heard the packed crowd singing, 'Rule Britannia'. It was a wonderful moment. I looked at Klingspor for some reaction but he did not seem to know the words or the music. As he left for the prison camp I said, 'I am glad you'll now have the chance of finding out the truth for yourself. You will see how false your propaganda was.' He looked at me with a small smile and said, 'I wonder.' And so did I.

THE FAR EAST WAR AND LIBERATION

Lieutenant-Commander Arthur Hezlet, RN

We left for the Far East just after D-Day in *Trenchant*, which had just been completed at Chatham dockyard. We were rubbing our hands, as there were likely to be plenty of targets. Unfortunately the Americans practically sank most of the Japanese fleet before we got there. We arrived in the Far East and made our first patrol outside Sumatra, mainly as an air/sea rescue operation for a B29 bombing raid on Palambang. We had various kinds of electronic gadgets to tell us when they were going overhead so that wasn't a very exciting patrol except that two small Japanese vessels came along, and we popped up with our gun and sank the pair of them. It was quite an exciting battle for they put up a fairly good fight with their machine-guns. But our 4-inch gun soon mastered them.

Although we knew the Japanese normally had no intention of being taken prisoner, we tried to cut off a section of them from what was obviously the commanding officer, and managed to get a few prisoners. We brought them back just in case they were of some use for intelligence purposes and I remember we suspected they were Korean and we thought, 'Let's see what the intelligence books say.' The book said the way to tell a Japanese from a Chinaman is by the big toe. The Japanese always use the one-thonged sandal which means the big toe is completely separate from the others; but we couldn't notice any difference in their toes. The other test of a Japanese (this is scarcely believable but was in the books) was to give them a banana to peel. Apparently a Japanese has a special way of peeling a banana: he cuts it diagonally in half and then he squeezes the ends out like toothpaste. But the trouble was that no-one in Great Britain had seen a banana for four years and where they thought we were going to get a banana from I don't know. Anyway we brought the prisoners back. We decided we didn't like the idea of Japanese being loose in a submarine so we kept them in the torpedo compartment with two armed guards all the time. That was the first time I had come face-to-face with the enemy.

For our second patrol we were sent inside the Malacca Straits with a body of eight commandos, commanded by a major. They were equipped with explosives and four fall-boats, and they were going to try and blow up a bridge in Sumatra which had a road and rail running over it. We found the bridge eventually and we went in that night and launched the commandos. But they found the current in the river too strong and they could make no headway at all. They were very upset having gone all that way for nothing, so after a conference with the major we decided to try again. The next night we landed them on the beach half a mile away from the bridge and they laid their explosives very satisfactorily. But as they withdrew they came across a native chap. They didn't want him to follow them but they didn't want him to tell the Japanese about the changes either. The major said, 'We'll have to knock him out and leave him on the beach.' So they turned to the sergeant and said, 'Knock him out.' The Sergeant tried, but this chap just shook his head, he couldn't be knocked out. So the subaltern hit him on the back of the head with a pistol and even that didn't knock him out. Then they thought, 'This is a bit much, we've been really rather nasty to this fellow,' so they gave him all the counterfeit money which they'd been given in case they were taken prisoner and left this poor half-stunned fellow on the beach by the bridge and started paddling off. They were supposed to come out on a compass course and after so many paddle strokes they were supposed to stop. However they paddled on past us out to sea and I couldn't see them anywhere. It began to get light to the east and I thought, 'I'm afraid they've had it,' and turned around and headed out to sea, practically running them down from behind. We got them all on board and by that time the bridge had been demolished by the explosive charges. This patrol was eventful. Subsequently we laid a minefield off Sumatra and then sank U-boat 859 off Penang on 23rd September.

Eventually the whole flotilla moved to Fremantle in Australia. The war was getting pretty close to the end – this was well into 1945 – and we did a patrol up into the East Indies from Fremantle. We knew that the Japanese were pulling their troops back into Singapore from all the outlying places in the East Indies with the intention of making a fighting retreat up the Kara Peninsula into Siam. They were using two cruisers from Singapore to fetch these troops. While we were passing through the East Indies one of these cruisers, the *Ashigara*, was seen going into Batavia by two American submarines. At that time I was very nicely placed to intercept I made a signal to the American command (it being an American operational area) asking permission to intercept in the Banka Straits, which was approved. We went into the top of the Straits at the same time as another smaller British submarine, an 'S' Class, did the same thing. We went alongside at night to discuss what we'd do. I said, 'The best billets are obviously inside the minefield and what we've got to do is put one submarine on each side of the minefield.' I was quite prepared to toss a coin for whoever went in for the better place and he began to say, 'Oh, I don't think you could go inside there.' I didn't give him another chance. I said, 'Right-o, you stay outside,' and we went round the end of the minefield, very close to the rocks. The depth of water in the straits was 15 fathoms, about 80–90 feet, fairly shallow but quite enough to dive under a ship if it tried to ram you. We waited on the surface to charge the batteries and got a report from the American submarines that the *Ashigara* was on her way north and that she had one destroyer with her. So for the rest of that night we waited on the surface and we sighted something at about three in the morning. It was quite dark, and we couldn't see whether it was the cruiser or the destroyer. I didn't want to dive because if you dive on a dark night like that you can't see through the periscope and you've lost the whole initiative, so I was determined to stay up until I'd solved this question and fired the torpedoes. I let him get far too close but there was nothing I could do about it. We were bow to bow and, as he went by, we swung to keep end on. I heard after the war that he did see us and thought we were a junk, but by keeping bow on to him we didn't give a submarine-shaped silhouette. But we got very, very close and I could hear his boiler room fans as he went past. Then I couldn't keep the swing up and he saw what we were and opened fire. All the shots went right over the top so I turned away and fired a stern torpedo at him. He saw it coming and turned away from the torpedo and the range opened stern to stern, very fast. I was still looking for the cruiser but there was no sign of her. Luckily we shook the destroyer off and went on with the patrol while he went on out to sea.

When daylight came we dived and waited and soon after daylight the *Ashigara* came in sight coming up the Sumatran side, without the destroyer. The destroyer had gone out to sea and this colleague of mine in the 'S' Class had a shot at him and he then turned on the 'S' Class, dropped depth-charges and probably said to the cruiser, 'I've got him, come on by. I'll sit on him while you go by,' not realising there were two of us.

The *Ashigara* then came up on the Sumatran side and we fired a full salvo of eight torpedoes, five of which hit her. She capsized after about half an hour and sank and 800 men were drowned: she had 2,000 troops on board. I let a lot of the ship's company have a look through the periscope and we stuck up so much periscope that the *Ashigara*, which hadn't sunk by then, saw it and opened fire with her anti-aircraft guns. Then we squeezed out past the minefield.

Sub-Lieutenant Dick Reynolds, RN

On 10th March the *Indefatigable* sailed from Sydney for the invasion of Okinawa. En route we disembarked at a US air-station at a remote Pacific Atoll called Ulithi. When we arrived there it was full of American naval and marine squadrons. We had been sworn to silence before we disembarked, so we were very conscious of security, but the Americans were talking quite freely about the invasion. They said, 'It's all right, you are in Ulithi and there is no communication between us and the outside world so you can say what you like.' We were soon briefed by them. A young intelligence officer got up – his words have stuck in my memory to this day. He said, 'You chaps have been fighting in the European theatre, there is one big difference. Those goddamn Germans fight to live, but now you are out here these bastard Japs fight to die.' Those were his exact words.

After sailing north, our task was to subdue all air movement of the Japanese on the islands of Sakishima Gunto. We entered operations there on 25th March. Avengers, Corsairs, Hellcats and Fireflies struck the various airfields. Seafires of 887/894 Squadrons provided low and medium defensive combat air patrols (CAP).

As most suicide attacks came in at very low level, the American system was to keep at least two squadrons of fighters on station to protect the fleet, rather than scrambling aircraft at the last moment. So you could at least be at the right height and, if you were correctly vectored, you would be in the right place. On April Fool's Day, 1st April Peter Roome, our batsman, came up to me before take-off and said, 'What a glorious morning Dick, I envy you being up there.' Everybody on deck was in shorts and sandals! After lunch we were told there was a raid developing to the west. Our senior Fighter Direction Officer, Ian Easton, an experienced pilot and FDO, had always placed us in a good attacking position on previous engagements. I always felt very confident with Ian as he had always got it right. On this day sure enough a big raid did develop but we didn't intercept it until it got into the fleet because they came in very low. The first the radar boys knew about it was when they were only ten miles away.

I got on the tail of a Zeke after he had already dived on *King George V*. I remember quite distinctly, he pulled up, I got on his tail again and managed to give him a burst. I clipped his port wing, he rolled over on his back and dived straight into a carrier which was enveloped in smoke and flames. I thought, you poor bastards. What I didn't realise was that it was my ship; as you can imagine, from 2,000 feet four fleet carriers look exactly alike. I then got on the tail of another Zeke who dropped a bomb on the destroyer *Ulster*, and hit her in the engine-room. He then turned for base but I stuck on his tail, overhauled him and shot him down with a long burst from dead astern. I remember flying past and seeing the pilot slumped in the cockpit – he went straight in the sea so that was that. Returning to the fleet, I was getting pretty low on fuel, but another Zeke appeared on our opposite course, I pulled around, got on his tail, gave him the rest of my ammunition and he went into the sea. So that was 1st April 1945, a day which will always be in my memory.

We had a method of identifying our ship on returning. We had a pivot ship, a cruiser, from which we would take a bearing to our own ship. The ships were always in the same relative position. When I landed I leapt down and there was this blackened flight-deck with a bloody great hole in the Island. That was the first time I realised the situation. The ship recovered all its aircraft safely, in spite of some arrester wires and barriers being out of action.

The sight on deck was unbelievable; a lot of chaps had been killed. The tragedy was that in those days we had our 'ready rooms' in the ship's Island which of course was the nerve centre of the ship, and that is how we lost so many fine people, including the ship's doctor and some very good aviators. Many of the pilots who were at readiness were killed. From that day our new ships, like *Ark Royal* and *Eagle*, all had their 'ready rooms' under the armoured deck. Our armoured flight deck had been pierced, only just, but that meant that the whole blast from the impact had gone through the softer 'flesh', for want of a better word, and had blown up most of the Island. Had it been an American carrier with a wooden deck it would have been a total disaster.

I went to report to the captain who was on the bridge with full whites and medal ribbons, as was the form in those days during actions stations. He looked at me and said, 'Well done.' He heard the R/T relayed to the bridge. I then went down to the wardroom and had a couple of gins. I had lost my cabin mate and best friend. But I couldn't think about it, I daren't. I flew that afternoon.

Sub-Lieutenant Ivor Morgan, RN

I was a pilot with 894 Squadron aboard *Indefatigable*, The sun shone in a cloudless sky at 0500 on 1st April 1945. I was not to fly that day, being temporarily grounded by an ear infection. My job that particular morning was that of Duty Pilot, to supervise flight deck movements – including the ranging and striking down of aircraft – noting the number of each as it took off (and, hopefully, as it returned), acting as liaison between the captain and Air Branch, and generally assisting Commander (Flying) Pat Humphries, known universally as 'Wings'.

As we waited for the fleet to turn into wind, I was struck by the fact that only the captain was correctly dressed in naval uniform. In order to afford some sort of protection against fire we all wore long trousers and long-sleeved shirts – blue for the ratings, khaki drill for the officers. Dominating the scene was the resplendent figure of Captain Quentin Dick Graham, in his high-necked Number Ten tropical white uniform, complete with medal ribbons from 1914 onwards.

'Wings' gave the order to start-up and soon the aircraft were roaring up the deck. Everything went smoothly, not a single machine was U/S and the spare aircraft remained on the deck until such time as they would be taxied forward preparatory to landing-on.

The first inkling I had of trouble was the sound of aerial firing and, looking upwards, saw two aircraft in a tail chase about 2,000 feet above the ship. At first I thought they were two of ours and it had only just registered that the leading machine had a radial engine, whereas our Seafires had in-lines, when it turned on its back and I distinctly saw the 'Rising Sun' roundels on its wings as the pilot commenced a power-dive directly at the spot where I was standing!

By this time all hell had broken loose. All of our guns, from 5.25s to pom-poms and additions, had opened fire, people were yelling. The captain gave a helm order, I rushed on to the main bridge, closed the armoured door behind me – and flung myself down full-length on the deck, together with everyone else.

We waited. The engine roar got louder and louder. There was no escape. This was it, this was how it was going to end. Pity, I thought, life is so enjoyable on the whole. I felt no fear, only a vague disappointment that the curtains were about to be drawn.

And then another thought struck me. I'd like to be there, as some sort of disembodied spirit, when my father opened the telegram. He was a dogmatic person, who would never entertain any arguments but his own, some of which were quite preposterous, nor would he ever admit to being in the wrong. I suppose to hearten me he would always say, 'They couldn't get me at Ypres, they won't get you either.' The sheer illogic of this used to annoy me intensely.

Well, at last, he'd be proved wrong. Yes, I did so hope that there was some way in which I could be a fly on the wall when he learned that I had been killed.

Then came the crash, followed immediately by flame and a searing heat. I choked. I could not draw breath. I believe I lost consciousness. I next remember opening my eyes to see all the recumbent forms near me. All immobile. All dead, I thought I must be dead too. I tried to raise my shoulders and found that I was able to move although no-one else followed suit. Oh well, if this was being dead it wasn't so bad after all. Interesting to find that there was indeed a life hereafter, a fact in which I had never had much faith.

'Port fifteen.'

The captain's voice brought us to our senses and we shambled rather sheepishly to our feet. He above all, in his 'ice cream' suit, had remained erect and in command. This was the moment for which he had trained since joining the navy as a thirteen-year-old cadet in 1914. And he did not fail.

From then on things moved fast. With certain communication lines out of action I was ordered below to assess damage and casualties, for we could now see that the kamikaze had crashed into the bottom of the island at flight deck level. Flames engulfed both forward and after bridge ladders so I swarmed down the thick, knotted manilla rope which had been rigged for just such an emergency.

As I made my descent I saw Pat Chambers staggering aft, his back covered with blood. Someone ran forward and guided him to safety. An Avenger, in the process of being taxied forward, had collided with the superstructure, engine and cockpit blown to smithereens. Of the pilot, there was no sign.

The Damage Control party was already hosing the flames and I could now see a gaping hole where the island sick bay had been. Being of small stature I was able to crawl through the wreckage and there they were, my comrades Al Vaughan and Bill Gibson, showing no sign of injury but both killed by the blast, which had removed most of their clothing. In the passage between the sick bay and the Fighter Ready Room lay Lieutenant Leonard Teff, also killed by the blast which, miraculously, had left untouched the man on each side of him. Looking upwards I realised that the bridge mess was no more.

On regaining the bridge I was relieved to see Pat Humphries on the flight deck. A last minute dash to his cabin for some forgotten article had undoubtedly saved his life.

'Sandy' Sanderson, our Flight Deck Engineer, and his party were already rigging a replacement for No. 3 barrier which had been destroyed. Twenty minutes later we were landing-on, Sub-Lieutenant Dick Reynolds of 894 Squadron holding aloft a gloved hand to indicate two victories.

As soon as I was relieved, I went below to the hangar where maintenance crews were working with every sign of normality. They had thought their last moment had come when, unable to see what was happening, a terrific explosion occurred right above their heads. Flaming petrol ran down the hangar bulkhead, presumably through a fissure in the flight deck, threatening to engulf men and machines alike. Under the leadership of CPO 'Jimmy' Green the fire was brought under control without having to resort to sprinklers.

'Right lads. Show's over. Back to work.' The Jimmy Greens of this world are worth their weight in gold.

I proceeded to the sick bay, where the Principal Medical Officer Surgeon-Commander Yates and his team – Surgeon Lieutenant-Commando Henry Towers and Surgeon-Lieutenant Musgrave, together with their 'tiffies' – had been working non-stop since the kamikaze struck at 0730. With over forty casualties dead, dying and/or seriously wounded, accommodation was hopelessly inadequate and the adjoining messdeck had been pressed into service as an auxiliary ward. There, upon mess tables, lay men too badly injured to survive. A steward with a hole in his head the size of a cricket ball, loosely plugged with cotton wool, a man with both legs missing. Between them were other casualties – men unrecognisable due to the burn dressings which covered head and body alike – and even as I looked for any of my own chaps, some were quietly slipping away into eternity.

I did find one, however, Able Seaman Gay, 894 Squadron's messenger, who was well into his forties when he joined up. Quiet, polite, conscientious, he was popular and respected by all. He sat, staring at nothing, in an advance state of shock.

If it had been the captain's moment, so had it been for the PMO. After fifteen hours at the operating table, he was ordered by his superior to take some rest. His reply was to order Captain Graham out of the Sick Bay in which, as a non-medical man, he had no authority. Only when, at 2300, it was obvious that he could do no more, did this fifty-five-year-old consent to turn in. The final toll of eleven dead and thirty-two injured but surviving, was in large measure due to his skill and leadership.

Lieutenant-Commander T. V. Briggs, RN

On Wednesday 9th May the bulk of the East Indies Fleet had just returned to their base at Trincomalee on the east coast of Ceylon, after extended operations in the Andaman Sea covering the Army's recapture of Rangoon from the Japanese. Just before entering harbour, in the early hours of that day, we had listened to the King's broadcast on VE-Day and in a state of great exhilaration were looking forward to celebrating onboard and ashore.

We had hardly finished securing to our buoys when Rear Admiral Walker, sent for me and told me to arrange for every ship to sail as soon as possible – a 'Top Secret' signal had been received that a Japanese cruiser had sailed from Singapore on a mission thought to be to relieve the Japanese garrisons in the Andaman Islands. After a feverish day and night of replenishing with fuel, stores and ammunition (though with just enough time to celebrate VE-Day by splicing the mainbrace), the Fleet sailed at daylight the next morning, Thursday 10th May. We headed for Car Nicobar, the central island of the Andamans, to cut off the cruiser before she could return to Singapore.

That night submarine reports were received that a Japanese

'Nachi' class cruiser and a destroyer had passed through the One Fathom Channel at the north end of the Malacca Straits on a northerly course at a speed of 17 to 20 knots. From this it was clear that we would have to maintain a speed of 17 knots to achieve an interception if we were to pass the Ten Degree Channel, south of Car Nicobar.

The next morning, Friday, the *Shah*, one of the four Escort Carriers, broke down and had to reduce speed to 8 knots. Along with an adverse wind for flying off this made it clear that we were unlikely to achieve the necessary rate of advance.

Then, at about midday, a 'bogie' was reported on radar 80 miles to the eastward (220 miles west of Car Nicobar), and we became almost certain that the Force had been sighted by Jap reconnaissance aircraft. Our course was altered to the southeast to make for the southernmost channel into the Andaman Sea – the Six Degree Channel, between Great Nicobar and Sabang at the northernmost tip of Sumatra. This would give us a better chance of intercepting the cruiser on her return southwards, and less chance of being sighted again by Jap recce aircraft.

At nightfall a Fast Force consisting of *Cumberland*, *Richelieu* and the 26th Destroyer Flotilla, were sent on to be fifty miles ahead at dawn so as to increase our chances. However the next day, just before midday, as no reports of the enemy had been received, it was decided to haul off to the southwest, and the Fast Force was recalled.

Then, at 6pm that evening, a report was received from the submarine *Statesman* that the Jap cruiser, escorted by three destroyers, had passed southwards into the Malacca Straits. This was a severe blow to our plans, but not unexpected, as we thought we had been sighted by the Jap recce aircraft the day before. Our only hope now was that the cruiser would try again, and come north from Singapore.

Sunday was spent in a position safely to the west of the Sabang Channel fuelling destroyers from the Four Escort Carriers so as to be ready for any eventuality. The plan then was to move at our best speed towards the Six Degree Channel during the night so we would be as close as possible to the southern Andaman Sea, which our quarry had to pass through. Then we were to reverse course in time to be clear of recce aircraft by daylight. Fortunately there was good weather cover.

On 14th May, the Fuelling Force (Royal Fleet Auxiliary *Easdale*, escorted by *Paladin*) arrived in the area, and we rendezvoused with them during the night – *Tromp* was fuelled. At midnight, both Forces were about 220 miles west of the Six Degree Channel, steering east towards it.

We were now coming towards the end of the fifth day in Operation Dukedom. I was fully occupied day and night dealing with the operational requirements. Important decisions had to be made almost every hour. At the back of my mind was the awareness that at last we in the East Indies Fleet had the chance of combating a large Japanese surface ship – after over a year keeping the Japs occupied with air and gun bombardments and supporting the army in Burma in the Indian Ocean whilst the Americans battled with them in the Pacific. It was a great and timely opportunity to prove our mettle: we must not fail. All eyes were upon us and one could feel the expectancy of everyone in the Fleet. My position was a key one, advising the admiral on the spot. I had been on the admiral's bridge and had not slept for four days.

As soon as it was dark that Monday night, the admiral told me I must get some sleep. I remonstrated with him and said I would prefer to keep awake as I would be in no condition coming out of a deep sleep if the signal came with the intelligence we were all waiting for. But he insisted, and at about 8pm I lay down my clothes on the floor of my cabin which was nearby and immediately fell into a deep sleep.

Then of course it happened.

At 2am I was awakened by the admiral. He showed me the 'Top Secret' signal, and wanted to know what we should do about it. It was information that the 'Y' Party had intercepted a

Jap signal indicating that some action was taking place at Sabang. A ship, probably an Escort vessel, was being sailed from Sabang. This was a real conundrum, and here was I trying to regain my full senses but, after being aroused, feeling very egg-bound.

This was not the clear-cut signal we had hoped for giving us information about the cruiser's movements. And there was a particularly difficult problem known only to me. I had a pact with Captain Power (D26), who had dropped into the Staff Office to see me after he had been summoned and briefed by the admiral on the day before we sailed. Our pact was that, if we sent him a signal ordering him to a position, it would signify that we had received the 'Top Secret' intelligence giving the cruiser's movements into the Andaman Sea. To launch him now with only a rather sketchy report that an escort had sailed would be contrary to that agreement. However, if the Jap cruiser was to try again, it seemed to me that the timing would be right for her to do so, and that if she did not do it now it would be unlikely that she would try at all. Furthermore, we had been at sea for five days after being in harbour only twenty-four hours after a previous twelve days operation – we could not stick around for much longer. Also the chances were becoming more and more remote. My training had taught me that when you get an enemy report you should send out your forces at full speed to intercept without delaying an instant. Usually you could call them back if it turned out to be a false alarm: however, in this case we did not want to have to break W/T silence and give the whole scheme away. The chance of this would have to be accepted. I therefore advised that if we could not get the cruiser, let us get the escort, or whatever was there. It would be better than waiting for the cruiser which might never come. I advised the admiral that we had better act now, and he agreed.

With some effort, as my mind was still clearing, I drafted the following signal:

To . . . D26 (R) AC21 CS5   From . . . BS3

PROCEED FORTHWITH WITH TWENTY SIXTH FLOTILLA AT 27 KNOTS TO SEARCH FOR AUXILIARY VESSELS CENTRE LINE 06 DEGREES 10 MINUTES NORTH 97 DEGREES 25 MIN-UTES NORTH 98 DEGREES 17 MINUTES EAST AT 2130GH 15 MAY. RETURN BY SAME ROUTE. TO RENDEZVOUS WITH FORCE 70. AIR SEARCH AND STRIKE FROM CARRIERS WILL BE ARRANGED. THE ABOVE ORDERS MAY BE CANCELLED.

The search indicated was the best estimate of where the enemy might be if they sailed from Sabang, and would lead us about as far south as possible without chancing the Force being seen from the shore. They had 400–500 miles to go. I picked 27 knots as I knew from my destroyer days that they could go this speed with two out of their three boilers, and thus as economically on fuel as possible at high speed.

We supplemented this signal with another sixteen minutes later: . . .

IF CANCEL 'MITRE' IS RECEIVED FROM C-IN-C EI OR BS THREE REJOIN ME.

This let the destroyer know that there was some question about the validity of the intelligence.

At 4am Operation Mitre was implemented by BS3, who then told CS5 to take command of Operation Mitre as he was taking the *Queen Elizabeth* back to fuel and rejoining on completion. We rendezvoused with the oiler at 7am and started fuelling at 8.20.

The subsequent chain of events was incredible.

To my utmost dismay a signal was received at about 0600 from AC21 saying that he was sending out an air search at 0820 of four Avengers. We had said in our operating signal that *we* would arrange air search. However we had not intended to do this before about noon, so as to enable 26 to get well to the eastward position where they could cut off any enemy forces in the area from retiring into the Malacca Straits. Unfortunately AC21's search would alert them and give them more time to escape. We wrongly thought we would have come to the same conclusion.

I should have made our intentions clearer. Now the damage had been done and, as the Carrier Force was now out of TBS touch it was better to leave things as they were and not break W/T silence – this with a heavy heart that my omission would prejudice our chances of success.

The next blow was the receipt of C-in-C, East Indies' signal at 1100 to cancel 'Mitre'. Before this, from about 0945 onwards, reports had come in from the air search that small enemy vessels had been sighted and attacked with bombs. At 1108 CS5 signalled to D26 to sink these enemy ships before returning. We received this signal in *Queen Elizabeth* at 1203, and immediately cast off and headed back to the Six Degree Channel at best speed.

Then, one of the search Avengers reported the presence of a heavy cruiser and destroyer, confirmed half an hour later as a '*Nachi*' class cruiser and '*Yubari*' class destroyer. The position given was about 150 miles east of the Six Degree Channel and 100 miles north of the Sumatra coast.

This was utterly unexpected and a great surprise. It was not thought that the cruiser could have passed northwards through the Malacca Straits without being sighted by our submarines, although from 12 May the patrol had been reduced from two to one. No intelligence signals had been received that a cruiser had sailed from Singapore. This was a devastating setback as the cruiser could regain the Malacca Straits at 20 knots, and D26 were not far enough advanced to intercept her. The early air search had, we considered, wrecked the operation.

D26, on receipt of C-in-C East Indies' signal to cancel 'Mitre' at about 1100, had continued on but at a reduced speed of 15 knots whilst he tried to sort out the conflicting orders. From BS3's operating signal, and with our pact in mind, he was under the impression that the cruiser was definitely there. On the other hand the C-in-C was the fountain of Ultra intelligence. He had also certainly received some of the air search's reports that auxiliary enemy vessels were in the area ahead. His action to carry on was therefore correct, and later was confirmed by CS5's signal at about noon to go on. Shortly after this he received the air search's report that the cruiser had been sighted, and exultingly went on again at once to 27 knots. As a result, only about 15 miles of advance had in fact been lost, which in the event did not prejudice the operation.

We pressed on through the Six Degree Channel to our rendezvous for the next morning, and as the night went on became more and more depressed when no action reports or sightings were received. Admiral Walker remarked to me, 'I shall probably be given a final shore job as a Rear Admiral and you will see out your time as Commander before we are retired.' Then at 0215, the signal office reported that part of a faint signal had been received '. . . cruiser, sinking . . .' at 0140. Suddenly our hopes were raised, but on reflection, having not received any action signals or sighting reports, we concluded that it must be some mistake, or the Japs planting a signal to deceive us. Our spirits drooped again, and it was not until about 9am we knew the truth, when we received a signal from the Commander-in-Chief congratulating us on sinking the Japanese cruiser *Haguro*. The hot damp air of the on-coming monsoon had deflected all D26's action signals upwards except that one faint one, so that we heard nothing through the night.

There was tremendous jubilation, especially as our casualties and damage were so small, and great pride that the East Indies Fleet had succeeded in the one major surface operation that presented itself, and in such a brilliant, epic night action by our destroyers, and the FAA operating as they were under the most difficult and hazardous conditions from Escort Carriers. As an operations officer, one learns that things seldom turn out as expected. Operation Dukedom was no exception. It was particularly nice, later, to receive a congratulatory signal from Admiral Fraser, the Commander-in-Chief of our British Pacific Fleet.

Lieutenant Ian Fraser, RNR

In June 1943 I was appointed as first lieutenant of an H-class submarine which was refitting in Sheerness. Eventually we sailed but where should we end up but in Londonderry! A boring bit of grey area as far as I was concerned.

We received a signal from the Admiralty asking for volunteers for special and hazardous service. I thought to myself, well, I'm married so they are not going to send me on anything particularly dangerous, which was a fallacy, of course. My navigator, Sub-Lieutenant David Carey, said, 'I'm fed up too. I'll volunteer with you.'

So we found ourselves in Rothesay and they said to me, 'Right, you're in command of an X-craft midget submarine. We want you to do six week's training at the top of Loch Striven. Which I did.

These submarines were 57 feet long. You could stay at sea in them for three weeks and they had a range of over a thousand miles. But I couldn't stand up in them and I'm only five foot four. Fortunately at that age I didn't get backache. These X-Craft had a speed of 6½ knots and if you went any faster you dived and couldn't stop diving. They were built in three pieces, each held together with 164 bolts so that it was possible to take the pieces apart, put a new battery in and even a new front end if you wished.

There were two methods of attack for X-craft. They had great long detachable tanks on either side, each of which held two tons of high explosive, which is what Godfrey Place* used. Place was a figure in the past by now, a prisoner-of-war. On our more

* see p.433

advanced craft we also carried six 200-lb. limpet mines which the diver would attach to the bottom of the target's hull.

The crew of an X-craft consisted of four people, the captain, the first lieutenant and two others, one of whom was a diver. We also had two more crews of four people known as passage crews because to get the X-craft from A to B you had a passage crew which stayed on board during the tow.

When we finished training we all went up to Eddrachillis Bay which is up in the north-west of Scotland. The X-craft were carried on the depot ship, HMS *Bonaventure*, which was an ex-Clanliner. They chose a Clanliner because it had very heavy derricks and could lift weights up to 27 tons out of the water. For six months we played about in and out of the Western Isles and the Orkneys and Shetlands, practising different things.

Then it was Christmas 1944 and the war looked nearly over. We didn't expect to go into action now. But all of a sudden they decided to send us out to the Far East. So the *Bonaventure* loaded six X-craft submarines, two down in the forward hold and four more on the after-deck, all cased in to look like deck cargo, all very secret. My wife was very anxious about me because the first time she had seen an X-craft she nearly had a fit because it was so small.

We sailed from the Clyde in January 1945. The voyage was like a world cruise. We went to the West Indies but we weren't allowed ashore because of all the secrecy. So we went to a secret bay where we swam and picked coconuts. Then we went through the Panama Canal, up to San Diego in California and on to Honolulu. After a month in Hawaii at a big rest camp, we went on to the Philippines.

All this time the Captain of the *Bonaventure*, Captain W.R. Fell, was flying all over the place trying to get us some target to attack. Eventually, in Sydney, he got together with Admiral Fife, the commander of submarines in the US Seventh Fleet. The Pacific war wasn't yet over then, and they came up with the idea of cutting submarine telegraph cables which the Japanese used to send their signals between Saigon, Hong Kong and Singapore.

On VE-Day we were in Brisbane, having a marvellous time. Then we went out on the Great Barrier Reef and practised cutting these cables. It seemed a waste of time to us. The divers used a hydraulic cutter to cut the cables and pure oxygen in their breathing apparatus, which can be very dangerous below a depth of about 32 feet.

We were waiting for a diver from the *Bonaventure* but they were taking so long that I said, 'Come on, David, I'll have a go,' and David Carey said, 'No, I'll have a go'. So he got into his diving suit and dived. The water was as clear as a bell so I watched through the night periscope as he cut the cable and gave the thumbs up and put his equipment away. Then he turned round and gave the thumbs down sign, which meant he was in trouble. He must have been poisoned by oxygen. Immediately I started to blow the tanks but he jumped off the side and we never saw him again. I had lost my First Lieutenant whom I had been with since we volunteered together.

When I got back to the *Bonaventure* they gave me another first lieutenant, 'Kiwi' Smith, a New Zealander. He was a brilliant number one and I was amazed how quickly we got on together.

Captain Fell was still trying to get us something to do. The American navy suggested we attack two Japanese cruisers: the *Takao*, which was lying at the top end of Singapore with its guns pointing up the Malay peninsula where the British army were advancing and the *Myoko* which was half a mile further up the Straits. Our boat, the XE3, was to attack the *Takao* and the XE1, led by Jack Smart, was to attack the *Myoko*.

So we were towed 600 miles by S-class submarines to the Straits of Singapore. Then we took over from the passage crew and were towed for about another twelve hours before slipping about 35 miles from the entrance to the Strait. There was an old British boom across the entrance, but when I got to it the gate was open, so we went through. Then we had eleven miles up the Strait to get to the *Takao*. Navigationally it was a bit worrying as there was nothing to get a fix on and we had to guess our course, more or less. Eventually I saw the cruiser through the periscope about a mile away, so I let each of the crew have a look: Kiwi Smith, Leading Seaman Jamie Magennis who was the diver, and Charlie Reid who was steering.

The *Takao* was lying in very shallow water: eleven to seventeen feet at high water and just three feet at low water. It would have been impossible for us to get under her, except that there was a five-foot depression in the sea bed, 500 feet wide and 150 feet long, over which the *Takao* was lying. The plan was to skim across the shallows, slip down into this depression and under the cruiser's hull. But I really didn't think it would be possible.

About 400 yards from the ship I put the periscope up to have a look around and saw a Japanese liberty boat with about forty men aboard only ten feet away. They were so close I could see their lips moving. We went deep immediately, but I'll never know why they didn't spot us.

Then we scraped along the sea bed towards the ship with only ten feet of water above our heads. We were hoping to go down into the dip at any moment, but suddenly there was an almighty crash as we bashed straight into the side of the ship. I felt sure the Japs must have felt the crash.

We were all sweating hard by this time, especially Magennis in his diving suit. After a breather we started the motor but the boat wouldn't budge. We were stuck – either in an anchor cable or jammed under the ship's curved bows. It took ten terrible minutes of straining at full power forward and back to free us. Then we came out 1,000 yards from the ship, turned around, and started a second attack.

This time we slipped down into the hole and under the *Takao*'s keel. I looked through the periscope and saw that the hull was only a foot over our heads and covered in thick weed. Magennis could hardly squeeze himself out of the hatch.

Then we had to wait while he laid the mines. He seemed to take forever and each time he made a noise I thought the Japs would be bound to hear it. He was only gone thirty minutes but it seemed like thirty days. I was very anxious to get away as it was already nearly four hours after high water. But all we could do was watch him through the night periscope and drink pints of orange juice. It was sweltering down there.

At last he got back and we could start to release the side charges. As we worked, he told us what a terrible struggle he'd had, fixing the mines. He'd had to cut away the thick weed and scrape away a thick layer of barnacles before the magnets on the mines would stick to the hull. He had stuck on six. He was exhausted.

The port charge fell away from the boat all right, but the starboard charge would not budge. The tide was falling so quickly that I decided we should get the hell out from under the ship and then free the starboard charge. So we set the motor at half speed ahead, but the boat wouldn't budge an inch, even at full speed. I was in a flat spin. I was sure the *Takao* had settled on top of us in the falling tide and we'd be stuck there for good.

For half an hour we went full speed astern and full ahead, with no success. I made a mental plan to abandon ship before the charges went off in six hours' time. But just as I was despairing, we felt a movement, and the XE3 climbed out from under the ship. It was such a relief to see daylight through the periscope.

Now we were sitting less than twenty feet down in perfectly clear water. Anybody looking over the side of the *Takao* would have thought, 'What's that bloody great rock down there?' I offered to go out in a diving suit and release the starboard charge, but Magennis insisted he could do it. So out he went with a bloody great spanner and for a couple of minutes he made a hell of a noise freeing the charge. They were the most anxious minutes of my life. All the time I was cursing him, cursing Captain Fell, and, more than anything, cursing myself for having volunteered for this madness. In the end the charge fell away and Magennis got back into the hatch. We were all exhausted but at last we could go. 'Home, James,' I said, 'and don't spare the horses!'

After that it was plain sailing. Down the Strait, through the entrance and out to sea where we picked up our parent submarine dead on time and were towed back to Singapore. Jack Smart in XE1 had failed to attack the *Myoko* as he'd been held up by Japanese patrol boats, so he'd dropped his side cargoes alongside the *Takao* and had come back.

When we got back to the *Bonaventure* I went up with the captain to look at the charts and the aerial photographs. The captain said, 'The aerial photographs show this cruiser with oil all over the place, but it hasn't sunk.' I tried to point out that it only had to go down two feet and it'd be on the sea bed. But he said, 'You'll have to go back and have another go at it.' So I said, 'All right, in ten days' time.' We weren't very happy about that, of course.

Two or three days later, when I'd rested up and written my patrol report, we were on deck watching a film. The film suddenly stopped and the captain said, 'I've stopped the film, Gentlemen, because the return to Singapore has been delayed. They've dropped a bomb on Hiroshima.' I thought, 'Thank Christ, it's been delayed.' Then, lo and behold, five or six days later they dropped the second nuclear bomb and the war was finished. So we didn't have to go back.

Later on that year I was awarded a VC. On my way back home they asked if I'd like to go to Singapore to see the *Takao*. So I went with a Japanese interpreter who took me on board the hulk. He opened the hatch and I could see that the whole ship had been blown to bits. It had virtually no bottom.

Jamie Magennis, who was also awarded a VC, and I went together to Buckingham Palace to collect our awards. Our wives came too. I've no idea what King George said to me; all I can remember is that he talked with a lisp.

Engine-Room Artificer Vernon Coles

In 1945 a new flotilla of midget submarines was formed and numbered 14th Flotilla. These comprised the new X-submarines, the XEs, the 'E' meaning for operations in the Far East against Japan.

In July 1945 we were told that XE1 and XE3 would enter Singapore and attack two cruisers. At this stage the Allies had broken every Jap code and the enemy knew it. So as to retain secrecy the Japs used ocean cables. One ran from Singapore to a shore station in Saigon. Another cable came out of Saigon and ran to Hong Kong and on to Tokyo.

The Americans asked if we could cut them and the immediate response was 'Yes'. We then had to think about how we would do it.

The boats chosen to do this were XE4 for Saigon and XE5 for Hong Kong. The crew of XE4 was captained by Lieutenant Max Shean, an Australian with Sub-Lieutenant Ben Kelly, myself as the engineer and two divers, Sub-Lieutenant Briggs and Sub-Lieutenant Adam Bergius. These boats were so small, we were packed in like sardines.

When we knew we were close by the cables we dragged a grapnel along the sea bed and after a couple of false alarms became anchored on to the first cable. Ken Briggs went out and cut it and came back into the boat with a smile on his face and approximately two feet of the cable to prove to the authorities that it had been done. The only problem for Ken was that he was operating in about 42 feet of water which was considered very dangerous to his breathing oxygen and helium. But he did it. The deepest one should operate was 32 feet.

We then moved position approximately ten miles to where the other cable was thought to be located and after a short while it was a repeat performance except that, on this occasion Adam Berguis went out and brought a length back in. When we arrived back at the depot ship HMS *Bonaventura* in Brunei

Bay, Labuan, we learned that XE1 had missed her target, the cruiser *Nachi*, completely. Max was asked if our crew would go straight back into Singapore and attack it. We said we would go, but we were a little anxious as the element of surprise had been lost as 'Tich' Fraser in XE3 had made a successful attack on *Takao*, for which he and Micky Magennis were awarded VCs.

Thank goodness the Japs packed in just as were about to sail.

Many years later we were told that the main purpose of cutting the cables was for the Americans to get a feeling about whether the Japs would fight on after all their recent reverses. They sensed the Japs would; they made up their minds and dropped the Atom bombs.

Some months later I had returned to large submarines and joined *Timeless* and in our journeying around Japan we visited Nagasaki where I saw the damage the bombs had caused. I had no compassion for the Japanese having seen at first-hand what they had done to British and Australian prisoners. But I do believe to this day that the dropping of the bombs saved my life and many, many thousands more.

Marine Peter Dunstan, RM

After the sinking of the *Prince of Wales* and *Repulse*, and as the fighting in Malaya came closer to Singapore, we Marines were marched to the barracks of the Argyll & Sutherland Highlanders. Colonel Stewart of the Argylls stood on a soapbox on the parade ground and welcomed us, saying, 'The Royal Marines and the Argylls had fought side by side in the annals of history and would do so again.' So we became known as the Plymouth Argylls Battallion. But about four hours later we were at fighting stations in the NAAFI. As we had lost everything when the ships went down, we had khaki jungle uniform given to us, and that was our sum total, along with a rifle or bayonet.

We did commando work up behind the Jap lines for about a

week. After that we were withdrawn back to Singapore. By this time the Japs were advancing down the north-west side of the island and they started to mortar our barracks. There was an Indian hospital alongside our barracks which was on fire and I was helping to evacuate it when I caught a mortar bomb splinter in the hand and shoulder. Out east, wounds go poisonous within the hour, and my hand blew up. I was given a Bren gun but I couldn't use it. So I had to hand it over and was sent to Singapore General Hospital. While I was there I used my good hand to help the eye surgeon.

About a week or ten days later we were told that we had surrendered. The Japs came in and said, 'Everybody out of the hospital within forty-eight hours.' Two of my marines died the following day. I was taken up to the prisoner-of-war camp at Changi Jail. On the way we were told to line up along the road because a Japanese general's car was going to pass by. As the car passed us, I felt completely numb. At the camp the feeling was just numbness, too. We just got on with it and kept our noses clean. We thought it would not last long.

Then the Japs said they were moving us to a new place where there would be hospitals and plenty of food. All lies, of course. They put 600 of us on each train, 35 men to each covered steel truck. Inside the trucks the heat was unbearable, you couldn't lie down and if you wanted to go to the toilet you got your mates to hold on to your hands and you stuck your behind out as the train was going. It took five days to get from Singapore to Ban Pong. When we arrived we were ordered off and marched, walked or struggled to the prison camp. On the way some Thais had laid out some wicker baskets full of food and they told us to take it and eat it. We'd hardly eaten for five days.

When we got to the prison camp it was under nine inches of water so we were ordered further up country, where we were set to work on the railway. Our base camp was at Tarsao and then we carried on to a camp called Kanu, which was where we did most of our construction work.

Almost the whole railway was constructed with hammer and chisel. The Japs would say, 'Right, start down here, hammer and chisel, two men, one hole, half a metre, finish – yasmi – rest.' So the chaps would hammer away and in a couple of hours they'd finish. So the Japs said, 'Ah, right, two men, one hole, one metre.' The men were still finishing a bit fast so, 'All right, two men, two holes, one metre each . . .' and so it would go on.

We lived in huts made of bamboo which we had to build ourselves. Just a bamboo platform eighteen inches off the ground and a palm-leaved roof over the top. No sides, so the mosquitos had a whale of a time. No blankets, except what you owned yourself. No clothes or food utensils were issued. So it was a pint mug of rice in the morning, then we were marched out of the camp and on to the railway before dawn. At midday they would let us stop for some more rice, then we carried on working until it was dark and we were marched back to the camp. For three months I never saw the camp I was living in. If it poured with rain, you carried on working, boiling sunshine or monsoon, you just carried on. We liked the monsoon because we had a bath.

At times we were made to carry blokes to work. They demanded so many men a day and if there weren't enough, they would go into the sick hut. If a man had an ulcer he was excused, but if he had malaria he was out on the track. We carried many men out on bamboo and rice-sack stretchers and they had to lie out on the side of the track, breaking rocks to make ballast. This was normal procedure. We couldn't see any future for our lives.

We had nicknames for all the Japs. One little swine was known as Silver Bullet because he had a bullet on his belt. At this particular cutting the chaps were working on bosun's swings, drilling the rocks for dynamiting. Silver Bullet would stand right on the edge of the cliff and if he thought you weren't working hard enough he would throw a rock at you. One day he slipped and landed in the river about two hundred feet below. It was very strange, how he slipped.

We had one we called the Mad Mongol. He was a Korean and the Koreans were worse than the Japanese. I was going to the toilet one night and I didn't bow or salute and he knocked the hell out of me. But it was a question of suspended animation. You just avoided any trouble that you could. I only got bashed twice in three-and-a-half years; I was lucky, I kept out of it.

The other occasion was when we were cutting down trees. I was working in a group of fourteen people, all of average height. I was six foot six. This Jap thought I was slacking because I couldn't get under the tree properly so he started to knock the stuffing out of me with a lump of bamboo. What made me do it I'll never know, but I clenched my fist and drew it back. When I realised what I was doing, I put it behind my back, but he had seen it. So he broke two other bamboos across my back which knocked the hell out of me. Then he dragged me up to this bridge and got two of my mates to lift a massive piece of wood onto my shoulder. He told me to take it up to the bridge. We were by then used to carrying heavy weights, so I did it and went back and said to him, 'OK, another one?' 'No, no, no, finish.' Physically they beat us but psychologically we beat them.

Just two days later I was up on the bridge which was known as the Pack of Cards because it collapsed five times. I was up there banging some nails in when it collapsed. I got scissored by this log above me. Even today I can't feel my leg. The best of it was that this little swine that had bashed me up two days before was the first one up on the bridge with the saw and he cut through this log and got me down.

Soon after that I got malaria and beriberi. That was two years after capture. We had no drugs, no quinine for malaria. The two doctors we had could do virtually nothing. I was sent down country to Tarsao and I got over the malaria somehow. I was one of the lucky ones; I had malaria four times in all, but my body reacted well and I got away with it. Other chaps are still getting malaria today and they still can't treat it. I got over the beriberi by drinking some fermented wine made from jungle leaves. I was lucky. But we lost a hell of a lot of people from cholera and malaria.

We saw only two parcels from the Red Cross in three-and-a-half years. When the war was over and we opened the Jap storehouses they were stacked high with Red Cross parcels. The Japs had been looting them. If they had allowed those parcels through, three-quarters of our boys would not have died.

It was a struggle to survive. You had a mate; if you didn't have a mate you didn't live. He looked after you and you looked after him. We were getting a few cows through at that time, one cow between six hundred and that was a month's supply. The cows were only the size of a large English calf.

Everything used to go into the pot except the tripe, for some reason. I used to get hold of it sometimes, take it down to the river and clean it. Then I'd boil it and eat it. We used to catch the blood from the beasts and let it congeal and slice it up and cook it on the fire. If nobody was looking we whipped the tongue out.

We were paid ten cents a day by the Japanese when they felt like it. An egg cost 25 cents when you could get it. Unfortunately we had chaps who thought that what was yours was theirs and so what I used to do was spend my money on bananas and sit there and peel the lot and scoff the lot. It was the only way. It was like a very bad dream.

When I recovered from malaria I learnt that there was a party going down river and I thought there might be a chance of escaping my present situation. So I swapped with this other marine and took his place. We got down river to where this railway repair workshop was, five kilometres from the (real) bridge on the river Kwai. I worked there for a while and then got a job in the sawmill, which is where I stayed for the last ten months of the war.

In early 1945 one of the first indications we had that things were really going our way was when we heard the sound of aircraft and saw our planes flying between the clouds and the sun. You can imagine the magnification of the planes in those conditions. It gave us the greatest pleasure to say to the Japanese, 'We've got bigger ones than that coming, you stand by.' That was the first time we were able to start getting back at them and give them a little bit of a wigging.

Then one evening we heard the sound of aircraft and saw twenty-one planes away in the distance. It was nearing sunset and as they turned the sun caught them and they lit up like little balls of fire. They formed a circle over the bridge on the river Kwai and they were playing ring o'roses. They took it in turns to dive down, drop their bombs and come back up again. We heard afterwards that they were Liberators and they'd missed the bridge and hit a prison camp and killed thirty-five of our own boys and nine Japanese.

Some time afterwards we saw a plane approaching so low that we could see the rear-gunner waving at us. The plane waggled its wings to say, 'All right, boys, we know you're there.' No. 2 and no. 3 came across with their bellies open and we watched as they dropped their bombs and glided away. That time they managed to hit the bridge and also a Japanese troop train quarter of a mile from our camp. The feeling of elation in our camp was something I'll never forget.

A Japanese officer in the workshops had a radio which had been doctored so that he could only receive Japanese broadcasts, but it kept going wrong. They found a prisoner in our camp who could repair it who also knew how to fiddle it and tune into the news on Radio Colombo. That was how we heard that the atomic bombs had been dropped. Then a Liberator came over dropping leaflets which told us the war was finished. Two or three days later a jeep came into our camp with a British Indian Army lieutenant and a sergeant, loaded up to the gunwales with food and ammunition. We had never seen a jeep before; we didn't know what it was. Within hours they were in contact with Rangoon telling them what supplies we needed.

One of my mates, Sergeant Tommy Locklin, was dangerously ill with cerebral malaria at the time and the padre came round and said, 'Come on, Locklin, you've got to pull out of it now, the war is over.' Tommy told the padre where to get off in a pretty unrepeatable way. But one of the first cases dropped by the Dakotas had fresh blood on ice for him and other prisoners. Tommy was given some of this blood and today he is as fit as I am.

Sergeant Terry Brooks, RM

I'd survived the sinking of the *Prince of Wales*, and had later been captured at the fall of Singapore and sent to Change camp. I was then moved to Ban Pong which was built on a dried up rice paddy which as soon as it rained, had a foot of water in it. Someone had been there before and they hadn't had a good time either. The vultures were walking up and down the street outside the camp – waiting for us to die. We had to build our own huts out of bamboo and we didn't have a clue how to do it. We learned later of course. The very first morning the camp was flooded and there were millions of ants floating around. Right in the middle of the hut was a huge great python and we all took off. Five months later, if the same sort of thing happened up in the jungle, the snake wouldn't last more than five minutes. We'd kill it and eat it. I was there four days and I caught sand fly fever – dengue – which is worse than malaria. I thought I was dying. I had to wait until it wore off. There was a doctor but he had no drugs, nothing. And then we started to walk to build a railway. We built the railway up to Kanchanaburi and then we crossed the river. For the next two years I was building and repairing the bridge over the River Kwai.

Eventually in 1944 they took all the officers away. A week before they went a senior British Officer came to me and said, 'I want you to take charge of the camp when we leave.' I said, 'Why me for God's sake? You have got army grades senior to me, Australian Army, Indian Army.' He said, 'I want you.' I said, 'What the hell for?' He said, 'Well, you are a Royal Marine.' I said, 'Give me forty-eight hours to think it over.' I weighed it all up. The first thing in my mind was survival. I thought that if I was in charge I would have less chance of being sent on to the railway again. So I said 'yes' and took over command of the camp. There were 8,000 men at the time but they got whittled away. Some were sent by ship to Japan. I was due to go, but wasn't fit enough. The ship was sunk. I lost two of my best corporals on that.

It was a nice job being in charge. As far as I was concerned there was only one crime and that was thieving from your mates and I instituted a rule that anyone found thieving from their mates would be given a damn good hiding. It happened once but not at my instigation! However, 'jungle law' prevailed and he was punished by his mates. There were some very strange moments. One day a man called to me and said, 'Cheerio, Terry,' and I said, 'What's the matter?' but there was no sound. I wasn't very well but I managed to get out to him and he was dead. In his pack there was seven pounds of rotting bully beef.

One day we were on parade, Tenco, five o'clock in the evening. I heard aircraft. Somebody said, 'Look up,' and I looked up and there were Liberators coming over, very low. I could see the bomb doors open and all the bombs as they fell. They went for the bridge, bang, bang, bang and I thought, 'God that one was near,' and I looked over and saw that our Number One hut was blazing. I dragged one lad out but for three days after that we were digging bodies out. We lost about nineteen men in that raid.

A short while later they wanted a party to build airstrips further down the isthmus and I was one of them. We marched 200 miles barefoot. It took us a fortnight. By this time I was pretty low. I think I was in a daze. I was down to six stone seven. The lads used to carry me to work because if you didn't work you didn't get any rations. I went blind for three months. It was frightening. That was the worst time. The lads used to go out and collect wild peanuts for me which was the only way to treat the disease. Somehow somebody got me on to a truck back to the main hospital. I laugh when you call it a hospital camp – you went there to die. There were Scottish doctors, Australian doctors, but hardly any drugs at all. I didn't think I was going to die; it never occurred to me.

But then came the day when I was standing at the door of the hut and the Japanese were marching along, changing their reliefs. There was something funny about them, I couldn't quite place it. So I decided not to come to attention – but they didn't notice. I thought, 'You bastards, it's over.' The next minute the British officers came and said, 'It is over.' We all sang 'God save the King,' and 'Abide with me'. Then we heard explosions all over the place. The Japanese soldiers and Korean privates and corporals were committing hari-kiri by blowing themselves to pieces. All the Japs we hated were dead. We saw them dead. We had to make our way to Bangkok, about sixty miles away. When we arrived they put us in a hangar. We were sitting there and we heard a sound which we all recognised but couldn't put a name to. It was the sound of a tea trolley being pushed along. In it came and it was pushed by a lovely blond German girl. Very embarrassing for her because noone could keep their eyes off her as she went round and round, poor girl.

One morning the Dakotas arrived and flew us off. They took us to an open air hospital and said, 'Get rid of all your clothes, keep your personal belongings and destroy everything else.' Then they gave us a pint bottle of beer each. I saw all the lads through. Then a nurse said, 'All right, Sergeant, you are in now.' I went through to the ward. I'll never forget the sight. A row of beds with mosquito nets all folded up and on each was a man sitting in his brand new green jungle clothes, crying. Never forgot it. We have all tried to forget, but we will carry these memories to the grave.

Petty Officer Alf Hunt, RN

I was a Petty Officer in change of the radio equipment in a flotilla of 8 MTBs. On 17 December the Japs started to land in Hong Kong. We were sent into Kowloon Harbour, a narrow stretch of water between Kowloon and Hong Kong. Two boats were sent in at about eleven o'clock that morning. I was on No. 12 boat. No. 26 went in with us. Of course the Japs were waiting for us. No. 26 caught fire and blew up. There were no survivors. We carried on down the harbour and fired torpedoes at Kowloon where they were embarking from the jetties but we got hit as we turned to come out. The Japs were firing at us from Hong Kong as well as from Kowloon. We had taken on aviation spirit for our engines and so we caught fire, but we were going at full speed, crashed straight into the jetties at Kowloon, and blew up. The skipper was alongside me on the upper deck and he took the brunt of the blast. The explosion blew me overboard. I was the only survivor.

I swam to Kowloon, a distance of about a hundred yards. There I got into a typhoon drain with a six-foot diameter. I was up to my waist in water. I had been hit; a bullet through my steel helmet had grazed my forehead. I still have quite a big scar. I was also hit on the arm and back and twice in the left leg with machine-gun bullets. I could just about hobble. I had a 45-revolver and ammunition. They had told us the Japs were taking no prisoners, but to be honest I hadn't got the guts to shoot myself. You have to be insane to do a thing like that, or very brave, and I was in between.

After twenty minutes or so I saw a little boat come along with three Japanese soldiers in it. So I took off my bandoleer of ammunition and my revolver and flung them into the water. They came and picked me up with a lot of shouting in Japanese and tied me up with barbed wire around my wrists, even though I was wounded. I still have those scars too.

When we got to land they put me on the back of an old lorry

and took me to their headquarters in Prince Edward Road. It was a European style house, beautifully decorated. They had knocked holes in the ceiling downstairs and holes in the roof, and they had a fire burning in the corner. It is cold in Hong Kong in December. That was my first night as a prisoner.

I felt very lonely. When I was interrogated on the first day they said, 'If you want to tell us anything you needn't because we know all we want to know about Hong Kong.' The only thing they didn't know, I didn't know either, which was what the naval Commodore's name was. He had been there only about six weeks.

I was treated reasonably well. The Japs used to bring me cigarettes or chocolate bars or something to eat, and would try to talk to me in English. The chef was Japanese, an army chap, but he looked after me very well and brought me plenty to eat. I was there about four or five days, I suppose. Then at eleven o'clock in the morning there was one big whoosh and a 9.2-inch shell from Fort Stanley came and knocked the house down. The only bloke I was sorry to see killed was the chef. Quite a few of the Japs were killed too. They whipped me out – I was still on a stretcher because I had a gammy leg – and into the Argyll Street prisoner-of-war camp. I was there for a month. There were a couple of doctors in Argyll, one Canadian and one British.

Hong Kong had surrendered by then. I had heard very little about the fighting. The Japs were putting out propaganda on loudspeakers. There was still quite a lot of shelling going on from Hong Kong on to the mainland by the British.

After about a month I could get around, and after Argyll Street I went to Sham Shui Po in Kowloon, a prisoner-of-war camp. It had been an old army camp but the Chinese had looted it and there was no wood left in it. We slept on concrete floors. There were about five or six thousand there. After only a few days we were sent to North Point on Hong Kong island. The camp had had mules or horses in it and was infested with flies.

We were there for a couple of weeks and then got sent back to Sham Shui Po. It was quite a march – ten miles each way.

In Sham Shui Po the food was awful. It was just rice and maybe a few bean sprouts or a bit of vegetable. Just a couple of meals a day and watery soup – enough to survive on, that's all. We did nothing in the camp for the first three or four months. We were just wandering around, walking round the electric fence. Most of the lads were captured with kit on them but I didn't have any. I just had a pair of shorts but I did scrounge bits and pieces off other lads. I had a pair of boots I took off a dead Canadian officer.

We were in Sham Shui Po until 27 September 1942. During that time we went on an outside working party on half a dozen occasions. We went to Kai Tak airport, the airport for Hong Kong, and were set to work extending the runway into the harbour, carrying big lumps of rock and dropping them into the harbour.

It was hard work. We worked from dawn to dusk. They didn't really beat me but you had to keep at it. Several of the lads got a good walloping. They hit with a cane or rifle butt, anything like that. We lost a lot of men. Diphtheria killed several hundred men. They attempted very little treatment for that. There were some 'Pot Pomang' crystals to gargle with but that was about all. English doctors looked after us. We had a Dr Jackson who was a navy doctor.

I was down to eight and a half stone from 12 stone 7lbs. I had beriberi and pellagra, which is like a scurvy complaint, but most of the lads had that. We ate just the same food every day. I don't think we ever had any meat. Once or twice they sent stinking fish and we had some rotten eggs – some of these hundred-year-old eggs, covered in mud, which are dug out of the river bed. There were no Red Cross parcels. But there was plenty of water.

Morale was always pretty good. If anyone said, 'We shan't ever get out of this,' they were dead in a couple of days. We slept on a concrete floor all those months. Eventually I got a blanket.

The Japanese told us to sign a form to say we wouldn't escape. At first we refused to sign it, so they paraded us on the parade ground, and wouldn't let us off that parade ground until we did sign it. They then fetched all the sick people out of the hospital. In the end the officer said 'We'll sign it and say it is under duress,' so that it didn't mean anything.

Then they split us into groups of ten and if one of your group escaped they'd shoot the lot of us. Quite a few did get away. They went in groups – to China, into Bias Bay. A New Zealand navy lieutenant got away and so did one of my colleagues, a petty officer called Maxwell Holroyd.

In our free time we were just wandering around doing nothing. We had a pack of cards and we played crib. We weren't allowed to write home. My mother didn't know anything until the war finished. The first thing she knew was that she had a card from the Australian Red Cross that I had written after our release to say I was safe and free. She didn't know for three-and-a-half years.

On 27 September we left Hong Kong for Japan on the *Lisbon Maru* which was a 6,000 or 7,000-ton freighter. Conditions were awful: there was no room to lie down. They couldn't push us into the for'ard hold so we were the ones into the main hold, right down in the bottom of the ship on top of the ballast. There were some terrible cases of chaps with dysentery and diphtheria on board. Several died during the next five days. We were allowed on the upper deck in groups, to go to the toilet. The food wasn't too bad. We did get bully beef and rice. I didn't see any element of compassion from the Japanese.

At seven o'clock in the morning on 1st October we were torpedoed by USS *Grouper*, an American submarine. She fired five torpedoes at us and only one hit, but that was right in the coal bunkers in the middle of the ship. It killed about eleven of the Japanese crew, but none of the POWs.

There were about 1,500 Jap troops on board. They were taken off during the following night. We were about one hundred miles outside Shanghai, near the Tusan Islands when they put all the hatch covers on stretched the tarpaulins over and battened us down. A few Japs were left on board with machine-guns to make sure we didn't escape. The conditions were hard to describe. Chaps dying there from diphtheria and dysentery. There was no air and the stench was terrible. I was right on the bottom of the ship yet I seemed to get fresh air. I don't know whether it was coming down a ventilator or what, but it wasn't bad right on the bottom. Our water bottles were empty and some of the lads were begging for water. You can cope without food but without water it's terrible. Eventually the Jap guards opened the hatch cover and dropped a bucket of piss down. That was the type of people they were.

About one o'clock the next day the ship took a list and started to sink. One of the lads got a knife and he stuck it up in between the hatch covers and split the tarpaulin. There was a mad rush as everyone pushed out and got on the upper deck. The first half a dozen were machine-gunned by the Jap guards on the bridge. Some of the lads in the aft didn't even get out, they were still battened down. I jumped overboard and they fired at us in the water. They were picking chaps off, using them for target practise. Then the guards were killed by our lads. I would think there were about eleven ships in the area within a mile radius. Small and bigger ships, navy boats and civilian boats – Japanese. But they didn't make any attempt to pick anyone up. They were just churning our chaps up with their screws, going in and out amongst them and firing at people in the water.

There were islands about four miles away and I thought, I am not going to get picked up, and I swam to these islands. I reckon I was ashore within an hour and a half. There was a hell of a tide going inshore. The problem was that some of the chaps went inshore and were swept in-between the islands and back out to sea again. They couldn't land. There was about 1,870 on board originally and 840 went down with her and about another 200 died within two weeks. About 200 of us got ashore onto Steep Island. There was a big lighthouse there and the first thing I saw on it was 'Chance Brothers, Smethwick, Birmingham, England'. This was on the side of the lighthouse. It was reassuring. There was a Chinese village on the island and they picked up quite a lot of the lads in sampans. It was brave of them because they didn't know what the Japs would do to them. We went to this little village and they gave us all the spare clothes they had.

When I got ashore I was terribly thirsty. On the beach there was a beautiful clear trickle of water coming down the rocks from above the cliffs. When some of us got there we lay on our stomachs and drank. It was beautiful, like nectar, and we climbed up the cut-out steps in the rocks. When we got to the top we found it was a toilet – all the Chinese used it as a toilet – but to us it tasted like nectar.

We were there for about four or five days. I think we just felt exhilaration at being alive. Three men got away. I had the chance but I said no, I would rather stick with the main crowd. The escapees went by sampan or junk to the mainland. Of course they told the whole story of the *Lisbon*.

The Chinese on the island fed us and did us proud, but they were frightened of recriminations. We gave them back all the clothes. They put us on a Jap navy boat and took us to Shanghai. The Jap navy, I must say, was very, very good. They gave us corned beef, condensed milk and blankets. The skipper of our boat spoke very good English because most of the Japanese navy were trained by the British.

We got to Shanghai about seven o'clock in the morning. Then we stood on the jetty until midnight and it was freezing. There were blokes who died on the jetty. Then they put us on board an old Japanese drumsteamer, the *Shin Se Maru*. It had already been on the bottom. It had cockles and shellfish on its inside, we didn't know if we would make it or not. Anyhow, it was uneventful and we got to Moji in Japan where they put us on the train. On this train they gave us what they call a 'Binto', which is like a little wicker basket with rice balls and dried fruit, fish and vegetables. It was quite good accommodation too. The train took us to Osaka.

I was among twenty-six of us taken off at Hiroshima where there was a military hospital. We were all ill with dysentery or diphtheria and only six of us came out alive. I had dysentery. I was passing a lot of blood too but I never gave up hope. I never ever once thought that I wouldn't make it. If you gave up the spirit, you didn't survive.

I then went to Osaka from there, into a hospital underneath the big baseball stadium and then I went into the main camp with the rest of the lads. They were all survivors from the *Lisbon, Maru*, between four and five hundred of us. They did feed us up a little bit and then we went out on working parties. I was in a steel works for a time, breaking pig iron, which was a very hard job – lifting big chunks of iron and throwing them down to break them up. I was down to about seven stone by then. Not everyone was emaciated – some wore it better than others.

Then I worked on the docks for about two-and-a-half years. We fared reasonably well. We never did any fishing. We could have a swim in the midday break but that was about all. The Japanese civilians weren't too bad at all. The Koreans guards were bastards. I suppose we lost between thirty and forty men. There was no contact at all with the outside world – no wireless, but some of the lads could understand Japanese and they read the newspapers.

My worst moment in those two-and-a-half years was being bombed by our own people. We got hammered in five different camps. These B.29s used to come over at about 40,000 feet and they looked like white ghosts in formations of twenty-seven. The next day they would be over at roof-top height. I saw three shot down. A couple of the crew were picked up as prisoners. They were treated badly. The Japanese weren't very friendly after all that heavy bombing. One of the lads got stabbed in the street. An old woman dashed out of the crowd and stabbed him. It didn't kill him, though.

We worked with women and I learnt the lingo pretty well. I shall always remember, just before the war finished, we were working on a barge and there was an elderly lady there having a midday meal. She had a chunk of meat, picked it up in her chopsticks and gave it to me – that was probably her month's meat ration.

The Japanese brought a lot of sugar from the islands and used it for aviation spirit. We used to unload it in two hundred kilo weight sacks. By now I was down to about six stone seven, that was the lowest I got down to. We were then told that they had dropped a bomb on Hiroshima and Nagasaki. We knew that something important had happened when the emperor spoke over the radio. Then the American planes started coming over and we knew it was over. They parachuted a couple of blokes into our air camp about 25th August, who were the scruffiest blokes I have ever seen. They hadn't had a shave or anything. Then they started dropping supplies and that was almost worse than the bombing. There were leaflets that warned us not to eat too much because our stomachs had shrunk.

We arrived in Southampton on 5 November 1945. I had six brothers, four of whom were pilots in the RAF and they had all survived. As a family we were very, very lucky. They didn't recognise me at first when they met me at the station. There was a lot of hugging. Then they took me home.

I was invalided out and given nineteen shillings a week pension. Then we got our compensation off the Japanese, £74.

Even after all these years I still get nightmares. I suffer from tinnitus. I am also claustrophobic and I can't stick it on public transport. Sometimes I relive the bit on the motor boat and see the skipper covered in blood. On *Lisbon* I see the water rising up around us and feel the terror.

Lieutenant Ronald Neath, RNVR

In 1945 every available battleship, aircraft-carrier, cruiser, destroyer, storeship and tanker was despatched from Britain to the Pacific theatre to join the Americans in the final assault on Japan. Although US forces had been taking the brunt, and would continue to do so, it was considered vital that there should be a strong British presence in the area when Hong Kong and Singapore were liberated.

The 35,000-ton battleship *Duke of York*, which I had joined in the previous winter as a junior gunnery officer, left Liverpool in April 1945. We celebrated VE-Day in Malta – not too exuberantly, I recall, for many of us were apprehensive about fighting the fanatical Japanese for perhaps a very long time to come.

After nearly going aground in the Suez Canal because of our heavy armament, we had a most unpleasant passage through the Red Sea where the frightful heat and funnel fumes brought on a lot of sickness, particularly among the engine-room staff. We were instructed to sunbathe as much as possible so as to avoid prickly heat and boils. Skin cancer was not treated seriously then.

Admiral Lord Louis Mountbatten spent time on board with us in Colombo, mingling with the whole ship's company by day and usually partying in the wardroom by night until the wee hours.

We received a great welcome in Australia but soon moved north, past the Great Barrier Reef and across the Coral Sea to Manus in the Admiralty Islands where we embarked our Commander-in-Chief, Admiral Sir Bruce Fraser. Then we moved on to the American base at Guam in the Marianas.

The Americans on the island entertained us royally. For a colleague and myself our allocated hosts on the first day ashore were none other than Henry Fonda, then a US naval officer, and a well-chosen female escort. Fleet Admiral Nimitz came on board two or three times, likewise Admiral 'Bull' Halsey, commanding the US Third Fleet, and General Carl Spaatz in charge of the US Army Airforce.

Nimitz and Fraser were the most impressive wartime leaders I met. Both were quiet men, with a great sense of humour, and were totally approachable, irrespective of rank. Fraser did not sleep much at night and when we were in harbour he would sometimes come up on the quarterdeck, where I, as a junior RNVR officer, frequently had the middle watch. If I was not busy he would engage me in a long friendly conversation, rarely talking about himself, but asking about me and what I hoped to do after the war.

Every day while we were at Guam the skies were full of planes, mainly US 'Superforts', mounting a constant air offensive on the mainland of Japan. There, too, we heard the sensational news of Hiroshima and Nagasaki.

We were at sea on VJ-Day, 15th August. The celebrations going on in London were broadcast over the ship's tannoy system but many of us felt resentful and had little inclination to listen, because we were sweltering in our anti-flash gear, closed up at full action stations in case Japanese kamikaze planes attacked the ship in a final fling.

We had to wait several more uncomfortable days, even having to scurry out of the way of a threatening typhoon, while waiting for General MacArthur to make up his mind about how and when the formal surrender should take place.

British warships had to cope with many problems in the Pacific. They did not have the same mobility as the ships of the US Navy. Even in a big battleship we seemed always to be short of fuel and fresh water. I was made aware of this when I managed to get myself invited for a relaxing day on board the USS *Iowa*.

On 27th August the *Duke of York* was the first British ship to enter Japanese home waters since the war had begun. That evening, together with the US flagship *Missouri* and the largest fleet of warships ever assembled, we dropped anchor in the shadow of Mount Fujiyama. Later, when the minefields had been cleared, we moved into Tokyo Bay and were given the place of honour next to the USS *Missouri* where the surrender ceremony was to take place. We had to lend our comfortable wardroom chairs for the VIPs to sit on, as well as our smart admiral's barge for Nimitz to make his various official visits.

In these final days the *Duke of York* as flagship overflowed with senior staff officers. There were also scores of press reporters, newsreel men and photographers on board all vying for accommodation – and a shower. In the scramble I had to give up my cabin.

As cities, Tokyo and Yokohama were terribly smashed. On two brief visits ashore we saw burnt out factories, wrecked machinery, huge craters filled with water and mountains of ashes and rubble as far as the eye could see – a wasteland of ruins.

During one of those days of waiting I found myself on duty in one of the destroyers which had anchored further up the bay close to the Tokyo waterfront. Suddenly, approaching the ship in a cloud of spray, a landing-craft was sighted which was full of figures waving frantically. As it drew near, an outburst of cheering was heard, getting louder and louder. These were the first Allied prisoners-of-war to be released, dirty, unshaven, haggard, yet exultant. Some waved in a bewildered sort of way, as if they could not believe we were real, or that what they saw was true. Scrambling on board, helped by dozens of willing hands, these men shook hands and embraced us wildly. But there were others who could not speak or move. Several were on makeshift stretchers – an awesome sight.

The Japanese made their formal surrender aboard the *Missouri* on the morning of 2nd September 1945. With a grand-stand view we were able to see the arrival of General MacArthur, Admiral Nimitz, numerous Allied and Commonwealth personalities as well as the top-hatted and bemedalled

Japanese representatives. Admiral Fraser signed for the United Kingdom, and the ceremony ended with a great display of Allied air power in which massed formations of B29 Superfortresses, Avengers, Helldivers and Corsairs zoomed low over the assembled ships.

In the evening there was an impressive and moving ceremony aboard *Duke of York*. Admirals Nimitz and Halsey, our own Commander-in-Chief, General Spaatz and almost all the Allied leaders were present on the quarterdeck to witness it. This was the ceremony of sunset. Allied and Commonwealth flags flew from the ships' yardarms and a massed band of the Royal Marines was drawn up under the great 14-inch guns of the after-turrets. As the sun went down, casting a pink glow over the peak of Fujiyama, Royal Marine buglers sounded the sunset call and then, to the accompaniment of rolling drums, the ensigns of all the Allied nations were ceremoniously lowered; last of all, the *Duke of York's* own White Ensign, the flag which had flown over every Royal Navy ship by day and night since the beginning of the war, was gathered in. The guard presented arms and the band played the hymn 'The day Thou gavest Lord is ended'. All around us the great American ships were silent, their crews facing towards the British flagship, and saluting. This was a magic moment and few of us dispersed without a tear.

INDEX

Locators in *italics* refer to major contributions.
Ranks are generally the highest referred to in the text.

553